T0374652

VÍT SMETANA
KATHLEEN GEANEY
(eds)

EXILE IN LONDON
THE EXPERIENCE
OF CZECHOSLOVAKIA
AND THE OTHER OCCUPIED
NATIONS, 1939–1945

CHARLES UNIVERSITY
KAROLINUM PRESS 2017

Reviewed by: Prof. Mark Cornwall (University of Southampton)
                   Dr. Pavel Seifter (historian and former Czech ambassador to the UK)

Cataloging-in-Publication Data – National Library of the Czech Republic

Exile in London : the experience of Czechoslovakia and the other occupied nations,
1939–1945 / Vít Smetana, Kathleen Geaney (eds) – First English edition – Prague : Charles
University, Karolinum Press, 2017
ISBN 978-80-246-3701-3
342.395.3 * 32-026.12:314.15-026.49 * (410.1) * (437) * (048.8:082) * (078.7)
- government–in–exile – 1939–1945
- political activities of exiles – 1939–1945
- exile – Czechoslovakia – 1939–1945
- World War II (1939–1945)
- London (England) – 1939–1945
- collective monographs
328 - Legislative process [15]

Cover photo: W. Churchil and E. Beneš in Leamington Spa in 1941.

ISBN 978-80-246-3701-3
ISBN 978-80-246-3732-7 (pdf)

CONTENTS

INTRODUCTION

Three quarters of a century ago, during the Second World War, the common state of the Czechs and Slovaks existed, from the legal point of view, only in the United Kingdom, where its government-in-exile resided. For the long and arduous six war years, the same was true for Poland. The governments of four Western nations (Norway, Belgium, the Netherlands and Luxembourg), as well as those of Greece and Yugoslavia, were moved to London after their countries had been occupied by Nazi Germany in 1940–1941. The capital of Great Britain thus in a way became the capital of free Europe as well.

The individual national stories naturally differed, both in general aspects and in details. Yet, a number of interesting parallels between them can be drawn. Just to mention one example: unlike the other governments, that of Czechoslovakia was created in a revolutionary way, achieving *de jure* recognition from the host country only in July 1941. Yet, it was still undoubtedly a remarkable success for the Czechoslovak representatives to attain this status, especially when compared to the failure of the Free French to achieve similar recognition.

Intensive research conducted in the archives, especially in the last three decades, has enabled us to observe and study the story of the European exile in London from a more detached and a more historical perspective. We are thus now in a position to wage a more profound debate not only about the political and military issues, but also about the various economic and social aspects of the individual stories of the governments-in-exile as well as about everyday life in the exile in general. To avoid national self-centrism, the Czechoslovak case needs to be analyzed in the international context and particularly in comparison with the cases of other countries whose governments found refuge in London.

To stimulate and abet such a debate, the British-Czech-Slovak Historians' Forum invited leading scholars in the field to a conference that took place in the Czernin Palace, the seat of the Czech Ministry of Foreign Affairs, from 6 to 7 June 2013. It was preceded by the annual Bruce Lockhart Lecture delivered by Richard Overy, on the topic of *British Political Warfare and Occupied Europe*, symbolically in the Thun Palace, the seat of the British Embassy in Prague. The conference itself was divided into five panels in which more than 20 historians from nine countries focused on various aspects of exile politics, the importance of armies-in-exile, the preparation of the post-war solution for the issue of minorities as well as the problem of media, education and propaganda in exile.

Eighteen participants eventually delivered their chapters for this volume while the special lecture by Richard Overy is also included. Of course, the authors could profit from the vast array of relevant literature on the topic of the exile, from which at least the collective monograph *Europe in Exile*, published in 2001, must be mentioned.[1] On the other hand, the research has moved forward further in the last one-and-a-half decades since that book was published. In particular, the authors of the current volume could make use of the large quantity of newly-released documents in their efforts to answer some crucial and intriguing historical questions. Their chapters thus seek the common characteristics and differences in the origin and structure of the individual exile representations in London, the ways in which the governments-in-exile dealt with their pressing social and economic problems and, of course, several of them strive to set the measure in which the governments-in-exile were able to influence crucial allied diplomatic negotiations.

There is no doubt that the Polish, Yugoslav and later also the Czechoslovak exile leaders failed to achieve their primary war aims as the introductory chapter by Detlef Brandes clearly demonstrates and those by Anita Pražmowska, Vít Smetana and also Radosław Żurawski vel Grajewski all but underline. But were they the only "losers" or can any similarities with the fate of the Western statesmen-in-exile and their plans be observed? The chapters by Chantal Kesteloot and Albert Kersten on the Belgian and Dutch exiles respectively help to draw a more colourful picture of the alleged "winners" and the others. Victoria Vasilenko, for her part, adds an important chapter on how the story of the exile has been treated by historians. It is all the more significant in that it deals with the ways that Russian (and Soviet) historiography has treated the topics of the Polish and Czechoslovak exiles, whose fate the Soviet Union had once affected so dramatically, in the politically most turbulent last three decades – that is from the *glasnost* period in the late 1980s to the Putin era.

The book *Europe in Exile* contained several chapters focusing on the role the military forces of several countries played in the exile. Another study of the topic, called *Exile Armies*, appeared three years later.[2] In contrast, this volume offers a truly comparative chapter by Zdenko Maršálek that assesses the relative importance of not only armies, but also of all the strategic

1   Martin Conway – José Gotovitch, eds., *Europe in Exile: European Exile Communities in Britain 1940–1945* (New York – Oxford: Berghahn Books, 2001).
2   Matthew Bennett – Paul Latawski, eds., *Exile Armies* (Houndmills, NH – New York: Palgrave, 2004).

commodities and equipment which particular governments-in-exile were able to offer for the allied war effort. Moreover, Maršálek's chapter clearly demonstrates how some of the problems faced by the exile representations, such as the problem of achieving maximum effectiveness from small armed forces, are topical even today, within the framework of current allied forces. This comparative view is fittingly supplemented by Blaž Torkar's detailed chapter on the Yugoslav armed forces in exile and their political importance, since probably no other country represented such a divergence of changing governments-in-exile and their (as well as Allied) attitudes to the resistance structures at home. The resistance activity in the occupied countries themselves was at least equally as important for Allied warfare as the military units in exile were. Yet, to achieve real efficiency, this had to be supported by the governments-in-exile in cooperation with the pertinent British authorities who provided weapons, ammunition and logistical support. The chapter by Mark Seaman represents an interesting probe into this broad topic as it points out the various practical problems entailed in British support for clandestine operations in such a far-away country as Czechoslovakia.

One of the major war aims of the Czechoslovak government-in-exile was to prevent the internal disintegration of the state in the future. The preparation of the post-war solution for the issue of minorities is thus deservedly a topic of three chapters. Those by Jan Kuklík with Jan Němeček on the one hand and by Matěj Spurný on the other differ slightly in their conclusions, thus reflecting the fact that discussion on this sensitive topic continues. Martin Brown's chapter assesses the ways this theme has been treated by English language historiography while René Petráš's brief contribution, the only one which is not devoted to exile problems, sets the issue into the historical context of the inter-war treatment of minorities.

Four chapters (those by Richard Overy, Erica Harrison, Jan Láníček and Dušan Segeš) deal with various aspects of propaganda, thus appositely demonstrating how significant this weapon was deemed to be not only by the exiles themselves but also by the British for the overall Allied war effort. The process of preparation for the post-war orientation of the liberated country in the important fields of education and culture is then covered in Doubravka Olšáková's chapter.

Of course, not all the national stories are adequately dealt with in this book, not to mention all the important themes. Still, the authors hope that the variety of the topics that really are covered as well as the quality of their treatment will prompt further discussion on the overall exile phenomenon, perhaps not limited to the Second World War, and might thus serve as a further incentive for intensification of research in the area in the future.

Vít Smetana

I. THE EXISTENCE AND CHALLENGES FACED BY THE EXILE GOVERNMENTS IN LONDON

LIMITED INFLUENCE: THE BRITISH AND THE GOVERNMENTS-IN-EXILE OF POLAND, CZECHOSLOVAKIA AND YUGOSLAVIA

DETLEF BRANDES

In this chapter, I provide a comparison of the British influence on three governments-in-exile and examine to what extent the British government used its power to promote its views.[1]

THE COMPOSITION AND POLITICAL ORIENTATION OF THE THREE GOVERNMENTS-IN-EXILE

Though the British government had great influence on the composition and political orientation of the Polish, Czechoslovak, and Yugoslav governments-in-exile, it used its power resolutely only in the case of Poland. Together with the French it forced a change of government from the pre-wartime *Sanacja* movement to a broad coalition of the former opposition parties with some moderate politicians from the old regime included. On three occasions Britain vetoed the removal of the Polish Prime Minister, General Władysław Eugeniusz Sikorski: once in June 1940 after the loss of the greater part of the Polish army in France, again in July 1941 during negotiations with the Soviet Union on the re-establishment of diplomatic relations, and, finally, in April 1943 after the withdrawal of the Polish divisions from Soviet territory. Britain not only relied upon Sikorski's popularity within Poland itself and on his competence and efficiency in government affairs, but also on his willingness to compromise with the Soviet Union. After his death it accepted the appointment of General Kazimierz Sosnkowski, a follower of Piłsudski, as Commander-in-Chief of the Polish army, since it wanted to avoid a crisis similar to that which had occurred in the Greek and Yugoslav armies, and, on

---

[1] The paper is based on my study *Großbritannien und seine osteuropäischen Alliierten 1939-1943. Die Regierungen Polens, der Tschechoslowakei und Jugoslawiens im Londoner Exil vom Kriegsausbruch bis zur Konferenz in Teheran* (München: Oldenbourg, 1988). It was translated into Czech under the title *Exil v Londýně 1939-1943. Velká Britanie a její spojenci Československo, Polsko a Jugoslavie mezi Mnichovem a Teheránem* (Praha: Karolinum, 2003). Since this chapter is to a great extent a very short summary of my books with 607 and 566 pages respectively, I will add footnotes only when I quote other publications.

the political front, backed Stanisław Mikołajczyk, leader of the Peasant Party, whom it was expected would also make concessions to the Soviet Union.[2]

In the case of Czechoslovakia, Edvard Beneš asserted himself despite opposition from France and partly also from Britain because of his many sup-porters among the political émigrés. The Slovak Milan Hodža, who had won a reputation as a proponent of far-reaching confederation plans for Eastern Europe, was not consistently supported by the British, despite their own confederation plans. Behind the façade of the Czechoslovak government and the so-called State Council, Beneš systematically built up a dominant posi-tion. This was only challenged by the Communists following the first Soviet military victories. The British government did not champion any of his com-petitors and was surprised when the official institutions of the Czechoslovak exile lost their internal political balance. A belated attempt to use the Foreign Minister, Jan Masaryk, as a conservative counterweight to the pro-Soviet ori-entation of the Czechoslovak government-in-exile and State Council failed because of his weakness and indecisiveness.

The Foreign Office defended General Dušan Simović, the symbol of Yu-goslav resistance and sacrifice for the Allied cause, against the attacks of the King, the queen mother, and his fellow ministers only until January 1942. Although King Peter and the Yugoslav government, shaken especially by the *Ustaša* terror within occupied Yugoslavia, depended totally on British sup-port, the Foreign Office hesitated to confront the clique of ministers, diplo-mats, and officers with Great Serbian inclinations and did not force through a new cabinet ready for attempts at conciliation in the national conflicts and at social reforms. Instead of demanding such a new cabinet, it was content with a series of half-hearted changes in the composition of the Yugoslav exile apparatus. Annoyed by the internal dissensions among Yugoslav politicians, the British eventually in August 1943 accepted a government of civil servants whose most important members had made their career under the dictator-ship of Peter's father, Alexander. The Foreign Office stuck to this solution, even though a group of younger politicians had just united against the Ser-bian and Croatian extremists and offered a democratic alternative. Only in July 1944, which was much too late, was a government headed by the moder-ate Croat, Ivan Šubašić, appointed.[3]

With the westward advance of the Soviet armies, British influence on the three governments-in-exile diminished. It could only achieve the tem-porary inclusion of some democratic ministers in the new Yugoslav and Polish governments dominated by the Communists. On the other hand,

2   Eugeniusz Duraczyński, *Rząd Polski na uchodźstwie 1939-1945. Organizacja, Personalia, Polityka* (Warszawa: Książka a Wiedza, 1993), pp. 240-242.

3   Dragovan Šepić, *Vlada Šubašića* (Zagreb: Globus, 1983).

Beneš anticipated Soviet wishes and appointed in Košice in eastern Slovakia a new government, in which Communists occupied almost one third of the ministries.[4]

GREAT BRITAIN AND THE EXILE ARMIES

Britain expected the governments-in-exile to recruit troops abroad and to support and control the resistance movements in their occupied home countries. In both respects the Polish government maintained a big lead over the other governments-in-exile. When the war began, it could rely on a colony of Polish workers in France and on the military units which had fled to Romania and Hungary following the lost September campaign. Upon Soviet entry into the war, the Polish government could also mobilize some of those prisoners of war and civilians who had been deported to the Soviet Union following Soviet occupation of eastern Poland.

The Czechoslovak army-in-exile was significantly smaller. Up until June 1941 it suffered from the refusal of the former fighters in the Spanish Civil War to take up arms in a so-called "imperialistic war on both sides." The British had of course no influence on the Czechoslovak units organized from 1942 on Soviet soil or on the Polish division mobilized after the departure of the Anders Army in late 1942. The Polish and Czechoslovak units in the West were engaged by the British in Africa, Italy, and Western Europe. Their pilots played an important role in the "Battle of Britain."

As the Yugoslav government did not succeed in evacuating at least part of the Yugoslav army prior to the sudden capitulation in April 1941, its forces were extremely small. They were filled with Slovene prisoners of war who had Italian citizenship. The Yugoslav units disintegrated when their Serbian officers protested against Simović's dismissal and when the British military authorities in Cairo supported the mutineers. The Yugoslav prisoners of war liberated by the Allies on Italian soil already expected the victory of the communist partisans and refused to submit to the discredited Yugoslav government.[5]

---

4   Toman Brod, *Osudný omyl Edvarda Beneše 1939–1948. Československá cesta do sovětského područí* [The Fateful Error of Edvard Beneš. Czechoslovakia's Road to Soviet Domination] (Praha: Academia, 2002).

5   Detlef Brandes, "Slowenische Exilpolitik zwischen Jugoslawien und Mitteleuropa 1941–1945," in *Historik na Moravě. Prof. Jiřímu Malířovi k šedesátinám* (Brno: Matice Moravská, 2009), pp. 555–572.

BRITAIN AND THE RESISTANCE MOVEMENTS

Only the Poles succeeded in forming an "underground state" with a governmental delegation, a political representation comprising the main parties, and an underground army. The Political Warfare Executive supported the resistance movements with propaganda over the radio; the Special Operations Executive delivered radio transmitters, money, some weapons, and transported parachutists to the resistance, though the governments-in-exile all complained about the insufficient scale of British help. Poles and Czechs were able to establish independent radio links with their homeland, but the British refused to grant the Yugoslavs an uncontrolled code. As a result, the Yugoslav government could not confer confidentially with its Minister of Defence, Draža Mihailović. With British acquiescence, the three underground armies should have confined themselves to acts of sabotage and saved their valuable squads for a general uprising shortly before the withdrawal of the Axis forces, but the uprisings in Warsaw, Central Slovakia and Prague led to defeats with terrible casualties. Since the *Ustaša* regime were practising a policy of wholesale expulsions and extermination, and the communist partisans were actively fighting to liberate some regional areas, the units of the Yugoslav home army, i.e. the *Četnici,* could not wait for an Allied Balkan invasion. The British and Yugoslav governments proclaimed General Draža Mihailović leader of the rebellion in Yugoslavia and the government-in-exile appointed him War Minister. Through this policy they became dependent on one of the competing parties, and what was more, of the Serb nationalist movement. British attempts to influence Mihailović's strategy directly and through military advisers failed. Though they quietly accepted Mihailović's collaboration with Italy, they demanded acts of sabotage especially against German lines of communication. Only after the defeat of the *Četnici* in the Battle of the Neretva in the spring of 1943 did the SOE switch to an initially cautious but later strong support for the partisans. Its effect on the policy of the successful and self-confident Communist Tito, however, was limited.

BRITAIN AND THE POLICIES OF THE GOVERNMENTS-IN-EXILE TOWARDS THE SOVIET UNION

Following the military successes of the Soviet armies, British influence on the governments-in-exile diminished. Relations between Poland and the Soviet Union were not only burdened by centuries of conflict, but also by the Soviet policy of repression and deportation in its occupation zone during the years 1939–1941, the treatment of the deportees in the vast areas of the Soviet Union, and the quarrel over the future common borders. Under British pressure, the Polish government sought to normalize relations with the Soviet Union after 22 June 1941 by building up a Polish army and welfare organization on Soviet soil. This new start was hindered not only by traditional Soviet distrust of any autonomous movement, but also by British policy. Britain withheld the promised equipment and arms for the Polish eastern army. Initially it demanded a transfer of the Polish divisions to the Caucasus in case of a Soviet collapse and later it wanted to dispatch these divisions to the Near East in order to strengthen its own troops. Sikorski's attempt to steer a middle course by transferring only part of the eastern army was thwarted by an agreement General Władysław Anders and Churchill made with the Soviet leadership.

The British knew that Sikorski was prepared to conclude a compromise with the Soviets with regard to Poland's former eastern provinces, but it did not press him into an early decision so as not to undermine the fighting morale of the Polish troops. The situation changed when the Soviet leadership broke off diplomatic relations with the Polish government, in reaction to the public controversy over the discovery of the corpses of Polish officers near Katyń, and formed the core of an alternative government. Now Great Britain exerted growing pressure on the government-in-exile to recognize the Curzon line as the Polish eastern frontier. As compensation, Churchill offered the Poles extensive territorial gains in the north and west as far as the Oder and Western Neisse including Stettin. When Mikołajczyk finally yielded, his colleagues in the government forced him to resign. Beneš, however, agreed with the British policy of avoiding anything that could endanger relations with the Soviet Union. Already in 1939, he had hinted to the Soviet ambassador in London that he would be prepared to cede the Carpathian Ukraine to the USSR.

THE PLANS FOR THE TRANSFER OF GERMAN MINORITIES[6]

During the Battle of Britain the disposition of the British public to a radical punishment of Germany increased and included support for a territorial reduction of Germany and the expulsion of Germans from Czechoslovakia, Poland, and the German provinces in the east. Eden's visit to Moscow in December 1941 produced a change also in the policy of the War Cabinet towards questions of nationality in East-Central Europe. Stalin had called for the return of the Sudetenland to Czechoslovakia, the cession of East Prussia to Poland, and the annexation of Istria and Venezia Giulia by Yugoslavia.

---

6   Detlef Brandes, *Der Weg zur Vertreibung. Pläne und Entscheidungen zum "Transfer" der Deutschen aus der Tschechoslowakei und aus Polen* (München: Oldenbourg, 2001 and 2005). In Czech: *Cesta k vyhnání 1938–1945. Plány a rozhodnutí o „transferu" Němců z Československa a z Polska* (Praha: Prostor, 2002).

After his return to London, Eden asked the Foreign Office Research and Press Service to draw up special studies on the question of the German-Polish, the German-Czechoslovak, and the German-Italian-Yugoslav borders, with only secondary attention to be paid to ethnic factors. If the conclusions suggested a need for population transfer, the Service was to submit a second paper based on the Greek-Turkish precedent, and also on the resettlement of the Baltic Germans by Hitler. Earlier in January 1942, the Service had argued that a confederation consisting of Poland after the loss of its eastern territories, Czechoslovakia, Hungary, and possibly Austria, if it was to survive without Russian help and be in a position to stand up to post-war Germany, could come into being only if it were strengthened by the addition of East Prussia, Upper Silesia, and the Sudetenland. The Greek experience after the First World War suggested that Germany could cope with a large number of expellees – the figure reached was three to 6.8 million – so long as the transfer was extended over a period of five to 10 years.

In the negotiations between Britain and the Soviet Union after December 1941, the opinions of both countries with regard to the so-called "transfer" of the Germans from East-Central Europe converged. The Foreign Office, however, did not succeed in its efforts to induce Beneš and the leader of the Sudeten Social Democrats to reach a compromise over the question of the scale of the transfer. In July 1942, the British War Cabinet agreed in principle to the transfer of German minorities to Germany after the war. After that decision Beneš resumed his conversations with Wenzel Jaksch. The exiled leader of the Sudeten German Social Democrats accepted Beneš's proposal to expel part of the German population on the basis of their collaboration with the occupiers. At the same time, the British ambassador warned Beneš against applying the criterion of war-guilt on an individual basis, since the resulting number of expellees might be too small. After protracted negotiations, London saw no possibility of changing Moscow's determination to impose a new Polish border at the Oder and the Western Neisse. Of course, other national minorities such as the Ukrainians, Hungarians, and Italians also suffered under the policy to create ethnically homogenous states.[7]

Although the Yugoslav government counted on the expulsion of the German and Hungarian minorities, its main goal was the "liberation" of the Croats and Slovenes residing on pre-war Italian territory. Since the dominant Serb ministers warned against too far-reaching territorial claims, the memorandum on the issue was submitted to the allies only in July 1943, but by then it

---

7   Detlef Brandes, Holm Sundhaussen, Stefan Troebst, eds., *Lexikon der Vertreibungen. Deportation, Zwangsaussiedlung und ethnische Säuberung im Europa des 20. Jahrhunderts* (Wien – Köln – Weimar: Böhlau, 2010).

was not taken into consideration because of the declining influence of the government-in-exile relative to the successes of the Partisans.

BRITAIN AND THE CONFEDERATION PLANS

British endeavours to induce the Yugoslav government to commit to the federalization of Yugoslavia after the war failed due to the stubborn opposition of the Serb ministers, which was strengthened by concern over the massacres in "Greater Croatia." At the beginning of the war, the Chamberlain government doubted whether Czechoslovakia should be restored, and accepted the French proposal to recognize a "National Committee" instead of a government-in-exile. *Vis-à-vis* Churchill's government, Beneš reached further stages of recognition without any concessions to the Slovaks. The Foreign Office did not support those Slovak politicians who called for the postwar federalization of Czechoslovakia, especially since Slovak troops fought on the Axis side against the Red Army.

The British government, diplomats and political advisers had come to the conclusion that developments in Eastern Europe during the inter-war period had proved that the states of East-Central and South-East Europe should join together in two confederations in order to form a barrier against renewed German and possible Soviet aggression. This proposal was supported by the Poles without reservations, while the Yugoslav Foreign Minister, Momčilo Ninčić, used the plan as an instrument in the inner-Yugoslav power struggle. The Czechoslovak government made its consent conditional on good Polish-Soviet relations. The Greek government, for its part, was only prepared to form a loose union with Yugoslavia. When the Soviet minister made clear to the governments-in-exile that Moscow rejected any confederation plans, Beneš and Ninčić made up their minds to travel to the Soviet Union. They wanted to dispel Soviet misgivings and to conclude treaties of friendship and mutual cooperation with Moscow in the hope of averting future Soviet interference in the internal affairs of their countries. The Foreign Office succeeded in dissuading Ninčić permanently and Beneš for the time being from their intentions. When the Soviets also turned down Beneš's proposal to conclude at least parallel treaties of assistance with Poland and the Soviet Union, Beneš confined himself to a plan to reach agreement on a 20-year treaty of friendship, collaboration, and mutual assistance with the Soviet Union which would be open to the future accession of Poland. The Polish counter-proposal of a quadrilateral pact which would include Poland and Great Britain was abandoned by the British Foreign Secretary at the conference of Foreign Ministers of three Great Powers in Moscow in October 1943. Nevertheless, it opposed Beneš's plan, which allegedly would have led to the creation of spheres of influence in Europe and to the isolation of Poland. In October 1943 Eden gave up his opposition to Beneš's projected trip to Moscow to conclude the treaty. After the conference at Teheran, it became more and more clear that British plans for the future of East-Central and South-East Europe could not be realized in the face of Soviet resistance and without strong American support. As a result, during the Warsaw as well as the Slovak uprising, Britain provided little help, since both states were *de facto* already situated in the Soviet sphere of influence.

BELGIUM IN EXILE: THE EXPERIENCE OF THE SECOND WORLD WAR

CHANTAL KESTELOOT

During the Second World War, Great Britain welcomed several governments-in-exile and numerous refugees.[1] Even though it was not the only country to act as a host, it was probably the most emblematic. As for Belgian civilians, it was their second flight to Britain as had been the case in 1914–1918. This time, however, the government also crossed the Channel in search of a safe haven. The following text describes the situation of both the refugees and their exiled leadership.

A FIRST EXPERIENCE: THE FIRST WORLD WAR

The German invasion of 1940 was not Belgium's first war, nor its first experience of exile. Indeed, German forces had also crossed the Belgian border in August 1914. This violent attack caused widespread destruction and fear, forcing more than one million people to flee: "Upwards of 400,000 refugees fled from Belgium to the Netherlands in the first three months following the outbreak of war. This was only the beginning of an enormous upheaval. An estimated 200,000 Belgian refugees arrived in France in the aftermath of the German invasion. Around 160,000 refugees remained on British registers at the end of 1916, this number dropping only slightly before the war ended."[2] Half of the August 1914 refugees had returned home by the end of the month or early September. More than half a million Belgians, i.e., 10 percent of the total population, nonetheless, spent the war years abroad, having no possibility of repatriation before the 1918 armistice. This event left deep wounds in the psyche of the nation and also involved having to come to terms with other cultures, customs, languages and religions. Britain had been rather welcoming towards the Belgian refugees, since Belgium had acquired an aura of heroism ("Brave Little Belgium") and was seen as the victim of unjust

---

1   For a global overview, see Martin Conway, José Gotovitch, eds., *Europe in Exile. European Exile Communities in Britain 1940–1945* (New York – Oxford: Berghahn Books/Soma-Ceges, 2001).

2   Peter Gatrell, "Refugees," in Ute Daniel, Peter Gatrell, Oliver Janz, Heather Jones, Jennifer Keene, Alan Kramer, and Bill Nasson, eds., *1914–1918 online. International Encyclopedia of the First World War* (Berlin: Freie Universität Berlin, 2014). Available at: http://dx.doi.org/10.15463/ie1418.10134.

treatment since its neutrality had been violated and because the Germans had massacred civilians during their invasion ("Poor Little Belgium").

This attitude of friendliness slowly evolved, modified during the war. In 1914, the refugees were clearly "at the heart of the discourse which opposed barbarians to civilized peoples"[3] and served as a strong incentive for mobilization. As time passed, a change became visible in the structures for aid distribution. These were private at first, but, as the initial enthusiasm waned, were gradually replaced by government programmes. The situation was comparable in the Netherlands and in France.[4] One of the interesting characteristics of private and public relief policies is the correlation between humanitarian relief and social stratification. During the summer and early fall of 1914, numerous local relief committees were founded to help the refugees. However, the estimated 2,500 active associations in Britain at the early stages of the war decreased in number as the conflict persisted. The ways in which relief was administered largely reflected 19th century social divisions, both regarding the refugees and the host countries. In other words, help for refugees from the upper and middle classes was not the same as that for the lower classes.

As the war continued, the necessity to find suitable occupations for the refugees became prominent. In the summer of 1914, no one expected a long war. At the time, Britain was grappling with a high unemployment rate and it was out of the question that refugees would compete with British workers on the job market. This situation improved steadily, first with an upturn in economic conditions that required additional labour, and then with the implementation of the Military Service Act, which came into effect in March 1916, and made single British men aged between 18 and 41 liable for military service. Two months later, in May, this was extended to include married men. By mid–1916, around 50,000 Belgian refugees were working in Britain. Integration, however, was not easy since labour cultures were totally different. Before long, the presence of Belgian refugees was believed to pose a threat to the British social protection system. The exiles, meanwhile, had become more organized; in certain cities they even occupied entire neighbourhoods, and had their own businesses. Sharing native space with non-natives in the long term, however, revealed strong dissimilarities which increasingly turned the stay of the refugees into a burden. This first experience is paramount to an understanding of how British society reacted to Belgian exiles when the Second World War broke out.

---

3   José Gotovitch, "Réfugiés et solidarité – Vluchtelingen en solidariteit," in Serge Jaumain, Michaël Amara, Benoît Majerus, and Antoon Vrints, eds., *Une guerre totale? La Belgique dans la Première Guerre mondiale. Nouvelles tendances de la recherche historique* (Bruxelles: AGR, 2005), p. 407.

4   For a general overview of this question, see Michaël Amara's study *Des Belges à l'épreuve de l'exil: les réfugiés de la Première Guerre mondiale. France, Grande-Bretagne, Pays-Bas* (Bruxelles: Editions de l'ULB, 2008).

THE OUTBREAK OF THE WAR ON THE WESTERN FRONT

The second German invasion took place on 10 May 1940 and was followed by the Belgian capitulation 18 days later. The King, like his father, decided to remain in Belgium, but the country's submission had created an entirely different context. During the First World War, King Albert remained head of the army, and Belgium was at war with Germany during the four years of hostilities. The Belgian government remained in exile in Le Havre in France for the duration of the conflict. The memories of the massacres of 1914 were very much alive in May 1940 and the Belgian population fled in huge numbers from the second German attack. From one-and-a-half to two million people sought refuge in France, most of whom went back home between July and September, while the rest remained, either willingly or because of the impossibility of returning to Belgium. Again, some refugees crossed the Channel: in the summer of 1940, around 15,000 Belgians arrived in Britain, a small figure compared to the 250,000 who came in 1914.

Besides Britain, the United States, mainly New York City, was chosen as a destination (especially by industrial and financial groups but also by members of the Belgian government-in-exile and by Jewish families). On top of that, around 1,000 Belgian Jews escaped to Portugal.

While the number of Belgians who sought sanctuary in Britain was much smaller than during the First World War, they were nevertheless the largest refugee community in the United Kingdom. According to figures from the Home Office, Britain hosted 22,758 refugees in October 1940. Of these, 14,500 were Belgian, 3,164 Polish, 2,250 French and 1,657 Dutch. Of course, the quantity of wartime refugees must be compared to the 250,000 who had arrived before.[5]

Having learnt from her previous experience, Britain was better prepared for the influx of refugees. This time different scenarios had been anticipated, the authorities having estimated that up to 500,000 refugees from Belgium and the Netherlands would arrive. This figure was later scaled down to 100,000, but, naturally enough, the social and financial consequences of the sudden appearance of such a number on British soil was feared. With the surrender of the Dutch army five days after the German invasion, the estimates turned out to have been largely exaggerated.

For those who made the journey across the Channel, the British government had no alternative but to provide welcome, while at the same time dreading the prospect of large-scale migration, especially of needy refugees. As had happened during the First World War, a certain amount of class

---

5   Colin Holmes, "British Government Policy Towards Wartime Refugees," in Conway, Gotovitch, eds., *Europe in Exile*, p. 14.

solidarity again came into play, with the poor being confronted with more obstacles than the wealthy, who were often hosted by their British counterparts. In order to relieve the pressure on the British Treasury, the business of meeting and helping the new arrivals to adjust to their new life was once more handed over to local voluntary organizations.

Of the approximately 15,000 Belgian civilians who arrived in Britain, most had been deprived of everything, having either been unable to take their belongings with them or having lost what they had on the way.[6] The majority stayed in London, at the so-called reception centres. The group was far from homogenous. The vast majority (63 percent) were Flemish women, children and older men, and two main social groups emerged: civil servants (3,000) and fishing communities. Among the first to come was the Belgian merchant marine. On 17 May 1940, the entire Belgian fishing fleet (507 vessels) had been requisitioned by the Belgian government and ordered to evacuate the coast. The old fleet had been seized and destroyed by the Germans in 1914, but by 1940 a new one had come into being, up to date, well equipped and motorized. Fifty percent of the ships arrived at British shores, from which one half were assigned to the fishing trade, and the remainder taken into service by the Royal Navy.

Another feature that distinguished WW2 refugees from those of the previous conflict was that the later arrivals benefited more from structures established by the Belgian authorities themselves. Both the parliamentary office (created in July 1940) and the Embassy helped smooth some of the bureaucratic hurdles faced by the newcomers. There was, nevertheless, a large degree of amateurism and chaos in running the operation.

Once more, the issue of refugee employment had to be considered. However, on this occasion the expectation was that the conflict could last for years, so the problem was tackled immediately. Unfortunately, as in 1914, Britain had a high unemployment rate and was again in the middle of a financial crisis, and, not surprisingly, the British authorities preferred to give work to their own citizens than to foreigners. On the other hand, in 1940, the Belgian authorities themselves decided to create positions for the refugees. The task was not an easy one, particularly so because London was often bombarded. Providing accommodation posed additional problems as there were very few places of refuge left. Since most of the refugees were women and children, it was decided to move them away from the capital. After the autumn of 1940, because of the Blitz, only one third of the Belgian refugees remained in London, the rest having been transferred to other districts in Britain. The question of work in the new, safer havens had now to be resolved.

---

6   See Luis Angel Bernardo and Matthew Buck, "Belgian Society in Exile: An Attempt at a Synthesis," in Conway, Gotovitch, eds., *Europe in Exile*, pp. 53-66.

This matter had progressively become a priority for the British authorities, too. A scheme was launched to make jobs available for the refugees but this of course was partially hindered by the language barrier. However, general mobilization came into effect in April 1941, and, by May 1943, 80 percent of the men and 40 percent of the women were employed. Clearly, the more successful handling of the problem this time around was also the result of the Belgian government's presence. The question of work was high on the agenda with the arrival in Britain of the chief Belgian ministers in late October 1940. The *Service Central des Réfugiés*, which came into being on 21 September 1940, slowly included within its remit the provision of health, education and jobs for Belgian nationals. By degrees, associations giving moral and spiritual support were also initiated. The exiled community was becoming increasingly organized, with access to schools, libraries, English courses, and sporting activities, as well as social gatherings such as the celebration of Belgian National Day, placed on a much firmer footing. Needless to say, the upturn in refugee life was reflected most among those who stayed in London or in areas where there were sufficient numbers to create a sense of togetherness.

EXILED GOVERNMENTS AND POLICY-MAKERS

Among those who left Belgium for Britain in the early summer of 1940 were anti-Fascists who had opposed Belgian neutrality, Socialist Party members, and officials of the Socialist Trade Union, who had links with British unions in the framework of the international trade union movement.[7] Included in these groups were Camille Huysmans, who had protected Jewish and German anti-Fascist refugees during the 1930s, Isabelle Blume, who had been active during the Spanish Civil War, and Max Buset, future head of the Socialist Party after the liberation of Belgium. These members of left-wing circles organized rapidly and were fully committed to backing the British war effort. The *"Office des Parlementaires belges"* was founded on 22 July 1940, essentially formed by socialist and progressivist liberals. Exile had acquired a quality of political activism. At the same time, most members of the Belgian government were scattered throughout in France, under two minds about whether to return to their occupied country or throw in their lot with the British. The German Führer, however, soon prohibited the first option by a decree issued on 18 July 1940. Undoubtedly, the situation was very different from what had prevailed in 1914–1918.

---

7   About this group, see José Gotovitch, *De Belgische socialisten in Londen* (Antwerpen: Standaard, 1981).

Marcel-Henri Jaspar, the Belgian Minister of Health, was the only minister who travelled to London in June 1940. He joined Camille Huysmans in creating a "shadow government." The British, however, were reluctant to recognize the Jaspar-Huysmans arrangement. In this context, the arrival in Otober 1940 of de Vleeschauwer, the one Belgian minister with legal powers outside Belgium itself, was a turning point. As Belgian Minister of the Colonies, de Vleeschauwer could have brought the Congo over to the British side, but he hesitated to do so. Moreover, he had been asked by Prime Minister Hubert Pierlot to join the other Belgian MPs in Vichy. De Vleeschauwer was close to the King and not very enthusiastic about abandoning what he considered the realm of legality to take part in a "governmental adventure" with left-wing politicians. On 15 August 1940, the Belgian MPs in London openly pledged their solidarity with the British by means of a manifesto. The text mentioned the strategic importance of the Congo, which the authors clearly wished would benefit the Allies, and objected to a separate peace. This stance was unambiguously perceived as a criticism of the royal capitulation of 28 May. Being the only Belgian minister with legal powers outside of Belgium, de Vleeschauwer, together with Camille Gutt who came to London soon afterwards on his own initiative, was able to form a temporary "government of two" with British approval. However, both Gutt[8] and de Vleeschauwer were concerned with the legitimacy of their actions and preferred to await the arrival of the other ministers, namely Paul-Henri Spaak and Pierlot,[9] who had been detained in Spain *en route* from France to London. Pierlot and Spaak reached London on 22 October 1940, thereby marking the start of the "government of four," and providing this "official" government with the authority of Belgium's last elected Prime Minister. Their work was at first centred on the four key ministries of the war period: Colonies, Finances, Defence, and Foreign Affairs. The British had been distrustful of many of the Belgian ministers, as well as of the legitimacy of the governement itself. However, with the advent of the Prime Minister, the new state of affairs, albeit grudgingly, was accepted.

The priority of the Belgian government was to appear convincing and to gain credibility after the events of the summer. They had a number of strategic assets to offer but needed political standing. The fact that King Leopold III had remained in Belgium further complicated the situation. Other countries had sent both their governments and their heads of state to London. It was

---

8   See Jean-François Crombois, *Camille Gutt, 1940–1945, les finances et la guerre* (Bruxelles-Gerpinnes: Quorum-Ceges, 2000).

9   See Pierre Van den Dungen, *Hubert Pierlot 1883–1963. La Loi, le Roi, la Liberté* (Bruxelles: Le Cri, 2010); Michel Dumoulin, *Spaak* (Bruxelles: Racine, 1999).

also important to win popularity in occupied Belgium, where the presence of the King was, at least for the moment, considered reassuring.

The difficulties facing the Belgian government-in-exile were therefore fourfold: to satisfy the British authorities, and more broadly the Allies, as to its legitimacy and determination, to win over the Belgian people, to maintain cohesion and dynamism in the ministerial group, and to assure the Belgian exiles of its concern regarding their fate and well-being.

Time was favourable with regard to furthering acceptance and legitimacy in Belgium,[10] but the whole business was exhausting. The ministers were only four in total and each had a considerable workload. Indeed, the number of tasks to be performed soon became impracticable and in early 1942 they decided to hire sub-secretaries of state, a post which had not formerly existed in the Belgian legislature. Most of the other ministers had remained in France but were expected to join their colleagues in London and take up office. By early 1941, however, it became clear that this was no longer an option from a political point of view. The situation was of course exceptional, but in practice they ceased to serve as ministers. Their portfolios were therefore shared among the four already in London and later also by the sub-secretaries. Meanwhile, another minister who had remained in occupied Belgium reached London and became Minister of Propaganda and Justice. Other nominations were also made and by the spring of 1943 the government would count 12 members in all.

RELATIONS WITH OCCUPIED BELGIUM AND THE (HOMELAND) RESISTANCE

During the first months of the war, communication between London and occupied Belgium was scant. The government-in-exile was frowned upon at first but this view modified as the war progressed. In the autumn months of 1940, Britain's bold stand against Hitler was admired by many Belgians.[11] Yet, by and large, information was limited to what was transmitted by radio. Indeed, in early September 1940, the BBC had begun to broadcast 15–minute news bulletins to Belgium twice daily, but, from July 1940, listening to

---

10   "Le gouvernement a continué à regagner petit à petit dans l'opinion le terrain qu'il avait perdu lors des événements de fin mai 1940. Il ne reste aujourd'hui plus grand-chose de l'extrême discrédit dans lequel il était tombé. Il n'est pas rare d'entendre faire son éloge par ceux-là même qui, il y a deux ans, le condamnaient avec une implacable sévérité et envisageaient de le faire traduire devant une Haute Cour." This opinion was expressed after two and a half years of occupation. Paul Struye, Guillaume Jacquemyns, *La Belgique sous l'occupation allemande (1940–1944)* (Bruxelles: Complexe/Ceges, 2002), pp. 176–177.

11   Voir Alain Colignon, "La Résistance 'de droite': une anglophilie par défaut?," in *Jours de guerre*, pp. 37–53.

these programmes was strictly forbidden.[12] The aim of the BBC reports was to counteract German propaganda strategies and to make the government-in-exile's decisions known to those at home, although the Belgians in London were not always satisfied with the tone and the news items selected. Clearly, the government wished to have the media under its own control. With the establishment of *Radio nationale belge* in October 1942, however, the Belgians had access to the air waves themselves.

Research has shown that the importance of the Belgian broadcasts from London was more imaginary than real. The number of listeners actually decreased during the war (40 percent initially but less than 25 percent by liberation) as German jamming became more effective from the end of 1942. In addition, *Radio-Bruxelles,* which the occupiers controlled, featured popular entertainment programmes and those Belgians who tuned in to "London" also liked to pick up other stations. Nevertheless, the London broadcasts did play an important role in conveying messages to the resistance movements, notifying interested parties of safe arrivals in London, and in disseminating government directives.

Radio was not the only means used by the government-in-exile to maintain relations with their compatriots in occupied territories. The Belgian ministers in London were also very much aware of the stringent rationing system enforced in the homeland, although with the threat of immediate confiscation by the German authorities, there was little that could be effectively done in terms of sending food supplies to alleviate the situation. However, the commitment was real and they did provide what help they could with the aid of private organizations.

The imposition of forced labour in Belgium in 1942 marked a turning point. The so-called *"Mission Socrate"* was launched to financially help those who tried to escape the measure.[13] The mission took time to get underway. The aim was to keep as many workers as possible out of German reach, but the fugitives still had to survive in occupied Belgium, where getting enough to live on was becoming a severe problem. It was equally imperative that those who refused the work mobilization should not be driven to commit violent acts to find food. The Socrates operation was organized with the help of traditional structures, particularly Catholic and socialist networks.

Relief for citizens who rejected the forced labour recruitment was linked to the question of financing the resistance. The government-in-exile had to decide which groups it should help. The issue of whether the *Front de l'Indépendance*

---

12   See Céline Rase, *Radio Bruxelles au pilori. Des ondes impures à l'épuration des ondes. Contribution à l'histoire de la radio, des collaborations et des répressions en Belgique (1939–1950)*, Thèse de doctorat inédite (Namur: Université de Namur, 2015–2016).

13   See Bernard Ducarme, "Le financement de la résistance armée en Belgique, 1940–1944," in *Courrier hebdomadaire du Crisp*, No. 476–477 (1970).

movement, which had communist tendencies but nevertheless recognized the government's legality, should be included was debated at length. A major concern for the Belgian politicians in London and for their State Security and Intelligence was the line these parties would take at the moment of liberation.[14] How would they guarantee the keeping of law and order? What part would the resistance, itself divided into markedly different currents, have in the political life of the restored state? The government's stance was that no resistance movement should be in charge of maintaining order. This was brought home in January 1944, when a clear message was sent through parachuted agents that the upholding of law and order would not be the responsibility of the resistance organizations, but that the authorities could, if necessary, request their assistance. This decision was accepted by all factions.

From December 1943, 15 million Belgian francs were sent to Belgium every month. The major portion of this was used to assist those on the run from work conscription (10 million), and the rest went to the various resistance movements. This help made clear the government-in-exile's commitment to supporting the homeland resistance.

PREPARING FOR THE POST-WAR REALITY

One of the main wartime concerns shared by both the Belgians at home and the government-in-exile in London was preparation for the post-war period. For this purpose, the gathering of reliable information was crucial. What were the main items of importance for citizens? How did Belgians at home feel about the government-in-exile? What were their priorities for the aftermath of the war? The answers proposed fuelled exchanges and discussions. The exiles kept track of developments from a distance and employed a certain amount of ideological filtering to gauge public opinion. At the same time, the circulation of information on decisions taken in London was felt to be paramount. The chief mediators in this regard were based in Brussels, mostly pre-war associates of the Prime Minister from the francophone Catholic milieu with whom he had preserved strong ties.

As the war continued, the government's preoccupation centred more and more on the situation that would come into being at the end of hostilities. The Commission for the Study of Post-war Problems (CEPAG) was founded in June 1941.[15] Three main tasks were identified: the immediate measures to

---

14   See Etienne Verhoeyen, "La résistance belge vue de Londres: ententes et divergences entre Belges et Britanniques: le cas du SOE," in *La résistance et les Européens du Nord/Het Verzet en Noord-Europa* (Bruxelles-Paris: IHTP/CREHSGM, 1994), Vol. 2, pp. 156–182.

15   See Diane de Bellefroid, "The Commission pour l'Etude des Problèmes d'Après-Guerre (CEPAG) 1941–1944," in Conway, Gotovitch, eds., *Europe in Exile* (2001), pp. 121–134.

be put into practice after the country's liberation, the political, social and economic reforms to be undertaken, and the maintenance of a smooth relationship with the British government and the Allies to help solve post-war problems. A lot of thought went into social improvement. Clearly, the aim was to find a remedy for the profound pre-war crisis in Belgian democracy which had stretched well into the year 1940. Several of the initiatives proposed are worth mentioning, particularly the outspoken desire to increase the role of the state in political, social and economic matters. On the domestic front, the goal was to achieve a more democratic and egalitarian society, while internationally a new world order was envisaged, with mutual respect among nations. After the war, several of these projects were implemented, most notably currency reform, the introduction of a social security system, and the creation of a State Council.

The issue of retribution for collaboration, in other words the "punishment of the traitors," was also an important concern. The government took decisive steps in December 1942 to broaden the legal provisions enacted after the First World War in this regard. In May 1944, jurisdiction for the dispensing of justice in this area was handed over to the military courts. This move was linked to information coming from occupied Belgium in connection with the conduct of the enemy and to the scale of the collaboration.

WHAT ABOUT THE BELGIAN ARMY?

Among those who went into exile in May and June 1940 were several hundred from the ranks of the Belgian army.[16] This was a much smaller number than, for example, their Polish counterparts and, unlike the Poles and the Czechoslovaks, they would not have any role to play in the Battle of Britain. The Belgian soldiers gathered in Tenby, in South Wales. Of the first group of around 600 men, some returned to France on 3 June 1940 since Belgium had not as yet surrendered. The remainder stayed put but had difficult times to endure after French capitulation on 18 June 1940. Many soldiers were hostile to the Belgian government which was still in France. Others had been taken aback by the King's actions, and to exacerbate matters even more, they had no meaningful dialogue with either government exiles in London or the British, who were preoccupied with their own forces. On 12 August 1940, however, a general staff and a fighting unit were created. These had at first a rather symbolic role but their status rapidly increased. Tensions, however, did not abate. Nor were they resolved by the formation of the Belgian government-

---

16   See Luc De Vos, "The Reconstruction of Belgian Military Forces in Britain," in Conway, Gotovitch, eds., *Europe in Exile* (2001), pp. 81–98.

in-exile. Resentment was real and officers were divided into two camps, one of which might be termed "democratic," the other "royalist" or even fascist. The state of general dissatisfaction was augmented even more by the lack of opportunity to fight the enemy, shortcomings in equipment, and relations with the policy makers in London.

In June 1942, the so-called *"Forces Belges de la Grande Bretagne"* joined the Allied war effort. At their head was Major Jean-Baptiste Piron, who had escaped from Belgium and arrived in Britain through Scotland in 1942. The brigade, which would bear his name, counted 5,000 men when Piron took charge. Some had participated in the earlier Abyssinian campaign. From 30 July 1944 Belgian troops began to arrive in Normandy and on 3 September the brigade crossed the French border and joined in the liberation of Brussels just one day later.

RETURN AND SILENCE

For the Belgians, the heroes of the Second World War were the soldiers (the first Belgian Brigade, the Brigade Piron), in contrast to the government-in-exile in London who came home on 8 September to meet with general indifference. Other displaced nationals only returned in the course of the summer and autumn of 1945. The exile experience did not have a long-lasting effect on Belgium in general. Indeed, in a broad sense, the event was muted. This is understandable for several reasons. Compared with the First World War, the Belgian presence in Britain was much smaller. In addition, when weighed against the depredations occupied Belgium and the conscripted labour force had to endure, along with the urgency of coming to grips with post-war problems, the London interlude seemed marginal enough. Another factor here was probably the royal question: the rupture between the King and his ministers had already taken place at the moment of Belgian capitulation, but the London sojourn contributed nothing to an improvement in the situation. All attempts by the government-in-exile to re-establish relations with the King failed. After the war, Socialists and Catholics took opposing positions on the royal question and mention of the London years would likely have been an unwelcome reminder to both of what might best be quietly left to one side. The policy-makers' experience with exile had been, on the whole, one of powerlessness and of dependence on their British hosts and, despite all the projects and plans devised in London, Belgium not Britain was where the great reforms would be decided upon.

On the other hand, the Piron brigade returned victoriously to become the real heroes in the liberation of Brussels. Although this remained a far cry from triumphant Gaullism, the role of the Belgian soldier in driving the enemy from the nation's capital nevertheless entered the country's annals of glory.

It was not until the 1970s, when a number of eyewitnesses started to share their memories, that the archives were opened and research into this episode of Belgian history could begin. Today, the exile and the part played by the Belgian government in London are acknowledged. What appears surprising, however, is the relative shortfall in the influence accorded them. Moreover, there seems to be no collective memory as such, only a number of individual figures each with his own individual story to tell. In this sense, the national experience of WW2 exile in Britain is not unlike that of the First World War, which likewise left few traces. On the other hand, the brunt of the earlier exile had been borne by civilians not policy makers or members of the armed forces. Indeed, for Belgians looking back on the First World War today the tendency is to focus increasingly on the plight of refugees, not surprisingly perhaps given the topicality of the issue. The British exile of 1940-1945, in contrast, has been largely forgotten.

A COLD SHOWER IN INTERNATIONAL REALITY: REDEFINING THE DUTCH INTERNATIONAL POSITION 1940-1945[1]

ALBERT E. KERSTEN

In 1951, the Dutch diplomat Joseph Luns expressed the opinion that Dutch diplomacy suffered from the consequences of a century long policy of aloofness and neutrality. He went on to say that from 1940, Dutch diplomats still acted as if the Netherlands should not get involved in international power politics. According to Luns, this was a major error because in international politics decisions were always taken at the cost of the weaker parties, i.e., small states. In the international setting, the Netherlands was a minor player. Therefore, it was better to play hard ball than to be polite and show an understanding for the reasoning and the views of the different Great Powers. Their purpose was to serve their own interests and Dutch diplomats should likewise put Dutch concerns first. Basically, Luns reproached his colleagues in the Dutch diplomatic service for a lack of awareness of how international power politics operated and of professional naivety.

Luns was a junior diplomat in Berne, Switzerland, when the Dutch government left Holland on 14 May 1940, four days after the country was attacked by Germany. The Dutch Foreign Minister, Eelco N. van Kleffens, and the Minister for the Colonies, Charles Joseph Ignace Marie Welter, had arrived in London on 11 May in order to coordinate policies with the British government. To the outside world it looked like cooperation between equal allies, but in fact the Dutch had consented to the stationing of British troops in the Dutch Antilles to protect the Shell refineries, which were essential to the RAF – an action which would have occurred anyway, with or without Dutch approval. The appearance of the two Dutch ministers in London was convenient, but not essential for the British move. The situation whereby foreign troops established a base on Dutch territory with the last-minute assent of the Dutch government was repeated in August 1941; on that occasion, the Dutch agreed to American troops taking up position in Surinam to protect

---

1   In general, this chapter is based on the following publications: Bert van der Zwan, Albert Kersten, Ton van Zeeland, eds., *Het Londens Archief. Het ministerie van Buitenlandse Zaken tijdens de Tweede Wereldoorlog* (Amsterdam: Boom, 2003); Albert E. Kersten, *Buitenlandse Zaken in Ballingschap. Groei en Verandering van een ministerie 1940-1945* (Alphen aan den Rijn: A. W. Sijthoff, 1981); *Documenten betreffende de Buitenlandse Politiek van Nederland 1919-1945. Serie C: 1940-1945*, 18 Vols. ('s-Gravenhage: Nijhoff, 1976-2004); Louis de Jong, ed., *Het Koninkrijk der Nederlanden in de Tweede Wereldoorlog*, Vol. 9, *Londen* ('s-Gravenhage: Nijhoff, 1979).

the bauxite mines, an event which had been planned without direct Dutch involvement. Bauxite was a vital raw material for the booming American war industry. In both cases the government-in-exile chose to play the role of a good ally and to make the best of the state of affairs that had arisen. From the perspective of Allied grand strategy, this was a wise decision, but from the Dutch point of view it was frightening to experience such measures taken by the allies, who did not even bother to consult let alone involve them in the decision-making process.

Dutch foreign policy had been one of detachment since 1839, the year when the Treaty of London was signed guaranteeing Belgian independence and confirming the division of the United Kingdom of the Low Countries, itself created as a result of the Congress of Vienna to be a barrier against France and French expansionist policies. The Dutch policy of aloofness and informal neutrality had been made possible by the so-called *Pax Britannica,* which protected the Dutch metropolitan territory in Europe and its colonial possessions in South-East Asia, Latin America and the Antilles. After the First World War, however, the Dutch government gradually became aware that this option was nearing its end. Membership in the newly created League of Nations made full neutrality impossible due to the obligation of participating in sanctions imposed by the decisions of the League's Council. The Dutch international position became even shakier after Japan and Germany left the League of Nations in 1933. Defining a new international position, on the other hand, proved well-nigh impossible because the principle of non-involvement in international power politics stood at the very base of Dutch thinking on foreign policy. The system of collective security as envisaged by the League did not work in practice but no real alternative existed. A dual set of non-aggression treaties with Germany and Great Britain proved unattainable. As a result, on the surface at least, the Dutch government sublimated its neutral position in the European security system as a contribution to peace in Europe, although it did try to come to an arrangement with potential allies in case of a German attack. The German invasion of 10 May 1940 brought a sudden, although not unexpected, end to this state of hallucination and self-deception.

The weak Dutch forces withstood the German onslaught for no more than five days. Indeed, the Commander-in-Chief had little option other than to surrender on 14 May. A major achievement was the fact that the Dutch Air Force, though small in size, had prevented a surprise raid on The Hague and had foiled the German plan to arrest Queen Wilhelmina and her government. The Navy, and all its ships then under construction, managed to escape to the safety of British harbours. After capitulation, some troops still put up a desperate fight in the Dutch region of Zeeland but had to give in on 18 May. Remnants of the Dutch army escaped via France to Great Britain. In the meantime, the government and Queen Wilhelmina made a separate, uncoordinated departure. The Queen ended up in Britain because the commander of the British man-of-war who picked her up along with members of her household turned down her request to be taken to the region of Zeeland, a position he made quite clear when he stated: "Majesty, I am in command." Needless to say, this approach was quite new to her. A small number of officials followed the government to Britain. Naturally enough, not only the Queen but all those involved were shaken and disillusioned.[2]

With the help of Dutch multinationals in the British Isles, such as Unilever and Royal Dutch Shell, the government-in-exile rented offices in Stratton House near Trafalgar Square in the centre of London. In addition to traditional government departments, new provisional institutions like the Temporary Auditor's Office were established. The administration was re-established in miniature, although some government units, such as the Ministry of Social Affairs and the Ministry of Education, were, necessarily, very small. In addition to the Secretary, one official, the Secretary's personal assistant, was appointed. Other departments were fully equipped due to their continuing duties. Among these were the Department of the Navy, the Ministry of Foreign Affairs and the Ministry for the Colonies. Despite the fact that some sections had problems finding competent staff among the Dutch community in Britain, the quality of the government services was considered sufficient by and large.

The unbalanced political structure, however, was an area that needed to be tackled. With the Queen and Cabinet functioning from London and both chambers of Parliament left behind in the occupied Netherlands, the system of democratic checks and balances was naturally no longer in place. With all participants working together in good faith, this might not have created a problem but the reality was that all concerned had diverging views on how to function in this exceptional situation. Under normal circumstances, the role of the monarch in the Dutch constitutional system was restricted. Although in theory commander of the forces, administrator of the colonies and endowed with the right to appoint and dismiss Cabinet ministers, in practice all these prerogatives had since 1848 been gradually made subject to approval by the Cabinet and Parliament. During the exile years in London, difficulties arose because the Parliament in its capacity as a balancing factor was not present and the Queen and the Cabinet disagreed on how to compensate for this absence. The Council of Ministers was divided on the issue. After the French armistice signed in June 1940, the 71-year-old Prime Minister, Dirk Jan de Geer, proved to be very defeatist. Without consulting Whitehall, he suggested to the Council that opportunities for negotiating a separate peace with Germany and an eventual return of the government to the Netherlands

---

2   de Jong, *Het Koninkrijk der Nederlanden in de Tweede Wereldoorlog*, Vol. 9, Londen, p. 24.

be explored. This proposal, however, met with opposition within the Council and was dropped. The Prime Minister then recommended that the government be transferred to the Dutch East Indies instead.

When the Queen was informed of what de Geer had in mind, she decided to dismiss him. After consulting those members of the Council whom she regarded as truly non-defeatist and pro-Allied, she made him resign and appointed the Minister of Justice, Pieter Sjoerds Gerbrandy, as Prime Minister in his place. He himself totally agreed with the procedure. In his opinion, as a result of the emergency situation, the Queen possessed the right to appoint and dismiss Cabinet Ministers at her own discretion. Some colleagues were pleased with the unquestionably pro-Allied attitude of the new Prime Minister but others were less enthusiastic about his accommodating attitude towards the Queen's unconstitutional behaviour. She was convinced she had no other choice than to take the lead, as her forefather William of Orange had done at the beginning of the war of independence against Spain in the 16th century, because the future of the Netherlands was at stake. In her mind, it was quite natural that she should carry responsibility for a pro-Allied government. Furthermore, she saw the exile as an excellent opportunity to change the Dutch political system by bringing an end to the complicated multi-party democracy and establishing a more authoritarian form of government which would increase the power of the head of state.

To some extent, the new Prime Minister Gerbrandy did not oppose these ideas nor did he communicate them to the Cabinet immediately. Without doubt, Gerbrandy was the most anti-Nazi member of the Dutch government-in-exile, but he was also an individualist, not a team player. On top of that, he proved to be a somewhat chaotic chairman at Cabinet meetings. This and other disagreements created tensions within the Cabinet time and again. On several occasions these escalated and led to the resignation of some members. Neither did he voice any dissent when the Queen called for the dismissal of individual Cabinet ministers because of personal dislike or alleged incompetence. Initially, the Queen in consultation with Gerbrandy tried to fill the resulting vacancies by making a reshuffle. After the loss of the East Indies in March 1942, however, the entire Cabinet was hauled over the coals and new members with strong personalities were appointed to important posts such as the Army, Finance and the Colonies. The move strengthened the energy and determination of the Council, but also brought internal disagreements to a head. Somehow in the process, Gerbrandy managed to change sides and lined up with his fellow ministers in an effort to restore the leading position of the Council of Ministers. In so doing, he lost the confidence of the Queen. She tried to tighten her grip on the Cabinet by nominating some recent escapees from the occupied homeland; these were a nuisance factor as far as Gerbrandy was concerned but did not undermine the solidarity of the

reconstructed Cabinet. In the winter of 1945, after the liberation of the southern part of the Netherlands, the Queen tried to get rid of Gerbrandy, but the
man she had earmarked to succeed him as Prime Minister, Foreign Secretary
van Kleffens, flatly rejected the offer. In fact, he made her understand that
both abroad and in the occupied Netherlands she and Gerbrandy were the
figureheads of the government-in-exile. The Queen gave in and Gerbrandy
kept his post. After the German capitulation in May 1945, he tendered her the
resignation of his government. She accepted but without a word of gratitude
for his services.

Diverging views on the shape of post-war Dutch society were the linchpin
of the conflict between the Cabinet and the Queen from 1942 onwards. Due
to her frequent contacts with subjects who had escaped from the occupied
Netherlands, she formed the impression, wrongly, that the old political and
societal system was no longer viable among Dutch people. Her way of in-
terviewing these so-called *"Engelandvaarders"* [England travellers] and their
subservience were the basis for the creation of this image. The drive to renew the political system fitted well with her own mindset of greater national
unity and a new society without the political divisions which had been present among the population of the Netherlands ever since the introduction of
equal representation and general suffrage in 1917. Whoever opposed her ideas
was declared "not-renewed" and essentially regarded as unfit to participate
in the process of opinion-building on the shape the post-war Netherlands
should take. From her point of view, Prime Minister Gerbrandy and most
members of the Cabinet belonged to this category. Therefore, within the
Dutch government-in-exile open debate on the arrangement of post-war society and government was practically impossible. However, as will be shown
in the following pages, this does not mean that there was no discussion at all.

Even before the German invasion of the Netherlands in May 1940 a large
Dutch community had settled in London. This was a mainly Calvinist society working in trade, insurance and banking. They had their own church at
Austin Friars, which was destroyed during the Blitz in October 1940. Most
members of the Dutch community in Britain were well off. During the days
of the German invasion the appearance of several thousand fugitives on all
kinds of vessels – a kind of Dutch civilian Dunkirk – was taken in hand by
several emergency committees. Their services continued until the refugees
found decent shelter and a source of income. The influx of the evacuees and
the arrival of the government gave a new impulse to the Dutch community in
Britain. In addition to normal social activities, celebrations marking national
holidays received a glamorous boost since Cabinet ministers and sometimes
even the Queen herself attended many of them in person. In addition, the

newcomers were provided with their own assembly rooms for meetings and recreation.

Paul Rijkens, one of those who spent the war years in Britain, was the Dutch President of Unilever. He took the initiative in establishing a weekly journal entitled *Vrij Nederland* [Free Netherlands]. The liberal Jewish correspondent Marcus van Blankenstein, who had been dismissed as a columnist by the leading Dutch newspaper *Nieuwe Rotterdamsche Courant* after complaints about his anti-Nazi comments, became editor-in-chief. Rijkens and van Blankenstein acted independently, to the dissatisfaction of the government-in-exile, which would have preferred the new publication to be a kind of official newspaper. The content was a mixture of news on the occupied homeland, events in the refugee community, articles glorifying Dutch history and obituaries on deceased Dutch people all over the world. It was read both in Great Britain and abroad. In the United States, a similar newspaper was established with the title *The Knickerbocker Weekly*. It worked on the same formula, and it, too, was out of the reach of the government-in-exile.

Vrij Nederland journalists were also involved in radio transmissions to the homeland. The Dutch broadcasts of the BBC were very much under the influence of the Dutch government. *Radio Oranje* [Radio Orange], on the other hand, was more effective because of its variety; not just news on the progress of allied war efforts and events in occupied Holland were addressed, but also songs, comedy and other leisure items were included. *Radio Oranje* had likewise been set up by a group of Dutch captains of industry and became very popular in the occupied Netherlands. It was the main instrument for official broadcasts by the Queen and Prime Minister Gerbrandy, whose familiar voices heartened their audiences with rousing speeches on the fight against the Germans and the Japanese, the certainty of allied victory and their hopes for a better Netherlands after the war. A similar station *De Brandaris* [Lighthouse] was launched on the short wave for Dutch sailors in the merchant navy to raise their spirits as they toiled to keep vital sea routes open.

It was more difficult to open other lines of contact between the government-in-exile and the occupied Netherlands. Initially communication went through neutral countries such as Spain or Portugal and it was not until 1942 that regular interaction between the government and its secret services on the one hand and the different resistance groups in the homeland on the other was made. This enabled the government to gauge the mood and attitude of the people, as well as what they had to endure under the occupation, and to gain an insight into opinions on post-war policies. It also enabled the passing of vital information for Allied combatants in the battle for liberation in 1944–1945.

FOCUS ON THE DUTCH EAST INDIES AND THE FAR EAST

Once established in London, the Dutch regarded themselves as the main ally of Great Britain. This was to some extent with good reason. In addition to the colonies in the Caribbean and Latin America, the Dutch administered the Dutch Indies in South-East Asia, an important producer of vital raw materials and agricultural products. The Japanese government had delivered its wish list for raw materials to The Hague and Batavia on 12 May 1940 and had asked for direct negotiations. The Dutch Royal Navy had crossed over to the British Isles, and most of the gold of the National Bank and the government had been deposited in London or the United States. In theory, the Dutch government could act independently, but in reality it was tied to British strategic interests. Although the Dutch regarded themselves as Britain's most important ally, it was a standing that did not yield any real dividends in terms of influence. An official in the Dutch Colonial Office remarked rightly that while it was good for the self-esteem of Foreign Minister van Kleffens to meet Foreign Secretary Anthony Eden every fortnight, it did not give the Dutch a finger in the pie when it came to British policy-making. On the other hand, the Dutch government-in-exile did not expend a lot of energy in forming relations with other exile governments. In all cases the Dutch Acting Envoys were lower ranking officials from the Ministry for Foreign Affairs or the Legation at the British government. In fact, until March 1942 the Dutch government-in-exile was mainly focused on developments in the Far East.

The Japanese call in May 1940 for discussions with the Dutch on the delivery of strategic raw materials such as oil, bauxite, rubber and quinine posed a grave threat for the Dutch. Initially, the Governor-General in Batavia, A. W. L. Tjarda van Starkenborgh Stachouwer replied that he did not have instructions at his disposal to answer the request. In July, a Japanese delegation headed by some Cabinet ministers arrived in Batavia and, much to their satisfaction no doubt, was lavishly entertained. Although formally neutral in the Far East, the Dutch government was in direct touch with Washington and London, and to a lesser extent also with Canberra, on the approach and tactics to be adopted for the talks with Japan. Officially, the Japanese had to reach agreement with the companies which produced the raw materials requested, but this was just a ploy to exempt the Dutch government from being the direct arbiter of the matter. Behind the scenes all moves were of course coordinated. The main goal was to stretch out the negotiations for as long as possible, reject Japanese proposals for long-term contracts and offer deals for only small quantities with a duration of three to six months maximally instead. When the negotiations were finalized in June 1941, restricted deliveries were made. The Dutch, however, joined the American trade blockade against

Japan in July 1941 and the export of significant amounts of strategic materials to the future enemy was stopped.

In the meantime, cooperation with the Western powers in South-East Asia was extended. In November 1940, the British and the Dutch naval commanders in the region met in Singapore on an informal basis to discuss cooperation in the event of Japanese aggression. Although the results were never confirmed by the colonial or metropolitan authorities, the discussions were continued in February 1941 on a broader basis. Furthermore, Australian and New Zealand representatives and experts from all the associated armed forces participated. The final meeting in April 1941 to complete the contingency plan was also attended by American observers. This was based on the premise that a state of war existed between Germany, Italy and Japan on the one hand and the British Empire and its allies on the other. The agreement did not specify any political commitment and required ratification by the governments concerned for implementation. Although it appeared rational to suppose that a state of war would also exist between the United States and Japan, the arrangement for obvious reasons did not take this as a point of departure.

The Dutch government did their utmost to make the next move in line with their British and American counterparts. In August they succeeded in getting a British guarantee for support in case of a Japanese attack, but ratification of the Singapore protocols was never agreed. In Washington, the Dutch were even more disappointed. They were particularly perturbed by the American economic embargo on Japan in July 1941 without any prior consultation or even notification, although such a measure could well result in a Japanese attack on the Dutch East Indies. Nevertheless, the Dutch followed suit and likewise proclaimed an embargo on Japan. Endeavours to gain a guarantee of American support in the event of a Japanese attack were a frustrating experience, too. Washington maintained its policy of keeping the Dutch in the dark about its Far Eastern policies. However hard he tried, the Dutch envoy Alexander Loudon was unable to get reliable information on the state of affairs. It was scant comfort that on the eve of the Japanese attack on Pearl Harbor in December 1941 this guarantee was finally given. The Dutch government, for their part, declared war on Japan shortly afterwards.

After the declaration of war on Japan, the Dutch became the junior partner in the alliance against the Asian enemy. The British Prime Minister Churchill went to Washington to coordinate with President Franklin Roosevelt the Grand Strategy against Germany and Japan. The Dutch were neither invited nor informed. On the other hand, military cooperation was implemented at staff level. In the Dutch Indies the inter-allied American-British-Dutch-Australian (ABDA) Command was created. Such collaboration was good in general terms but crucial decisions were made in Washington, London and Canberra. Due to the rapid Japanese advance in Malaya and towards Australia, the Command was dissolved and the Dutch had to face the Japanese onslaught alone. Before the Japanese landed on Java, the Dutch Navy had battled the Japanese and was destroyed in the Java Sea. On 8 March 1942, Dutch forces in the East Indies signed an armistice with Japan. The Governor-General decided to stay and became a prisoner of war. Core elements of the East Indian administration were evacuated to Brisbane, Australia, together with remnants of the Air Force and the Navy. The Dutch Navy felt betrayed by the American naval commander because of the early discontinuance of the ABDA-Command.

Foreign Minister van Kleffens felt comparable frustration. Alerted to the Churchill-Roosevelt consultations around New Year 1942, he hurried to Washington to make sure that this time the Dutch had a place on the Allied driving seat. Unfortunately, he failed once again. The Combined Chiefs of Staff (CCOS) for Allied warfare was an exclusive British-American institution. The Dutch had to be content with the acceptance of a Dutch mission to the CCOS. This was occasionally invited to CCOS meetings and was also allowed to raise issues of concern. The one political body the Dutch gained membership of was the Pacific War Council, which was located both in Washington and London. The Washington Council, however, ceased de facto to exist in mid-1942; the London Council was not very influential either since real decisions were taken by the CCOS or at high level political meetings.

The sole consolation for the Dutch government was in May 1942 when President Roosevelt proposed the raising of diplomatic relations between the Netherlands and the United States to the level of ambassadors. In a way, this was a palliative for Dutch grievances. Ever since 1919 the Dutch government had been attempting to place an ambassador in Washington but had been refused on the grounds that the US was simply following the British government's lead in this matter. The Dutch were of the opinion that they were entitled to this status being the second largest colonial empire after Great Britain. Whitehall, on the other hand, had only granted such standing to countries that had been part of the First World War alliance. The Dutch government eagerly consented to FDR's proposal and Alexander Loudon handed his diplomatic credentials to President Roosevelt on 7 May 1942. The Dutch decided to make use of the situation and take a sort of revenge against the British government. It accepted the proposal for raising relations to ambassadorial level, but made the British appointee wait till 2 September 1942 for the ceremony of formally presenting his letters of credence to Queen Wilhelmina.

INTER-ALLIED POSITION IN MID-1942

After the Japanese conquest of the Dutch East Indies, the contribution of the Netherlands to the Allied war effort was substantially reduced. The claim of being the most important ally of Great Britain had evaporated after the German invasion of the Soviet Union in June 1941 and the Japanese attack on Pearl Harbor six months later. This change in the composition of the alliance against Germany and Japanese entry into the war forced the Dutch to reconsider both their current and post-war international position. They could no longer continue to refuse to have any diplomatic relations with the Soviet Union. Although trade relations had already been established in the early 1920s, nonetheless the fact that the Dutch delivered rubber and bauxite from the East Indies to the USSR after June 1941 as part of the allied war effort was significant. From a political point of view, with the United Nations Declaration of January 1942 the establishment of diplomatic relations appeared to be a mere matter of course. The Queen, however, remained adamant in her rejection of the move, as she had in 1933 and against the wishes of the government when the Soviet Union joined the League of Nations. The Queen would not send a representative to a state that had murdered relatives of her Romanov grandmother. Van Kleffens' Soviet counterpart Vyacheslav Molotov, however, insisted that temporary arrangements for the duration of the war were not negotiable and the Foreign Minister confronted the Queen with the Kremlin position. Initially she persisted in not complying, but with the whole Council supporting him, Van Kleffens succeeded in getting a royal "let us do it" in August 1942.[3]

Although less important from the Allied perspective, Van Kleffens and the Council were also eager to re-establish diplomatic relations with the Holy See. Ties had been severed in 1925 because of a budget initiative on the part of the orthodox Calvinist party in Parliament with the opportunistic support of among others the Social Democrats. Similarly with regard to this issue, the Queen favoured waiting until the war was over when the Dutch people themselves could decide whether or not to resume relations with the Vatican. Again it was Van Kleffens who faced up to the Queen on the question. The staunch Frisian stood his ground but so, too, did the Queen. It was only after the Cabinet threatened collective resignation that she finally gave in and signed the document accrediting the young Calvinist diplomat Mark van Weede as Envoy to the Holy See.

Van Kleffens had worked very hard to get the Queen's consent for the normalization of relations with the Soviet Union and the Holy See. In both cases he was not afraid to pursue his objective despite the strong opposition of the

---

3   Kersten, *Buitenlandse Zaken in ballingschap*, p. 142.

Queen. In comparable disputes, other members of the government had fallen or would fall out of the Queen's favour. It is remarkable that Van Kleffens' working relationship with the Queen remained stable and that she appreciated his expertise. As already mentioned, at the end of the war she planned to make him Prime Minister. Van Kleffens, however, refused and made her stick to the popular and stubborn Gerbrandy.

Of a different nature was the necessity to implement the Allied principles of the Atlantic Charter of August 1941, in which F. D. Roosevelt and Winston Churchill proclaimed the basis of their cooperation and of the post-war world order they envisaged. Grudgingly, Churchill consented to the right of self-determination for the colonies. Before American entry into the Second World War, the Dutch government had made known their intention to initiate a post-war revision of the constitutional relations between the motherland and its colonies. It was a non-committal statement. In October 1942, the new Minister for the Colonies and Deputy Governor-General of the Indies, Hubertus Johannes van Mook, drafted a radio speech to be given by the Queen on 7 December, one year after the Pearl Harbor attack. In this speech, she was to reveal a substantial plan for the equal status of the metropolitan country and the colonies in Asia and Latin America within the Kingdom. Basically, it was meant to be a kind of federation. During a visit to the United States, he formed the impression that such an offer would give the Dutch a lot of political credit in American eyes since public opinion there was rather critical of the unforthcoming attitude of the British on the post-war decolonization of India. Van Mook's scheme provoked intense debate within the Council of Ministers. Most members opposed it. On the other hand, the Indonesian member, Raden Soejono – recently appointed to make the Council appear to reflect the make-up of the Kingdom as a whole – labelled it insufficient. Why not be more generous and offer complete independence? Total free choice could lead to autonomy within the Kingdom and such a move would not imply that the Indonesians held an anti-Dutch stance. Rather it would mean that they were pro-Indonesian just as the Dutch were pro-Dutch. Soejono's logic was too long a stride for his colleagues in the Council as was Van Mook's proposal. The result of the protracted discussions was rather meagre: the announcement of a post-war conference of representatives with equal status from all parts of the Kingdom to discuss its future structure. The speech given by the Queen on the issue proved to be a great success in the United States. In the East Indies, most people were informed of its content only after the Japanese capitulation in August 1945.

REDEFINING THE DUTCH INTERNATIONAL POSITION

Until the occupation of the Dutch Indies by Japan in March 1942, the Dutch government focused on developments in the Far East and tried to influence American and British policies in the area. After Pearl Harbor, strategic and military cooperation on an equal footing temporarily became a reality in the ABDA-command. However, as noted earlier, among the Combined Chiefs of Staff, the Dutch remained in the backseat of the main decision-making political body in Washington for the Far East. The upgrading of the Dutch diplomatic mission in Washington and London to ambassadorial level brought some consolation, but it did not hide the fact that the Dutch goal of being a player in allied decision-making had been an illusion.

Deprived of their main asset, the Dutch East Indies, Dutch politicians began the process of rethinking and redefining the future international position of the Netherlands. Foreign Minister van Kleffens was the central figure in the exercise. In 1942, he was 48 years old. After an earlier career in the Foreign Ministry, he was made Envoy to Berne in June 1939, but before he could leave for Switzerland to take up the post, he was appointed Foreign Minister. Van Kleffens was an expert on international law. He remained for many years a bachelor until he married Margaret Horstmann, the daughter of one of the directors of Standard Oil. He was not a great diplomat or negotiator since his thinking tended to follow strictly legalistic lines. According to President Roosevelt's confidant Harry Hopkins, van Kleffens was afraid of his own shadow; the American diplomat and Envoy to the Dutch government-in-exile, Anthony Joseph Drexel Biddle noted that he could be rude when presenting proposals but could be easily put in place by responding in like manner. Van Kleffens was a creative personality, conservative, well aware of belonging to the Dutch elite and holding a restricted perception of diplomacy as the art of maintaining political and security relations between states. In his view, monetary and economic issues did not belong to the core business of diplomacy, which was a strange approach for the Foreign Minister of a country whose main international activity was in fact trade and services.

Van Kleffens' point of departure for the post-war international order was the League of Nations. This organization, in his view, had failed to keep peace because it was a universal institution. A consequence of this global principle was that states had a say on matters in which they had not the slightest interest. Therefore, according to him, instead of one international peace-keeping organization it would be better to create a set of regional security groupings in which the Great Powers, i.e., the United States and Great Britain, would also be members. He was likewise of the opinion that membership should be confined to peace-loving nations. In line with this conception, he divided the world into six areas, not defined by landmass in the geopolitical sense but by territories bordering oceans. It is likely that he got his basic inspiration for this from the regional North Atlantic security scheme of his Norwegian colleague, Trygve Lie, launched in 1941. Van Kleffens developed Lie's idea into an international security plan. To some extent, Van Kleffens' reasoning was based on the dissolution of the League of Nations, which had proved to be a disappointment, but it is also probable that frustration caused by the lack of Dutch influence within the League made him turn his back on a worldwide approach to international security. He considered the League had failed because its decisions were hindered by states which had no actual interest in disputes outside their own spheres of concern. For example, Latin American countries had a word on European and Asian disagreements. This mechanism opened the door to extraneous interlinking and made conflict resolution more difficult. It was van Kleffens' belief that the sixfold demarcation he proposed would bring an end to this problem and only those with a real stake in the matter at hand, nationally or internationally, would, within various multiple panels, participate in decision-making on particular issues.

It is remarkable that van Kleffens restricted the Great Powers to just the United States and Great Britain. Undoubtedly, it was for ideological reasons, and because of the vehement opposition of Queen Wilhelmina, that he did not include the Soviet Union in the group. Indeed, it was not until late 1942 that the Netherlands recognized the USSR. It is also worth asking why van Kleffens did not include France. Even though France surrendered to Germany following defeat in June 1940 and established a new fascist state in Vichy, it seems somewhat illogical that its status as a colonial power should be ignored and the country omitted from future international leadership. Did the leader of the Free French, General de Gaulle, not represent the better side of France? Not surprisingly, van Kleffens did not regard Germany and Japan as peace-loving states and therefore they were excluded from his plan. But what about China? Was it discounted because of the complex relationship the Dutch sometimes had with China owing to its proximity to the East Indies and its international influence was therefore undesirable? All in all, the postwar system of security that van Kleffens devised was based on a disputable selection of Great Powers.

For the Netherlands, the structure of six regional security organizations created a potentially influential international position. Because of its colonies in the Caribbean, South America and South-East Asia, it would become a member of four such groups and would be involved in international decision-making. Van Kleffens was aware that it would no longer be possible for the Dutch to continue their policy of aloofness and neutrality and that they would have to engage internationally. In that case it appeared better to participate in power politics than to be sidelined and without influence.

Basically, it was a good scheme as far as creating an international position for the Netherlands went, but was it realistic? Could Washington and London be convinced that this was the ideal master plan for post-war international security? Within the Dutch government the proposal was applauded by the Cabinet and Queen Wilhelmina. Outside the Dutch circle, however, enthusiasm was moderate. During the state visit of Queen Wilhelmina to Washington in August 1942, van Kleffens tabled his plan at a meeting with President Roosevelt, but the American statesman did not show any real interest. A similar reception was given by the State Department. The British government was likewise unsupportive. Van Kleffens did not present his proposal to the other governments-in-exile except for the Belgians. The Belgian Foreign Minister, Paul-Henri Spaak pointed out that economic, social and monetary aspects also needed to be taken into account. Van Kleffens, however, disliked this broader scope and Dutch-Belgian dialogue on the matter ended. On the other hand, discussions between Spaak and the finance ministers of both countries in 1943 led to a treaty on a customs and an economic union, the future Benelux, which was signed without the involvement of van Kleffens.

Both Washington and London favoured an international approach to post-war security under the leadership of the Great Powers and did not show interest in any alternative put forward by the other Allies. Reaching an agreement between the United States, Great Britain, the Soviet Union and China proved to be a very complex operation. The Dutch were treated like all the other small Allied Powers and this was something they had to accept. They were invited to attend Allied conferences on post-war issues such as the Hot Springs Conference on Food and Agriculture and tried to acquire a seat on the associated steering committees. This, however, did not pave the way for more influence on Allied post-war policies. Frustration increased but Van Kleffens did not give in to such feelings. In his perception, the Netherlands was a middle-sized power and, as was the case with Canada and Australia, deserved fairer treatment. He was convinced that like these countries, the Netherlands represented a vast economic reserve for post-war reconstruction. Furthermore, the Dutch regarded themselves as different from the other Allies in exile. They possessed the wherewithal to finance their own policies and activities; they belonged to the "haves" in contrast to the "have-nots" who were dependent on outside sources for their very existence. However, these self-promoting concepts were not productive and did not lead to any increase in influence among the international Allied community during the Second World War.

Van Kleffens continued to promote the Netherlands as a middle-ranking power during the remaining years in exile. His first notable endeavour in this regard was in his role as a self-appointed advocate of the less powerful Allies in a letter addressed to the editor of *The Times* of 25 March 1943, entitled *Great and Small Nations: Shares in Shaping of Policy. Democracy in Action.* Referring to an article published on 23 March on the role of the United States, Great Britain and the Soviet Union as guardians of the post-war world order with no mention of the other Allies, he maintained that this was sponsoring oligarchy not democracy. The dominant position of the Great Powers in international matters was vindicated, according to the earlier writer, but the views of the less important states were not to be ignored, although these should carry less weight because the decisive criteria were size and power. Van Kleffens contended that this was an outdated concept. In national affairs, he claimed, this principle had been abandoned with the introduction of democracy and general elections. It was difficult to understand, he argued, how in international affairs democratically-minded people could feel justified in attaching more weight to the voice of the Greater Powers than to that of smaller ones, some of which in fact might not necessarily be small at all. Van Kleffens' intention was to underline that the principle of the equality of states declared in the Peace of Westphalia of 1648 had to be the basis of relations between the Allies. For practical purposes, however, the lesser Allies could temporarily forgo their rights in order to realize a collective goal such as the defeat of Germany and Japan in the ongoing war. The legalistic argument of van Kleffens notwithstanding, it was generally assumed that the Great Powers would make the decisions during the peace negotiations. His letter to *The Times* was hardly more than nuisance value as far as they were concerned. Cordell Hull, for instance, refused to comment on the article, while German radio used it for anti-Allied propaganda. Once again van Kleffens' initiative fell on deaf ears.

On the other hand, van Kleffens was more successful in day-to-day diplomacy. After the Italian surrender in September 1943, the small Allies were confronted with two *faits accomplis*. Firstly, the United States and Great Britain without consulting the other Allies agreed to the terms of an armistice with Italy. Secondly, the two powers in question only informed the other Allies five days after signing the accord. Stalin, furious at this slighting behaviour, insisted on forming an inter-Allied commission to prevent such incidents in future dealings with Italy. Within the commission, the British, Soviet and American authorities were to negotiate on an equal basis on belligerent and armistice affairs concerning the European theatre of war. The commission was established under the title European Advisory Commission (EAC) and its members were Great Britain, the United States and the Soviet Union.

During his fortnightly meeting with Anthony Eden on 29 September 1943, van Kleffens tabled the issue of membership of the EAC. Van Kleffens proposed the appointment of a Dutch representative as well as one from the lesser European Allies. Eden did not reject the idea out of hand. However, the Foreign Office was much more in favour of consulting the Allies on an individual basis in cases where specific interests were at stake. Van Kleffens was incensed at this decision. According to the British report, van Kleffens had "gone off the deep end." He would never accept a mere consultative role in matters which affected the Dutch government directly and made clear that the small Allies were quite capable of representing each other's interests in the EAC. Although the Foreign Office's chief official Sir Alexander Cadogan left van Kleffens with the impression that the proposal was reasonable, the opposite proved to be the case. In his diary, he wrote: "These little powers are inclined to get on the high horse [...] but in the end it's the Great Powers who carry the burden. After all, the contribution that Holland has made to the winning of the war is in the order of .0001 percent."[4] The Foreign Office opposed granting the lesser Allies membership in the EAC because in the long term they might gain more influence than was actually desired. During a meeting of the foreign ministers of the Big Three in Moscow, van Kleffens' suggestion was vetoed. The EAC became a three-power institution. Van Kleffens had lost this battle to have a voice in Allied decisions concerning post-war Europe but did not give up the fight.

During the second phase of the campaign to gain a seat at the EAC-table, van Kleffens cooperated with other governments-in-exile. They discussed post-war issues within different groups and van Kleffens tried to use the fruit of these consultations to confront the Big Three. He submitted to the State Department a document put together with representatives of the other small Allies on conditions for an armistice with Germany. In May-June 1944, he convinced his Belgian, Norwegian and Luxemburgian colleagues to send an identical memorandum to the British, American and Soviet governments on membership of the EAC. It was presented on 9 June, three days after D-Day. Ultimately, the memorandum provided enough leverage to get at least some involvement in EAC affairs. Thanks to a British initiative the small Allies were kept informed of the proceedings and, finally, in 1945 they joined its many working committees. Although, by and large, the input of the small Allies was much closer to the initially proposed consultative role than to the desired full membership, it gave van Kleffens some satisfaction to know that he had managed to get the small Allies to act in unison for a good cause. It was, however, his sole success in the area. His opposition to the inequality in the constitution of the United Nations Organization owing to the veto power of the five permanent members of the Security Council was of no avail despite the support of Canada and Australia. In fact, the claim that there was an intermediate category of states between the Great Powers and the small was internationally rejected.

---

4   Quoted in M. van Faassen, *In de marge. Het Nederlands buitenlands beleid in de jaren 1943-1945*, in: Zwan, Kersten, van Zeeland, eds., *Het Londens Archief*, pp. 15-16.

In addition to the post-war international world order, the treatment of Germany after the end of the war was an important issue for the Dutch government-in-exile. The German attack of 10 May 1940 had deeply wounded the Dutch. The nation had been awakened from a self-indulgent dream and confronted with the reality of occupation and of exile international power politics. Germany could no longer be trusted. For that reason, van Kleffens excluded Germany from membership of a regional security organization in his spring-1942 plan. At the same time, he was aware that within the European context Germany was too important to be ignored or isolated altogether. Germany would be punished for starting the war in 1939, but in his opinion the penalty was not to be as harsh as that imposed in Versailles at the close of the First World War. In his view, such treatment would only foster feelings of revenge among the German population and this was precisely what had to be avoided. His thinking on the matter developed in the direction of binding Germany within European cooperation organizations. Because coal and nitrogen were vital to modern warfare, he drafted a plan for an international organization to control the production and distribution of both commodities. In contrast to other members of the government, his approach was rather moderate. In 1943, discussing a memorandum prepared by van Kleffens on the post-war attitude to Germany, some of his colleagues criticized his moderate stance. They were in favour of complete dismemberment of the state, the dismantling of German industry, and a large annexation of German territory. Van Kleffens opposed such severe retribution and succeeded in convincing the majority of his colleagues to follow his policy with regard to defeated Germany. However, when the Germans started to destroy the Dutch infrastructure after Operation Market Garden in September 1944, van Kleffens plotted a new course. He now looked favourably at the idea of annexation and the payment of huge reparations. In turn, the group preferring more measured treatment became the minority. After the conclusion of the war, successive Dutch governments continued to advocate these policies but were frustrated by opposition to them by their war-time allies.

CONCLUSION

The Second World War proved to be a clear dividing line in the history of the Netherlands. Until the German invasion of May 1940, the nation had deluded itself into believing that its policy of neutrality was an important contribution to preserving peace in Europe. This self-image was shattered and it took a whole decade for the country to redefine its international position. The government-in-exile in London made the first endeavours in this respect but encountered no interest from the other Allies. At the same time, they themselves showed little concern for the other governments-in-exile, who could have been their natural partners. As if by reflex, they focused on gaining recognition by the Allied Great Powers of their international position and the important contribution the Dutch Kingdom could make to the war against Germany and Japan. This strategy resulted only in prolonged frustration. Basically, the Dutch were right in their opinion that their colonial empire was an important asset in the war. Yet, they did not seem to grasp the fact that economic and financial clout had to be backed by military might. In comparison with the armed forces of Britain and America, or indeed those from Canada and Australia, Dutch martial capacity was quite modest.

Was the ensuing frustration self-inflicted? Had Foreign Minister van Kleffens' concept of a set of regional security organizations materialized, it would have given the Kingdom a level of international influence it had never reached or even aspired to since its establishment in 1813. A century of international isolation had bred complacency and self-deception. In 1940, the daydream came to an abrupt end with no alternative to take its place. In terms of enhancing self-esteem, the attempts by the Dutch exile to have a say on the post-war international order was helpful. It was a means of taking stock of the new environment that would emerge, the new international reality. On the other hand, the conception of the Netherlands as ranking midway between the Great Powers and the lesser Allies was not very conducive to accommodating to the actual state of affairs that was developing. The most important step forward was the realization by the Dutch government of the necessity of cooperation with other states in defence of territorial integrity. In all the post-war plans, this became the accepted point of departure. The process of dealing with the other Allies and of fine tuning its own position on various issues was more difficult. The immediate post-war history is full of striking examples of modification and refinement and was not confined to the annexation of German territory. The decolonization of the East Indies/Indonesia was the main problem for five years until the country finally achieved full independence in December 1949. On a similar pragmatic note, the Netherlands chose the path of Atlantic and European integration and by 1950 had regained confidence in its future. No longer a colonial power for all intents and purposes, the Netherlands would become a state embedded in its West European and Atlantic context. However, that is another history.

BETWEEN SCYLLA AND CHARYBDIS: THE POLISH GOVERNMENT-IN-EXILE'S POSITION WITH ITS ALLIES AND IN POLAND, 1940–1945

ANITA J. PRAŻMOWSKA

On 29 June 1945 the British and US governments withdrew recognition from the Polish government-in-exile in preparation for the eventual acceptance of the Soviet-sponsored government which had been established in the liberated territories in Poland. For the Poles this was a tragic blow in particular because all military resources available to the government-in-exile, which were not insignificant, had been pledged to the British war effort.

In Polish historiography and in accounts of the origins of the Cold War written in the West, the point at which the Western powers abandoned Poland to the Soviet Union is variously traced to the German attack on the Soviet Union, the British and US collaboration in the defeat of Germany or to one of the two major war-time conferences, the Teheran or the Yalta Conference. The word used to define the historic process whereby Britain and the US failed to honour their debt of gratitude to the Polish government-in-exile, is "betrayal." And, indubitably, it was a betrayal, since the British used Polish manpower for the duration of the war. The Polish infantry had been deployed in North Africa and in Italy. In 1944 Polish soldiers fought under British command on the North European front where they remained until the end of hostilities in Europe. Polish air force squadrons, built up in the United Kingdom from crews who had made their way out of occupied Poland, operated within the structure of the Royal Air Force. Polish naval units which avoided capture by the Germans became part of the British naval war effort. This extensive employment of Polish resources and manpower took place in spite of the fact that throughout the war the British and the US governments refused to make an unequivocal commitment to the restoration of pre-war Poland to the map of Europe. In principle it was always understood that when the war ended Poland would once more be independent, but the question of its borders was left unclear because of the growing importance of the Soviet Union to the Allied war effort. The Soviet Union acting in concert with Nazi Germany had occupied eastern parts of Poland in September 1939. The word "betrayal" carries connotations of premeditation and self-interest and stands in contrast to a painful historic determinism in which the actors see the perils of a situation but have no option other than to try and navigate the rapids as best they can.

The phrase "between Scylla and Charybdis" seems to be a particularly apt image for the course of historic developments relating to Poland's fate during the war. The Encyclopaedia Britannica states: "To be 'between Scylla and Charybdis' means to be caught between two equally unpleasant alternatives." This was exactly the strait which the Polish government-in-exile had to negotiate. After the German attack in September 1939, the destruction of the Polish state by military action, and partition between Germany and the Soviet Union, the alternatives came down to that of annihilation or of joining forces with the Allies, who clearly would have their own policies towards Germany and their own long-term interests. Irrespective of what these were, Poland would never be an absolute priority for the British wartime government. This means that while historians might fix on one specific historic moment when the future of Poland was consigned to the Soviet sphere, in fact whatever date is chosen will merely be symbolic because the Polish government-in-exile and its military leadership were throughout the war always perilously steering a course between the rocks of Scylla and the whirlpool of Charybdis.

THE POLISH GOVERNMENT-IN-EXILE

Although the creation of a government-in-exile in France on 3 October 1939 was sanctioned by a clause in the Polish Constitution which allowed for the president to appoint a successor in an emergency, the final composition of the government-in-exile was not what the members of the pre-war military regime wanted.[1] Headed by Władysław Sikorski, an opponent of the Piłsudski coterie, it was supported by the leaders of the key pre-war political parties. The most important issue nevertheless was that of relations between the government-in-exile and the host country, first France and, after it had fallen, the United Kingdom. Sikorski was determined that Poland, although defeated by Nazi Germany, should not be reduced to being an object in future talks, but should in fact be a full, active member in wartime alliances and all post-war peace conferences. He reasoned that this could only be achieved if Poles made a significant military contribution to the Allied war effort.

In this he was supported by party leaders who had managed to escape from Poland and gravitated to France and naturally also by the military leadership who, although opposed to Sikorski, supported his plans for active participation in the war. Until French capitulation, they and the government-

---

1   Magdalena Hułas, *Goście czy intruzi. Rząd polski na uchodźstwie, wrzesień 1939 – lipiec 1943* [Guests or Intruders. The Polish Government-in-Exile, September 1939 – July 1943] (Warszawa: Instytut Historii PAN (1996), pp. 12–15.

in-exile busied themselves with the difficult task of building up military units in France. Inevitably, political and economic dependence on the French authorities as well as a lack of manpower limited the scope of this task. At the same time, the consensus on the need to become France's ally disguised a deeper unease over whether France and Britain, an increasingly important partner in the war against Germany, would ensure that Poland was restored to the map of Europe after the war. This key question directly impacted on the way the government-in-exile planned for the dispersal of the Polish military forces mustered in France. Sikorski was of the view that the Poles should not hold on to any units to liberate Poland when the time came but that they should aim to become involved in all the French and British theatres of war. His opinion prevailed.[2]

BRITAIN'S FIGHTING ALLY

The fall of France destroyed the precariously built-up Polish military potential, the role of which had been to fight as much as to secure political influence. Only 23 percent of Polish manpower was evacuated from France to the United Kingdom. This was still a formidable force of approximately 27,000 battle-hardened men, but since Britain did not intend to open a second front in Europe in the foreseeable future, their effectiveness was limited for the time being. The painful question of dependence on the host country once more resurfaced. The part which the Poles could play in British plans for the defeat of Germany and the dilemma of Britain's attitude towards the Soviet Union, an aggressor state which had collaborated with Germany in the destruction of Poland in September 1939, became an important issue in debates within the Polish exile community in the United Kingdom.[3] In France the Poles could be confident that the European war effort would be a priority. Even though France sought to protect its imperial possessions overseas, Europe was central to French military thinking. This meant that the Poles in France could hope for a quick resumption of hostilities. They also assumed that France would continue its pre-war policy of building anti-German alliances with the East European states.

The German defeat of France spelled an end to those expectations. Although the government-in-exile found sanctuary in London, it was inevitable that British imperial interests would broaden the focus of military and politi-

---

2   This subject was more extensively discussed by Anita J. Prażmowska in "Polish Military Plans for the Defeat of Germany, and the Soviet Union, 1939–41," in *European History Quarterly*, Vol. 31, No. 4 (2001)., pp. 591–608.

3   Maria Pestkowska, *Uchodźcze pasje* [Exile Conflicts] (Paris: Editions Dembiński, 1991), pp. 63–67.

cal concerns. British thinking on the war against Germany was that it was going to be a long one and economic resources would be crucial in all long-term military plans. Nevertheless, the Polish government-in-exile and the British government, which after the fall of France was led by the redoubtable Winston Churchill, proceeded to formalize military collaboration between the two allies. From August 1940 onwards a number of agreements were signed creating the basis for the expansion, deployment and utilization of Polish military units, fighter and bomber squadrons, and naval forces in the British war effort. Sikorski was determined that nothing would be held back in the quest to gain British gratitude which would, he hoped, be repaid after the war. In the internal conflicts which tore the Polish government and the military leadership apart, Sikorski benefited from Churchill's direct involvement in the politics of the governement-in-exile. Sikorski's willingness to discuss the resumption of relations with the Soviet Union, even before Operation Barbarossa, chimed with Churchill's inclination to plan for future collaboration with Moscow, too. Here again the dilemma of how the government-in-exile could make sure that Poland would be liberated after the defeat of Germany came to the fore. The more Sikorski committed Polish resources to the British war effort, the more his own government's prospective influence, and the ability of their military to ultimately free the homeland, was expended. On the other hand, if the Poles were to try to pursue an independent course by perhaps retaining troops until the end of the war, they risked a loss of status within the Allied camp.[4]

ARMED RESISTANCE IN OCCUPIED POLAND

Sikorski and the government-in-exile could not overlook the fact that in the occupied territories resistance movements would emerge which would very likely think differently from the way the government-in-exile did. No Polish politician or military leader worth his salt could ignore the fact that this was exactly what had happened during the First World War and its aftermath, when the Dmowski-Paderewski Committee established in Paris and destined to become the first Polish government was upstaged by the administration which emerged in Poland in the wake of the German withdrawal in November 1918. Led by Józef Piłsudski this authority proceeded to govern and to build up its defence forces without reference to either the French or the British governments. This recent historic precedent served as a warning to Sikorski who felt that he had to establish control over any armed resistance in Poland.

4   Anita Prażmowska, *Britain and Poland, 1939–1943. The Betrayed Ally* (Cambridge: Cambridge University Press, 1995), pp. 67–68.

After Poland's defeat in September 1939, the first resistance groups which emerged in the Polish areas under Soviet and German occupation were organized by military leaders. They had guns and ammunition and also the necessary organizational and soldierly skills to mount some form of opposition to the aggressors. The socialist and peasant parties were less successful in their ability to come up with a military response. But Sikorski knew that the organized resistance movement, in due course to be known as the Home Army (*Armia Krajowa*), was likely to represent the political ideas of the Piłsudski camp, which he was determined to sideline in post-war Poland. He therefore sought to bring the armed struggle under the control of the government-in-exile. In principle at least he achieved this end. The Home Army accepted the government-in-exile as the legitimate Polish government, a decision influenced no doubt by the fact that the Sikorski leadership was their only source of arms and military equipment. The Home Army commanders and the government-in-exile planned and hoped that the liberation of Poland would be won by the émigré Poles in collaboration with their Western allies to the exclusion of the Soviet Union. They therefore prepared for a national uprising that would coincide with the final battles in the West. Unfortunately for them, by 1942 Churchill in coordination with the US agreed that the Mediterranean would be the first priority, and since all earlier proposals for an offensive in the Balkans had been abandoned, no military action in the East was authorized.[5] The critical element in Allied strategies for the defeat of Germany in Europe was the Soviet Union's entry into the war.

THE GRAND ALLIANCE: BRITAIN, THE UNITED STATES AND THE SOVIET UNION

On 12 July 1941 Britain signed an agreement with the Soviet Union to aid each other during the war and not to enter into separate treaties with the enemy. Reliance on the Soviet Union to defeat Nazi Germany in Europe was of critical importance to British political leaders.[6] On 30 July Sikorski likewise reached an accord with the Soviet Union. Although the Soviet Union refused to make any commitment on the restoration of Poland's pre-war borders, nevertheless Sikorski gambled that the arrangement with Moscow would enhance his standing among the Allies. His thinking was affected by the fact that Stalin had consented to the formation of Polish military units into which Poles living in areas incorporated into the Soviet Union after September 1939 would

---

5   Leon Mitkiewicz, Z Generałem Sikorskim na Obczyźnie [With General Sikorski in Exile] (Paris: Instytut LiterCKI, 1968), pp. 68–70.
6   Anita Prażmowska, *Britain and Poland, 1939–1943*, pp. 82–86.

be recruited. If Sikorski's plan that the government-in-exile would make a tangible, namely military, contribution to the joint war effort were to succeed, then Polish manpower would be needed. This could only be found in the Soviet Union. Hence the complex compromise: in return for tapping into an apparent unlimited supply of Polish recruits in Soviet territory, the government-in-exile would increase its influence with Britain and the US. Sikorski calculated that the new enlisted men could strengthen the British war effort in the Middle East and North Africa, and bring more soldiery to the United Kingdom in preparation for the eventual opening of the North European front. [7]

But in his desire to consolidate and increase Polish repute with the Allies, Sikorski had to contend with the fact that postponement of Allied entry into Northern Europe and the opening of a second front, boosted the importance of the Soviet war effort. The stalling of the German thrust into the Soviet heartland and then the reversal of that relentless progression, symbolized by the fighting around Stalingrad, meant that from the beginning of 1943 Soviet strength and endurance became more important than ever to the Allies. Since the main brunt of fighting in Europe was borne by the Soviet Union, and the British and US invasion of northern France did not take place until late spring 1944, the Poles' input to the war effort could no longer secure them a place at the table alongside the Allied triumvirate.

NO WAY BACK

The Poles' tragedy was that their tactic of trying to prevent the British and the US from according the Soviet Union the status of an equal ally, which was to be achieved by increasing Poland's military contribution to the joint endeavour, was ineffective. Until the end of the war, the Polish government-in-exile made formidable attempts to be a genuine fighting ally. Nonetheless, even though the Polish armed forces under the command of the government-in-exile were deployed in support of British military objectives, this had no impact on the situation in occupied Poland. Crucially, however, the Soviet Union did not trust the Polish government-in-exile and in due course the troop formations which had been built up in the Soviet Union and which theoretically might have entered Poland once Germany was defeated were withdrawn to fight under British command. The evacuation of Polish units from Soviet territory to Iran took place in two stages. The first, as a result of which approximately 44,000 Polish soldiers and civilians were transferred to British control, was completed on 24 March 1942. The second, in August the

---

7   *Ibid.*, pp. 89–94.

same year, numbered a further 70,000. The British Middle East Command proceeded to train all those capable of military service for action in North Africa and Italy.

For the Polish government this major shift in how their human resources were to be used in the closing stage of the war had momentous political implications. From this time, the Polish contribution to the Allied war effort was more closely and irreversibly linked to the course of military action pursued by the Western Allies. This happened even though at this stage no commitment to the restoration of Poland to its pre-war borders had been made. The Soviet decision to permit the departure of the Polish units meant that the government-in-exile was further sidelined. Then, following the German discovery of the mass graves of Polish officers in Katyń, an area which until the summer of 1941 had been under Soviet control, relations between the two governments collapsed altogether. On 25 April 1943 the Soviets broke off relations with the Polish government-in-exile. Soviet political and military leaders refused to have any more dealings with them and a new Polish organization, comprising Communists and left wing Socialists, was duly formed in the Soviet Union. This was later transformed into the first post-war administration in Polish areas liberated by the Red Army.

On 4 July 1943 Sikorski died in an air accident off the coast of Gibraltar. The tragedy removed the only Pole who might have safely navigated the perilous diplomatic journey between absolute dependence on the British and the need to recognize the ineluctable Soviet position in the Grand Alliance. We will never know whether his hope of re-establishing relations with the Soviet Union had a realistic prospect of success, but there is no doubt that by turning its back on the government-in-exile, the Soviet leaders rid themselves of an obstacle to their aim of determining the course of post-war developments in Poland.

TEHERAN AND AFTER

By the time the three wartime leaders met in Teheran in November 1943, the Polish government-in-exile had been reduced to an irrelevance. Thus, it was not the decisions made during the conference that decided the future course of events. They merely confirmed the existing state of affairs.

After the lifting of the siege of Stalingrad the Red Army took the initiative on all fronts. In November Kiev was secured and this opened the way to Romania and Poland. The unthinkable scenario was unfolding in front of the Poles' eyes, that of Soviet entry into Polish territories while British and US dependence on the Red Army's continuing advance increased. At the same time, arrangements were being made for the deployment of approximately

70,000 Polish men on the Italian front. For the government-in-exile, even before the convening of the Teheran Conference, all the diplomatic signs were ominous. The British refused to intervene in the crisis caused by the discovery of the Katyń graves. It likewise would not support the Poles when Moscow withdrew diplomatic recognition.

From the Soviet Union came indications that plans were being prepared to create a pro-Soviet Polish administration. Its authority was to be strengthened by the formation of Polish forces which would fight with the Red Army. The Soviet commanders made no effort to contact the leaders of the resistance in occupied Poland, which suggested that there would be no military collaboration with the Home Army in the defeat of the Germans. Decisions made at the Teheran Conference to which the Polish government had not been invited, confirmed this state of affairs. Among the many complex issues discussed by the Big Three, Poland was a contentious topic in view of the presence of the Polish government-in-exile in London, the anticipated British use of Polish units in Italy, and the impending opening of the Second Front which was now postponed until 1944. During the Teheran talks Stalin was led to understand that what mattered most to Churchill was that the Soviet military push continue and the Polish question was not to be an obstacle to that. What was already known in diplomatic circles, namely that Poland would not regain the eastern territories the Soviet Union laid claim, was now formally agreed.

THE WARSAW UPRISING: THE LAST THROW OF THE DICE

Since neither Britain nor the United States was willing to confront the Soviet Union with demands for a commitment that the fate of Poland be determined by the Poles only, the government-in-exile and the leadership of the Home Army had to decide how Poland might be liberated and a first post-war administration established. Clearly, the military units which had been so painstakingly built up in the West could not be brought back to the homeland. They had been pledged to fight alongside the British so their role in the liberation of Poland was not a realistic possibility. A parachute brigade had been put together and trained for active service in Poland when German control would weaken. However, even that unit was handed over to Churchill when he requested it for use in the disastrous Operation Market Garden around the town of Arnhem during 17–25 September 1944.

The perilous situation in which the Polish government found itself in 1944 called for a reappraisal of goals and strategies. But by then there were few options. In the circumstances an earlier plan for a national uprising which would be coordinated with Allied entry into Poland was once more considered. However, when the commanders of the Home Army in Warsaw made the decision to stage an uprising in the capital, the objectives had been scaled down. Its purpose now was to take control of Warsaw in order to prevent the Soviets from installing a puppet regime. In the full knowledge that neither the British nor the US air force would be in a position to support the rebellion, the leaders of the Home Army calculated that the German occupation authorities were abandoning the city. They therefore started hostilities on 1 August 1944.[8] The ferocious fighting which engulfed the town lasted for 63 days with the Germans returning to confront the insurgents in the largest urban fighting of the Second World War. The Soviets predictably refused to help and furthermore refused permission for British planes, which could have flown from Italian bases, to refuel. The Home Army and the skeleton government structures which had been built up under the occupation were destroyed in the battle against the troops brought by the Germans into the city.

The Warsaw Uprising was the last attempt, possibly doomed from the outset, made by sections of the government-in-exile and the Home Army command to reverse the fatal journey into oblivion.

The debate on the painful and limited choices which faced the Polish government-in-exile during the war should include an analysis of the situation which confronted the other two major players in the drama, the Soviet Union and Great Britain. If both pursued policies which seemed to offer the Poles few alternatives and precious little support, then their own priorities in the fight for survival are by necessity an important element in the picture. These issues, however, remain beyond the scope of this chapter.

---

8   Anita J. Prażmowska, *Civil War in Poland, 1942–1948* (Houndmills: Palgrave/Macmillan, 2004), pp. 101–103.

FROM RE-EMERGENCE TO UNCERTAINTIES: THE CHANGING POSITION OF CZECHOSLOVAKIA IN LONDON THROUGHOUT THE SECOND WORLD WAR

VÍT SMETANA

The position of Czechoslovak political refugees in London during the Second World War was unique among the other émigré communities not just because they had been first to find sanctuary there or had arrived even before the outbreak of hostilities. Unlike the other exile governments, that of Czechoslovakia did not simply move across the Channel as a body but had to be established there in a revolutionary manner and undergo a long and tiresome struggle before achieving recognition. Since that experience has been amply described several times already,[1] I will confine myself to drawing some parallels and add assessments of the fascinating process. In the second part of the chapter, I will focus on the impact that the gradually strengthening bond between Czechoslovakia and the Soviet Union had on British-Czechoslovak relations as well as on the overall perception of Czechoslovakia and its representatives in Britain in the later stages of the war.

THE THORNY PATH TO RECOGNITION

While there was no apposite figure on hand from the Czechoslovak side in London to influence Whitehall policy between 15 March 1939, the day the Germans occupied Prague and what was left of Bohemia-Moravia, and the British declaration of war, it became clear by the summer of 1939 that the most suitable figure for any such role would be Edvard Beneš, the second president of Czechoslovakia who had resigned a few days after Munich and fled to Britain (and thence for half a year to the United States). Although he was certainly not popular among many British politicians and officials, they were increasingly aware that they would not be able to avoid accepting Beneš as the leader

---

1   See e.g., Johann Wolfgang Bruegel, "The Recognition of the Czechoslovak Government in London," in *Kosmas – Journal of Czechoslovak and Central European Studies*, Vol. 2, No. 1 (1983), pp. 1–13; Michael Dockrill, "The Foreign Office, Dr Eduard Benes and the Czechoslovak Government-in-Exile, 1939-41," in *Diplomacy & Statecraft*, Vol. 6, No. 3 (1995), pp. 701–718; Jan Kuklík, "The Recognition of the Czechoslovak Government in Exile and its International Status 1939-1941," in *Prague Papers on History of International Relations*, Vol. 1 (1997), pp. 173–205.

of Czechoslovak action in exile.[2] Accordingly, the British did not support French attempts to outmanoeuvre him in the first months of the war. Nevertheless, the question as to the form such exile activity should take remained. The Foreign Office was soon flooded with memoranda asking for recognition of Beneš's team, initially (and unsuccessfully) as a government-in-exile, subsequently (and successfully) as the Czechoslovak National Committee seated in Paris, and finally, in the spring of 1940, as a government-in-exile. Nonetheless, the process of recognition was stalled by disagreements among the Czechoslovak exiles themselves and primarily by British respect for the position of several countries (and their critical attitude towards Beneš) that were not yet at war, such as Hungary and Italy. It was only after these nations had shifted their policies more clearly towards support of Germany, France had collapsed, and Britain's own situation had become gravely critical, that the Foreign Office (and then the British government, now headed by Winston Churchill) decided to take the Czechoslovaks on board and recognize, in July 1940, the Provisional Czechoslovak government.

If there was one single person who more than any other deserved credit for securing almost instant recognition once the grand strategy had made it possible, then it was undoubtedly Robert Bruce Lockhart. He had spent several years in Czechoslovakia as a commercial secretary in the early 1920s, now served in the Political Intelligence Department (P.I.D.), and had been appointed as liaison between the Foreign Office and Czech and Slovak exiles soon after the outbreak of war. For months, he had been supplying the Foreign Office with analyses based largely on information collected by the P.I.D., mostly from refugees. Indeed, these were sometimes far from objective, but their effect supported the Czechoslovak cause.[3] Lockhart's activities, his dozens of cleverly argued memoranda made many officials think seriously about what they considered a bold step, unprecedented from the legal point of view.

Neither Edvard Beneš, now the "Czechoslovak President," nor the members of his government were satisfied with their provisional status. It was Winston Churchill who gave the green light for the process of full recognition, following his visit to the Czechoslovak military unit stationed in Leamington Spa in April 1941. However, this development soon became mired in legal niceties as a result of the Dominions' reluctance to grant such status. This was especially the case with Australian officials as well as with General Jan Smuts, Prime Minister of South Africa, who disliked Beneš personally and had al-

2   "With all his faults Dr. Benes appears to be the only experienced and really able leader among the Czech exiles," Frank Roberts of the Foreign Office's Central Department wrote for instance. The National Archives of the United Kingdom, London (henceforth TNA), FO 371/22899, C 17805/7/12, Roberts' minute, 8 November 1939.

3   The weekly summaries were edited in *Great Britain Foreign Office Weekly Political Intelligence Summaries*, Vol. I, Oct. 1939 – June 1940 (London: Kraus International Publishers, 1983).

ready been against recognition of his government in 1940.[4] Some authors, both British and Czech, have wondered why the Foreign Office consulted the Dominions on the matter and whether the move was not merely a pretext for procrastination.[5] On the other hand, the War Cabinet clearly aimed at having home and Commonwealth foreign policy co-ordinated in time of war. It was in fact Foreign Office experts, such as William Strang, who first sought to overcome the Dominions' resistance – only to be stymied by the Secretary of State for Dominion Affairs, Viscount Cranborne. This setback notwithstanding, they quickly came up with a compromise solution that would leave out the humiliating adjective "provisional" from the exile government's official title, while maintaining a legal distance. Nevertheless, another political directive was needed for the granting of full *de iure* recognition. This came only in consequence of the hasty Soviet readiness to recognize the Czechoslovak government-in-exile, just days after the German attack on the USSR on 22 June 1941. At that point, Foreign Secretary Anthony Eden realized the threat posed by a dramatic rise in Soviet influence over the Czechoslovak public as well as over exile politicians as a result of British non-recognition and found a means to overcome the Dominions' reservations. The British government granted full recognition on 18 July 1941, just a couple of hours after the Soviets had done so.[6]

Irrespective of all the delays, British recognition of the Czechoslovak government in 1941 was in fact little short of a miracle.[7] The Czechoslovak Republic had become legally re-established on British soil with Edvard Beneš as its head. Although, as many Czechoslovak exiles saw it, the British needed two years for something that the Soviets managed to grant in two weeks, this comparison is hardly sound. The Kremlin rulers could easily make a foreign policy U-turn twice in two years and present both as part of a continuous line

---

4   "The memory of the commitments of the last war should counsel caution," Smuts wrote, and concerning Beneš he added: "I frankly dislike Benes's persistence. He has already occasioned too much trouble." TNA, FO 371/24289, C 7646/2/12, Smuts to Halifax, 8 July 1940; FO 371/26394, C 4078/1320/12, Roberts' minute, 22 April 1941.

5   Martin David Brown, *Dealing with Democrats. The British Foreign Office and the Czechoslovak Émigrés in Great Britain, 1939 to 1945* (Frankfurt am Main: Peter Lang, 2006), p. 99; Libuše Otáhalová, Milada Červinková, eds., *Dokumenty z historie československé politiky 1939-1943* [Documents from the History of Czechoslovak Politics 1939–1943] (Praha: Academia, 1966) [henceforth *DHČSP*], No. 204, p. 249, note 1.

6   On 17 July 1941, the War Cabinet agreed that it was "very desirable" that full recognition should be announced the next day, in order to "avoid undue emphasis being placed on the full recognition by Russia." Bodleian Library, microfilm, CAB 65/19, WM(41)71, 17 July 1941. The Dominions were given a mere 17-hour time frame to express their possible dissent. Of course, it was neither welcomed, nor expected. For further details on the process of full British recognition, see Vít Smetana, *In the Shadow of Munich. British Policy towards Czechoslovakia from the Endorsement to the Renunciation of the Munich Agreement (1938-1942)* (Praha: Karolinum, 2008), pp. 244-277.

7   Cf. Bruegel, "The Recognition of the Czechoslovak Government in London," p. 1.

in Soviet foreign policy. British foreign policy, on the other hand, at least respected certain rules of international law and the constitutional procedures of individual countries. Beneš in fact offered a *modus vivendi* – a "theory of juridical continuity" with respect to the pre-Munich republic and his own presidential function. However, since this was based on the illegality of everything that had been agreed under threat of force, its acceptance by the British authorities would have meant that British involvement in the Munich Agreement and subsequent negotiations had been illegal from the outset. The juridical continuity of the Czechoslovak Republic in this regard clashed with a like continuity in British foreign policy. Although by 1941 most British politicians and officials agreed with the view prevailing in the Foreign Office already in October 1938 that Munich had been a debacle,[8] it was something else to say that the Prime Minister's signature on an international agreement was invalid from the very beginning. Not even Churchill and Eden were ready to go that far, despite the fact that they had acquired much of their prestige from criticism of the appeasement policy.

Thus recognition of the Czechoslovak government was accorded as a revolutionary act, unprecedented and unparalleled from the legal point of view. What General de Gaulle did not achieve in four years in Britain, Beneš managed to get in less than two, even though their original positions had not been dissimilar. (And Beneš shared with the French general his "often baseless suspicions of Britain."[9]) Indeed, the leader of the Free French really did struggle to gain British recognition; in 1941 he even sought Beneš's support to attain the goal.[10] True, before 1940, Beneš had been far more notable a figure than de Gaulle. For 20 years his name had been intrinsically connected with Czechoslovakia and therefore his claim to lead the state structures in exile was less questionable than that of Charles de Gaulle. On the other hand, by 1941 de Gaulle was able to muster military forces whose number far exceeded those of the Czechoslovaks.[11] There were perhaps three reasons for the difference in treatment accorded to the two men and their efforts by Britain.

---

8   Donald Lammers, "From Whitehall after Munich: The Foreign Office and the Future Course of British Policy," in *The Historical Journal*, Vol. 16, No. 4 (1973), pp. 831–856.

9   Elisabeth Barker, *Churchill and Eden at War* (London: Macmillan, 1978), p. 32.

10 On 17 October 1941, the French diplomat Maurice Dejean asked Beneš to agree to a common French-Czechoslovak statement whereby all pre-Munich treaties between France and Czechoslovakia would automatically become valid again, something that would help de Gaulle and contribute to the recognition of his committee. Beneš refused, arguing that Munich had been a terrible blow to the Czechoslovak people, one that could not be so easily overcome. Hoover Institution Archives, Stanford University, Palo Alto (California) (henceforth HIA Stanford), Eduard Táborský Collection, box 5, folder "Czechoslovakia – Relations with France," Beneš's memorandum on his talk with Dejean, 17 October 1941.

11 Probably the best book on the topic of de Gaulle's exile in Britain is: François Kersaudy, *De Gaulle et Churchill. La mésentente cordiale* (Paris: Perrin, 2001) [Czech translation by Pavel Starý: *De Gaulle a Churchill. Srdečná neshoda* (Praha: Themis, 2003)].

Firstly, unlike de Gaulle, Beneš could prove that he had the support of the resistance organizations at home as well as that of the leaders of the government of the Protectorate of Bohemia and Moravia.[12] Secondly, many of the French exiles in London were highly critical of de Gaulle and made no secret of their feelings when talking to influential British contacts.[13] Beneš, for his part, either managed to come to terms with his opponents, at least temporarily in 1939-1940 (Lev Prchala, Štefan Osuský, Milan Hodža), or to convince prominent British circles of the insignificance of his adversaries. Apart from Milan Hodža, who left for the United States in 1941, Beneš's Czechoslovak opponents in London were virtually nonentities and the British authorities treated them as such, especially if their activities seemed to undermine the Allied war effort.[14] Thirdly, there was a clear feeling on the part of Churchill, Eden, and many other British politicians and officials that Britain owed something to Czechoslovakia. Although only a few explicit statements along those lines can be found in the relevant documentation,[15] it was probably one of the reasons behind the miracle of the successful creation and recognition of the whole state apparatus of Czechoslovak institutions on British soil.

The Czechoslovak exiles, however, expected much more – preferential treatment as a way of repaying the "Munich debt." Instead, they encountered the slowness of bureaucratic machinery and, always, subordination of their lot to major strategic priorities and overall political directives. To most Czechoslovak exiles this seemed as intentional procrastination and a continuation of the "Munich policy" and provided, at the least, an incentive to look for an alternative foreign policy course that would replace reliance on the West.

"President Benes' policy is to commit us, our policy is to avoid commitment." This is how Roger Makins, the then head of the Foreign Office's Central

---

12   As late as January 1942, Eden rejected de Gaulle's proposal that he should take over the Special Operations Executive's French section with the following words: "It would not, we fear, be prudent to rely [...] on the assumption that the National Committee enjoys the adherence, open or secret, of a very large majority of French citizens." Cited in Barker, *Churchill and Eden at War*, p. 48.

13   Ibid., p. 44.

14   See Jan Kuklík, Jan Němeček, *Proti Benešovi! Česká a slovenská protibenešovská opozice v Londýně 1939-1945* [Against Beneš! The Czech and Slovak Anti-Beneš Opposition in London 1939-1945] (Praha: Karolinum, 2004), esp. pp. 369-411.

15   There are, however, exceptions. See e.g., Archiv Ministerstva zahraničních věcí ČR [Archive of the Foreign Ministry of the Czech Republic], Prague (henceforth AMZV), fund Londýnský archiv – důvěrný [London Archive – Confidential] (henceforth LA-D), box 61, 169/dův/41, Gustav Winter's report on his talk with Miss Davies, director of the Labour Party's publication department, 20 January 1941. Similarly, John Monro Troutbeck of the Foreign Office's Central Department wrote as early as 1 September 1939 in a memorandum: "On moral grounds we cannot hold ourselves wholly blameless for their [the Czechoslovaks'] current plight." TNA, FO 371/22899, C 13304/7/12, Troutbeck's memorandum, 1 September 1939.

Department, summed up in one of his minutes the core of continued tensions between Beneš and the Foreign Office.[16] The President constantly criticized the British for "lack of policy," and for being unprepared for a possible German collapse. In his mind this was connected with the uncertain status of the former Czechoslovak territories ceded to Germany, Hungary, and Poland in 1938.[17] All his initiatives in this matter, however, failed as a result of Britain's adherence to the US government's policy of non-commitment in territorial matters. Although Whitehall was considering breaching this principle in response to Soviet demands for securing the territorial acquisitions gained in 1939/40, it did not want to do so in the case of "minor allies," including Czechoslovakia. Hence the relatively poor outcome from Beneš's next diplomatic offensive from the spring of 1942 that aimed at the "undoing of Munich." Instead of guaranteeing the pre-Munich Czechoslovak borders, the British government merely pledged that in the final settlement of the Czechoslovak frontiers at the end of the war it would "not be influenced by any changes effected in and since 1938."[18] It would appear from Beneš's subsequent policy that he then realized he was approaching the very limits of the commitment he could hope to obtain from Britain during the war.[19] Only in March 1945 did the British government agree to grant the Czechoslovak government "full political authority" (rather than "sovereignty") over the territory of Czechoslovakia within the frontiers of 31 December 1937.[20]

IN THE SOVIET EMBRACE

Until 1942, it seemed that Czechoslovak foreign policy was directed primarily at achieving close co-operation with Poland. This was in line with the highly elaborated British plans for federalization of the area lying between Russia

16   TNA, FO 371/26388, C 13503/216/12, Makins' minute, 28 November 1941.
17   House of Lords Record Office, London, Bruce Lockhart Papers, diary No. 38, 9 August 1941, 16 August 1941, 28 December 1941. For further details see Vít Smetana: "Robert Bruce Lockhart and His Patronage of Czechoslovak Exiles and Their Political Programme in Britain during the Second World War," in Andrew Chandler, Katerzyna Stokłosa, Jutta Vinzent, eds., *Exile and Patronage. Cross-Cultural Negotiations beyond the Third Reich* (Berlin: Lit Verlag, 2006), pp. 167–177.
18   TNA, FO 371/30835, C 7210/326/12, Eden to Masaryk, 5 August 1942, Masaryk to Eden, 5 August 1942; Edvard Beneš, *Šest let exilu a druhé světové války. Řeči, projevy a dokumenty z r. 1938–45* [Six Years of Exile and the Second World War. Addresses, Speeches, and Documents from the Years 1938–45] (Praha: Družstevní práce, 1946), pp. 473–475, here p. 474.
19   Potentially much more important was another British pledge from the summer of 1942 – to support transfers of national minorities after the war as a method of solving a perennial problem of East-Central Europe. For further details see the chapter by Jan Kuklík and Jan Němeček in this volume.
20   Vilém Prečan, "British Attitudes towards Czechoslovakia, 1944–45," in *Bohemia*, Vol. 29, No. 1 (1988), pp. 73–87.

and Germany.[21] Thus the British supported the plan for a post-war Czechoslovak-Polish confederation and agreed that this should have friendly relations
with the Soviet Union. By the end of 1942, however, Polish-Soviet relations
had proved to be an insurmountable obstacle to any such arrangement and
Beneš and his government decided to secure above all an alliance with the
USSR.[22]

It was this decision and the attendant circumstances that led to a conflict
with Foreign Secretary Anthony Eden, a man whom the Czechoslovaks had
by then found a major supporter.[23] In June 1943, Beneš returned from a trip
to the United States.[24] He had had several opportunities to talk to Roosevelt,
especially about the need for post-war co-operation with the Soviet Union.
The two men agreed on many issues and both were protagonists of the "con-
vergence theory," which foresaw not only continued co-operation between
the Soviet Union and the western Great Powers after the war, but admitted
also the possibility that democracy could and perhaps even should be affected
by certain progressive social trends that had been implemented in the Soviet
model. Back in London, Beneš informed Eden that he had secured the support of Roosevelt, Secretary of State Cordell Hull, Under-Secretary Sumner
Welles, and his deputy Adolf Berle for the idea of a Soviet-Czechoslovak
treaty. British surprise, however, met with an American denial. Indeed, State
Department officials said that none of them had ever even spoken about such
a treaty. Upon this, Eden put Beneš in a rather tight spot and his hasty "ex-
planations" were hardly convincing.[25] Moreover, Eden took umbrage at the

21 See e.g., András D. Bán, ed., *Pax Britannica: Wartime Foreign Office Documents Regarding Plans for
a Post-bellum East Central Europe* (Boulder – Highland Lakes: Columbia University Press, 1997).

22 For further details see Smetana, *In the Shadow of Munich*, pp. 244–277; Brown, *Dealing with Democrats*, pp. 219–250. On the topic of Polish-Czechoslovak relations, see Jan Němeček, *Od spojenectví k roztržce* [From Alliance to Quarrel] (Praha: Academia, 2003). A Polish study on the same
subject that comes to entirely different conclusions is Marek Kazimierz Kamiński, *Edvard
Beneš kontra gen. Władysław Sikorski. Polityka władz czechosłowackich na emigracji wobec rządu Polskiego na uchodźstwie 1939–1943* [Edvard Beneš versus General Władysław Sikorski. The Policy
of the Czechoslovak Government-in-Exile Towards the Polish Government-in-Exile 1939–1943]
(Warszawa: Neriton, 2005).

23 See Vít Smetana, "Beneš a Britové za druhé světové války" [Beneš and the British during the
Second World War], in *Na pozvání Masarykova ústavu* [Upon the Invitation of the Masaryk Insti-
tute], Vol. 1 (Praha: Masarykův ústav, 2004), pp. 73–86, here p. 83.

24 For further details see Jan Němeček, Helena Nováčková, Ivan Šťovíček, eds., "Edvard Beneš
v USA v roce 1943. Dokumenty," in *Sborník archivních prací* [Collection of Archival Works], Vol.
49 (1999), pp. 469–565.

25 National Archives and Record Administration, College Park – Maryland, RG 59, Department of
State File 860F.00/1009 and European War 1939/28633 1/2, Welles's record of his talk with Beneš,
17 May 1943, record of Berle's talk with Beneš, 31 May 1943; TNA, FO 371/34339, C 8317/2426/G,
Halifax to Eden, No. 2978, 29 June 1943, Halifax to Eden, No. 3029, 2 July 1943; FO 371/34338,
C 7493/2462/G, Eden to Nichols, 30 June 1943; Jan Němeček, Helena Nováčková, Ivan Šťovíček,
Miroslav Tejchman, eds., *Československo-sovětské vztahy v diplomatických jednáních 1939–1945, Do-
kumenty* 1–2 [Czechoslovak-Soviet Relations in Diplomatic Negotiations 1939–1945. Documents

fact hat Beneš only revealed his real intention under pressure, having spoken about a trilateral treaty with Poland's participation before his departure to the United States. He also realized that Poland, on whose behalf Britain had declared war in September 1939, was being left out in the cold.[26]

Furthermore, in 1942 Britain had tentatively agreed with the Soviets on the so-called *self-denying ordinance*, forbidding the Great Powers from concluding treaties with "minor allies." In such treaties, the British saw the danger of a European split. Eden's categorically negative attitude made Beneš postpone his trip to the USSR.[27] However, at the Moscow conference of Foreign Ministers in October 1943 in Moscow, Eden unexpectedly endorsed the treaty having found its proposed wording quite benign and generally acceptable. Another reason for Eden's consent lay in US evasiveness. Although State Department experts considered such treaties obsolete and saw the Czechoslovak-Soviet Treaty as a tool whereby the Russians could strengthen their increasingly dominant position on the European continent,[28] the British did not get *any* support from Washington for their opposition to the treaty. Indeed, when the topic was raised at the Moscow conference, Cordell Hull simply apologized and said he was not familiar with all the details.[29] Thus, as in many other similar situations, the Americans refused to risk a conflict with the Soviets because of an issue that was not of global importance and left it entirely to the British to play the role of the "bad guy."[30] The British then felt that they had no choice but to back down.

Yet, it is not entirely clear to what extent the Czechoslovak-Soviet Treaty of 12 December 1943 actually hampered Anglo-Czechoslovak relations in the long run. On the one hand, Eden telegraphed the following words from Moscow: "I trust we shall offer Beneš no bouquets. His part in this business seems to have been to tell half-truths to either side, making as a result a good deal

I-II], 2 Vols. (Praha: Státní ústřední archiv v Praze, 1998–1999) (henceforth ČSSVDJ), Vol. 1, No. 264, pp. 525–528, Beneš's record of his talk with Eden, 30 June 1943. However, we do not know whether Beneš discussed the issue of a Soviet-Czechoslovak treaty with President Roosevelt, since no record of that talk is deposited in Roosevelt's files.

26   For further details see Vít Smetana, "The British, the Americans and the Czechoslovak-Soviet Treaty of 1943," in *Czech Journal of Contemporary History*, Vol. III (2015), pp. 5–24.

27   Jaroslav Hrbek, Vít Smetana et al., *Draze zaplacená svoboda. Osvobození Československa 1944–1945* [Dearly Paid Freedom. The Liberation of Czechoslovakia 1944–1945], Vol. 1 (Praha: Paseka, 2009), pp. 57–58.

28   Geir Lundestad, *The American Non-Policy towards Eastern Europe: 1943–1947* (Tromsö – Bergen – Oslo: Universitetsforlaget, 1978), pp. 150–151.

29   Library of Congress, Washington, D.C., W. Averell Harriman Papers, box 170, undated handwritten notes of W. A. Harriman and J. C. Dunn; *Foreign Relations of the United States* (Washington: US Government Printing Office) (henceforth FRUS), 1943, Vol. I, pp. 625–26, Charles Bohlen's record of the 6th meeting of the trilateral conference, 24 October 1943.

30   Cf. Petr Mareš, "Československo na sklonku 2. světové války" [Czechoslovakia at the Close of the Second World War], in Jakub Čermín, ed., *Národ se ubránil, 1939–1945* [The Nation Resisted Successfully] (Praha: Národní osvobození, 1995), pp. 93–98, here p. 94.

of unnecessary mischief." He also called Beneš a *petty intriguer*.[31] On the other hand, on 6 January 1944 Churchill wrote to Roosevelt from Marrakesh about the talk he had had with Beneš two days earlier: "Beneš has been here and is very hopeful about the Russian situation. He may be most useful in trying to make the Poles see reason and in reconciling them to the Russians."[32] In fact, this is what almost happened. In a concerted effort to make Prime Minister Stanisław Mikołajczyk and the other Poles agree to the Curzon line as the Polish eastern border, Beneš was to play the role of a vanguard in the Allied persuading campaign. However, his interference in the Polish-Soviet dispute was utterly unacceptable to the Poles, even though Roosevelt repeatedly recommended him as an intermediary.[33]

In British materials from the turn of 1943/44, we find expressions of fear that the Soviet Union was starting to build an exclusive sphere of influence in Eastern Europe.[34] Nonetheless, Beneš's Soviet policy – especially when compared to the fruitless frontal resistance of the "intransigent" London Poles – was regarded as quite realistic within British government circles. This was all the more so because they did not know the details of his recent negotiations in Moscow which accompanied the signing of the Soviet-Czechoslovak treaty and culminated in Beneš's plea for co-ordination of Czechoslovak and Soviet foreign policies.[35] What British officials loathed were the methods that Beneš sometimes used rather than the visible substance of his policy. For its part, from early 1944, Czechoslovak diplomacy clearly sought to improve relations with Britain and obtain concrete assurance of her continued interest in Czechoslovakia.[36]

Yet, the friendly British attitude at the time certainly had its geo-strategic limits. The British government, like that of the United States, was neither

31 TNA, FO 371/34340, C 12497/515/12, Archibald Clark Kerr to Foreign Office, No. 86, 25 October 1943.
32 Warren F. Kimball, ed., *Churchill and Roosevelt, the Complete Correspondence*, Vol. II. (London: Collins, 1984), C-533, 6 January 1944, pp. 650–651.
33 For further details see Vít Smetana, *Ani vojna, ani mír. Velmoci, Československo a střední Evropa v sedmi dramatech na prahu druhé světové a studené války* [Neither War, nor Peace. The Great Powers, Czechoslovakia and Central Europe in Seven Dramas on the Eve of the Second World War and the Cold War] (Praha: Nakladatelství Lidové noviny, 2016), pp. 320–321, 328–329.
34 See e.g., Detlef Brandes, *Großbritannien und seine osteuropäischen Alliierten 1939-1943. Die Regierungen Polens, der Tschechoslowakei und Jugoslawiens im Londoner Exil vom Kriegsausbruch bis zur Konferenz von Teheran* (München: R. Oldenbourg Verlag, 1988), p. 552.
35 Archiv vneshnei politiki, Moskva [Foreign Policy Archive, Moscow] (henceforth AVP), fund 06 – Collection of Molotov's Secretariat, opis 5, papka 33, delo 401; *ČSSVDJ*, Vol. 2, No. 58–70, pp. 121–189. See also Hrbek, Smetana et al. *Draze zaplacená svoboda*, Vol. 1, pp. 69–72; Vojtech Mastny, *Russia's Road to the Cold War: Diplomacy, Warfare, and the Politics of Communism, 1941–1945* (New York: Columbia University Press, 1979), p. 136.
36 See Prečan, "British Attitudes towards Czechoslovakia, 1944-45." As late as 2 September 1944, Frank K. Roberts commented on one of Beneš's speeches: "Dr. Benes is certainly playing up now to the west." TNA, FO 371/38975, C 11241/11241/12, Roberts' minute, 2 September 1944.

willing to sign any far-reaching treaty with Czechoslovakia, nor to negotiate an agreement on the administration of liberated Czechoslovak territory,
since, until the last weeks of the war, it seemed highly unlikely that the Anglo-American armies would ever actually get there. Thus the Czechoslovak
exile leaders, supported by British Ambassador Philip Nichols, only managed
to extract a vague declaration of continued British interest in maintaining
most friendly relations with Czechoslovakia after its liberation, presented
by the British Foreign Secretary in the House of Commons on 2 August 1944.[37]
Eden was unwilling to go beyond that, pointing out that Czecho-Slovakia was
not "popular in any quarter of this house just now, and Dr. Benes is much
distrusted. All this may be unjust, but it is a consequence of what is regarded
as Dr. Benes's over-eagerness to obey Moscow's behest. Unfriendly people
describe Dr. B. as Stalin's jackal."[38]

Meanwhile, Czechoslovak public diplomacy proved to be quite inept in
dispelling this kind of stereotyping. Viktor Fischl, one of the most far-sighted
officials in the Czechoslovak Foreign Ministry, had already suggested in February 1944 that Czechoslovakia should tone down the ambivalent impact of the
Czechoslovak-Soviet Treaty by some common Anglo-Czechoslovak initiatives
and he saw the creation of the Czechoslovak Committee in the House of Commons as an ideal start. This was underscored all the more by the fact that all the
other allies, including the Soviet Union, had already set up such committees.[39]
However, due to delays on both sides, it took another four and a half months
before the establishment of the Committee under the chairmanship of the
Conservative MP Hamilton Kerr was announced at a meeting of the House.[40]

The achievements of this body in the subsequent nine months of its existence were unimpressive, to say the least. On 10 April 1945, the Committee's secretary, Vera Haslop, wrote to Hubert Ripka, the Czechoslovak State
Minister in the Foreign Ministry and Beneš's most efficient collaborator in
the field of foreign policy. After stressing how much she had the Czech cause
at heart, she pointed out the utter ineptitude of most Czechoslovak politicians and officials to make Members of Parliament, including those on the
Labour benches, feel interested in the Czechs and their affairs. There was, she
maintained, a complete lack of imagination in every function they organized
and in the way they dispensed hospitality and organized meetings: "There
has been an utter lack of presentable people to talk to Members, people who

---

37   *Parliamentary Debates, House of Commons*, 5th Series (London: His Majesty's Stationery Office),
     Vol. 402, 2 August 1944, Cols. 1418–1419.
38   TNA, FO 371/38922, C 9449/63/12, Eden's minute, 15 July 1944.
39   AMZV, LA-D, box 61, 1215/dův./41, report by Viktor Fischl "Anglická reakce na čs.-sovětskou
     smlouvu" [English Reaction to the Czechoslovak-Soviet Treaty], 7 February 1944.
40   Ibid., 4853/dův./44, report by Viktor Fischl on the issue of the Czechoslovak Committee in the
     British Parliament, 27 June 1944.

speak the sort of English which does not have to be retranslated, and the sort of people who are acceptable to English people. If I live to be a hundred I shall not forget our terrible lunch with [Minister of Social Welfare, Ján] Bečko, and I shall not forget that most of the Czech hospitality has been on similar hopeless lines." However, she set these "qualities" against the virtues of the men of the Czechoslovak armed forces who were "nice, competent, well-mannered," looked "right to English eyes" and "could make an infinitely better job of the Czech-British public relation than has been done so far." She rightly concluded that it was "a most urgent time for making the people of England understand the Czechoslovak position vis-à-vis the U.S.S.R." and Britain and that it had to begin with Parliament.[41]

In spite of such reservations, the official Czechoslovak interpretation of the alliance treaty with the USSR seemed increasingly plausible – namely that the country had become part of the Soviet security sphere without losing any of its liberty and sovereignty thereby. Thus, throughout 1944, the British Foreign Office expected that Czechoslovakia's international position would not be complicated after the war; potential problems were to be sought within the state itself (such as the question of national minorities or the status of Slovakia).[42] Also, the US State Department gradually came to realize that it was natural for Czechoslovakia to lean towards Moscow in security matters. However, this did not necessarily mean that the country was to be left entirely in thrall to the Soviets. Some key experts and diplomats (Charles Bohlen and Averell Harriman) even formulated the idea that Czechoslovakia was a real "test-case" of Soviet sincerity and readiness to co-operate with the West, given the lengths to which Beneš had gone to accommodate Moscow's wishes and aspirations.[43] The first signs that Stalin regarded these gestures as insufficient and preferred to assume a more authoritative tone in his policy even towards compliant Czechoslovakia had already come in the final stages of the war – with Soviet ambivalence regarding the uprising in Slovakia, the conquest of Sub-Carpathian Russia or Ruthenia, the refusal to allow Western diplomats to enter Czechoslovak territory liberated by the Red Army, and,

41 HIA Stanford, Ivo Ducháček Collection, box 25, env. 14, Vera Haslop's letter to Hubert Ripka, 10 April 1945.
42 TNA, FO 371/38931, C 1902/239/12, Roberts' minute, 15 February 1944, C 4882/239/12, Roberts' minute, 19 April 1944.
43 Archiv Ústavu T. G. Masaryka [Archive of the T. G. Masaryk Institute], Praha, box 153, Beneš's record of his talk with Harriman, 27 May 1944; NARA, RG 59, Records of Harley A. Notter, 1939–45 – records of the Advisory Committee on Post-War Foreign Policy, 1942–45, box 84, record of the 14th meeting of the Subcommittee on Problems of European Organization, 3 March 1944. See also the State Department analysis sent to President Harry S. Truman on 4 May 1945, cited in: Petr Mareš, "Čekání na Godota. Americká politika a volby v Československu v květnu 1946" [Waiting for Godot. US Policy and the Elections in Czechoslovakia in May 1946], in Soudobé dějiny [Contemporary History], Vol. 4, No. 1 (1997), pp. 7–25, here p. 8.

finally, the ostentatious pressure that Soviet People's Commissar of Foreign Affairs, Vyacheslav Molotov, exerted on Jan Masaryk during the critical votes at the UN founding conference in San Francisco, to which the Czechoslovak Foreign Minister responded with feeble obedience.[44]

However, immediately before Beneš and his Ministers' return home via Moscow, major British newspapers including *The Times* and the *Daily Telegraph* predicted an optimistic future for Czechoslovakia, pointing out the friendly cooperation of Russia secured by the treaty of 1943. They also paid tribute to Beneš's efforts in exile for the sake of his country. Most commentators foresaw that Czechoslovakia would have to deal primarily with various internal problems similar to those which would be faced by the governments of other liberated countries. The Catholic *Tablet* represented a dissenting voice. It criticized Beneš's policy towards the Poles on the one hand and the Russians on the other, which had culminated in Czechoslovakia's recognition of the puppet "Lublin government" just before the Yalta Conference. It condemned Beneš as the man who had used his good strategic position to undermine the efforts of Central European nations to secure their future independence through closer mutual association. He still saw the Habsburg shadow everywhere, which was probably one of the reasons why he had so swiftly abandoned talks with the London Poles on the first indications that Moscow was not in favour of them – a year before the Soviet government broke diplomatic relations with the Polish government-in-exile. The *Tablet* predicted that as somebody who really hated totalitarianism, Dr. Beneš would not feel comfortable amongst real Kremlin men like Bierut and Tito, and also pointed out that the Soviets now had at least three tools at their disposal to exert pressure on him whenever they so wished: the Lublin government (through renewed claims for the disputed Těšín district), the Ukrainians (through the possible annexation of Carpathian Ruthenia), and above all the Czechoslovak Communists (through the permanent threat that he might be replaced by someone else if he tried to act independently).[45]

---

44   AVP, fund 06 – Collection of Molotov's Secretariat, opis 7, papka 51, delo 820, Masaryk's exchanges with Molotov and Vladimir Nikolaevich Pavlov. See also Vít Smetana, "Concessions or Conviction? Czechoslovakia's Road to the Cold War and the Soviet Bloc," in Mark Kramer and Vít Smetana, eds., *Imposing, Maintaining, and Tearing Open the Iron Curtain. The Cold War and East-Central Europe, 1945-1989* (Lanham – Boulder – New York – Toronto – Plymouth: Lexington Books, 2014) pp. 55-85, here pp. 61-62; Hrbek, Smetana et al., *Draze zaplacená svoboda*, Vol. 1, pp. 255-310; Vol. 2, pp. 17-20, 27, 30, 61-64; Jan Němeček, "V sovětském objetí. Prezident a vláda v osvobozených Košicích 1945" [In the Soviet Embrace. The President and the Government in Liberated Košice in 1945], in Stanislav Kokoška et al., *Nultá hodina? Československo na jaře 1945 ve strategických souvislostech* [The Zero Hour? Czechoslovakia in the Spring of 1945 in a Strategic Context] (Praha: Euroslavica, 2011), pp. 21-29.

45   HIA Stanford, Eduard Táborský Collection, box 6, folder "Reviews of the British Press Prepared by the Information Service of the Czechoslovak Ministry of Foreign Affairs," surveys for 22 and 10 February 1945.

Admittedly, these were prophetic words, although they by no means represented the prevailing opinion among British political circles at the cusp of war and peace in Europe. Ambassador Sir Philip Nichols departed for Prague confident that it should be possible to prevent Czechoslovakia from falling completely within the Soviet orbit. He even formulated a very concrete agenda on how Britain could contribute significantly towards realizing that objective – especially by strengthening cultural and commercial ties and by providing assistance in re-establishing the Czechoslovak air force.[46] Although Britain was successful in fulfilling these particular goals,[47] this was not enough to forestall the aggressive march of the Czechoslovak Communists, backed by the Soviet ally, towards securing complete power, which was achieved in less than three years.

46   TNA, FO 371/47107, N 2839/365/12, Nichols to Warner, 14 March 1945.
47   For further details see Mark Cornwall, "The Rise and Fall of a 'Special Relationship'? Britain and Czechoslovakia, 1930–1948," in Brian Brivati, Harriet Jones, eds., *What Difference Did the War Make?* (Leicester: Leicester University Press, 1993), pp. 133–134.

THE FACTORS SHAPING THE INTERNATIONAL POLITICAL STATUS AND THE FOREIGN POLICY OF THE CZECHOSLOVAK AUTHORITIES IN EXILE, 1939–1945

RADOSŁAW PAWEŁ ŻURAWSKI VEL GRAJEWSKI

The disaster that confronted the Czechoslovak state as a result of the Munich Agreement[1] created a completely new political situation in which the Second Czechoslovak Republic was forced to exist. Prague ceased to be an ally of France and part of her system of collective defence. The influence of both Western powers, France and Great Britain, on what was happening in Czechoslovakia, and their interest in the country's affairs, rapidly diminished. The new state having been deprived of an important segment of her previous territory had become defenceless from a military point of view[2] and was no longer in a position to face down growing German political pressure. Czechoslovak attempts to avoid additional conflicts and further losses failed against the demands made by the Hungarians and the Poles. On top of that, the state was weakened even more by discord between the Czechs and Slovaks themselves. However, the Second Republic continued to enjoy full international recognition and the legitimacy of her authorities was, generally, not questioned.[3]

The invasion of Czechoslovakia by the German Wehrmacht and the occupation of Prague on 15 March 1939 greatly changed the situation. The United States of America, as well as France and Great Britain, refused to recognize the German action as legal. Nevertheless, after some hesitation, London and Paris eventually accepted the existence of the Slovak state on *de facto* (though not *de jure*) grounds, and both were poised to take the same course with re-

---

1   *Documents on German Foreign Policy 1918–1945. From the Archives of the German Foreign Ministry*, series D (1937–1945), Vol. 2, *Germany and Czechoslovakia 1937–1938* (London: His Majesty's Stationery Office, 1950), No. 675, pp. 1014–1016, Agreement Signed at Munich Between Germany, the United Kingdom, France, and Italy, 29 September 1938.

2   For a discussion about the possibilities of defending Czechoslovakia in 1938, see: Karel Bartošek, "Could We Have Fought? — The 'Munich Complex' in Czech Policies and Czech Thinking," in Norman Stone, Eduard Strouhal, eds., *Czechoslovakia: Crossroads and Crises 1918–88* (Basingstoke: Macmillan, 1992), pp. 101–119.

3   On the other hand, the Czechoslovak envoy in Washington, Col. Vladimír S. Hurban, did not notify the American authorities of the Munich Agreement, the resignation of Edvard Beneš, and the appointment of Emil Hácha as the new President of the republic.

gard to the Protectorate of Bohemia and Moravia but were prevented from this move by the outbreak of war on 1 September 1939.

The completely new situation changed the position of Beneš and his political allies considerably. At first, the destruction of the Second Czecho-Slovak Republic was considered by Britain and France to be a violation of the Munich Agreement, and the subsequent German attack on Poland brought both countries into war with the Third Reich. This change in circumstances presented Czechoslovak emigration with the opportunity to make a political comeback. Beneš, however, having resigned from presidential office in October 1938, was in fact a private person, a former president of Czechoslovakia, no matter how well known in the political world. So in September 1939 he could represent nobody but himself and a small group of his political collaborators. This situation notwithstanding, the bravery of the Czechoslovak diplomats, among others Štefan Osuský and Vladimír Hurban, coupled with the friendly attitude of host countries allowed the retention of some important diplomatic posts for future Czechoslovak action in exile, most notably the embassies and consulates in the United States, France, Great Britain, the Soviet Union, and Poland. Although it was an undoubted success for the Czechoslovak émigrés, still nobody could provide an answer to the question as to what government those diplomatic missions actually referred to. All had renounced obedience to the government in the Protectorate but no other recognized authority existed as representative of the Czechoslovak state and its people in international relations. In reality, the stance taken by Washington, London, Paris, Moscow, and Warsaw towards Czechoslovak diplomats in exile was more an act of protest against German conduct, than an indication of any particular political line the governments of the respective countries were going to adopt in their approach to the Czechoslovak question. Nonetheless, the fact that the four Great Powers had sanctioned the diplomatic posts on their territories, and simultaneously rejected the legality of the German action in Prague allowed Beneš and his circle to proclaim the idea of the continued existence of the First Czechoslovak Republic albeit temporarily under German occupation.

From the point of view of the Western powers, however, the situation was by no means so clear-cut. Both Paris and London made a clear distinction between Czechs and Slovaks. In the first months of the war, they were not prepared to tie themselves to any notion of rebuilding the Czechoslovak state. On the contrary, this was still very much an open question in both capitals and was the main reason why attempts to obtain recognition of an interim Czechoslovak government-in-exile had failed in autumn 1939. The deep divisions among émigré Czechoslovak politicians served as an official excuse for the refusal. In point of fact there was rivalry and wrangling between

Beneš, Osuský and Milan Hodža.[4] Osuský, the Czechoslovak envoy in Paris, and Hodža, the former Prime Minister of Czechoslovakia, were supported by the French government. Beneš, in turn, had better relations with British politicians but, by and large, was regarded as *persona non grata* in France. In spite of serious reservations, London eventually came to accept Beneš, as leader of Czechoslovak political emigration but was still strongly against the formation of any Czechoslovak government-in-exile. The French authorities, on the other hand, were much more amenable to the idea of such a government but not with Beneš as its Prime Minister. The views of France and Great Britain on the international political status of the Czechoslovak exile were also influenced by their policy towards Italy (one of the signatories of the Munich Agreement); towards Hungary which was locked in a bitter territorial dispute with the Czechs and Slovaks over South Slovakia and Carpathian Ruthenia; and towards Poland, an ally in the war against Germany, but which was also in conflict with the Czechs over the region of Cieszyn/Těšín, Silesia. Both Allied Powers had to take the attitude of all three states into account. As yet, Italy and Hungary were not at war, and Paris and London wanted to avoid any step that might push them into open military collaboration with Germany. Poland already had its own government as well as a sizable army in exile (ca. 80,000 men) and it made no sense to rekindle a quarrel over frontiers that neither France nor Britain was prepared to guarantee to either the Poles or the Czechs.

The situation was made even more complicated by the existence of the Slovak state, which was *de facto* recognized by the Western Allied Powers, and also by that of a functioning government in the Protectorate of Bohemia and Moravia. The net result of all those factors was that only a Czechoslovak National Committee, not a Czechoslovak government, was recognized, first by the French government on 14 November[5] and then by the British on 20 December 1939.[6] For France, the Czechoslovak National Committee represented

---

4   For more detailed information concerning the internal conflicts among the Czechoslovak politicians in exile, see Jan Kuklík, Jan Němeček, *Proti Benešovi! Česká a slovenská protibenešovská opozice v Londýně 1939–1945* [Against Beneš! The Czech and Slovak Anti-Beneš Opposition in London 1939–1945] (Praha: Karolinum, 2004); Idem, *Hodža versus Beneš. Milan Hodža a slovenská otázka v zahraničním odboji za druhé světové války* [Hodža versus Beneš. Milan Hodža and the Slovak Issue in the Resistance Movement Abroad During the Second World War] (Praha: Karolinum, 1999).

5   Archiv Ústavu Tomáše Garrigua Masaryka [Archive of the Institute of Tomáš Garrigue Masaryk], Prague (henceforth AÚTGM), fund 37, sign. 5, 67 pages, Š. Osuský's note to E. Daladier, 13 November 1939, p. 10 (English versions, pp. 15–20), E. Daladier to Š. Osuský, 14 November 1939, p. 11.

6   Archiv Ministerstva zahraničních věcí [Archive of the Ministry of Foreign Affairs], Prague (henceforth AMZV), Londýnský archiv – důvěrný [London Archive – Confidential] (henceforth LA-D), oddíl [section] 4, regál [shelf] 70, No. 129 (or No. 160), President Beneš's letter to Lord Halifax and Lord Halifax's letter to President Beneš, both 20 December 1939); The National Ar-

the Czechoslovak people; for the United Kingdom, the Czechoslovak peoples; but neither was prepared to allow that it represented the Czechoslovak state.

At the same time the Czechoslovak émigré groups tried to make use of the Czechoslovak army in France as a tool to obtain political recognition of a Czechoslovak government-in-exile. This attempt met with partial success thanks to the Czechoslovak-French military agreement[7] signed on 2 October. Thus, the recognition of some provisional Czechoslovak government-in-exile became part of the political debate between the Czechoslovak emigration and the allied governments, thereby making it difficult for Paris and London to remove the question from the agenda of negotiations with Beneš and Osuský. On the other hand, however ready to support Czechoslovak military initiatives both allied governments might be, they were keen to avoid any political commitment towards the future status of the former Czechoslovak territories, preferring to keep an open mind on the issue.[8]

The transformation of the Czechoslovak National Committee into the Provisional Czechoslovak government became the main aim of the Beneš group after recognition of the Committee had been granted in December 1939. Nevertheless, 1940 opened with a new crisis in internal relations among the Czechoslovak émigrés and even more intense jostling for position between Beneš and the two Slovak politicians, Osuský and Hodža. On top of that, the cluster of anti-Nazi German Social Democrats from the Sudetenland, headed by Wenzel Jaksch, also tried to influence attempts to reach a solution for the future of the former Czechoslovak borderland region. The interminable altercations provided both Allied Powers with a readymade excuse for turning down recognition of the Czechoslovak government. Clearly, any chance of success in that enterprise would depend on reconciliation between the opposing Czechoslovak groups.

In the first half of 1940, possibilities for effective action by the Czechoslovak exiles were limited by three circumstances, all outside their control. The first was the lack of will on the part of the Allies to proceed from recognition

---

chives of the United Kingdom, London (henceforth TNA), Foreign Office (henceforth FO) 417/40, C 20702/7/12, p. 115.

7   *Dokumenty československé zahraniční politiky. Od rozpadu Česko-Slovenska do uznání československé prozatímní vlády 1939–1940 (16. březen 1939 – 15. červen 1940)* [Documents on Czechoslovak Foreign Policy: from the Breakup of Czecho-Slovakia to Recognition of the Czechoslovak Provisional Government (16 March 1939 – 15 June 1940)] (Praha: Historický ústav AV ČR, 2002), No. 110, p. 241, Agreement between French Prime Minister E. Daladier and Czechoslovak Minister to France Š. Osuský, 2 October 1939.

8   As regards the British attitude towards the question of the organization of the Czechoslovak military units in the first months of the war, see Radosław p. Żurawski vel Grajewski, "Kwestia utworzenia czechosłowackich jednostek wojskowych w Wielkiej Brytanii w początkowym okresie II wojny światowej (wrzesień – grudzień 1939 r.) [The Question of Creation of the Czechoslovak Units in Great Britain in the Initial Stage of the Second World War]," in *Acta Universitatis Lodziensis. Folia Historica*, Vol. 89 (2012), pp. 151–174.

of the Czechoslovak National Committee to the next stage, that of the Czechoslovak Provisional government. Both Paris and London had long been content with the former designation and evinced no desire for fresh negotiations on the matter. The second, favourable in terms of furtherance of Czechoslovak plans, was a change of government in both France and Britain. The third and perhaps decisive factor was the military disaster in France in May – June 1940. At a stroke, this eliminated French opposition to recognition of the Provisional Czechoslovak government and simultaneously completely scuppered support in Paris for the anti-Beneš faction led by Hodža and Osuský.

The recognition of the Provisional Czechoslovak government by Great Britain on 21 July 1940 was undoubtedly an important success for Beneš and his cohorts,[9] yet, even so, the Foreign Office did not commit itself to any programme concerning the rebuilding of the Czechoslovak state after the war. Indeed, the wording of the recognition was constructed in such a way as to preclude any overt reference to the Czechoslovak state. British attitudes on the matter were being formed by several evolving conditions at the time. The first, Hungarian and Italian influence on British foreign policy in general, including the Czechoslovak question, diminished, especially after the declaration of war by Italy on 10 June 1940. Consideration for the Polish position, hostile to Beneš personally and as leader of the Czechoslovak émigrés, as well as to the existing Protectorate government, ceased to carry much weight in British decision-making after the French military *débâcle*. At the same time, a traditional British aversion to making concrete commitments with regard to Central European states still played an important role. Nevertheless, the incentives to support Beneš and recognize the Provisional government were numerous and can be listed as follows:

- the danger of aggravating internal Czechoslovak dissension by further deferment,
- the need to build respect for the United Kingdom in the eyes of the Czechoslovak public and to strengthen its Western orientation,
- strong pro-Czechoslovak lobbying by the Labour Party and the Political Intelligence Department, and the favourable attitude of the new British Prime Minister, Winston Churchill, to the Czechoslovak issue,
- the isolation of Great Britain in the war against Germany, a situation that enhanced the value of any ally still prepared to fight,

---

9   AMZV, LA–D, section 4, shelf 70, No. 129 (or 160 or 162), Lord Halifax's letter to President Beneš, 21 July 1940. See also Jan Kuklík, "The Recognition of the Czechoslovak Government in Exile and Its International Status 1939–1942," in *Prague Papers on the History of International Relations* (Prague: Institute of International Relations, 1997), pp. 173–205.

–   the presence of a batch of small states (Norway, the Netherlands, Belgium) with governments-in-exile in London, each with a political and military potential similar to that of the Czechoslovaks while Czechoslovakia itself was unrepresented in the group.

For the whole of the following year until June 1941 the main factor influencing Czechoslovak foreign policy was the fact that Great Britain was the only power still at war with Germany. This largely determined Beneš's diplomatic and political programme. In such circumstances the United Kingdom became the main focus of efforts to obtain full recognition of the Czechoslovak government-in-exile and to jettison the humiliating, at least in Czechoslovak eyes, epithet "provisional."

Relations between the Czechoslovaks and their British partners during the war were shaped by two categories of concern. The first were incidental and their influence was short-lived. The second defined the contours of diplomatic interaction between both beleaguered combatants in the long-term. In the first group were:

a.   The Battle of Britain (August – September 1940) which totally engaged the time and energy of the British government and British public opinion,
b.   The Balkans campaign (April 1941), which appeared more immediately urgent to London than resolution of the Czechoslovak question,
c.   The residual influence on British policy exerted by those "men of Munich" still present in the Churchill cabinet, such as Neville Chamberlain, Lord Halifax and Jan Smuts, who was personally ill-disposed towards Beneš.

In the second group were:

a.   juridical reasons (important in the Anglo-Saxon legal and civil context), which restrained or delayed decisions by the Foreign Office,
b.   political reasons, which pressed the British authorities towards acceptance of Czechoslovak demands,
c.   practical reasons, anxiety in the Foreign Office about the future of intelligence collaboration between London and the resistance in the Protectorate, which was felt to be under the control of President Emil Hácha and his government.

Among other factors affecting the British approach to the Czechoslovak question between July 1940 and June 1941 might be mentioned serious reservations to the idea of reconstruction of the former Czechoslovakia. These had been in existence for a long time and were only officially abandoned in Churchill's speech to the Czechoslovak army on 18 April 1941.[10] The Foreign Office also constantly refused to accept the uninterrupted continuity of the First Czechoslovak Republic and to give any guarantee with regard to future frontiers. However, this was not simply the case with Czechoslovakia only but also with other countries in the same bracket, such as Poland and Yugoslavia. London wanted to avoid any commitments in that area and sought to avoid involvement in territorial squabbles among its allies.

With respect to the final affirmative decision on full recognition of the Czechoslovak government-in-exile, this was influenced in part by successful lobbying by prominent British friends of Czechoslovakia, particularly Robert Bruce Lockhart, against a backdrop of opposition among the British Dominions to any such move. Mention should of course be made, too, of the crucial fact that the Soviet Union granted full recognition without hesitation or equivocation, thus spurring London to do likewise lest Britain lose its prestige in Central Europe and even leadership of the anti-German coalition.

The events of July 1941 changed the relationship the Czechoslovak authorities in exile had with their allies. Great Britain was no longer the only power at war with Germany or the bedrock on whom the fate and international status of the Czechoslovak émigré structures depended. The entry of the Soviet Union into the war and its support for Czechoslovak demands gave Beneš and his team an effective weapon for exerting pressure on the Foreign Office. At the same time, it raised the value in British eyes of working closely with the Czechoslovaks since they enjoyed excellent relations with Moscow and could be useful both in gathering information about the Soviets as well as helping to coordinate the work of the joint British and Soviet intelligence services. Later the Czechoslovaks could also be pressed to modify the lukewarm and distrustful attitude of other allies towards the Stalin regime.

For the whole of the following year, the focus of Czechoslovak diplomatic efforts was on obtaining a declaration from the British rescinding the Munich Agreement. This alone would not put paid to that particular national calamity but would strengthen Beneš's hand considerably in discussions on the question of Czechoslovak boundaries after the war and, concomitantly, the fate of the Czechoslovak Germans. After protracted negotiations, which finally ended in August 1942, the British government proclaimed that its future policy would no longer be influenced by the Munich Agreement. However, it still refused to guarantee the future borders of Czechoslovakia or to recognize the

---

10   For Churchill's speech to the Czechoslovak army, see *Bitva o Československo v britském veřejném mínění. K třetímu výročí mnichovské dohody sestavili B. Beneš a J. Šuhaj* [Battle for Czechoslovakia in British Public Opinion. Composed by B. Beneš and J. Šuhaj on the Occasion of the Third Anniversary of the Munich Agreement] (Londýn: Čechoslovák, 1941), p. 69.

uninterrupted existence of the First Czechoslovak Republic.[11] In September 1942, the French National Committee headed by General Charles de Gaulle was more forthcoming by committing itself to support the restoration of Czechoslovakia within the frontiers that had existed before September 1938.[12]

The end of 1942 and the beginning of 1943 were the decisive months of the war. The British victory at El Alamein, the Allied invasion of French North Africa along with the German disaster at Stalingrad gave firm grounds for expecting that the Axis powers would eventually lose the war, and this was duly noted by Czechoslovak diplomats in their negotiating strategies. Although Czechoslovak-British relations were still good, the Soviet factor in Czechoslovak policy became gradually more pronounced. Soon it appeared clear that the idea of a Czechoslovak-Polish confederation, which had the approval of the British and been under discussion since 1940, would be abandoned as a result of pressure on the Czechoslovaks by Stalin who was opposed to any confederations in Central Europe that might prove an obstacle to his plans for hegemony in the region. However, it is also worth mentioning that both potential partners in the planned confederation were under the influence of their different historical and political experiences, which made a meeting of minds on the issue difficult although not impossible. The Poles all too aware of the long, dramatic narrative of their struggle against Russian domination and the fresh crimes perpetrated against their country by both the Germans and the Soviets in the wake of the 1939 Ribbentrop – Molotov Pact were surprised and indeed shocked by the Czechoslovak attitude towards the Soviet Union and Beneš's idea of building a future security system based on collaboration with Moscow. They looked askance at any such idea viewing it as decisive proof of Czechoslovak political blindness and naivety. Simultaneously, the Czechs remembering their history of resistance against Germanization and the *Drang nach Osten*, and with Britain and France's betrayal at Munich in 1938 still fresh in their minds, could not believe the Poles would be so foolhardy as to entrust their future security to an alliance with the Western countries only. Eventually, Czechoslovak policy in this area was subordinated to Soviet demands, while Polish-Soviet relations were broken off a short time later in April 1943 after the Soviet massacre of thousands of Polish officers at Katyń in 1940 came to light.[13]

---

11   AMZV, LA-D, section 4, shelf 70, No. 137, A. Eden to J. Masaryk, 5 August 1942, p. 29 (English version), p. 1 (Czech version); English version also in: TNA FO 371/30835, C 7210/326/12, print between pp. 35–43.

12   Jan Němeček, Helena Nováčková, Ivan Šťovíček, Jan Kuklík, eds., *Československo-francouzské vztahy v diplomatických jednáních (1940–1945)* [Czechoslovak-French Relations in Diplomatic Negotiations (1940–1945)] (Praha: HÚ AV ČR – SÚA – Karolinum, 2005), No. 105, p. 176.

13   For further details see Piotr S. Wandycz, *Czechoslovak-Polish Confederation and the Great Powers 1940–1943* (Bloomington: Indiana University Publications, 1956); Eugeniusz Duraczyński, "*ZSRR wobec projektów konfederacji polsko-czechosłowackiej (1940–1943)* [The USSR in Relation to the Pol-

Both British and Czechoslovak diplomats in their quest for good relations with the Soviet Union agreed that a precondition to gaining Moscow's confidence would be to give her a free hand in the Baltic states and eastern Poland and to guarantee Stalin his say on the post-war political order in Europe. It seems that one of the foremost aims of the Czechoslovaks in 1943 was to sign a treaty of alliance and cooperation on post-war Europe with the Soviet Union. The rationale behind this objective was, firstly, that such a treaty would secure the Czechoslovak state against any future German threat, and, secondly, as Beneš saw it, would safeguard Czechoslovakia against unconstrained interference by Moscow in the country's internal affairs, in the event that the Red Army was present in Czechoslovakia, if such a formal agreement were not in place. Moreover, good relations with the Kremlin would strengthen Czechoslovak's hand in its territorial conflicts with neighbouring countries, Germany, Hungary, and Poland, as a result of the justifiable expectation that the Soviets would protect Czechoslovak interests.

Other more general but nonetheless important factors in the long-term played a part, too. Some were objective in nature, others more subjective. The fact that the decision-making process among the Czechoslovak émigrés was largely centralized is one. All important questions were decided personally by President Beneš. Indeed, other members of the government were very often not even informed about the details of negotiations. Next, the strong pro-Soviet sentiments of the majority of the exiled Czechoslovak politicians combined with their trust in the good intentions of the USSR should be borne in mind. At the same time, many nourished prejudices against Western countries, especially Britain and France, for their part in the Munich Agreement. Another constant feature of Czechoslovak diplomacy was hostility towards Poland linked with permanent attempts to weaken her international position.

ish-Czechoslovak Confederation (1940-1943)]," in *Dzieje Najnowsze* [Contemporary History], Vol. XXIX, No. 3 (1997), pp. 129-153; Marek K. Kamiński, *Edvard Beneš kontra gen. Władysław Sikorski. Polityka władz czechosłowackich na emigracji wobec rządu polskiego na uchodźstwie 1939-1943* [Edvard Beneš versus General Władysław Sikorski. The Policy of the Czechoslovak Governments-in-Exile towards the Polish Government-in-Exile 1939-1943] (Warszawa: Neriton, 2005); Idem, *Edvard Beneš we współpracy z Kremlem. Polityka zagraniczna władz czechosłowackich na emigracji 1943-1945* [Edvard Beneš in Cooperation with the Kremlin. The Foreign Policy of the Czechoslovak Governments-in-Exile 1943-1945] (Warszawa: Instytut Historii PAN, 2009); Tadeusz Kisielewski, *Federacja środkowo-europejska. Pertraktacje polsko-czechosłowackie 1939-1943* [The Central-European Federation. The Polish-Czechoslovak Negotiations 1943-1945] (Warszawa: Ludowa Spółdzielnia 1991); Jan Němeček, *Od spojenectví k roztržce. Vztahy československé a polské exilové reprezentace 1939-1945* [From Alliance to Rift. Relations between the Czechoslovak and Polish Exile Representations 1939-1945] (Praha: Academia, 2003); Eduard Táborský, "A Polish-Czechoslovak Confederation. A Story of the First Soviet Veto," in *Journal of Central European Affairs*, Vol. 9, No. 4 (1950), pp. 379-395; Rudolf Žáček, *Projekt československo-polské konfederace v letech 1939-1943* [The Project of the Czechoslovak-Polish Confederation in the Years 1939-1943] (Opava: Slezský ústav Slezského zemského muzea, 2001).

This attitude was hidden behind a putative desire for close Czechoslovak-Polish cooperation, couched under what would be for the Poles unacceptable conditions, i.e. voluntary subordination to the Soviets as per the Czechoslovak pattern. Another dictate behind the Czechoslovak position was enmity towards Germany, Hungary, and towards the autonomous tendencies of the Slovaks. All those issues made the Czechoslovak authorities in exile more inclined to look for Soviet acquiescence in implementing the radical solutions envisaged. Mention might also be made of Beneš's own strong leftist ideological views along with his old pan-Slav sympathies as well as his personal ambition to be in company with the representatives of the Great Powers and play the role of a bridge between East and West. Yet another consideration was a perceived threat from the Czechoslovak Communist Party members, which animated Beneš in his efforts to convince Stalin that his team was just as loyal to the USSR as they were and that a future government of Czechoslovakia in his hands would be a better option for Moscow than anything the Communists might come up with. Finally, fears of conflict with either the Soviet Union or the Western powers should not be overlooked. The first was seen as most likely to have control of Czechoslovakia by the end of the war and thus be in a position to install a government of its choosing in Prague and also to prevent, if it so wished, the return of Beneš and his team from exile. As far as the future frontiers of Czechoslovakia, expulsion of the German population,[14] and post-war economic aid were concerned, all were vital but still unresolved questions and all depended on the stand the United States and Britain would take.

From the beginning of 1944, and shortly after the Czechoslovak-Soviet agreement had been signed, a change in the international orientation of the Czechoslovak exile could be observed. Significant tension in Czechoslovak-British relations, as a result of the treaty that Beneš had signed in Moscow in December 1943,[15] remained, but the influence of both Anglo-Saxon powers was waning while that of the Soviets was on the rise during the whole of 1944. Whether fairly or not, Beneš was labelled a voluntary vassal of the Soviet Union and this description stuck, serving as a ready excuse to further reduce Western engagement in the Czechoslovak question. The belief in Washington and London that Czechoslovakia belonged to the Soviet camp became very apparent during the Slovak uprising. Effective relief for the insurgents

---

14   For more details on the attitude of the Czechoslovak authorities in exile towards the Sudeten Germans see Francis D. Raška, *The Czechoslovak Exile Government in London and the Sudeten German Issue* (Praha: Karolinum, 2002).

15   For the text of the Czechoslovak-Soviet agreement of 12 December 1943, see: TNA FO 371/38920, C 2068/35/12, pp. 153–155. See also Vojtech Mastny, ed., "The Beneš–Stalin–Molotov Conversations in December 1943. New Documents," in *Jahrbücher für Geschichte Osteuropas*, Vol. XX, No. 3 (1972), No. 1, pp. 376–380.

proved to be well-nigh impossible without cooperation from the Soviets[16] and the experience of the uprising in Warsaw was exposing the fragility of trust in the good intentions of the Kremlin towards neighbouring countries. At the same time, it had become clear that the Western powers stood no real chance of influencing behaviour in Moscow without provoking an open quarrel with Stalin for which there was no appetite. Beneš refused to admit, perhaps even to himself, that his trust in the good intentions of the Soviets was based on misconceptions and that his ignorance or misreading of the nature of the Soviet regime led him to play Stalin's game in regard to Carpathian Ruthenia. While making desperate efforts to avoid conflict, Beneš was aware that the military occupation of the province by the Red Army would determine its future, and was motivated by the fear that any firm opposition on his part to Kremlin moves to incorporate the territory could lead not only to the loss of Carpathian Ruthenia but also Slovakia. As a result, he pretended that true responsibility for the situation lay with the nationalist Ukrainian officers in the Red Army and he eventually accepted the solution imposed by Stalin.

In the last months of the war, one of the most important goals of the Czechoslovak authorities in exile was to go home. The two factors at play here were time and events on the ground. On the one hand, there was concern that a return via Moscow would put them at the mercy of the Soviets. On the other, their continued presence in London might lead to the establishment of a puppet communist government in Prague in their absence, one that would be completely dependent on Moscow and that might ultimately prevent their homecoming altogether.

Unfortunately, all the nagging doubts about Moscow's good faith were proved right. The isolation of the Czechoslovak authorities after leaving London meant that a single Czechoslovak decision-making hub ceased to exist. Hitherto there had been a functioning entity providing direction and guidance but the sojourn in Košice meant that the returnees were no longer in contact with members of the government still in London and, compounding the confusion, that two, sometimes even three, separate bodies were propounding the Czechoslovak line on various issues: first President Beneš and his coterie, next Prime Minister Zdeněk Fierlinger and his group dominated by the Communists, and then on top of that Minister Hubert Ripka left to his own devices in London. It is difficult to speak of any common cohesive strategy between these different centres, even in matters as fundamental as the entry of US troops into Prague. The influence of Beneš in shaping the foreign

---

16   Vilém Prečan, *Britové, Sověti a povstání* [The British, the Soviets and the Uprising], in Idem, *V kradeném čase. Výběr ze studií, článků a úvah z let 1973–1993* [In the Stolen Time. A Selection of Studies, Articles and Deliberations from the Years 1973–1993] (Brno: Doplněk – Ústav pro soudobé dějiny, 1994), pp. 78–98.

policy position of Czechoslovakia, heretofore overwhelming, was in rapid decline. Nevertheless, right till the end the President adopted the facade, which in his view allowed him to remain in the game, of pretending to the Western allies that everything, or almost everything, in Czechoslovak-Soviet relations was in order and of declaring in his public addresses his belief in the good intentions of the Kremlin and the benefits flowing to Czechoslovakia from having such an ally as the Soviet Union. In so doing, Beneš by his own personal authority and the dignity of the office of the President of the Republic vested in him strengthened the communist influence (and thus the Soviet) in the government of Czechoslovakia, with no hint of protest and also no note of disapproval at the terror tactics of the NKVD in areas occupied by the Red Army. Cut off from meaningful communication, the once leading player had become a mere observer of the political scene. By his refusal to take a moral stand lest such a course entail conflict with the Soviet Union, the president's ability to speak out in defence of the independence of Czechoslovakia had been drastically weakened. In those circumstances he could only passively cheer from the sidelines as Patton's army advanced into the Czech Lands. With control of the government in communist hands, he could take no official action in the name of the Czechoslovak people that might have developed the situation advantageously at a decisive moment for the future of his country.

POLISH AND CZECHOSLOVAK GOVERNMENTS-IN-EXILE (AND THE IMPACT OF SOVIET FOREIGN POLICY) IN RUSSIAN HISTORIOGRAPHY

VICTORIA V. VASILENKO

In the first years of the Second World War, there seemed to be a chance that the Polish, Czech and Slovak nations* would share one road after the war on the basis of the Polish-Czechoslovak confederation project which was being developed by the governments-in-exile. Paradoxically, they did travel together in a similar direction but under completely different circumstances: the diverging strategies of the Polish and Czechoslovak exile authorities, clearly visible in 1943, led both, as it later turned out, into the Soviet Bloc.

The Polish and Czechoslovak governments-in-exile were only of marginal interest to Soviet historians. However, the lifting of ideological restrictions and the wealth of archival sources declassified, primarily in the 1990s, made a significant impact on the research agenda in Russia. In this chapter, I give a short overview of contemporary Russian historiography dealing with the governments-in-exile of Poland and Czechoslovakia, with the focus on works I consider most important, while also highlighting some key developments in Soviet policy towards these governments.[1]

Russian historiography has been developing certain themes in opposition to the methodology and assessments of the Soviet era but in some respects follows from or draws on its precursor. That is why some of the basic views of Soviet historians on the governments-in-exile are worth mentioning to reveal the evolution and peculiarities of contemporary approaches.

Soviet historians mostly characterized the Polish and Czechoslovak Communists as the "single progressive political force" among the Polish and Czechoslovak communities in contrast with the "reactionary" émigré governments who acted to the detriment of their peoples' interests and could hardly claim to represent them. The word "émigré" was defined in such a way as to

---

*   I shall henceforth employ the term "Czechoslovak," thus following Edvard Beneš's concept, as this terminology was for obvious reasons used in all exchanges involving the Czechoslovak government-in-exile.

1   The recent detailed analysis of the contemporary Russian historiography of Soviet-Polish relations in the 20th century in the context of political developments by Inessa Iazhborovskaia, one of the leading Russian scholars of contemporary Polish history, is available in the Russian-Polish monograph: A. V. Torkunov, A. D. Rotfeld, eds., *Belye piatna – chernye piatna: Slozhnye voprosy v rossiisko-pol'skikh otnosheniiakh* [Blank Spots – Dark Spots: Difficult Matters in Russian-Polish Relations] (Moskva: Aspekt Press, 2010), pp. 737–767.

stress the lack of support those so labelled enjoyed in their home countries. At the same time, it helped to explain the natural progression to both a "people's democracy" and a "socialist commonwealth" in the region, as well as to underlining the positive role played by the Soviet Union. This approach also implied that the émigré "anti-historical" political forces did not deserve thorough examination. When the activities of the governments-in-exile were alluded to in general surveys of the history of Poland and Czechoslovakia, they were subjected to fierce criticism. Only in the 1980s did more substantive works make their appearance.[2] Among them, the studies carried out by Valentina Parsadanova into Soviet-Polish relations[3] and those by Ivan Pop into Soviet-Czechoslovak affairs, already published in 1990, should be mentioned in particular.[4] In addition, Soviet historians argued that the policy of Great Britain, a host of exile governments, towards the Polish and Czechoslovak questions contradicted the peaceful aspirations of the Polish, Czechoslovak and Soviet peoples, since it supported the open hostility of the Polish government to the USSR which worked to the detriment of Poland, and also had a negative influence on the more pragmatic Czechoslovak authorities. In fact, these views in a sense represent the ideas and assessments of the Soviet leadership in the Second World War. By and large, despite the different strategies towards the Soviet Union which the Polish and Czechoslovak governments employed, the tone of the historical material on both exile authorities was almost identical.

While the Soviet literature dealt chiefly with the "brotherly fight" against the common enemy and often depicted the heroism of the Soviet-backed forces as they battled their way to power in Poland and Czechoslovakia,[5] contemporary research in Russia is, to a significant extent, devoted to more controversial topics in Soviet-Polish and Soviet-Czechoslovak relations during the war years on the basis of the declassified archived Soviet documents published in recent decades. The Soviet Union's endeavour to increase its security during the Second World War, especially after 1943, the key component of which was the setting up of a chain of dependent contiguous countries, added fresh difficulties to already fraught Soviet-Polish relations as well as to its more neutral ties with the Czechoslovaks.

---

2   V. V. Vasilenko, *Pol'skoe emigrantskoe pravitel'stvo i pol'sko-britanskie otnosheniia v gody Vtoroi mirovoi voiny* [The Polish Émigré Government and Polish-British Relations in the Years of the Second World War], Summary of Kandidat Nauk's Thesis (Tomsk, 2006), available at: www.tsu.ru.

3   V. S. Parsadanova, *Sovetsko-pol'skie otnosheniia v gody Velikoi Otechestvennoi voiny, 1941–1945* [Soviet-Polish Relations in the Years of the Second World War] (Moskva: Nauka, 1982).

4   I. I. Pop, *Chekhoslovakiia – Sovetskii Soiuz 1941–1947 gg* [Czechoslovakia – the Soviet Union 1941–1947] (Moskva: Nauka, 1990).

5   See *Pamiat' o sovmestnoi bor'be: O sovetsko-pol'skom boevom bratstve v gody bor'by s nemetskim fashizmom* [Memories of Fighting Side by Side: On Soviet-Polish Combat Brotherhood in the Years of the Fight Against Fascism] (Moskva: Politizdat, 1989).

In Russian historiography, studies of the Polish authorities in exile re-
volve around three broad interrelated themes: repression, armies formed in
the USSR, and Poland in the post-war settlement, in particular the role of
the government-in-exile in the measures imposed by the Big Three. While
research on the first two topics is also present in regard to Czechoslovakia,
most attention is paid to Edvard Beneš's alleged desire to have his country
join the Soviet Bloc (which was certainly not the case) and to the question
of Sub-Carpathian Russia or Ruthenia. Attention is also paid to Soviet policy
towards the German-sponsored Slovak state. The exile authorities of Poland
and Czechoslovakia are referred to as "governments in emigration" (which is
considered a middle-of-the-road expression), "governments-in-exile," "émigré governments" (again mostly a neutral term) or simply the governments
of Poland or Czechoslovakia (in the Polish case, this applies until roughly
mid–1943 when the Soviet-backed political forces started to come to the fore;
to characterize the period after that time, the term "the London Poles" is often
applied).

The Polish-Soviet agenda, however, was larger and was determined by
the strategic importance of Poland's position as neighbour to the USSR in
Joseph Stalin's calculations, coupled with bitter Polish memories of the 1939
Red Army campaign against the Second Republic, the most invidious being
the questions of *kresy* and the massive repression of their population. Given
its location between the USSR and Germany, it is hardly surprising that Poland was of pivotal interest to the Soviet leadership, particularly Stalin, who,
especially from 1941, envisaged the country becoming a key component in
the Soviet sphere of influence, to wit its security belt. On the other hand, the
Second Polish Republic had been a central constituent part in the so-called
cordon sanitaire around the Soviet Union in the inter-war period. To this
complex setting might be added a long history of mutual mistrust and misunderstanding, with the suppression of Polish aspirations for independence
during the Romanov era, further exacerbated by negative experiences from
the Soviet-Polish war of 1919–1921. Bilateral relations were generally tense,
with a strong undercurrent of unneighbourly sentiment, although there had
been a trend towards normalization in the late 1920s – early 1930s,[6] on both
sides of the border.

Thus, in the years of the Second World War, Stalin had few expectations
of cooperation from the Poles and was very suspicious of their intentions.

---

6   See L. N. Nezhinski, "SSSR i Pol'sha v 1934–1935 godakh: upushchennye vozmozhnosti?" [The
    USSR and Poland in 1934–1935: Lost Opportunities?], in E. Duraczynski and A. N. Sakharov, eds.,
    Sovetsko-pol'skie otnosheniia v politicheskikh usloviiakh Evropy 30–kh godov XX stoletiia [Soviet-Pol-
    ish Relations in the Political Conditions of Europe in the 1930s] (Moskva: Nauka, 2004), pp. 106–
    111.

However, his policy of repression was restricted, primarily by international but also by intra-Polish factors.

There are few personal accounts from those who witnessed or, to a limited extent, participated in the policy-making of the time, and the existing official documentation seldom touches on motivation. Against this backdrop, the diary and the selected correspondence with Russian and foreign correspondents by Ivan Maisky, Soviet ambassador to the United Kingdom, and later Deputy Foreign Minister and academician, is an invaluable resource for the study of Soviet policy towards both governments-in-exile in the context of Soviet-British relations, and the broader Allied diplomacy. First, the material provides an insight into the Soviet policy-making process itself: on the one hand, Maisky had little to no information on how Stalin reached his conclusions, on the other hand, he made his own, often discerning and revealing, judgments which seemed to uncover some of the motives of the Soviet leader. Second, this prominent diplomat's line of reasoning seems a good indication of the Soviet pattern of thinking. According to the diary, Maisky, in his exchanges with British officials, for example, explains why the smaller nations on the Soviet border should be friendly towards the Soviet Union: they were neighbours after all, and the USSR was much bigger in terms of population. This was mentioned in his memoirs published in 1975,[7] but can be found in more detail in his diary, a part of which has been published in recent years.[8] Third, Maisky describes some significant events, such as the signing of the Soviet-Polish treaty of 30 July 1941, his conversations with the British leadership concerning the Katyń Massacre, his talks with Eden on 10 March 1943 about post-war problems and the subject of confederation in particular (the British record of this meeting was published earlier), and the like. Fourth, Maisky enables us to get an idea of the attitude of a Soviet diplomat to the exile governments' leadership – often sarcastic and sceptical, though tolerant. Nonetheless, one should take the constraints of the system into account with regard to what might or might not be prudently expressed.

The reassessment of the Polish government-in-exile performance was activated by research into Stalin's crimes and repression that was stimulated by the newly-opened archival documentation in the early 1990s. The findings soon highlighted the significance of the so-called Anders Army, which was formed from Poles deported to the Soviet Union after annexation of the Polish eastern areas.

---

7   I. M. Maisky, *Vospominaniia sovetskogo diplomata, 1925–1945 gg* [Memoirs of a Soviet Diplomat, 1925–1945] (Moskva: Mezhdunarodnye otnosheniia, 1987), p. 144–145.

8   I. M. Maisky, *Dnevnik diplomata. London. 1934–1943* [Diary of a Diplomat. London. 1934–1943], in 2 vols., Vol. 2, part 2: *22 iiunia 1941 – 1943 god* [22 June 1941– 1943] (Moskva: Nauka, 2009), p. 235.

The formation of a Polish army had already appeared on the Soviet agenda in 1940. At first, after the invasion of Poland the previous year, Stalin wanted to remove the Polish question entirely by decapitating the nation, as exemplified in the Katyń massacre, the wholesale deportations from the former *kresy*, and other brutal measures. But in the summer and autumn of 1940, Stalin's policy changed, probably in line with Germany's military successes. Oppression was replaced by open support for Polish culture, a softening in the imposition of Soviet socio-economic structures, and steps to organize Polish military units from POWs, although this last was hampered because the officers chosen often made their participation conditional on the consent of the Polish government-in-exile.[9] Then, in June 1940, Władysław Sikorski, the Polish Prime Minister, having run into difficulties in creating a Polish army in the United Kingdom, attempted, via the British, to encourage the establishment of such an army in the USSR. However, this resulted in a crisis in the Polish government-in-exile, and the Foreign Office memorandum was revoked.[10] In the end, the decision to build up a Polish military unit, which would be disguised as part of the Soviet army, was taken by the Soviet leadership only in early June 1941.[11]

After diplomatic relations between the USSR and Poland's government-in-exile had been regularized, the formation of the Polish army in the Soviet Union became a matter of mutual interest for the Polish and Soviet governments, but their objectives differed: the USSR was in sore need of manpower, whereas the Polish government wanted a military-political instrument to facilitate a return to Poland. The documents, especially the minutes of the Stalin-Sikorski talks in December 1941, demonstrate that this army was, perhaps, the only trump card the Poles had in their relations with Stalin. Sikorski's consent to the army remaining in the USSR, contrary to British demands, made a very favourable impression.[12] In 1942, after the soldiers and their families had been evacuated, bilateral relations drastically worsened. In particular, work conditions at the Polish Embassy in Moscow became almost impossible. Many scholars (e.g., Natalia Lebedeva, Valentina Parsadanova,

---

9   "Stalin, Beriia i sud'ba armii Andersa v 1941–1942 gg" (Iz rassekrechennykh arkhivov) [Stalin, Beria and the Fate of the Anders Army in 1941–1942 (From the Declassified Archives)], in *Novaia i noveishaia istoriia*, No. 2 (1993), pp. 59–90. Then in Berling's conversations with Beria and Merkulov there was a puzzling mention of a mistake made in regard to Polish officers. I. S. Iazhborovskaia, A. Iu. Iablokov, V. S. Parsadanova, *Katynskii sindrom v sovetsko-pol'skikh i rossiisko-pol'skikh otnosheniiakh* [The Katyń Syndrome in Soviet-Polish and Russian-Polish Relations] (Moskva: ROSSPEN, 2001), p. 130.

10   A. F. Noskova, ed., *Pol'sha v XX veke. Ocherki politicheskoi istorii* [Poland in the 20th century. Essays on Political History] (Moskva: Indrik, 2012), p. 303; Iazhborovskaia et al., *Katynskii sindrom v sovetsko-pol'skikh i rossiisko-pol'skikh otnosheniiakh*, p. 128.

11   "Stalin, Beriia i sud'ba armii Andersa v 1941–1942 gg", p. 62.

12   *Dokumenty vneshnei politiki* [Foreign Policy Documents], Vol. XXIV: *22 iiunia 1941 – 1 ianvaria 1942* [22 June 1941 – 1 January 1942] (Moskva: Mezhdunarodnye otnosheniia, 2000).

and Albina Noskova) argue that the episode was a landmark. The way had been opened for more British interference and for the Polish government to be clearly perceived as British-sponsored. There is some indication that the Polish exile authorities were, to a significant extent, aware of the effect of the developments. In late February 1943 the Polish authorities mentioned the possibility of cooperation between their underground forces in occupied Poland and Soviet units and even the return of the army to the USSR.[13] Stalin held out the possibility of negotiations, but soon the situation had changed again. Stalin broke off diplomatic relations with the Polish authorities in exile, officially because of their position on the Katyń massacre, but also, in Maisky's words, "to explode the Sikorski government and to clear the way for a more democratic and friendly Polish government [...]."[14]

Edvard Beneš, the President of Czechoslovakia's government-in-exile, no doubt regarded Sub-Carpathian Russia as an important Czechoslovak asset. Indeed it is one that seems to have had a role in proving that Czechoslovak intentions to develop closer ties with the USSR were serious, although it is unlikely that the Czechoslovak leader prompted the idea of incorporating Ruthenia into the Soviet Union. Moscow, however, found Beneš's rather noncommittal position on the issue, especially at the end of the war, an indication of his untrustworthiness. Valentina Mar'ina, a leading Russian specialist on contemporary Czech and Slovak history, in her pioneer work "Trans-Carpathian Ukraine (Sub-Carpathian Russia) in the Policy of Benes and Stalin: 1939–1945," which is accompanied by a corpus of documents published in the USSR, Russia and the Czech Republic, points out that quite a few important questions should be left unanswered, primarily because some important Russian archival collections are still closed to researchers while, at the same time, some Soviet decisions may simply not have been documented.[15]

The Polish-Czechoslovak confederation project has received attention from Russian scholars only in the last decade. The scheme highlighted the ability of the Polish and Czechoslovak governments-in-exile to develop relations on a new, constructive and friendly basis, but it was a goal worth striving for only in British and, to a certain extent, American eyes, given the United Kingdom's support for a federalist solution in the area. The research Mar'ina presents in her two-volume work on Soviet policy with regard to the

---

13   The Soviet record of the Stalin – Romer talks was published in 2008: "Stalin i Pol'sha. 1943–1944 gody. Iz rassekrechennykh dokumentov rossiiskikh arkhivov [Stalin and Poland. 1943–1944. From the Declassified Documents of the Russian Archives]," in *Novaia i noveishaia istoriia*, no. 3 (2008), pp. 104–137. Practically at that time, in February 1943, the Union of Polish Patriots was created; in April the Wasilevska request to form the Kościuszko Division was agreed by Stalin.

14   Maisky, *Dnevnik diplomata. London. 1934–1943*, Vol. 2, part 2, p. 272.

15   V. V. Mar'ina, *Zakarpatskaia Ukraina (Podkarpatskaia Rus') v politike Benesha i Stalina. 1939–1945 gg* [Trans-Carpathian Ukraine (Sub-Carpathian Russia) in the Policy of Beneš and Stalin. 1939–1945] (Moskva: Novyi khronograph, 2003), pp. 164–169.

Czecho-Slovak question demonstrates that the Soviet attitude to the project was likely to be based on analyses by a (Soviet) official from the Narkomat of International Affairs (NKID), Nikolai Novikov.[16] In late January 1942 Novikov stressed that a confederation would not be in the Soviet interest because it was an Anglo-Polish, as well as Czechoslovak, attempt to create a buffer between the Soviet Union and "external Europe."[17] Mar'ina and also the well-known scholar of Soviet Bloc formation, Leonid Gibiansky, show that any such confederation in the region was considered contrary to the Soviet good, and there was not only mistrust of Polish but also of Czechoslovak motives, despite all Beneš's efforts.[18] There was a chance that a confederation clause might have been included in the Soviet-British treaty of May 1942, a move which would later have complicated Soviet policy in the region. At the same time, the Soviet tactic was not to reveal clearly the USSR's real attitude to the Western powers until the proper moment and, simultaneously, attempt to steer the governments-in-exile in the desired direction, that is, to make them put a stop to the project themselves.[19] As Gibiansky notes, this was among the first instances of such diplomatic ploys by the Soviet Union in pursuing its goals in Eastern Europe.

In a recent, almost one thousand-page long, collective monograph on Poland's political history in the 20th century, Valentina Parsadanova, a prominent historian of Soviet-Polish relations in the Second World War, stresses that the Allies' acknowledgement that NKVD actions on Polish territory complied with international law was one of Stalin's successes at Yalta. This opened the road for the suppression by force of the underground state. Besides, Parsadanova clearly demonstrates that the provisional government (the Lublin Poles) needed reorganization, including more trusted politicians, since until spring 1945 it had practically lost even the little support it had because of its repressive policy and the visible presence of Soviet personnel in the army and key agencies (also for objective reasons, as there was a lack of Polish cadres).[20]

---

16   He was had of the Fourth European Division.

17   V. V. Mar'ina, *Sovetskii Soiuz i chekho-slovatskii vopros vo vremia Vtoroi mirovoi voiny 1939–1945 gg* [The USSR and the Czecho-Slovak Question during the Second World War 1939–1945], in 2 vols., Vol. 2, *1939–1945 gg* (Moskva: Indrik, 2009), p. 108.

18   Mar'ina, *Sovetskii Soiuz i chekho-slovatskii vopros vo vremia Vtoroi mirovoi voiny 1939–1945 gg*, Vol. 2, p. 108; L. Ia. Gibiansky, "Problemy Vostochnoi Evropy i nachalo formirovaniia sovetskogo bloka [The Problems of Eastern Europe and the Beginning of the Soviet Bloc Formation]," in *Kholodnaia voina. 1945–1963 gg* [The Cold War. 1945–1963] (Moskva: OLMA-PRESS, 2003), pp. 108–110.

19   In view of this it is understandable why Ivan Maisky's wording was milder than that of Aleksandr Bogomolov, Soviet ambassador to the governments-in-exile.

20   A. F. Noskova, ed., *Pol'sha v XX veke. Ocherki politicheskoi istorii* [Poland in the 20th century. Essays on Political History] (Moskva: Indrik, 2012), pp. 416, 417, 427, 428, 449, 450.

A number of scholars (e.g., Albina Noskova, Vladimir Volkov[21]) argue that it was not in the interest of the Soviet Union for its activities in the region to appear as occupation. That is why, for example, the term "the Polish Workers' Party" emerged, implying that it had no connection with the Comintern, which was formally dissolved in May 1943.[22] At the same time, it was most important to have appropriate authorities in place in the region whom the Red Army could work with[23] and, where possible, to use the national military units formed in the USSR for liberation.[24] Both factors were present in the Soviet Union's dealings with the governments-in-exile, even though they worked differently in practice.

Due to the Czechoslovak President's strategy of coming to terms with the USSR (50 percent to the West and 50 percent to the East), the Soviet-Czechoslovak treaty of friendship, mutual assistance and post-war cooperation of 12 December 1943 was the first agreement to be concluded and acted as a precedent. For the Soviet Union, its completion also served as a declaration of friendly relations after the break with the Polish government-in-exile. Though problems still existed in releasing Czechs, Slovaks, Ruthenians ("Carpathian Ukrainians" who numbered 10,000 or so[25]) from various camps, and with the organization of the army (the First Czechoslovak Battalion), these did not affect the Soviet-Czechoslovak concord to the same extent as similar problems had Soviet-Polish relations for three main reasons: Czechoslovakia was of less strategic importance to Stalin than Poland, the policies of the Beneš government did not arouse much concern, and there were fewer people from pre-Munich Czechoslovakia in the USSR.

Given the individual strategies pursued by the governments-in-exile and the distinctive conditions prevailing in each of the countries liberated, different patterns of Soviet domination developed, which are discernible in the case of Poland and Czechoslovakia. Gibiansky places both countries in separate groups: Poland, together with Romania and Hungary, was a state

---

21   Director of the Institute of Slavic Studies (previously the Institute of Slavic and Balkan Studies) in 1987–2004, died in 2005.

22   V. K. Volkov, "U istokov kontseptsii 'sotsialisticheskogo lageria' [At the Origins of the Concept of 'the Socialist Camp']," in *U istokov "sotsialisticheskogo sodruzhestva:" SSSR i vostochnoevropeiskie strany v 1944–1949 gg* [At the Origins of "the Socialist Commonwealth" in 1944–1949] (Moskva: Nauka, 1995), p. 12.

23   See Albina Noskova's detailed study of Stalin's consideration of different combinations in regard to the Polish authorities in: A. F. Noskova, "Stalin, pol'skie kommunisty i sozdanie Pol'skogo komiteta national'nogo osvobozhdeniia (po novym dokumentam arkhivov Rossii) [Stalin, Polish Communists and the Formation of the Polish Committee of National Liberation (Based on the newly available documents from the Russian archives)]," in *Novaia i noveishaia istoriia*, No. 3 (2008), pp. 3–21.

24   Volkov, "U istokov kontseptsii "sotsialisticheskogo lageria," pp. 15–19.

25   *Chekhoslovakia v XX veke: ocherki istorii* [Czechoslovakia in the 20th century: Historical Essays], in 2 vols., Vol. 1 (Moskva: Nauka, 2005), p. 405.

which experienced "direct Soviet interference" in imposing "people's democracy" and where the harshest policy was implemented; in Czechoslovakia, along with Bulgaria, in contrast, "the Soviet influence was important but compounded with the internal socio-political situation."[26]

In short, the research agenda dealing with the Polish and Czechoslovak governments-in-exile has considerably broadened in Russia. Studies of many aspects of bilateral relations (and other issues) have been reconsidered or initiated on the basis of the wealth of archival sources which has become available in the Russian Federation and abroad in recent decades. In this venture, historians from the Institute of Slavic Studies have primarily taken the lead. Noteworthy too, however, is the work which has been done in bringing to light important documents in the Russian archives mainly by scholars from the Institute of Slavic Studies and the Institute of World History (both from the Russian Academy of Sciences) dealing with Soviet repression, the role of the USSR in establishing "people's democracies" in Poland and Czechoslovakia as well as other countries of the region,[27] the place these nations had in Allied policies,[28] and the like.

On the other hand, many historians admit that a lot of questions remain unanswered or that only indirect evidence is available. While further research, together with publication of relevant archival documents, is needed and is underway,[29] it would also be fruitful to devote more attention to the study of mutual perceptions and misperceptions, and to the meaning attached to terms such as "cooperation" for example in Soviet-Polish and Soviet-Czechoslovak relations in the context of Allied diplomacy. This would deepen our understanding of the motives of the different players and the failure of mutual expectations.

---

26 Gibiansky, "Problemy Vostochnoi Evropy i nachalo formirovaniia sovetskogo bloka," pp. 117–121. The third group – Yugoslavia and Albania.

27 See *Sovetskii faktor v Vostochnoi Evrope. 1944–1953. Dokumenty* [The Soviet Factor in Eastern Europe. Documents], Vol. 1., *1944–1948 gg* (Moskva: ROSSPEN, 1999); *Iz Varshavy. Moskva, tovarishchu Beriia...: Dokumenty NKVD SSSR o pol'skom podpol'e. 1944–1945 gg* [From Warsaw. Moscow, to Comrade Beria...: The Documents of the Ministry of Internal Affairs of the USSR about the Polish Underground] (Moskva – Novosibirsk: Sibirskii khronograf, 2001), etc.

28 See O. A. Rzheshevsky, *Stalin i Cherchill'. Vstrechi. Besedy. Diskussii: Dokumenty, kommentarii, 1941–1945* [Stalin and Churchill: Documents, Conversations, Discussions: Documents, Commentaries, 1941–1945] (Moskva: Nauka, 2004). The publication of the Maisky diary and correspondence was also carried out under the auspices of the Institute of World History.

29 There are important publication projects on Soviet-Polish relations which are being conducted under the auspices of the Russian-Polish Center for Dialogue and Understanding. See *Otchet o deiatel'nosti Fonda "Rossiisko-pol'skii tsentr dialoga i soglasiia" v 2013 g* [Report on the Activities of the Russian-Polish Center for Dialogue and Understanding in 2013], available at: http://rospolcentr.ru/tabid/227/ArticleId/170/language/ru-RU/Default.aspx.

II. THE ARMED FORCES OF THE OCCUPIED COUNTRIES AND THEIR POLITICAL SIGNIFICANCE

TOGETHER INTO BATTLE: THE ARMIES IN EXILE: CONSIDERABLE VALUE OR "A DROP IN THE OCEAN"?

ZDENKO MARŠÁLEK

INTRODUCTION: RESISTANCE-IN-EXILE AS INDIVIDUAL "NATIONAL STORIES"

Today, the history of the Second World War and the related resistance-in-exile is a topic of great interest in the countries that had their governments-in-exile in Britain during the war. Practically all of the affected states have already compiled the history of their respective military units in relative detail, especially with regard to the combat deployment of their particular formations or the personal stories of individual participants.[1]

However, the history of the military resistance-in-exile is often perceived by particular national historiographies mostly from the perspective of their "own" histories, i.e. of the history of their own national resistance, relations with the world powers, internal problems and several other aspects. As a result, individual "national stories" of the Second World War and of resistance-in-exile have been created.

The basic interpretation has not changed much since the war years, when the primary goal of creating a "resistance story" was propaganda. However, this interpretation remained in place also after the war when the heroic resistance stories helped to put together a picture (once again propagandistic) of the "all-national struggle against the oppressors." This image was designed to raise the self-confidence of citizens after occupation, but also (and especially) to create a generally acceptable consensus around which the nation could unite again. The rate at which motifs of heroism and national cohesion were accentuated is quite similar to the ancient tribal myths of the early Middle Ages; however, the societies in the previously occupied countries

---

[1] In terms of historiography and taking decades of research into consideration, it is necessary to stress the importance of the extensive multi-volume work *Polskie siły zbrojne w drugiej wojnie światowej* [Polish Armed Forces in the Second World War], especially Volume II, Part 1, 2: *Kampanie na obczyźnie* [Campaigns Abroad] (London: Instytut Historyczny im. gen. Sikorskiego, 1959, 1975, henceforth *PSZ*). Despite enormous difficulties and given the fact that the work was produced in post-war exile circles, without close ties to the mother country and without the support of its authorities, this series, when compared with the compendia of the resistance-in-exile history of other occupied lands, remains an extraordinary piece of work even from today's perspective.

often and willingly "accepted" this story and adopted it into their *common (shared) memory*.[2]

Emphasizing national aspects, as well as the needs of propaganda, also often leads to a disproportionate highlighting and an overestimation of the importance of the given country and its units-in-exile (the same phenomenon occurs with the resistance movement in the occupied homeland) within the frame of the overall war effort. It is remarkable how deeply even these stereotypes have penetrated into the *common memory* of individual nations.

On the other hand, such interpretations likewise emphasize the intricate fates of small or relatively small nations in the middle of a conflict between world powers, the necessity they have to pursue – or at least to try to pursue – their own objectives and to push through their own demands in relation to the "big" countries. This factor is common to practically all the countries in question.

Individual "national stories" are, however, mutually quite disparate. It is noteworthy that while the motif of being "underestimated" or "neglected" by the Great Powers is present in the common memory of practically all the nations mentioned, it is also true that historians as well as society as a whole in these countries do not pay much attention to the "national stories" of other occupied countries – even if these countries are their geographical neighbours. Attempts at mutual comparison and subsequent syntheses have been relatively neglected.[3]

In this regard, very little has been done in the field of historiography. Along with some others, the interesting collection edited by Martin Conway

---

2   Among the most regarded works on this topic is Pieter Lagrou, *The Legacy of Nazi Occupation: Patriotic Memory and National Recovery in Western Europe, 1945–1965* (Cambridge: Cambridge University Press, 2000). Probably the most famous French example has been summarized concisely by L. Michelet: "Au moment de la liberation de la France, en 1944, le conditionnement des esprits était déjà un fait accompli: la version médiatique des faits, qui a été fort peu contestée depuis lors, était la suivante: la France a été libérée par le général de Gaulle, par la Résistance et par les Forces françaises libres (FFI)." Louis-Christian Michelet, "La contribution militaire française a l'effort de guerre allié (1941–1945)," in *Guerres mondiales et conflicts contemporains*, No. 177 (Janvier 1995), p. 7.

3   It is not a coincidence that the first global synthesis on the governments-in-exile published in the Czech Republic was written by a German historian: Detlef Brandes, *Exil v Londýně 1939–1943: Velká Británie a její spojenci Československo, Polsko a Jugoslávie mezi Mnichovem a Teheránem* (Praha: Karolinum, 2003). It was first published as: *Großbritannien und seine osteuropäischen Alliierten 1939–1943: die Regierung Polens, der Tschechoslowakei und Jugoslawiens im Londoner Exil vom Kriegsausbruch bis zur Konferenz von Teheran* (München: Oldenbourg, 1988). Note the significant fact that the translation did not appear until 15 years (!) after the original work. Moreover, because it focuses on the countries from the eastern part of Europe and on the question of their incorporation (or not) into the future Soviet sphere of interest, it did not provide an overall comparison of all the governments-in-exile existing among the western Allies (notably in Great Britain).

and José Gotovitch, belongs among the relatively few exceptions.[4] The book offered a number of short overviews of particular exile armies (Norwegian, Czechoslovak, French, Dutch), in comparison with the Belgian "example" which was described in more detail.[5] However, reasonable and honourable though the intentions are, they only go half-way: the particular overviews are solid and very useful but little emphasis is placed on mutual comparison.

But only by mutual comparison can realistic views on the significance of the given nations' contributions be acquired. The issue in question is not just a mere comparison of the official "national" stories. Indeed, several fundamental matters, from the process of gaining official recognition of the exile representations, through negotiations about the extent of powers to be allotted, to purely military questions, share a common base. Very often, the British authorities addressed many concerns, especially the more complex ones, globally, i.e., in the same way towards all governments-in-exile. Using a comparative approach to the topic can lead to very inspiring conclusions. Thereby, we can differentiate between constant, aberrant or purely unique aspects.

The same complex issues pertaining to the governments-in-exile apply also to the military. Here too, mutual comparison will help us to understand better the real significance and importance of individual governments-in-exile and their military units for the British. The relationship between the British and individual governments-in-exile in the military area also involved complex bilateral negotiations. That is why the basic stipulations of the initial mutual agreements on the existence of individual national armed forces on British territory were very similar, as were matters related to equipment, soldiers' pay, legal powers, the basic organizational charts of the specific armies, operational subordination during actual fighting, the very important issue of recruitment of a particular state's citizens into its army-in-exile on British soil,[6] and the like.

---

4   Martin Conway, José Gotovitch, eds., *Europe in Exile: European Exile Communities in Britain 1940–1945* (New York – Oxford: Berghahn Books, 2001). Three years later, another similar collection was published: Matthew Bennett, Paul Latawski, eds., *Exile Armies* (Houndmills, NH – New York, Palgrave, 2004).

5   Nevertheless, it is worth mentioning that the military issues and the particular armies-in-exile were only one, albeit the most important, topic of the individual articles and of the book in general.

6   Individual "national" stories of the history of the resistance-in-exile usually mention problems related to the forcible recruitment of their respective citizens in Britain, but only rarely emphasize the fundamental impact of general British measures, such as the *Allied Forces Act 1940* or the *Allied Powers (War Service) Act 1942*, which formed the general background to this complex issue. Indeed, the crucial importance of the second mentioned Act was almost immediately noted by Pavel Hartmann, "The Allied Powers (War Service) Act," in *The Modern Law Review*, Vol. 6, No. 1/2 (December 1942), pp. 72–75. Pavel Hartmann (1905 Pilsen – 2003 New York) was a Czech refugee who had served in the Czechoslovak army-in-exile in France and Britain as an artillery lieuten-

The actual formation of exile military units by individual governments-in-exile fulfilled the most important objective, i.e., the political task – they represented not only the most visible proof of existing resistance but also an important attribute of the enduring statehood of these nations. However, the soldiers themselves as well as the politicians wished also for active participation in the struggle, inasmuch as this would demonstrate their commitment not only "outwards," towards the Allies, but also "inwards," i.e., towards their own soldiers and the population in the occupied homeland. This objective was achieved and the "national stories" are full of examples of bravery and success in combat of airmen, mariners, infantrymen and tank crews. But what was the real military value of the exile armed forces and what was their actual significance? Did they represent a real or even important military force or were they just symbolic units? From this perspective, were there any differences between these individual armed forces and if so, what were they?

ARMIES-IN-EXILE AND THEIR MILITARY ORGANIZATION

The organization of the first exile units began even before the actual start of the war proper when volunteers from occupied Czechoslovakia began to gather in Poland.[7] The build-up of the first significant units formed by exiles, however, began in France in September 1939, where the Czechoslovak and also, even at this stage, the Polish exiles managed to create numerous armed units. The Polish exiles formed a not negligible army of 84,000 soldiers, organized in four infantry divisions, two mountain and one mechanized (armoured) brigade and a substantial air force[8]; the Czechoslovaks tried to form their proportionately eight times smaller human resources into one large ground unit and air force.[9] It is not common knowledge that during the

---

ant prior to being temporarily released from the army to complete his doctorate in law at the University of Oxford.

7   Although the seeds of the Czechoslovak military units in Poland began to emerge (in semi-official terms) in the spring of 1939, their existence was legally confirmed only after the outbreak of war, on 3 September, 1939, when the Polish president signed a decree on the establishment of the so-called *Czech and Slovakian Legion*. Its numbers were supposed to comprise not only emigrants from occupied Bohemia and Moravia, as well as Slovakia, but also people living in Poland who had Czechoslovak citizenship or nationality. The units were built on a voluntary basis. However, due to lack of time, the commanders managed to organize only about one thousand men.

8   Witold Biegański et al, *Polski czyn zbrojny w II wojnie światowej: Walki formacji polskich na Zachodzie 1939–1945* [Polish Action in the Second World War: Battles of Polish Formations in the West, 1939–1945] (Warsaw: Wydawnictwo Ministerstwa Obrony Narodowej, 1981), pp. 51–60, 113–123.

9   The Czechoslovak authorities were able to muster no more than 11,400 soldiers, which could form only a single, undermanned "light" infantry division. The significance of the active and notable commitment of Czech airmen, especially fighter pilots, in the air battles over France was much greater. Vojenský ústřední archiv - Vojenský historický archiv Praha [Central Mili-

last month of the French campaign, another army-in-exile was to arise on French soil: immediately after the German invasion, the Belgian authorities mobilized all serviceable men (especially the younger ones) and sent them to areas in the rear where they were trained to become replacement units for the casualties suffered by the regular Belgian army. After the collapse of Belgium they were transported to southern France. The intention was to train them in order that they would form the core of a new, future army, which would work alongside French military forces.[10]

Armies-in-Exile in France, June 1940

army-in-exile	total numbers (circa)	of the total number, airmen	full-scale large units		incomplete large units under formation	
			divisions	brigades	divisions	brigades
Polish	85,000	7,000	2	1	2	2
Czechoslovak	11,500	950	–	–	1	–
Belgian	100,000	?	–	–	1	–

Regarding the building of the armies-in-exile, it is interesting that the Poles negotiated the establishment of their first division in France even before the start of the war.[11] In addition, at the last moment before the outbreak

tary Archive – Military History Archive] (henceforth VÚA – VHA Prague), collection Náhradní těleso – Velká Británie [Depot Centre – Great Britain, henceforth NT – VB], f. 50, No. 164, Číselný přehled čs. zahraniční armády za roky 1939–1940 [Numerical Overview of the Czechoslovak army-in-exile during 1939–1940]. However, when assessing the mobilization efforts of Poles and Czechoslovaks and their contribution to the cause of the Allies, we have to consider that about one half of the men were recruited from compatriot communities in France (approximately 44,700 Poles and 7,600 Czechoslovaks). These men could therefore also have been mobilized by the French army. Thus, the real assets were "only" the refugees from the occupied countries (approximately 38,000 Poles and 3,500 Czechoslovaks). Nevertheless, these men included experienced officers and trained specialists, including highly regarded airmen.

10   The new recruits were incorporated into the so-called *Centres de recrutement de l´armée belge* (C.R.A.B.). A total of 100,000 men represented a significant potential but, due to lack of time, it was not possible to organize and train them as valuable field units. Indeed, if the French Army had managed to hold the front, the Belgian Army would have been of far greater value than its Polish and Czechoslovak counterparts. For details, see Service historique de la Défence à Vincennes (henceforth SHD), sign. 7 N 2731, effectifs des troupes belges en France (4 juin); 7 N 2744, documents concernant les troupes belges stationnés en France; 7 N 2476, dossier 3, constitution d'une division belge (5 juin 1940), tableaux des effectifs des militaires belges stationnés en zone non occupée à la date 1ᵉʳ août 1940.

11   SHD, sign. 7 N 2476, dossier 1, accord entre le gouvernement français et le gouvernement polonais concernant la création d'une division polonaise en France. The negotiations took place during the visit of high-ranking Polish military officers to France in May 1939. Witold Biegański, *Wojsko Polskie we Francii 1939–1940* [*Polish Army in France, 1939–1940*] (Warszawa: Wydawnictwo

of hostilities, towards the end of August 1939, the Polish Navy made the very significant decision to send its three large destroyers to Britain.[12] Both steps later proved to be the foundation for developing the further organization of the Polish armed forces in exile (*Polskie Siły Zbrojne*).

It is however true that these remarkable and (seemingly predictive) pre-war steps represented only unsystematic exceptions.[13] Neither Poland nor any other country had a detailed plan of action in the event of its territory being completely occupied. The building up of the exile forces took place in an improvised manner in response to developing circumstances.

After the defeat of France, new governments-in-exile were established in addition to the Polish and Czechoslovak governments, and thus a "family" of exile representations was established on British soil (besides the Poles and Czechoslovaks, the Dutch, Norwegian, Belgian and Luxembourg governments, as well as the Free-France-movement were already set up during the summer of 1940). All of them tried to create as strong an army as possible as one of the most visible aspects of their statehood.[14]

The political importance of the units-in-exile was indisputable. However, from a purely military point of view, they had no practical value for the Allies unless they were fully operational. This meant that they had to be compatible and able to operate together with standard allied formations or within their structure. Any unit could be useful to a given superior commander only if it could be deployed in a similar manner to any other unit, i.e., when it had the same structure and organization as the British formations.

Paradoxically, from this perspective, the army branch that satisfied these requirements most was the most complex strand of the armed forces, the air force. The Allies managed to incorporate almost flawlessly all the airmen into the overall structure of the Royal Air Force, either by forming "national" squadrons or by directly shifting individual pilots to British units, thus utilizing the potential of every single airman as much as it was physically pos-

---

Ministerstwa Obrony Narodowej, 1967), p. 55. For an overview of the negotiations about forming Polish units in France during the entire inter-war period, see *PSZ*, Vol. 1, p. 90.

12   Their deployment against the Germans in the Baltic Sea by the Poles would not have made any sense but they represented a real, valuable and welcome reinforcement for the *Royal Navy*. In the early years of the war, Britain suffered from a critical lack of smaller escort- and anti-submarine vessels. The acquisition of "only" three destroyers with experienced crews should thus not be underestimated.

13   According to the original intent from May 1939, the Polish division in France was not supposed to constitute a basis for the army-in-exile. On the contrary, the Polish Command considered the division to be, more or less, a symbolic demonstration of the common struggle of the Western Allies and the Polish army, defending its own country on its own front in Poland.

14   Very good general overviews of the particular armies are contained in the above mentioned books by Martin Conway and José Gotovitch and Matthew Bennett and Paul Latawski. Thus there is no need to repeat the basic facts here.

sible.[15] Similarly, the incorporation of the naval forces was also successful by and large. However, the most difficult challenge proved to be the integration of the ground forces.

Thus, already in the fall of 1940, British army circles faced the problem of how they should incorporate the relatively small exile armies of their allies, which mostly had just a few thousand troops available. After lengthy negotiations, it was decided to organize them in the form of independent brigades, with an ideal number of 5,500 soldiers prescribed.[16] From a propaganda point of view, and also from a purely military perspective, this was a convenient solution since a brigade represented a so-called Large Field Unit – on the same level as full-scale field divisions with more than 15,000 soldiers. From an organizational point of view, the concept of brigade groups was flexible, in terms of the "ideal" *Tables of Organization and Equipment* (TO&E), and thus allowed a smaller number of battalions, batteries, and the like to be established, according to recruitment possibilities in the individual armies. It also enabled the quick expansion of brigades to the prescribed number or above if required (or better to say if possible). A further advantage of such a solution was the fact that British divisions were used to conducting their combat operations with brigade groups of various strengths. This meant that the operational integration of the exile brigade groups into the structure of the British armed forces posed no theoretical problem. This basic organizational

---

15   An interesting counterpoint to the utilization at very short notice of foreign airmen in the RAF is offered by Alan Brown in his article in the Conway, Gotovitch book, pp. 167–182. Brown pointed out the serious objections expressed by British military figures to absorbing Polish and Czechoslovak airmen in the ranks of the RAF Even in the very critical period of summer 1940, many British officers at various levels raised doubts about the skills these men had as airmen and soldiers, as well as their level of training: "We don't know if there are any pilots worthy of the name," wrote Archibald Boyle, then Director of Intelligence. Ibid, p. 169. In terms of choice, some British politicians and soldiers mistrusted Czechoslovaks even more then the Poles: "Anthony Eden told the War Cabinet on 19 June that, although he was prepared 'to take off any Czechoslovak troops who wished to leave' [France after its defeat in June 1940], he would 'much prefer to embark Polish troops'." Ibid, p. 168. Behind these opinions were fears of weaker Czechoslovak integrity owing to their multinational character, as well as the alleged strong influence of communist propaganda among Czechoslovak units.

16   The all-embracing aspect of this act has usually been neglected by individual national historiographies. However, the exile authorities at that time were aware of the complexity of the British approach, as could be demonstrated by the Czechoslovak example. On 8 December 1940, the Czechoslovak exile Ministry of Defence received a British proposition for organizing ground forces. In addition, on 5 April 1941, the relevant Tables of Organization & Equipment (TO&E) were provided. Czechoslovak officers closely monitored British negotiations with the other governments-in-exile during the winter and spring of 1941 and, on 5 April 1941, they reported: "The Brigade Headquarters received a new regulation of how the structure of the Czechoslovak ground forces shall look like. This new structure has to be achieved by about May. Such organized Brigade Groups will be formed by all allied armies apart from the Polish army, which will have an Army Corps." For details, see VÚA – VHA Prague, coll. Ministerstvo národní obrany – Londýn [Ministry of Defence – London], f. 3, No. 23, Válečný deník MNO–II./3.odd., 1940–41 [War Diary of the 3rd Section of the Department II of the Ministry of Defence, 1940–41].

concept thus applied to all exile ground forces in Britain and represented one of their significant similarities. Nevertheless, the actual number of troops within the individual exile forces varied greatly.

From the perspective of numbers, among others, the Poles were in the best situation.[17] As a result they were able to organize two fully-manned brigade groups in Britain and one in the Middle East area (and other units, as well), and later to go far beyond the horizon of independent brigade groups and form higher units in accordance with the standard British TO&E – in the Middle East area, for example, an entire army corps was established;[18] in Britain, the Poles decided to utilize their more modest manpower as efficiently as possible and to establish a full-scale armoured division[19] and a parachute brigade,[20] which could be incorporated into the British army structure, more or less like the normal, standard units. The other governments-in-exile were in a far worse situation. They usually had a maximum of a few thousand men available. The exile Royal Yugoslav Army at first formed only a single battalion,[21] the Belgian and Dutch formations in the West European theatre of war, despite the fact that they were officially called "brigades," were merely symbolic units as well.[22] The Czechoslovaks stood roughly in the middle be-

---

17 Right after the evacuation from France in July 1940, a total of 27,614 Polish soldiers (including 6,429 airmen and 4,432 soldiers in the Middle East) were available to the Polish government-in-exile. Biegański, *Walki formacji polskich na Zachodzie*, p. 207.

18 In the Middle East, the so-called *Carpathian Independent Brigade Group* (*Samodzielna Brygada Strzelców Karpackich*; correctly translated, this unit should be called the *Independent Brigade of the Carpathian Rifles*) that fought alongside the British Forces in the Western Desert was, thanks to the soldiers released from internment in the USSR, expanded into the 2nd *Army Corps* with nearly 50,000 soldiers. From the end of 1943, these soldiers were fighting in Italy (with two infantry divisions, one armoured brigade, an artillery group and other units).

19 The 1st *Armoured Division* (1 *Dywizja Pancerna*) was officially established in 1942 under the command of the highly experienced general, S. Maczek.

20 The 1st *Independent Parachute Brigade* (1 *Samodzielna Brygada Spadochronowa*) was established in 1942 but did not reach its required full strength until its deployment in Operation Market Garden in September 1944.

21 The issue of the Yugoslav battalion is dealt with in the article by Blaž Torkar in this volume: "The Yugoslav Armed Forces in Exile: From the Yugoslav Royal Guard Battalion to the Overseas Brigades."

22 The Belgians organized their ground forces (*Brigade Piron*) as a light composition of several independent motorized companies, supported by a handful of artillery units and a squadron of armoured cars, with a total of 2,200 men. The Dutch unit (*Prinses Irene Brigade*) was organized in a similar way but was even weaker, having only 1,200 soldiers. Apart from these brigade groups, the Dutch and Belgians formed some small sub-units for special duties (*commandos* and parachute troops). For a comparison of the individual exile-ground-units, see the following popular work: Nigel Thomas, Simon McCouaig, *Foreign Volunteers of the Allied Forces 1939-45* (Oxford: Osprey Publishing, 1991). A very short overview of the Czechoslovak case in comparison is presented by Zdenko Maršálek, *Dunkerque 1944-1945. Ztráty Československé samostatné obrněné brigády během operačního nasazení ve Francii* [Dunkirk 1944-1945. Casualties of the Czechoslovak Independent Armoured Brigade Group during Operational Deployment in France], (Praha: Nakladatelství Lidové noviny, 2011), pp. 22-26.

tween these two extremes. They could not aspire to form a classic field division but hoped to build a full-strength brigade group. From the beginning of 1943 they also followed the Polish example of maximum efficiency and thus concentrated on organizing an independent armoured brigade group.[23]

Ground Field Units of the Armies-in-Exile Actively Fighting in France and Italy, Summer 1944[24]

army-in-exile	total numbers (ca.)	full-scale large units		incomplete (underpowered) or non-standard large units	
		divisions	brigades	divisions	brigades
Polish	65,000	3	2	–	–
Czechoslovak	4,300	–	–		1
Belgian	2,300	–	–	–	1
Netherlands	1,200				1
Greek	3,500				1

The table clearly demonstrates that practically all the armies-in-exile deployed their ground forces in the form of independent brigade groups, more or less underpowered. The only exception was the Poles who went far beyond the level of "symbolic" or partly-available units as was the case with the other units.

The ranking of the "military usefulness" of individual exile armed forces seems to be in direct relationship to the table printed above: only the Poles managed to deploy real battle-worthy formations. The Czechoslovaks were relatively close to fulfilling the TO&E of an armoured brigade group with

---

23   From the original number of 3,010 soldiers available in December 1940, the Czechoslovak brigade group only managed to increase its numbers to 4,300 men by late August 1944, when this unit, called the *Czechoslovak Independent Armoured Brigade Group*, left Britain for France. Even the maximally reduced prescribed numbers (TO&E) called for more than 4,600 soldiers. For the Brigade's TO&E in detail, see Gustav Svoboda, "Československá samostatná obrněná brigáda ve Velké Británii" [Czechoslovak Independent Armoured Brigade Group in Great Britain], in *Historie a vojenství* [History and Warfare], Vol. 43, No. 6 (1994), pp. 74–105.

24   The *Norwegian Independent Brigade Group* (in 1944 *circa* 3,500 men strong) was not included in the above table because it was not deployed in the battlefield until towards the end of the war. It was trained for the possibility of an allied invasion of Norway. Only individuals and minor units "saw action," one of them being a unit of *commandos* in the Scheldt estuary and another a mountain company in Lapland, which fought alongside the Red Army.

It is also necessary to mention the Jewish Brigade Group, which was formed in the summer of 1944 and fought in Italy from November 1944 at a strength of about 5,000 soldiers. For details, see Morris Beckmann, *The Jewish Brigade: An Army with Two Masters, 1944–1945* (Staplehurst: Spellmount, 1998).

a significant number of tanks; the Norwegian brigade was stationed in Britain and did not "see the action,"[25] while the Belgian and Dutch formations were of very limited combat value.

Similar disparities in numbers can also be found in the individual exile-air-forces: the Poles formed over 15 squadrons with about 20,000 airmen, the Czechoslovaks four squadrons with only one-tenth of the Polish numbers. The Norwegians also managed to set up four squadrons, while the Belgians and Dutch were each able to organize only two squadrons on the British Isles.[26]

MILITARY VALUE A COMPLEX QUESTION: NOT LIMITED TO SOLDIER NUMBERS

It has often been said in the Czech Republic that when the British compiled "rankings" of the governments-in-exile based on their respective contribution to the common war effort, the Czechoslovaks were placed last in 1941.[27] However, is it even possible to compile such "rankings" and, if so, based on what criteria?

What is not clear from the numbers mentioned above is why the Czechoslovaks should have come last in the ranking instead of second, behind the Poles. Indeed the conclusion drawn represents the typical viewpoint of a landlubber from Central Europe: in addition to ground units and air squadrons in the European theatre of war, there were a lot of other contributions that could be made.

For example, the importance the British attached to the three Polish destroyers has already been mentioned. The Netherlands' ground forces had fewer than 2,000 troops in Britain, but the Dutch government-in-exile had a relatively strong military navy at its disposal.[28] Its combat value was

---

25 For the Norwegian army-in-exile, the description by Chris Mann in the repeatedly mentioned Conway, Gotovitch book is focused more on naval and air-force matters rather than on ground forces. For more details see e.g., Julian Holmås, *Historien om Skottlandsbrigaden 1940–1945* (Porsgrunn: Forlaget Grenland, 1997). For the general background, see e.g., Patrick Salmon, ed., *Britain and Norway in the Second World War* (London: HMSO, 1995).

26 The squadrons organized outside Britain are not mentioned here, e.g., Dutch air units in Australia and Ceylon, as well as the Belgian units in Africa. Interesting and worth noticing is the fact that two Dutch squadrons in Britain became operational as early as June 1940 and, during the first months of fighting, the 320th Squadron used to fly their domestic Fokker T.VIII planes, evacuated from Holland. Nico Geldof, *De Operaties van 320 Squadron 1940–1946* (Maarssen: Uitgeverij Geromy BV, 2006).

27 It has been said that the frustration of President Beneš at this ranking was one of the reasons for issuing the order to assassinate Reinhard Heydrich.

28 During the Battle of the Netherlands in May 1940, the largest part of the Royal Dutch Navy (*Koninklijke Marine*) was deployed in the Netherlands East Indies. Among the other vessels that were carrying out their duties in home waters, several managed to flee to Britain, including

clearly greater than the entire combat value of the ground forces of all the governments-in-exile combined (with the possible exception of the Polish forces). The relatively numerous armed units from their colonies should also be considered when assessing the Dutch and Belgian war effort.[29]

However, the military importance of the exile allies was based not only on the number of units, aircraft or maritime vessels. During this time, the Dutch government-in-exile still controlled a huge colonial empire, including its pearl, the Netherlands East Indies. The colony itself not only had its own substantial army and air force for its own protection,[30] but, most importantly, it supplied the Allies with many strategic primary raw materials, such as crude oil, rubber and timber. As shown in the following table, crude oil production in the Netherlands East Indies in 1938 represented "only" 2.8 percent of total world production. Nevertheless, there were only six countries in the world

World Crude-Oil Production, 1938[31]

	Country	Total (Thousands of Barrels)	Percentage of World Production
1	US	1,213,254	60.7 %
2	USSR	224,714	11.2 %
3	Venezuela	190,232	9.5 %
4	Iran	77,230	3.9 %
5	Netherlands East Indies	55,120	2.8 %
6	Romania	47,850	2.4 %
7	Mexico	36,000	1.8 %
8	Iraq	32,100	1.6 %
...	...	...	...
Σ	Total	1,997,579	100 %

some ships still under construction. The Dutch government-in-exile had 5 light cruisers, 8 destroyers, 1 great mine-layer, 2 gun-boats, and a significant number of submarines and small ships at its disposal. For a history of the Dutch Navy, see Philippus Meesse Bosscher, *De Koninklijke Marine in de Tweede Wereldoorlog*, Volume I–III (Wever: Franeker, 1984, 1990). For a brief overview in English, see Henry Trevor Lenton, *Navies of the Second World War: The Royal Netherlands Navy* (London: MacDonald & Co, 1968).

29   For example, the military force of the Belgian Congo (*Force Publique*) grew to nearly 40,000 soldiers. Among others, it deployed one full brigade group for the Abyssinian Campaign in 1941, which fought bravely against the Italian colonial army.

30   In December 1941, the *Koninklijk Nederlandsch-Indisch Leger* counted nearly 85,000 men and 400 aircraft, but their combat value was significantly limited by inadequate organization and training, inexperience in modern warfare and obsolete weaponry.

31   Basil B. Zavoico, "Foreign Oil Developments in 1938," in *Bulletin of the American Association of Petroleum Geologists*, Vol. 23, No. 6 (June 1939), p. 949. Available at: http://archives.datapages.com/data/bulletns/1938–43/data/pg/0023/0006/0900/0949.htm.

producing more than two percent; more than 55 million barrels represented a tremendous amount and the Netherlands East Indies thus constituted the fifth largest producer worldwide. The importance of rubber and timber production was even greater.

Even after the Netherlands East Indies were occupied by Japan in 1942, the not negligible resources of the Dutch colonies in the Caribbean area (Netherlands West Indies) were still available. In particular, the production of bauxite in Surinam was of enormous, strategic importance, as can be seen in the following table:

World Production Of Bauxite, 1938[32]

	Country	Total (metric tons)
1	France	682,440
2	Hungary	540,718
3	Yugoslavia	396,368
4	British Guiana	382,409
5	Surinam (Neth. Guiana)	377,213
6	Italy	360,837
7	US	315,906
8	USSR	250,000
9	Netherlands East Indies	245,354
10	Greece	179,886

In terms of the Allied war effort, none of the other Dutch Caribbean colonies had important mineral resources. The huge refineries on Curaçao Island, however, were processing a substantial amount of crude oil from Venezuela (the third largest oil producer in the world) and providing related logistical and transport support services. Another ally, Belgium, was able to offer significant raw material resources from the Belgian Congo, where, mainly, copper, cobalt, gold and diamonds were mined. After the defeat of the British in Malaya, rubber production gained significance. Of paramount strategic importance was the mining of uranium ore in the Shinkolobwe Mine, which provided the material necessary for the development of the atomic bomb.

---

32 Herbert A. Franke, M. E. Trought, "Bauxite and Aluminum," in *Minerals Yearbook*, 1940, p. 653. Apart from the countries mentioned here, other sources were of minor importance by comparison. It can be seen how much of the world production of bauxite was taken over by the Axis powers until the first months of 1942 (France, Hungary, Yugoslavia, Italy, Greece, and the Netherlands East Indies). The crucial importance of the Surinam mines is thus clearly evident.

The allied coalition fought on other fronts, on the ground and in the air, but at a strategic level, the most important battlefield comprised the maritime routes that enabled the transport of supplies. Thus, during the time when the strategically fundamental battle for the Atlantic was raging, practically until the middle of 1943, literally every cargo boat counted. In this sphere of operations, Greek and Dutch merchant fleets played a key role, but the most important was the Norwegian ally. While Norway had only a very small army in Britain, its merchant fleet was put at the disposal of the Allies. Prior to the war, the Norwegian merchant fleet was the fourth largest fleet in the world, and about 4 million gross registered tons of shipping sailed the oceans under the Norwegian flag.[33] Norwegian tankers, by all accounts, transported one third of the total volume of crude oil taken to Britain throughout the war.[34] Indeed it has been claimed that the Norwegian merchant fleet was "a weapon mightier than a million men in the battlefield."[35] The contribution made by the Norwegian fleet to the war effort is underscored by its losses, which amounted to half of the entire fleet.[36]

The "ranking" of usefulness of the exile allies looks quite different from these perspectives. Indeed, the Poles and (especially) the Czechoslovaks were only able to offer manpower, which had to be dressed in British uniforms, equipped with British weapons and fed with British food.[37] As mentioned earlier, because of the limited possibilities for deployment, we can estimate that in terms of "price – performance" ratio the Czechoslovak and Polish ground forces, and those of the other small allies, were "quite expensive" for the British and were more costly and less convenient than their British counterparts.[38]

---

33 In December 1939, the Norwegian merchant fleet consisted of 4,308 vessels with a total of 4,756,000 gross tons. *Statistisk Årbok for Norge, 1939.* Det Statistiske Sentralbyrå, Oslo 1939, p. 131. After the invasion of Norway, some vessels larger than 500 gross tons came under German control. Their number (273 ships) looks significant, but most of them were of a smaller type and represented only about 1/8 of total Norwegian tonnage. The Allies were supported by 1,078 ships with 500 gross tons or more. For an overview of the important sources, see http://www.warsailors .com/freefleet/nortraship.html.

34 In 1940, about 39 percent of all Norwegian merchant vessels were tankers (1.8 mil. tons); see http://www.warsailors.com/freefleet/shipstats.html.

35 The British merchant fleet lost about 11.7 million gross tons during the war, i.e., 54 percent of its total tonnage at the beginning of the war. Ian Friel, *Maritime History of Britain and Ireland* (London: The British Museum Press, 2003), pp. 245–250. This means that the Norwegian merchant fleet could replace a significant part of (future) British losses.

36 During the war, 570 Norwegian merchant ships were lost and 3,638 sailors died. Indeed, out of a total of 23 million tons of all allied merchant ships lost during the war, 10 percent were Norwegian. See http://www.warsailors.com/freefleet/shipstats.html.

37 It is worth mentioning here that apart from their warships, the Poles also offered their small merchant fleet. However, all they could add to the common war effort were 35 merchant ships with *circa* 117,000 gross tons. Biegański, *Walki formacji polskich na Zachodzie*, pp. 61, 69. This is quite a modest tonnage, but, as we know, all contributions counted, no matter how little.

38 We should mention here that each individual exile army had its own copious apparatus, such as a Ministry of Defence, General Staff, headquarters of the individual armed branches, vari-

On the other hand, Czechoslovakia, for its part, contributed to the economic side of the war effort, too. The Allies were able to capitalize on the results of the pre-war activities of Czechoslovak export companies, especially in the Middle East, among which the most important was a Tehran arms factory of significant production capacity. A unique aspect in this regard is represented by the output of branches of the *Baťa* shoe company in many countries of the world – as well as weapons, soldiers need boots and, in many respects, the production of boots is as important for conducting warfare as munitions factories.

Yet another area of military cooperation and a contribution made by the small allies to the common war effort was in the technical field, such as in the release of licenses for high-quality weaponry. The British were using several licensed weapons, Czech, Polish, Belgian, for example.[39] Similarly, also in this area, the "national stories" include plenty of myths related to the fundamental importance of this or that weapon or system. The best-known is, of course, the *Bren* machine gun, used by the British in huge quantities throughout the war. Czechoslovak people were and are properly proud of this invention. However, lack of comparison led to a certain overrating of its importance. The British themselves complained already during the war that it was practically impossible to attend any meeting or lecture on Czechoslovak-British friendship without hearing, over and over again, the "story" of the miraculous machine gun. The *Bren* was undoubtedly an excellent weapon, but it is good to realize that if this had not been the case, then a different gun would have been selected, and it would not have mattered significantly if the quality of such a gun was a little worse or a little better. Light machine guns do not win wars. It would therefore seem whatever type of gun the troops used would not have any real impact on the strategic situation on the battlefield. Nevertheless, there were some exceptions. It was not the Czechoslovak *Bren*, but, for example, the very advanced and up-to-date Dutch *Hazemeyer* naval anti-aircraft control firing system with tri-axially stabilized mounting, which significantly improved the very problematic effectiveness of the

---

ous recruitment depots and training centres, etc. The officers-to-soldiers ratio was thus quite disproportionate – too many generals, too few privates.

39   The Canadian army (and later the British army as well) introduced the Belgian *FN HP* pistol; the Czechoslovak light machine guns *Bren* were used extensively by nearly all the armies of the Commonwealth; practically all British-built tanks after 1940 were armed with Czechoslovak 7,92 heavy machine guns *Besa* (another Czechoslovak machine gun *Besa*, with a caliber of 15 mm, was also used, but less widely); all AFVs on both sides of the conflict were equipped with the revolutionary Polish rotary periscope invented by Rudolf Gundlach (a system still in use today). While some weapons were introduced to the British and Commonwealth armies on a license basis, the development of other weapons was not completed until during the war years, in close cooperation with British experts, for example, the Polish 20 mm anti-aircraft gun *Polsten*, or the famous mine detector, developed under the supervision of Józef Kosacki, which was used for the first time during the Second Battle of El Alamein.

anti-aircraft defence on British warships. Its importance can be seen in the significant reduction of losses to the British fleet from air attacks after its introduction in 1942. Thus, this system had a considerable impact at the operational and possibly also strategic levels.[40]

Real military value also includes cooperation on other technical projects. The Polish contribution in implementing the *Ultra* project was of essential importance. This takes us to yet another area, namely espionage and the employment of home resistance for intelligence tasks. But this topic would require a separate chapter.

Another issue that should be mentioned is the somewhat intangible "psychological contribution" the small allies made in terms of propaganda value and in boosting morale among British civilians and the armed forces, especially before June 1941 when Britain "stood alone" against Germany. One particular feature in this respect has been suggested, specifically that Britain's playing host to the governments and forces-in-exile reinforced the British in their belief that they were "doing the right thing" and "helping those weaker than themselves" against tyranny.

It is also important to observe the mutual relations among individual exile armies. In this area, the attempt by the Polish and Czechoslovak governments to introduce a project of confederation appears to be quite unique.[41] It was not an accident that relatively close cooperation on the military field was established at the same time as these negotiations peaked at the end of 1941. The Poles were very helpful in the initial organization of the Czechoslovak unit in the Soviet Union; a very successful chapter was written by the common struggle during the defence of Tobruk, during which a Czechoslovak battalion was subordinated to the command of a Polish brigade group. This move solved the problem of the insufficient compatibility the undersized exile units had with the British army.[42] It is interesting that the British attempted to adopt a similar measure in 1944, when they wanted the underpowered *Czechoslovak Independent Armoured Brigade* to closely cooperate with

40   The disadvantages and inefficiencies of the heretofore promoted "impassable umbrella" with the use of inaccurate but mass fire from the outdated 40 mm Vickers ("pom-pom") anti-aircraft cannons were clearly demonstrated by the tragic fate of *Force Z* (battlecruiser HMS *Repulse* and battleship HMS *Prince of Wales*), sunk by Japanese aircraft in December 1941 off the east coast of Malaya, north of Singapore.

41   The first study published on this topic was received with great interest: Piotr S. Wandycz, *Czechoslovak-Polish Confederation and the Great Powers, 1940–43* (Bloomington: Indiana University Press, 1956).

42   The Czechoslovak 11th *Infantry Battalion – East* was subordinated to the command of the *Polish Independent Carpathian Brigade Group* from the end of October 1941 to the beginning of 1942. Their deployment at the static, well-fortified sector meant that large casualties were avoided. During Operation Crusader in 1941 both of these units achieved the important task of securing the entire western third of the defence perimeter of Tobruk.

the Polish 1*st Armoured Division* on the Western front.[43] But 1944 was not 1941 and similar cooperation with the Polish exile army, however convenient this might have been from a military point of view, would certainly present a difficult diplomatic problem. The political orientation of the Polish and Czechoslovak governments-in-exile had completely separated by then.

CONCLUSION: HOW TO PLAY WITH THE GREAT POWERS?

As we can see, not even the purely technical warfare contribution of the exile allies can be measured only by the number of troops or field units formed. The question is much more complex.

However, from the military perspective, what matters most is whether the exile armies fulfilled their main task – to help their respective governments push through their political goals, i.e., not only liberation of the homeland but also restoration of full sovereignty. While the contribution of the exile armies was generally recognized, it was also clear that it was considerably limited. In the final analysis, political decisions were of much greater importance than the actual military performance of the armies-in-exile. The soldiers in all the exile armies fought stoutly. While even their bravest deeds could not have reversed any possible unfavourable decisions made by the Great Powers, the common struggle represented, at the least, a moral obligation that had to be taken into account. That was probably the maximum which the troops of the small allies could achieve.

But power calculations can be deceptive. The ability of the governments-in-exile to influence the decisions of the Great Powers was limited and they had no choice but to strive to find some kind of *modus vivendi*. Some succeeded better than others. From the Czechoslovak, and indeed a Central European perspective, the most important issue was the forthcoming relationship with the Soviet Union.[44] The Czechoslovak exile representation was able to return home from London, even though in a significantly modified form, and President Beneš resumed his office, even though only temporarily. On the other hand, not even a relatively strong army-in-exile or the bravery of

---

43   A group of officers was even sent to the 1*st Polish Armoured Division*, already fighting in Normandy. VÚA – VHA Prague, collection Čs. samostatná obrněná brigáda – velitelství [Czechoslovak Independent Armoured Brigade Group – Headquarters], f. 166, No. 220, Brigade order No. 210 from 6th September 1944.

44   For a distinctive brief on the complex development of mutual relations between the Czechoslovak exile representation and the "Big Three" powers and the other allies, see the relevant chapters of Jaroslav Hrbek, Vít Smetana et al, *Draze zaplacená svoboda. Osvobození Československa 1944-1945* [Dearly Paid Freedom: The Liberation of Czechoslovakia, 1944-1945] (Praha – Litomyšl: Paseka, 2009).

its sailors, airmen, tankers, parachutists and infantrymen helped the Polish government-in-exile, which clashed fundamentally with the Soviet Union.[45]

What then are the conclusions of this chapter? I strongly recommend focusing further research on the importance of the exile armies from wider perspectives, to attempt to find the answer to the question of their real military value for the Allies and to free ourselves from the more or less propaganda stories and myths, which in many respects still persist today.

The best method to do this is by mutual comparison, which will allow us to see which aspects, moments, approaches, solutions, and the like, were constant between the British and all the governments-in-exile, and which were unique or variable. Such an approach would allow us to better understand the relations between the British and the governments-in-exile generally as well as the specifics of bilateral connections.

Nevertheless, the primary issue is to find out how individual governments-in-exile managed to "do the impossible" and how they found appropriate solutions for the many, mutually contradictory requirements: how to put in place an organizational structure that would satisfy not only the prestigious requirements of the exiles themselves but also the purely military needs of the great Allies, how to acquire the necessary "laurels on the battlefield" while avoiding heavy causalities and, at the same time, achieve, at least partially, some of their own military and political objectives.

So, if there is a question to be seen, hidden inside the title of this project, it is: "What is to be revisited here?" In the field of military history, I strongly recommend that it should be just those narrow, mythic and "self-centred" stories of individual nations.

The problem of achieving maximum effectiveness from small armed forces that confronted the governments-in-exile of several countries during the Second World War and their attempts at resolution can be inspiring even today. Finding an optimal balance between simultaneous needs is still an open question with small European countries seeking not just to symbolically represent their own political orientation, and thus gain political points within the structures of allied forces but, at the same time, make a valuable contribution from the military point of view.

---

45   For that matter, the relationship of the Polish and Czechoslovak exiles in Russia can be demonstrated by a tragic but symbolic contradiction. In March and April of 1940, the Czechoslovak representatives managed to negotiate with the Soviets for the departure of two transports of soldiers interned in the Soviet Union after the Polish campaign in September 1939. Shortly after the end of the Russo-Finnish war, the internees were released to go to imperialist France to reinforce the bourgeois exile-army that was fighting Germany, which was, at that time, on friendly terms with the Soviet Union. Despite this fact, the Soviets let the Czechoslovak soldiers go. However, during the exact same days when the Czechoslovaks were leaving Odessa for France, the Soviets were murdering thousands of interned Poles in Katyń, Kharkov and elsewhere.

THE YUGOSLAV ARMED FORCES IN EXILE: FROM THE YUGOSLAV ROYAL GUARD BATTALION TO THE OVERSEAS BRIGADES

BLAŽ TORKAR

After the successful coup in Belgrade on 27 March 1941, which was carried out by pro-British generals in the Yugoslav Royal Army, General Simović formed a new government and soon after the Axis forces attacked the country on 6 April 1941, the Yugoslav government, King Peter II and a few members of his military staff went into exile. In retrospect, the Mirkovic (Simović) coup still appears to be one of the most unrealistic, or even romantic, acts of defiance in modern European history. Not only did it threaten to divide a precariously unified country, but it was also bound to provoke a hostile German reaction, against which the Serbs could call on no external assistance whatsoever to support them. The Royal Yugoslav Army surrendered on 17 April 1941 after 11 days of fighting against the Axis powers. The Simović government was welcomed into the family of governments-in-exile in London in June 1941. General Bogoljub Ilić was appointed Minister of Defence and Chief of Staff, while General Borivoje Mirković became commander of the Royal Yugoslav Air Force. In the following years, the Yugoslav drama unfolded in a number of theatres: militarily in the homeland, and politically and diplomatically in London, Cairo, Washington, and Moscow.[1]

The term in office of each of the five prime ministers who presided over the government under King Peter II during the next four years corresponded to a particular phase in the existence of the Yugoslav establishment in exile and its pursuit of attainable and unattainable goals. Simović carried the flag of "27 March" (the coup) to London, joined the grand alliance, and established the first links with Draža Mihailović's resistance movement at home. Simović was also accused of sharing responsibility for the almost immediate collapse of the Yugoslav army's resistance.

The government of the next Prime Minister, Slobodan Jovanović (in office from 12 January 1942 till 26 June 1943) included Mihailović, who was appointed Defence Minister and Commander-in-Chief of the Home army fighting in

---

1   John Keegan, *The Second World War* (London: Random House, 1997), p. 152; Gorazd Bajc, *Iz nevidnega na plan: slovenski primorski liberalni narodnjaki v emigraciji med drugo svetovno vojno in ozadje britanskih misij v Sloveniji* [From the Invisible Out in the Open: Liberal Nationally Conscious Primorska Slovenes in Emigration during the Second World War and the Background of British Missions to Slovenia] (Koper: Zgodovinsko društvo za južno Primorsko: Znanstveno-raziskovalno središče Republike Slovenije, 2002), p. 65.

the occupied territory. However, Jovanović failed to overcome internal dissension and restore confidence in relations with the British. The problem lay in the Yugoslav government's request for free and uncontrolled clandestine radio communication with Mihailović and his friends within the Axis-controlled territory, a demand consistently rejected by Britain and which led to a deepening distrust between both governments. The British were motivated not only by security concerns but also by the desire to halt the activities of extremist groups and prevent reports of tension among Yugoslav political émigrés in London from reaching the centers of resistance in the occupied homeland.

Miša Trifunović formed what came to be a transitional government (26 June – 10 August 1943). Within six weeks he had paved the way for a government of civil servants, eliminating the quarrelling politicians and inducing King Peter to address, in a broadcast to Yugoslavia, all "national fighters" without regard "to what temporary name they may be fighting under." At the time this was seen as an act of conciliation towards the partisans. Trifunović was followed by Božidar Purić (10 August 1943 – 8 July 1944), who moved the government's seat to Cairo but his backing of Mihailović failed to ensure the return of the monarchy and stem the advance to power of Tito and his partisans. The fifth and last Prime Minister of the government-in-exile was the former *ban* (governor) of Croatia, Ivan Subašić (8 July – 2 November 1944), who initiated "indirect negotiations" between King Peter II and Tito, which resulted in the ultimate liquidation of the government-in-exile and the establishment of a Tito government in Belgrade under a transitional regency.[2]

The Allies strengthened their contacts with both resistance movements by sending military missions. They provided each with a great deal of military and financial aid, which Tito and Mihailović used not only for fighting against the Axis, but also in the civil war.

In addition to Mihailović, who was active on the ground, the capitulation was not accepted by a small section of the Yugoslav Royal Army which had fled to the Middle East. The group consisted of seven generals, 114 officers, 54 non-commissioned officers, and 229 privates. 232 of them were in the air force, 127 in the navy, and 45 in the infantry. They managed to salvage one Yugoslav submarine, two torpedo boats, 27 planes, and eight flying boats.[3]

2   For more about the Yugoslav government-in-exile see Detlef Brandes, *Großbritannien und seine osteuropäischen Alliierten: 1939-1943. Die Regierungen der Tschechoslowakei und Jugoslawiens im Londoner Exil vom Kriegsausbruch bis zur Konferenz Teheran* (München: Oldenbourg, 1988); Veselin Đuretić, *Vlada na bespuću: internacionalizacija jugoslovenskih protivrječnosti na političkoj pozornici drugog svjetskog rata* [Governments at Crossroads: Internationalization of Yugoslav Contradictions on the Political Stage of the Second World War] (Beograd: Insitut za suvremenu istoriju, 1982); Bogdan Krizman, *Jugoslovenske vlade u izbjeglištvu: Dokumenti* [Yugoslav Governments-in-exile, Documents] (Zagreb: Globus, Arhiv Jugoslavije, 1981).

3   Krizman, *Jugoslovenske vlade u izbjeglištvu*, p. 132.

As early as April 1941, the first talks opened in Cairo between representatives of the Yugoslav government-in-exile and British officials. The British offered assistance to the Yugoslav Royal Air Force with a view to incorporating some units within the RAF. A plan proposed by Simović to form a conglomerate Yugoslav group made up of refugees and volunteers was adopted. The British demanded that the Yugoslav Royal Air Force be stationed in Amman, and the Yugoslav Prime Minister offered seven planes they had managed to save. Later on, General Ilić's request for the navy to remain under the Yugoslav flag was granted. There was a long debate on where to station the Yugoslav Royal Army units because the British were waiting for the consent of the governments of Canada, the US, and the Union of South Africa, where it was intended part of the Yugoslav Air Force would be sent. When this approval arrived, they had to decide how many units should remain in the Middle East and how many should go to Canada, the US, and elsewhere. The Yugoslav government-in-exile maintained that the main military center should be in the Middle East, as close to the Balkan theatre of war as possible and Simović wanted the Yugoslav contingents to form the nucleus of the future Allied invasion army.[4]

The Council of Ministers of the Yugoslav Royal government dispatched special military missions to Palestine, the US, South Africa, Canada, and South America. The Palestine mission was headed by Colonel Franc Stropnik, that of South Africa by Major Dušan Babić, Canada by Colonel Dragutin Savić, and South America by Colonel Mirko Burja. Their task was to organize recruitment and work in liaison with diplomatic emissaries and emigrant organizations.[5]

On 26 June 1941, Churchill met with Simović and the Yugoslav Foreign Minister, Momčilo Ninčić. He was in favour of the Yugoslav government having its own infantry, air force, and navy, and promised help in setting them up. At the meeting, it was agreed with the British army that: the Yugoslav infantry would have around 300 officers, non-commissioned officers (NCOs), and privates, and the number would be increased by recruiting Italian prisoners of Yugoslav descent. A motorized battalion would be formed with the assistance of the Yugoslav Committee from Italy, and the British would take responsibility for supplies and equipment. Representatives of the Yugoslav Committee from Italy would be given permission to visit British prisoner-of-war camps. At the time the Yugoslav government-in-exile had roughly 50 pilots and 22 more were expected to arrive from the Soviet Union.

---

4   Đuretić, *Vlada na bespuću*, pp. 38, 39.

5   Dušan Plenča, *Međunarodni odnosi Jugoslavije u toku drugog svjetskog rata* [International Relations of Yugoslavia during the Second World War] (Beograd: Institut društvenih nauka, 1962), p. 122.

It was decided to establish an air-force combat unit in the Middle East. The Yugoslav pilots would be trained in Canada and seamen in Great Britain.[6]

On 30 June 1941, representatives from the Yugoslav Royal Army met with the British General Ismay. They confirmed the decisions reached at the meeting of 26 June and agreed on some further details. The First Battalion was to be established in the Middle East, followed by four more battalions or a regiment. The plan was also to form a motorized battalion, but the British did not promise to provide the equipment. In addition, they agreed to engage Ivan Marija Čok and the Yugoslav Committee from Italy to begin immediately recruiting volunteers for the battalion from among the Italian prisoners of war. The British had already made it clear that due to the changed situation everything would not proceed according to plan, including the recruitment of soldiers for the Yugoslav army-in-exile. The British also wanted to use some Yugoslavs for special operations as members of ISLD and SOE missions to penetrate Yugoslavia. As well as assisting the formation of the Yugoslav armed forces in exile, the British goals in Yugoslavia were mainly to support guerrilla warfare and sabotage operations. One has to be aware that the military importance of the Yugoslav armed forces in exile was symbolic rather than operational.[7]

At the end of June 1941, the First Battalion of the Royal Yugoslav Guards (later the Yugoslav Royal Guard Battalion) was formed at Camp Agami, near Alexandria, Egypt, and later in Haifa, Palestine. At first the battalion had 505 men, the majority of whom (411) were Slovenian volunteers from the Littoral Region (under Italy), who were transferred from British custody to the Yugoslav Royal Guard Battalion. The battalion also included 78 Serbs (mostly officers and NCOs) as well as 16 Croats and comprised a headquarters company and four rifle companies under Major Živan Knežević. He was replaced in January 1942 by Lieutenant Colonel Miloje Dinić. The battalion numbered 47 officers, 44 NCOs, 389 privates and 25 Czech military bandsmen.[8]

Simović and George Rendel began discussing the reorganization of the Yugoslav Royal Air Force on 17 October 1941. The Yugoslav government-in-exile largely counted on the air force to provide the most effective military and material support for the resistance movement in Yugoslavia. Simović asked the British military forces in the Middle East for assistance and also advocated the independence of the future Yugoslav air-force units. Following the initial grand plans for the formation of the Yugoslav Air Force, gradually more realistic assessments of the potential operation of the Yugoslav

---

6   The National Archives of the United Kingdom, London (henceforth TNA), Foreign Office (henceforth FO), 371/30248, R 7053/2235/92; Krizman, *Jugoslovenske vlade u izbjeglištvu*, p. 158.
7   TNA, FO 536/8, Draft, Future Employment of Yugo-Slav Forces, October 1943.
8   Krizman, *Jugoslovenske vlade u izbjeglištvu*, p. 43.

Air Force were produced. It was decided to form a fighter, a hydroplane, and a bomber squadron. It was also agreed to send missions to South Africa, the US, Canada, Southern Rhodesia, and South Africa, where it was envisaged Yugoslav airmen would be recruited and trained. The British accepted the Yugoslav plan and thus a hydroplane squadron was established in Abu Qir together with a fighter and a bomber squadron. The hydroplane squadron was especially successful and dynamic, whereas more was expected from the fighter squadron.[9] The hydroplane squadron flew into Abu Qir on 22 April 1941, and the British provided accommodation and a liaison officer. It was named the Yugoslav Squadron and fell under the command of No. 230 Squadron. The unit operated effectively until the so-called "Cairo Affair" (see below) in early 1942, after which it was dissolved.[10] The fighter and bomber squadrons never came to be as active as the hydroplane squadron. There are several reasons for their lack of success, the major being the death of some pilots, and the lack of discipline in the Yugoslav air force.[11]

The formations were thus under British command in the Middle East and operated as special Yugoslav units within the British military forces. All of the military plans made by the Yugoslav Royal government, however, were thwarted by the Cairo Affair in early 1942, as a result of which the government and military leaders could no longer count on the allegiance of a large group of men who renounced their loyalty to the newly-appointed commanders. The Cairo Affair was a dispute between old air-force officers who were loyal to generals Simović, Ilić, and Mirković, and young infantry officers (the Major League) who had gained the most in the March 1941 coup. The young officers used Simović's replacement on 11 January 1941 to begin appointing their own men to key military positions. This led to a decrease in the morale of the exile Royal Army, a decline in the momentum of mobilization, and increasingly colder relations with the British.[12] All of Mirković supporters were sent to the 244th Provisional Battalion or the King's Own Royal Regiment, where they were no longer under Yugoslav command. Air-force officers thereby became the biggest victims of the scandal. Subsequently, the leadership of the Yugoslav Royal Air Force also slowly disintegrated.[13]

In September 1942, the status of the Yugoslav Royal Army in exile in the Middle East was as follows: a guard battalion with 741 soldiers was active

9   Bojan B. Dimitrijević et al, *Kraljevsko vazduhoplovstvo 1918–1944. Vojno vazduhoplovstvo Kraljevine SHS/Jugoslavije 1918–1944* [Royal Aviation 1918–1944. Military Aviation of the Kingdom of Serbs, Croats and Slovenes/Yugoslavia 1918–1944] (Beograd: Institut za savremenu istoriju, 2012), p. 489; Đuretić, *Vlada na bespuću*, p. 43.

10 Dimitrijević, *Kraljevsko vazduhoplovstvo*, pp. 494–95; Krizman, *Jugoslovenske vlade u izbjeglištvu*, p. 159.

11 Dimitrijević, *Kraljevsko vazduhoplovstvo*, pp. 494–95.

12 Đuretić, *Vlada na bespuću*, pp. 50, 52.

13 Dimitrijević, *Kraljevsko vazduhoplovstvo*, pp. 513, 514.

in Palestine; after the Cairo Affair, the Yugoslav Royal Air Force units were broken up, with 48 officers, 73 non-commissioned officers, and 35 privates inducted into British units, and 49 officers, 39 non-commissioned officers, and 20 privates enrolled at the training centre in Rhodesia. At the same time, 40 air-force and non-commissioned officers were in training in the US. The navy had three vessels with 26 officers, 28 con-commissioned officers, and 45 seamen.[14]

On 19 February 1942, Lieutenant Colonel Milan Prosen assumed command, and began to turn the Yugoslav Royal Guard Battalion into an effective fighting unit. In late February 1942, the battalion was ordered to Tobruk to relieve the Czechoslovak battalion, but was then diverted south to join the 11th Brigade of the 4th Indian Division in the east Libyan desert. In April, the battalion retreated to Halfaya Pass, then to Mersa Matruh, and in July 1942 joined the British 9th Army in Palestine, which was guarding the Haifa Oil refinery. During all this time, intense efforts were being made to recruit as many Yugoslavs as possible, including Slovenians, from British prisoner-of-war camps into the Yugoslav army, but this did not always proceed in accordance with Yugoslav plans. On several occasions, the British prohibited recruitment of the Yugoslavs (i.e., former Italian soldiers) and therefore the Slovenian ministers in the Yugoslav government-in-exile had to continuously press the Yugoslav Prime Minister to convince the British authorities to grant permission. The requests were often ignored by their colleagues in the Yugoslav government, which showed that clear opposition and lack of interest in establishing an effective Yugoslav army-in-exile existed.[15]

In January 1943, Lieutenant Colonel Franc Stropnik took command of the battalion with Major Josip Rijavec as his deputy. The battalion numbered 850 well-trained officers and men and was part of the 25th Brigade and the 10th Indian Division.

On the whole, the British were satisfied with the battalion, unlike members of the Yugoslav government-in-exile. Fighting on behalf of the British army was not what the Yugoslav government-in-exile and the representatives of the Yugoslav Committee from Italy had in mind, especially fighting against an army, in which members of the Royal Guard Battalion had once served.[16]

The Yugoslav government-in-exile planned to send the battalion to Yugoslavia in order to reclaim the Yugoslav western borders. In addition to

---

14   Plenča, *Međunarodni odnosi Jugoslavije*, p. 123.
15   Yugoslav Archives (henceforth JA), Collection No. 103 (Government-in-Exile of the Kingdom of Yugoslavia), Fascicle No. 7, Description units 62–67, Minister Krek to Prime Minister Jovanović, 6 October 1942; Ivan Rudolf's Private Archive (henceforth PAIR), Roll No. 8, Rudolf Marušiču, Middle East, 21 May 1944, pp. 3, 4.
16   TNA, FO 536/8, Major Hatch, Report on visit to 1 BNR Yugoslav GDS, 20 December 1943.

this battalion, which had already been equipped, other battalions would be formed. As already mentioned, the Serbian officers and the Yugoslav government-in-exile were growing increasingly disenchanted with the battalion, which was mainly composed of Slovenians. At the same time, they were becoming more and more disgruntled with the existing state of affairs and at this precise time a partisan military mission joined them and began to advocate joining Tito's partisan-overseas brigades.[17]

In addition to antagonism between the pro-Serbian officers and the enlisted men, by the end of 1943, one-sided information regarding conditions in the homeland were circulating in the Middle East. From mid–1943, the only alternative source of information was from the *Nova Jugoslavija* radio. Resistance to official propaganda was increasing among the soldiers as was their support of Tito. At the end of 1943, 35 soldiers rebelled. Others followed and in January 1944 the first group decided to leave the Royal Guard Battalion and join Tito's overseas brigades, which had been formed with Allied support in liberated South Italy in November 1943. Soldiers of the Royal Guard Battalion no longer trusted Mihailović and the Yugoslav government-in-exile. King Peter II also stopped backing Mihailović and in September 1944 publicly called on all members of the Yugoslav army-in-exile to join the Yugoslav National Liberation Army.[18]

The decline in Mihailović's fortunes started when he decided early in the struggle to interrupt his guerrilla activities pending a hypothetical Allied landing in Yugoslavia. The shrinking number of his followers and later accusations of working with the collaborator General Nedić and the Italians further weakened Mihailović's position. In contrast, Tito's movement was joined by a growing number of peasants and workers, victims of German reprisals, whose extraordinary mobility enabled them to move from one end of the country to the other, time and again escaping the rings closed around them by the Wehrmacht. Tito's call for political and social reforms, and equality for the different nationalities and religious groups appealed to vast sections of the population. These factors would weigh heavily in favour of the Partisans in determining the final outcome of the civil war.

After the Tehran Conference, the Allies recognized Tito's National Liberation Army as the only legitimate armed force in Yugoslavia, but they also knew that Tito wanted to establish a communist regime. A compromise was sought between Tito and the King, which led to the conclusion of the first Šubašić-Tito agreement on 16 June 1944 on the island of Vis. The British "sponsored"

---

17   Albert Klun, *Iz Afrike v narodnoosvobodilno vojsko Jugoslavije* [From Africa to the National Liberation Army of Yugoslavia] (Ljubljana: Partizanska knjiga, 1978), pp. 131–132.

18   JA, Collection No. 103, Fascicle No. 7, Description units 62–67, The attitude of the Yugoslav Royal Government regarding the disposal of the officers and men concerned as follows, p. 1; Bajc, *Iz nevidnega*, pp. 208, 209.

this accord and they demanded the terms be respected; they followed subsequent proceedings closely until the elections to the Constituent Assembly in
November 1945. From the very beginning of the war, the Western Allies, or
more specifically the British, had built their policy towards Yugoslavia with
the aim of engaging as much of the German armed forces as possible there. At
the same time, they wanted to preserve their own position in post-war Yugoslavia because they were well aware of the power and political orientation of
the partisan movement. They realized that the best they could hope to achieve
was to make Yugoslavia rebuild itself as a united and independent country.
Therefore in 1944 they tried to resolve the Yugoslav issue and supported a policy of compromise between the government-in-exile and Tito in Yugoslavia,
while seeking to keep Tito's liberation movement as independent of Soviet
influence as possible. The third vital goal in British policy towards Yugoslavia
until 1944 was to prevent civil war after the German retreat. The agreement
required joint hostilities against the common enemy and also stipulated that
the Yugoslav government-in-exile should include no elements inimical to the
Movement of National Liberation. It further stated that the National Liberation Committee did not consider the question of the monarchy an obstacle to
collaboration between the Committee and the Yugoslav government-in-exile,
since both had accepted the principle that the peoples of Yugoslavia would
decide on the organization of the state after the war. In London, however, the
Foreign Office was reluctant to accept these statements at their face value.
The King, moreover, had not been mentioned in the agreement.[19]

The Churchill-Tito meeting at Caserta on 12 and 13 August 1944, regarded
at the time as satisfactory, was followed soon afterwards by suspicions on
the British side that Tito was using British-supplied arms and ammunition
against his fellow countrymen, while Tito, for his part, apparently due to
the presence of a few American officers who had remained with Mihailović,
complained that the Allies were still supplying arms to Chetniks engaged in
fighting the Partisans. London's immediate objective was to secure as soon
as possible the establishment of a united Yugoslav government as agreed at
Caserta. Tito maintained that his National Committee already exercised full
authority throughout the country and that the government-in-exile should
confine itself to representing Yugoslavia with the Allies, in concert with the
National Committee. Already in September Churchill had reached the conclusion that the opportunity to facilitate King Peter's return to his homeland
by agreement with Tito had been missed in 1943. Now Britain could only

---

19   A documented volume on the Šubašić government titled "Vlada Ivana Šubašića" was published
in 1983 by the Croatian historian and former Yugoslav royal diplomat Dragovan Šepić, who
served as head of the Prime Minister's office in this government and traveled with them to Belgrade and Moscow.

act in conjunction with Moscow. The Churchill-Eden visit to Moscow took place in October 1944. Churchill took the initiative in suggesting overall "predominance" in the Balkans be shared between Britain and the Soviet Union, which was agreed to by Stalin. In the case of Yugoslavia the "50–50"[20] division in percentage terms represented, in Churchill's view, a common policy for Britain and the Soviet Union "without any thought of special advantage to themselves."[21]

During the complicated negotiations, which took Šubašić from Belgrade to Moscow and back again to Belgrade and London, the main consideration for Tito appears to have been ensuring recognition by the Allies of the government which he was to head. Otherwise, he indicated, the agreements would be of no interest to his movement. A new situation had arisen with the liberation of Belgrade by Tito's troops in October 1944, which marked the end of the guerrilla phase of Tito's struggle. The second Tito-Šubašić agreement was concluded on 2 November 1944. It laid down that Tito's Anti-Fascist Council would remain the supreme legislative body when Tito's Committee and the Šubašić government merged; in due course the united body would announce elections to determine the future government of the country; during the period of transition the status of the monarchy would be maintained through the establishment of a regency council consisting of three regents but King Peter would remain abroad until the question of the country's future regime was resolved. It was also agreed that Marshal Tito would hold the posts of Prime Minister, Minister of Defence, and Commander-in-Chief, while Šubašić would merely be a member of the government. Finally, after accusing Šubašić of having exceeded his authority in reaching an agreement on the regency without consulting him, King Peter re-appointed Šubašić Prime Minister with a view to his joining the United Yugoslav government. Wrangling over the composition of the Regency Council dragged on for weeks, until the question was finally settled by the Big Three's decision at Yalta to recognize jointly the new united government of Yugoslavia.[22]

With the Šubašić experiment of a united Yugoslav government in full swing in the autumn of 1944, it seemed that Great Britain, the United States, and the Soviet Union were following parallel, though not always identical, policies with regard to Yugoslavia. This unified policy was consecrated in

20 Cf. Albert Resis, "The Churchill-Stalin Secret 'Percentages' Agreement on the Balkans, October 1944," *The American Historical Review*, Vol. 83, No. 2 (1978), pp. 368–387.
21 National Archives and Records Administration, College Park, Md. (henceforth NARA), M 1642, Roll 86, Yugoslavia: Churchill's Comments to King Peter on Tito-Subasich Agreement, 21 Nov. 11. 1944, pp. 1–2; Matjaž Klemenčič, *Ameriški Slovenci in NOB v Jugoslaviji* [American Slovenes and National Liberation War in Yugoslavia] (Maribor, založba Obzorja, 1987), pp. 152–153.
22 Llewellyn Woodword, *British Foreign Policy in the Second World War* (London: H.M.S.O, 1962), Vol. III, p. 352.

February 1945 at the Yalta Conference, where Roosevelt, Churchill, and Stalin recommended to Tito and Šubašić "that the agreement between them be put into effect immediately." The Yalta meeting adopted two further resolutions, submitted by Churchill and Eden, and reluctantly agreed to by Stalin. The first proposed that the composition of the *Antifašističko veće narodnog oslobođenja Jugoslavije* (AVNOJ) be extended to include members of the last Yugoslav Parliament not compromised by collaboration with the enemy, in order to establish a temporary parliament; the second, that legislative acts passed by the AVNOJ be subsequently ratified by a Constituent Assembly. These recommendations were cabled to Tito and Šubašić.[23]

This was the last British effort at ensuring the principle of legal continuity in the transition from the old to the new Yugoslavia. However, in the following months Churchill seems to have had second thoughts on his Yugoslav policy. In March 1945, he communicated to Eden that he had reached the conclusion that Britain's role should be one of "increasing detachment" towards Yugoslavia and his inclination was to back defeated Italy against Yugoslavia as head of the Adriatic. Eden in reply recalled that British policy was based on the "50–50" agreement, "the principle of which is in effect that Yugoslavia should be a sort of neutral area between the British and Soviet zones of interest," providing protection for the British position in Greece and, to a lesser extent, in Italy.[24]

In early 1944, a large part of the units in the Middle East joined the Yugoslav National Liberation Army. Purić's government nonetheless continued to recruit a number of war prisoners from the Italian army. There were around 3,000 of these in Algiers, but the government did not have sufficient officers and British support to train them, and so all of the men remained without work. Approximately 2,200 were included in the Yugoslav pioneer companies that worked as a cheap labour force, and the remaining 800 awaited enlistment. In February 1944, a labour battalion was formed in agreement with the British command with a view to being included in the Yugoslav army. A third group was selected to join the air force but six months later the British had still not sent them to the Middle East, and so they worked as auxiliary staff with British units. After Tito spoke to British representatives in Italy, bases were formed for including soldiers of Yugoslav descent in the Yugoslav National Liberation Army. The Yugoslav government-in-exile tried in vain several times to conclude a military agreement with Great Britain, but

23   Jože Pirjevec, *Trst je naš!: boj Slovencev za morje (1848–1954)* [Trieste Belongs to Us!: The Fight of Slovenes for the Sea] (Ljubljana: Nova revija, 2007), p. 291.
24   Woodword, *British Foreign Policy*, Vol. III, pp. 364–369; Anthony Eden, *The Reckoning, The Eden Memoirs* (London: Cassell, 1965), pp. 523–524.

London kept postponing any such move until the question of the formation of the Yugoslav army-in-exile had been resolved.

In the end, the British and the Allies found the solution in the Šubašić government and the Yugoslav National Liberation Army. In other words, the British waited for the majority of the Yugoslav army-in-exile to opt for either Tito or Mihailović. They granted Tito's request of 22 March 1944 that the Slovenians and Croats who had served in the Italian army be allowed to enrol in the Yugoslav National Liberation Army units in southern Italy. Thus by the end of 1944, the majority of Yugoslav soldiers had decided to support the Yugoslav National Liberation Army and Tito, especially after King Peter II's call in September 1944.[25] With the establishment of the united Yugoslav government on 7 March 1945, the long story of the Belgrade agreement finally came to an end. The Royal Yugoslav Forces were disbanded on 7 March 1945 with the officers and men given the choice of joining Tito or becoming refugees.

25   Đuretić, *Vlada na bespuću*, p. 55.

"THE MOST DIFFICULT COUNTRY": SOME PRACTICAL CONSIDERATIONS ON BRITISH SUPPORT FOR CLANDESTINE OPERATIONS IN CZECHOSLOVAKIA DURING THE SECOND WORLD WAR

MARK SEAMAN

This chapter will seek to examine some salient features of the Anglo-Czecho-slovak prosecution of the clandestine war against Nazi Germany. Of course, it will not attempt to chronicle each individual operation but rather focus on how relations between the British and Czechoslovak secret agencies helped shape the course of events. In particular, the thesis will seek to emphasize the practical considerations that limited operational opportunities and suggest that these pragmatic difficulties substantially contributed to a marginalizing of Czechoslovakia in the broader "Secret War" fought by the Allies.

The description of Czechoslovakia as "the most difficult country" was made by Group Captain Ron Hockey, the wartime commanding officer of the Royal Air Force's No. 138 (Special Duties) Squadron. His opinion merits due attention as he was the first pilot to fly a successful wartime operation to Czechoslovakia (PERCENTAGE) and later had the distinction of delivering the ANTHROPOID, SILVER A and SILVER B teams of agents in a single opera-tion in December 1941: "Undoubtedly the most difficult country in which we operated was Czechoslovakia – a long flight, all over enemy territory, much high ground (the Tatras and associated ranges), flights only in the winter to benefit from the long nights, so terrain was often snowbound, and no recep-tion facilities in Czechoslovakia."[1] This statement by a highly-experienced participant in special duties flying underpins the main thrust of this chapter.

In spite of Britain's collusion in the Munich Agreement of September 1938 that so fatally compromised the sustainability of the pre-war Czechoslovak Republic, intelligence relations between the two countries underwent some-thing of an improvement in the following months. This, somewhat surpris-ing, state of affairs seems to have been inspired by several factors: a rupturing of the Czechoslovak intelligence's relationship with its French counterpart; a consequent need on the part of the Czechoslovaks to find a new intelligence partner; a British recognition that with war impending, an intimate connec-tion with a sophisticated and professional intelligence service (closely focused upon securing information on Nazi Germany) was highly desirable.[2] This en-

---

1   *The Proceedings of the Royal Air Force Historical Society*, No. 5 (February 1989), p. 20.
2   Igor Lukes, *Czechoslovakia between Stalin and Hitler* (Oxford – New York: Oxford University Press, 1996), pp. 150–4.

hanced relationship did not have long to develop. Harold Gibson, the Secret Intelligence Service (SIS) head of station in Prague, recognized that time was limited and, in addition to the day-to-day exchange of information with his Czechoslovak colleagues, he laid contingency plans for their evacuation in the event of a German invasion. His chartering of a Dutch commercial airliner proved prescient and on 14 March 1939, shortly before the arrival of the Nazis, Colonel František Moravec and the senior staff officers of Czechoslovak military intelligence, together with their operational funds, were brought to the United Kingdom. Their secret archives, having been entrusted to Gibson's care, followed them to London by diplomatic courier over the next fortnight.[3] Thus, although Britain had already forged an intelligence "special relationship" with the French as war against Germany loomed – a topic that deserves greater attention by historians than has been expended on it to date – the events of March 1939 appeared to foster a strong justification for a new, "special relationship" with the now exiled, but active, Czechoslovak military intelligence.[4]

There were a number of other Anglo-Czechoslovak connections in the field of secret services. In the spring of 1938 SIS had established a department, Section D, that was charged with undertaking clandestine warfare and its head, Major Laurence Grand, travelled to Czechoslovakia three times in 1938 to discuss cooperation with the local authorities on sabotaging armaments factories in the event of a German occupation.[5] Meanwhile another officer, soon to feature among the most influential figures in Britain's covert war effort, Lieutenant-Colonel Colin Gubbins, first visited Czechoslovakia in October 1938 as a member of the British mission to oversee the implementation of the Munich Agreement. He found the work disagreeable and his sympathies very much lay with Czechoslovakia, considering it "a thoroughly decent democratic little nation."[6] Gubbins subsequently joined MI(R), the War Office's equivalent of Section D, where his empathy for Czechoslovakia was reinforced by similar sentiments possessed by his closest colleague, Captain Peter Wilkinson, who had arrived in Prague in October 1938 to learn Czech and witnessed firsthand the German invasion the following year. After the outbreak of war both officers served with the British No. 4 Military Mission to the Polish and Czechoslovak armies in France and Wilkinson produced an upbeat

3   The group's arrival was reported in many British newspapers including *The Daily Telegraph*, *Morning Post* and *Daily Mail* on 15 and 16 March 1939. See Keith Jeffery, *MI6* (London: Bloomsbury, 2010), p. 308.
4   Jeffery, *MI6*, pp. 289–94; Paul Paillole, *Fighting the Nazis* (New York: Enigma Books, 2002), pp. 53–4.
5   Mark Seaman, ed., *Special Operations Executive – A New Instrument of War* (Oxford: Routledge, 2006), p. 10.
6   Peter Wilkinson and Joan Bright Astley, *Gubbins and SOE* (London: Leo Cooper, 1993), p. 33. Dr. Hugh Dalton, later the Minister of Economic Warfare, described Gubbins as "pro-Pole, pro-Czech and intelligent." Ben Pimlott, ed., *The Political Diary of Hugh Dalton, 1918–40, 1945–60* (London: Jonathan Cape, 1986), 18 November 1939, p. 314.

report on the potential for clandestine operations in Czechoslovakia. But in as early as the autumn of 1939, the complexities of inter-allied relations concerning clandestine affairs were all too evident. A conflict of interests already existed between British agencies (that pre-dated the notorious SIS-Special Operations Executive (SOE) rivalry) with the result that SIS sought to exclude MI(R) from contact with Moravec. However, Gubbins and Wilkinson found a way around this impasse and, taking advantage of the fact that Czechoslovak headquarters were based in Paris, went to France to see its commander, General Sergej Ingr. They were informed by Ingr that he possessed regular courier routes into his homeland, had an effective operational base in Yugoslavia and even a wireless link to German-occupied territory that handled 40 messages a day. Under these circumstances, the MI(R) officers deduced that there was little need to offer assistance from their organization's meagre resources.[7]

Ingr's confident assertions must have come as something of a relief. MI(R) propounded a doctrine based on the assumption that, in spite of the German occupation of Czechoslovakia and Poland, "secret armies" could operate effectively in pursuit of both national and Allied interests. It was MI(R)'s job to devise the means of supporting these movements but following the sweeping German victories of 1940 and 1941 it became clear that the viability of clandestine action in these countries had radically altered. Nazi Germany now dominated the Continent and menaced a beleaguered Britain that relied upon the width of the English Channel, the Royal Navy and the Royal Air Force's Fighter Command for its immediate survival. MI(R) shifted its attention to the preparation of a British "resistance" movement to meet the expected invasion, thereby rendering any schemes of taking the fight to Germany through the occupied nations a far lesser priority.

The direction of British clandestine activities underwent another major change in July 1940. The concepts developed by Section D and MI(R) and their implementation were controversially removed from the custody of SIS and the War Office. Following Churchill's legendary instruction to "set Europe ablaze," the prosecution of clandestine warfare was placed under the auspices of Dr. Hugh Dalton, the Minister of Economic Warfare. In keeping with Dalton's socialist convictions, his vision was of citizen armies inspired by workers' groupings rather than the paramilitary doctrines propounded by MI(R). However, Dalton was too intelligent a politician to fail to grasp the necessity of retaining the services of several of the leading members of Section D and MI(R) including Gubbins and Wilkinson - although Grand himself was rudely ejected.[8]

---

7   Wilkinson and Astley, *Gubbins and SOE*, p. 48.
8   Mark Seaman, ed., *Special Operations Executive*, pp. 18–19.

Wilkinson, of MI(R) and, later, SOE recognized that the early plans for Czechoslovakia needed to be amended, "contrary to the popular view, it was quite unrealistic to imagine that secret armies in Central Europe could be equipped by long-distance flights from the United Kingdom." He still had faith in finding a land route to sustain resistance movements but events were to show that this was overly optimistic and that air supply was far and away the most practical.[9] There was also a strong emotional investment inherent in working with Britain's exiled allies and the need to meet (or appease) their expectations was manifest. Wilkinson conceded that by the summer of 1941, SOE and the British Joint Planning Staff "had virtually ruled out the support of patriot forces in Eastern Europe on any significant scale as requiring too great a diversion of effort from the bombing of Germany."[10] The problem was telling the Poles the bad news and SOE's senior management took the line of least resistance, "Dalton and Gubbins and, for that matter, Perkins, Hazell and I, were so deeply committed to the Polish cause that we funked facing them with the realities of their situation." The result was that the SOE and Polish planners drifted off into a world of fantasy, "So we played along with them and, on Gubbins's instructions, over the next twelve months I wasted hours in make-believe joint planning with the Polish general staff working out the logistic requirements of a full-scale airborne invasion of German-occupied Poland which both they and I knew could not possibly take place."[11]

Both at the time and in many subsequent analyses of resistance, the logistic practicalities of providing material support to these irregular forces tend to be either overlooked or misunderstood. The initial British plans in the first years of the war were for trickle feeding illegal supplies of weapons and explosives across neutral frontiers. The seismic strategic shift of 1940/1 saw resistance movements isolated from Allied supply and support. Limited resources and shifting priorities were to put immense pressure on relationships between allies who only understood a fraction of the competing priorities of the other. For the British, with their policy being formed under the auspices of the War Cabinet, the Chiefs of Staff and the Ministry of Economic Warfare, there was now a distinct requirement for the gathering of intelligence and the prosecution of clandestine operations that would accrue the most benefit to Allied strategy. No country could be accorded a most favoured nation status on grounds of sentiment (other than by the type of charade described by Wilkinson) and if an agent needed to be sent to Norway to secure intelligence on the German battleship *Tirpitz* or a team of saboteurs had to be

9   Peter Wilkinson, *Foreign Fields* (London: I.B.Tauris, 1997), pp. 108–109. Wilkinson's theories of finding a "backdoor" into the Reich never fully left him and he devoted much effort and personal endeavour to Operation CLOWDER – a scheme to penetrate Austria via Slovenia.
10   Ibid., p. 124.
11   Ibid., p. 124.

despatched to attack the Norsk Hydro "Heavy Water" plant, the needs of the Czechoslovak sections of SIS and SOE along with Moravec's own preoccupations were to be relegated to a lesser priority. In practical terms, the type of question asked by the British was what was more important: finding out the structure and stability of Czechoslovak resistance movements or developing French sabotage networks in readiness for D-Day?

There was another determining factor in shaping the British attitude towards their allies. Broadly speaking, the Foreign Office and the secret services questioned the desirability of facilitating "political" missions to occupied Europe. They interpreted them as being detrimental to their more favoured operations that infiltrated agents tasked either with gathering military intelligence or carrying out specific sabotage operations. This British singularity of focus was not confined solely to its relations with the Czechoslovaks but was also applied to the other allies – notably the French (although their homeland's geographical proximity to the United Kingdom meant that they were less beset by logistical difficulties).

Meanwhile, the relationship between the Czechoslovak and British clandestine services underwent a reorientation as the number of allies exiled in London grew. The status enjoyed by the Czechoslovaks and Poles in the opening period of the war was radically changed by the arrival in 1940 of new co-belligerents who offered an expanded range of opportunities to help sustain the Allied war effort. Moreover, as the Allied grand strategy evolved, it was clear that the primary focus would switch to those clandestine operations that were likely to have the greatest impact on the preparation of a Second Front.

Perhaps as a result of the broadening perspectives, the Czechoslovaks were subjected to some adverse comment by their British peers. In his memoirs Peter Wilkinson stated that in the early days of SOE, while a colleague "was dealing so successfully with the Poles, I was doing my best to wake up the Czechs." A subsequent meeting between Beneš, Ingr and Moravec with leading members of SOE (Dalton, Gubbins and Wilkinson) secured a commitment that two dozen Czechoslovak volunteers from the army-in-exile would be made available for training.[12] But soon a pressing need arose to insert a wireless operator into the Protectorate to maintain SOE/resistance links that would be separate from SIS contacts. However, this was denied to them, "we got as far as the air-field only to be 'gazumped' at the very last moment by the SIS who produced an agent who, they claimed, was to be given

12 Wilkinson, *Foreign Fields*, p. 108. An account of the Czechoslovaks' training in Scotland is provided by an SOE officer who instructed them; Ernest van Maurik, *You Must be Paterson*, Vol. I, pp. 77-79 (private memoir in author's possession).

higher priority than Riedl [the SOE-trained wireless operator]."[13] This was by no means an unusual occurrence and was neither an indication of the lack of importance attached to Czechoslovak operations nor necessarily proof of the primacy of SIS. As the number of flights increased, "star" ratings were accorded to operations to help prioritize them and identify the best means by which the British secret services and the Royal Air Force could utilize the very limited number of aircraft available for clandestine flights.

A paper submitted by SOE to the Chiefs of Staff in July 1941 included estimates of the number of RAF aircraft sorties required to facilitate sabotage action and to build up "secret armies" in Nazi-occupied Europe. The eventual figure was 584 sorties for the former and 1,750 for the latter. SOE's paper was first examined by the Joint Planning Staff and they "recommended that subversive activities be given preference over Secret Armies." The Chiefs of Staff concurred in this assessment not least as it was perfectly clear that there were insufficient aircraft to render all SOE's aspirations feasible.[14] Moreover there was very strong opposition from the senior ranks of the RAF to any dilution of the bombing offensive against Germany. The Chief of the Air Staff, Air Chief Marshal Sir Charles Portal, offered an uncompromising statement of his position to a senior SOE officer, "your work is a gamble which may give us a valuable dividend or produce nothing. It is anybody's guess. My bombing offensive is not a gamble. Its dividend is certain; it is a gilt-edged investment. I cannot divert aircraft from a certainty to a gamble which may be a gold-mine or may be completely worthless."[15] Although a second Special Duties squadron, No. 161, was formed in 1942, it was hardly surprising that there were still not enough aircraft to go round to meet SIS's and SOE's immediate needs, never mind sustaining massed bodies of resistance fighters in Central Europe.[16]

The British Chiefs of Staff Committee, while playing a role in determining the allocation of aircraft to assist clandestine operations, was also forming policy, by means of the directives it issued to SOE, on the scale of support that was to be devoted to Czechoslovak resistance. The records chart an early optimism felt by the Chiefs of Staff regarding the potential of operations against the Nazi occupation forces with an unstated assumption that such action

---

13   Wilkinson, *Foreign Fields*, p. 108. Gubbins offered his own comments on the cancellation of the flight in a letter to the Air Ministry, The National Archives of the United Kingdom, London (henceforth TNA), AIR 20/2901. It was a lucky let-off for Riedl as Gubbins noted that the aircraft had failed to return from its SIS operation. Otmar Riedl was eventually dropped on Operation BENJAMIN on 16/7 April 1941.

14   TNA, AIR41/84, COS(41)147(0) of 21 July 1941 cited in Special Duty Operations in Europe, RAF Narrative, Air Historical Branch, p. 5.

15   Cited in M. R. D. Foot, *SOE in France* (London: HMSO, 1966), p. 13.

16   The first unit, No 419 Flight, was formed in August 1940 and was enlarged into No. 138 Squadron in August 1941. The second squadron, No. 161 Squadron, was formed in February 1942.

would divert enemy forces away from the main Allied battlefronts. But then a different appreciation steadily formed in London that saw Czechoslovakia accorded a lower priority with the result that the nation consequently slipped down the list of countries to which scarce resources should be allocated. Nevertheless, the Czechoslovak sections of both SOE and SIS gamely continued to attempt the insertion of personnel into Bohemia-Moravia although the combination of geographical challenges and the competition for the limited number of aircraft made this particularly difficult. Czechoslovakia's long distance from the United Kingdom resulted in flights of around 10 hours' duration but such lengthy sorties were too hazardous to be undertaken during the short summer nights. This dilemma necessitated winter operations flown during the long nights of darkness but the time of year ensured that adverse weather conditions became the norm. One, early, important sortie illustrates the problem. In December 1941 a rare break in a run of bad weather gave Ron Hockey the opportunity of reducing the operational backlog by dropping – in one flight – no less than seven agents, comprising three separate teams, ANTHROPOID/SILVER A/SILVER B. This epic undertaking saw 16 personnel aboard the aircraft (instead of the Halifax bomber's usual six men crew) and included the agents who eventually assassinated Heydrich.[17]

The difficulties of mounting Czechoslovak operations from the United Kingdom can be clearly discerned in the record of Gubbins's meetings with Dr. Beneš and General Ingr in February 1942. On the 20th "M" [Gubbins] was invited to visit Beneš who complained that the British Foreign Office's "Men of Munich" were still preventing adequate British recognition of the Czechoslovak cause. Beneš also expressed concern over the paucity of Czechoslovak aircrew posted to No. 138 Special Duty Squadron "and that he could not allow such flights [to Czechoslovakia] to be performed only by Polish or British personnel." That apart, he was, broadly speaking, satisfied with his relations with SOE, something that Gubbins echoed, "At the moment our work with the Czechs is more straightforward and the collaboration more forthcoming from their side than with any other country with which I have to deal."[18] A week later, on the 27th, Gubbins discussed with Ingr the delay in despatching six sabotage teams that had been occasioned by the fact that there were only three Halifax aircraft available "of which never more than two were serviceable at a time." Other topics on the agenda comprised the training of a Czechoslovak special duties aircrew (that Beneš had also raised in discussion) and an SOE undertaking to give parachute instruction to Ingr's regular army personnel. Gubbins concluded by stating, "The Czechs are being excep-

---

17   TNA, AIR27/956, Entry 28 December 1942 in No. 138 Squadron Operations Record Book; and Hockey's logbook on display in the Imperial War Museum.

18   TNA, HS 4/9, Memo from M [Gubbins] to CD [Sir Frank Nelson], 21 February 1942.

tionally cooperative and helpful. At the moment I trust them more than any other of our Allies, and I feel that any job which they say they will carry out, they will attempt it to the last ounce."[19]

While high level discussions in London offer insights into policy, a 1943, SIS-sponsored operation, IRIDIUM, provides a case study of the practical difficulties of attempting air operations to Czechoslovakia. The operation was originally scheduled in December 1942 but could not be attempted owing to weather conditions. It was attempted twice in January and three times in February but each time the aircraft had to turn back owing to weather. It was tried again on 14/15th March 1943 but the aircraft failed to return.[20] Although a high proportion of operations were completed at this time, IRIDIUM was not the only casualty; four aircraft transporting 10 agents and equipment were lost.[21] An analysis of the operations on behalf of SIS for the March 1943 lunar period offers interesting comparisons between the different target countries. Eight parachute operations were completed to France (with two uncompleted), the only two operations attempted for Belgium failed, Norway had one success with two agents dropped while another operation met with disaster when the aircraft and two agents were lost. Holland had a similar record with one agent dropped and another aircraft (together with its agent) shot down. But operations to Czechoslovakia proved to be a complete disaster with two abortive operations (IRIDIUM and BRONZE) resulting in the loss of seven agents, two aircraft (one each from No. 138 and No. 161) and all 15 members of their crews.[22]

In addition to the pragmatic, day-to-day relationship between SOE's Czechoslovak Section and Moravec's organization, there were attempts to provide a formal structure for developing policy. An Anglo-Czechoslovak Planning Committee was formed to discuss current issues and formulate a strategy for future activity in occupied Czechoslovakia with the intention that this would culminate in the rising of the "Secret Army." The minutes of a meeting held on 2 December 1942, seem to replicate the aspirational discussions described by Wilkinson in the early "planning stages" with the Poles.[23] The perception held by some historians of the British secret services being constantly at loggerheads is somewhat discounted by clear evidence that SIS and SOE worked closely together with the Czechoslovaks in planning operations. Meetings held at Moravec's Bayswater headquarters were attended by

19   Ibid., Memo from M [Gubbins] to CD [Sir Frank Nelson], 27 February 1942.
20   TNA, AIR 27/1068, No. 161 Squadron Operations Record Book.
21   TNA, AIR 27/956, No. 138 Squadron Operations Record Book; AIR 27/1068, No. 161 Squadron Operations Record Book.
22   Ibid.
23   TNA, HS 4/9, "Record of Anglo-Czech Planning Committee Meeting on 2 Dec 42," 7 December 1943.

SIS, SOE and Czechoslovak officers and there is ample evidence of a complex yet apparently harmonious collaboration.

By 1943 SOE had transformed itself into a highly potent Allied secret service with its efforts recorded in the reports it made to the Chiefs of Staff. In turn, the latter issued annual directives to SOE and those for 1943 grouped Czechoslovakia and Poland together with a reaffirmation that the main priority was to be the sabotaging of "German communications to the Russian Front." While resistance forces should be prepared to undertake "organized military action when the German hold is weakened," supplying them in readiness for future operations "should not be allowed to interfere to too great an extent with the provision of material for sabotage which can be carried out now." Poland and Czechoslovakia together occupied fourth place in a list of the six most important locations for operational activity.[24] The SOE report for the period April to October offers a succinct assessment of Czechoslovakia's importance and the level of British support for resistance activity in the Protectorate. It does not pull its punches, "There is hardly any direct communication with the Protectorate and reliable intelligence is scanty. There is at present little active resistance; President Beneš in a speech on 16 September, 1943, could only claim that Czechs were not giving active assistance to the Germans. The Protectorate appears to be becoming incorporated as a province of the Reich." Information on the true state of affairs was so limited that SOE was obliged to estimate the strength of resistance by the type and number of criminal charges that appeared in Nazi public announcements about the victims of executions. The nuanced statement, "The Czech General Staff maintain with conviction that remnants of the underground organisation are still in existence," was qualified by an assertion that confirmation of the claim was impossible due to "the lack of reliable communications" as "the only W/T station in operation is not regarded as a reliable source."[25] The immense difficulties in reaching Czechoslovakia by air featured yet again and the document stated that getting there was "almost impossible" due to German night fighter defences – but this observation signally underestimated the array of other challenges facing every flight over the Reich. Even a proposal that Czechoslovak personnel be inserted from Yugoslavia or flown in from bases in Italy was vague and imprecise, and its practicality was doubtful. Nevertheless the RAF and the British secret services soon grasped the need to investigate the possibilities offered by new bases in territory liberated by the Allies.

---

24   TNA, CAB 80/68, COS(43)142(0), Chiefs of Staff Memorandum of 20 March 1943 "Special Operations Executive Directive for 1943."
25   Ibid.

The early aspirations of Section D and, more specifically MI(R), had been frustrated by the practicalities of war. It had simply proved impossible to arm secret armies in Eastern Europe when the allocation of aircraft was insufficient and the targets were so far from British bases. Now, the Allied control of North Africa and southern Italy seemed to offer some degree of optimism due to marginally more advanced launch points and flight routes that did not take the aircraft across the heartland of the Reich. A decision was therefore taken in the autumn of 1943 to attempt Czechoslovak air operations from the Mediterranean.[26] The idea seemed to have much to commend it but events proved that the logjam of bad weather, too many operations and too few aircraft that had been the litany regarding sorties flown from the United Kingdom was merely transferred to new bases at Algiers and Bari. By the middle of January 1944, the BARIUM and CALCIUM agents were ready for despatch but the Polish flight that was to undertake the Central Europe operations suffered two fatal crashes. The remaining aircraft had to return to the United Kingdom to fetch reinforcements. SIS made representations to SOE in the Mediterranean to see if they could help provide facilities for their teams but the response was not encouraging – SOE had 12 Polish and one Czechoslovak operation scheduled in front of BARIUM and CALCIUM. The airwaves then buzzed with instructions from London arguing that meetings in SOE's Baker Street offices, SIS's Broadway Head Office and the Air Ministry had come up with apparent solutions but these did not readily convert to the prevailing situation in Algiers and Bari. The moon period imposed its own schedule and any inaction or prevarication could lose not just a day but impose a delay of months for the implementation of an operation. There was no doubting the commitment to try and complete Czechoslovak operations and even "pickup" sorties were discussed using Dakota, Hudson and Lysander aircraft to land on enemy-occupied territory to deliver and collect personnel.

But perhaps more significantly, Czechoslovakia and Poland were far from being the most pressing priority for Allied strategists. The Second Front demanded that supplies be delivered to those resistance forces that would help facilitate a successful Anglo-American invasion. The arming of Polish, Czech and Slovak partisans was desirable but secondary to building up a viable resistance movement in those countries through which the Anglo-American invading forces would be passing. The British watched for results (or potential) in various theatres of operations and took a pragmatic view regarding logistical support that was perhaps most notably evident in their willingness to provide support to communist resistance movements in the Balkans.

The RAF statistics are imperfect but those that are available give a clear indication of the priorities for air supply to occupied Europe. From 1943 to

---

26   TNA, AIR 41/84, Special Duty Operations in Europe, RAF Narrative, Air Historical Branch, p. 254.

1945, 8,651 aircraft sorties were attempted to France from the United Kingdom of which 5,632 were successful. During the same period there were 529 (342 successful) to Belgium, 630 (372 successful) to Holland, 102 (77 successful) to Poland and 19 (14 successful) to Czechoslovakia. The tonnage of supplies ranged from 8,455.5 to France, 484 to Belgium, 554 to Holland, 37 tons to Poland and one ton to Czechoslovakia. Scandinavia did well too with 933 tons to Norway and 678 to Denmark.[27] The importance (and difficulty) of operations to Czechoslovakia is further confirmed by records of air supply from the Mediterranean. 11,632 sorties were attempted to Yugoslavia, delivering 16,469 tons of supplies. Italy had over 4,000 sorties (538 personnel dropped) and Greece more than 2,000 sorties. Czechoslovakia had 119 sorties, 39 successful with 58 tons of stores dropped and 42 personnel inserted.[28]

The facts do not lie. Early wartime British doctrine suggested the potential of a substantial Allied focus upon resistance in Czechoslovakia was significant but the demands of war forced the amendment of such hopes and, in particular, the practicalities of air supply relegated Anglo-Czechoslovak efforts to a minor, subsidiary role. The bravery of the volunteer Czechoslovak agents and resistance fighters has few equals in the history of the Second World War. Similarly the valour of the RAF aircrews who faced immense challenges simply in getting the men and supplies to the dropping zones is the stuff of legend. Their deeds offer important counterbalances to the measured and unsentimental decisions of committees and steering groups whose difficult task was to plan the Allied victory from the relative safety of their London headquarters.

27   Ibid., Appendix H.
28   Ibid., Appendix I.

III. PREPARING IN EXILE A POST-WAR SOLUTION OF THE MINORITIES QUESTION

WAS THERE AN ALTERNATIVE TO THE "TRANSFER" OF GERMAN MINORITIES FROM CZECHOSLOVAKIA AND POLAND DURING THE 1939–1944 DISCUSSIONS ON POST-WAR EUROPE BY THE GOVERNMENTS-IN-EXILE?

JAN KUKLÍK – JAN NĚMEČEK

The question of the expulsion and resettlement of the German population from Czechoslovakia and Poland, which took place from 1944–1947, is a controversial subject and one that is still open for discussion, even with regard to terminology.[1] The transfers agreed at Potsdam in 1945 were preceded by mass movements of population, including those of displaced persons. The policy of resettlement had already been started by Hitler in 1939/1941 in the case of the so-called *Volksdeutsche*.[2] According to the terms of "General Plan Ost," Poles were to be moved to Siberia in order to make room for German settlers. In all, over one million Polish inhabitants from the Polish western areas were expelled to accommodate more than 800,000 *Volksdeutsche* from the Baltic states, the USSR and other parts of Europe.[3] Forced resettlement was also frequently used by the Soviet leader Stalin.

The resettlement of the German population was agreed to in principle by all three Allied Great Powers as a solution for both territorial and minority problems and is closely connected with the negotiations of the Big Three on Germany and Central Europe from 1943 until the Potsdam Conference. In this chapter we would like to examine if alternatives to this decision had been considered during the wartime period when the Czechoslovak and Polish governments-in-exile had their seat in London.

The idea of the expulsion of Germans from Czechoslovakia and from Poland can be traced to the beginning of the home resistance movement with the most implacable support for the notion coming from the military. In the case of Czechoslovakia, the Munich Agreement[4] was the most important step

---

1   Philipp Ther, *The Dark Side of Nation-States. Ethnic Cleansing in Modern Europe* (Oxford: Berghahn Books, 2013), pp. 1–15.

2   The National Archives, London (henceforth TNA), Foreign Office (FO) 371/34461, C 12443, Foreign Office Research Department memo of August 1943.

3   Anna C. Bramwell, "The Resettlement of Ethnic Germans, 1939–41," in Anna C. Bramwell, Michael Marrus, eds., *Refugees in the Age of Total War* (London: Unwin Hyman, 1988), pp. 122–123.

4   Recently Jan Kuklík, Jan Němeček, Jaroslav Šebek, *Dlouhé stíny Mnichova* [Lasting Shadows of Munich] (Praha: Auditorium, 2011), pp. 45–135.

that led to the complete break-up of the country in March 1939. From the Czech perspective, the agreement in concern was not only an unjust solution to a disputed minority question but also one of the most tragic and fateful moments in Czechoslovak history. For the Czech resistance movement both at home and abroad, "Munich" represented a theme with a deep moral and emotional resonance and a radical redress was sought. It is also necessary to stress that the leaders of the Sudeten German Party, acting on direct instructions from Berlin, rejected not only the Statute for National Minorities prepared in 1938 by the Czechoslovak government to deal with some irregularities in Czechoslovak minority policies[5] but also almost complete national autonomy proposed by President Edvard Beneš during the September crisis of 1938.[6] The first document that expressly mentioned the necessity to expel the German population from Czechoslovakia and return to pre-Munich frontiers was a memorandum prepared by Zdeněk Peška in August 1939 based on the programme of the national resistance movement at home.[7] The leadership of the democratically-minded home resistance had reached the decision that the Czech-German question could be solved only by adopting expulsion as an emergency measure to safeguard the future of the Czech nation *vis-à-vis* the Czechoslovak-German borders.

A similar conclusion is evident in the case of Poland. Already during the visit of the Polish Prime Minister, Władysław Sikorski, to London in November 1939 the Polish government-in-exile proposed the cession of East Prussia to Poland, explicitly specifying the "removal of Germans from it as well as from the rest of Poland."[8] The Polish state had been attacked by both German and Soviet forces, but Polish diplomats, realistically, chose to concentrate more on the war with Germany.[9] During his time in London, General Sikorski privately told the British that he "does realize perfectly well that the reconstruction of Poland in her pre-war frontiers is very problematic. If it proves impossible to recover from Russia what has been lost, he aims at finding compensation elsewhere which would at the same time increase Poland's security. In this connection his mind is turning towards East Prussia [...]."[10] On 19 February 1940, the Foreign Minister, August Zaleski, in his brief to Polish embassies argued that East Prussia had never been an integral part of ethnic Germany. Poland was prepared to adopt a liberal approach towards its Jewish

---

5   Jan Kuklík, *Czech Law in Historical Contexts* (Praha: Karolinum, 2015), p. 112.

6   Kuklík, Němeček, Šebek, *Dlouhé stíny Mnichova*, pp. 35–36.

7   See Jitka Vondrová: *Češi a sudetoněmecká otázka 1939–1945. Dokumenty* [Czechs and the Sudeten German Question. Documents] (Praha: Ústav mezinárodních vztahů, 1994), No. 6, pp. 21–23.

8   See also TNA, FO 371/24470, C 1762, Memo of 29 January 1940 handed to the Foreign Office.

9   Jacek Tebinka, *Polityka brytyjska wobec problemu granicy polsko-radzieckiej 1939–1945* [British Policy Towards the Polish-Reich Border Problem 1939–1945] (Warszawa: Neriton, 1998), pp. 81–82.

10   TNA, FO 371/23131, C 19288.

and Ukrainian minorities but not towards Germans. The German minority was depicted as an enemy element and a possible future fifth column. German atrocities against the Polish population gave Poland the right to demand that the "hangmen" should leave Polish territory and coexistence between Polish and German inhabitants was seen as impracticable for the future.[11] The Polish military leadership went further and at the beginning of April 1940 added, for strategic reasons, territories in East Prussia, Pomerania and Upper Silesia. New Polish frontiers on the Oder and the Lusatian Neisse rivers and a common border with the "Czech Lands" in the area of Žitava meant the acquisition of 77,000 km² with seven million inhabitants, and, therefore, the likelihood of expulsion of the German population to Germany or the making of exchange arrangements.[12] The stand taken by the Polish home resistance movement was comparable when it demanded the "return" of land east of the Oder and the Neisse.[13] The Polish home resistance advocated the expulsion of all Germans from this area pointing to the measures the German occupation forces had applied in Poland. The Foreign Office regarded such plans as premature but, at the same time, did not want to commit the British government to the pre-war Polish frontiers, even though it was not prepared to recognize the Soviet annexation.[14]

In the case of Czechoslovakia there is a direct connection between the idea of transfer and the difficulties faced by the Czechoslovak leaders abroad in their efforts to secure "redress for Munich" and the restoration of Czechoslovakia within its pre-Munich frontiers.[15] On 21 June 1940, Beneš officially asked the Foreign Office for British acceptance of this objective.[16] The Czechoslovak Provisional government-in-exile was recognized by Britain on 21 July 1940 but with certain reservations regarding the juridical continuity of the Czechoslovak state, its future frontiers and the authority of the Czechoslovak government over Czechoslovaks in Britain. It was clear that Whitehall policy was still influenced by the Munich Agreement, which in the British view was valid until violated by Hitler on 15 March 1939. Moreover, the British government, in the years 1938–1940, maintained that the cession of the Czechoslovak

---

11 Tadeusz Cieślak, Stefania Stanisławska, Stanisław Zabiełło, Włodzimierz T. Kowalski, Jarosław Jurkiewicz, eds., *Sprawa polska w czasie drugiej wojny światowej na arenie międzynarodowej. Zbiór dokumentów* [Polish Administration during the Second World War on the International Scene. Collection of Documents] (Warszawa: Państwowy Instytut Naukowe, 1965), No. 87, pp. 140–141.

12 Wojciech Wrzesiński, *W stronę Odry i Bałtyku. Wybór dokumentów (1795–1950)* [Towards the Odra and the Baltic], Vol. 3 (Wrocław – Warszawa: Oficyna Wydawnicza, 1990), No. 3, pp. 12–19.

13 Ibid., No. 4, pp. 19–20.

14 Anthony Polonsky, *The Great Powers and the Polish Question, 1941–45. A Documentary Study in Cold War Origins* (London: London School of Economics – Orbis Books, 1976), pp. 16–18.

15 Vít Smetana, *In the Shadow of Munich. British Policy towards Czechoslovakia from the Endorsement to the Renunciation of the Munich Agreement (1938–1942)* (Praha: Karolinum, 2008), pp. 108 and following.

16 Jan Kuklík, *Czech Law in Historical Contexts*, pp. 122–123.

territory inhabited by a substantial proportion of the German population was a fair solution when the system of protection under the auspices of the League of Nations had collapsed.

Beneš asked for a British declaration on the non-validity of the Munich Agreement on the second anniversary of its signing. The Foreign Office, however, refused to make such a wide-ranging statement and proposed a compromise presented on the BBC by Winston Churchill on 30 September 1940.[17] Churchill stressed that the Munich Agreement had been "destroyed" by Hitler on 15 March 1939. According to Churchill the British government "refused to recognize any of the brutal conquests of Germany in Central Europe and elsewhere [...] and have made the restoration of Czechoslovak liberties one of our principal war aims." On 11 November 1940, the Foreign Office added that Churchill's statement likewise dealt with the question of the frontiers established as a result of the Munich Agreement, but that the British government "did not want to commit itself to recognizing or supporting the establishment of any particular frontiers in Central Europe, and this covered also what had been agreed at Munich."[18] The British decision regarding Czechoslovak frontiers was thus (as with Poland) postponed until the end of the war. For many other reasons, too, (including the question of Slovakia) Britain did not want a return to pre-Munich borders.

It was not until the *de jure* recognition of the interim Czechoslovak state authority in London, however, that the concept of the expulsion of the German minority acquired a real political foundation. Beneš's position was strengthened after the German attack upon the USSR. Straightaway, the Kremlin changed its attitude towards the "Czechoslovak case" and was prepared not only to recognize Beneš and his government-in-exile in London but also to conclude an agreement on cooperation in military matters. Soviet recognition of the government-in-exile in July 1941 implied the re-establishment of Czechoslovakia within its original boundaries. Britain, too, accorded *de jure* recognition to the Czechoslovak government-in-exile on 18 July 1941 but was not ready to forgo its principal reservations concerning the Czechoslovak frontiers and authority over the Sudeten Germans.[19]

Beneš used the term "transfer" in diplomatic negotiations with the British in a memorandum on "Czechoslovak Peace Aims" of 3 February 1941 in connection with the restoration of Czechoslovakia to its pre-Munich frontiers.[20] Beneš originally coupled the principle of transfer with a possible adjustment of Czechoslovak borders, and this link would, to varying degrees, persist in

17   Jan Kuklík, Jan Němeček, Jaroslav Šebek, *Dlouhé stíny Mnichova*, pp. 146–152.
18   *Dokumenty československé zahraniční politiky* [Documents on Czechoslovak Foreign Policy], Vol. B/2/1 – 1940–1941 (Praha: Ústav mezinárodních vztahů, 2006), No 81, pp. 191–192.
19   Kuklík, Němeček, Šebek, *Dlouhé stíny Mnichova*, pp. 152–167.
20   Vondrová, ed., *Češi a sudetoněmecká otázka*, doc. No. 47, pp. 84–92.

his proposals until the very end of the war.[21] This represented an alternative to the more radical views propounded by some in his cabinet and especially by the home resistance. It was expected that the cession of territory would not only reduce the size of the German minority in Czechoslovakia (with up to 800,000 remaining) but would also justify the transfer of those minority leaders who had committed the worst offences against the state. As it happened, the Foreign Office objected to the "quilt principle," questioning its feasibility and also the limited scope of its criteria.[22] The documents therefore do not support allegations that Beneš was the most radical or "dogmatic" advocate of transfer among exile politicians in London. [23]

In January 1942 Beneš published an article on the organization of post-war Europe in *Foreign Affairs* in which he referred to the question of national minorities. Transfer was seen as one option. However, he rejected a simple return to the inter-war system of international minority protection and called for recognition of individual "human democratic" rights and the "national rights" of minorities as a group. He discussed this idea repeatedly with the British ambassador to the Czechoslovak government-in-exile, Philip B. Nichols, and the concept of individual rights as opposed to minority rights was seen as another possible solution to minority problems.[24]

In January 1942 Beneš issued a memorandum regarding "the question of the frontiers of the Czechoslovak Republic," in which he argued that neither the Munich Agreement "nor the decision regarding the frontiers with Poland and Hungary were binding for any Czechoslovak government."[25] He linked the non-validity of the Munich Agreement with a final settlement of Czechoslovak frontiers. Simultaneously, he suggested the transfer of a substantial portion of the German minority in tandem with the cession of a limited segment of Czechoslovak territory.

The military aspects of the transfer were discussed by Beneš and the Czechoslovak commanders-in-chief on 22 January 1942. Beneš mentioned the expulsion of at least two million Germans and the ceding of small sections of border regions. The Czechoslovak army was making preparations for active participation in the occupation of Germany near the Czechoslovak borders.[26] With regard to cession, the Ministry of National Defence developed a detailed

---

21   Kuklík, Němeček, Šebek, *Dlouhé stíny Mnichova*, especially pp. 136–212.

22   This stand was confirmed by William Strang during his conversation with Ray Atherton, 19 March 1943 (TNA, London, FO 371/34396, C 3518).

23   Recently, see Matthew Frank, *Expelling the Germans, British Opinion and Post-1945 Population Transfer in Context* (Oxford: Oxford University Press, 2008), p. 45.

24   TNA, FO 371/39012, C 2212, Nichols to the Foreign Office, 20 August 1943.

25   *Československá zahraniční politika v roce 1942. Dokumenty československé zahraniční politiky* [Czechoslovak Foreign Policy in 1942. Documents on Czechoslovak Foreign Policy], Vol. B/3/1 (Praha: Ústav mezinárodních vztahů, 2010), No. 2, pp. 53–61.

26   Archiv bezpečnostních složek [Security Services Archives], Praha, S-183-1.

plan in November 1942. The proposed relinquishment of territory could reduce the number of Czechoslovak Germans by 360,000.[27] In conjunction with this, the military commanders advocated their own territorial demands at the expense of Germany, especially in Silesia.

On 21 January 1942 the British Foreign Minister, Anthony Eden, asked Beneš to devise a formula to resolve the Munich issue that would serve as an acceptable compromise between the Czechoslovak and British views. The Czechoslovak president set out the Czechoslovak standpoint as follows: a) any decision regarding Czechoslovakia after September 1938 was not valid in international law since any such directive would have been imposed on Czechoslovakia and b) the pre-Munich legal status of Czechoslovakia should be restored and confirmed by the victorious allied countries during official negotiations concerning post-war organization.[28] For the Foreign Office the question of "repudiation" of Munich was closely connected with the idea of the transfer of German minorities and also with a proposed Central European confederation. The British government was prepared to repudiate Munich and to recognize the Czechoslovak government's jurisdiction over the Sudeten Germans on condition that agreement was reached between Beneš and the spokesman for the Sudeten Germans in exile, Wenzel Jaksch, on adequate representation of the Sudeten Germans in the State Council. Official renunciation of Munich was made yet more difficult for Britain because of Czechoslovak-Polish disputes over Těšín. Negotiations between Jaksch and Beneš were deadlocked because of Jaksch's refusal to agree to even a limited transfer of the German minority.[29] Accordingly, Beneš, citing the stance the Soviet Union had taken, asked Eden for an explicit British declaration regarding Munich. On 21 April 1942, the Foreign Office agreed to the possibility of recognizing pre-Munich Czechoslovak frontiers but suggested that no public pronouncement be made in this respect.

The situation changed dramatically after the assassination of Heydrich and, more especially, the resulting German retaliation against Czech civilians. The Czechoslovak position was also strengthened by Soviet diplomacy. The re-establishment of Czechoslovakia to its pre-Munich borders was confirmed by the Soviet People's Commissar of Foreign Affairs, Molotov, on 9 July 1942, two days after the compromise on British repudiation of Munich.[30] The British were ready to denounce the Munich Agreement provided their differ-

---

27   Ibid., report by Lt. Col. B. Bosý-Sklenovský, 24 November 1942.
28   *Československá zahraniční politika v roce 1942*, Vol. B/3/1, No. 20, pp. 99–104.
29   Francis D. Raška, *The Czechoslovak Exile Government in London and the Sudeten German Issue* (Praha: Karolinum, 2002), pp. 179–180.
30   Jan Němeček, Helena Nováčková, Ivan Šťovíček, Miroslav Tejchman, eds., *Československo-sovětské vztahy v diplomatických jednáních 1939–1945* [Czechoslovak-Soviet Relations in Diplomatic Negotiations 1939–1945], (Praha: Národní archiv, 1998), No. 171, pp. 348–351.

ent view concerning its initial validity was not challenged. At the same time, they were willing to improve the international status of the Czechoslovak government-in-exile. Eden immediately informed the British War Cabinet about the outcome of negotiations and asked for approval of the principle of German minority transfer from the states of Central and South-Eastern Europe. On 5 August 1942, he confirmed that Churchill's statement of 30 October 1940 still represented "the attitude of His Majesty's government in regard to the arrangements reached in Munich." The British still maintained their reservations concerning final Czechoslovak borders but stressed that "in order to avoid any possible misunderstanding" the frontiers had to be decided by the end of the war and "that they will not be influenced by any changes effected in and since 1938."[31]

The earlier moderate views on the Czech side were radicalized by the involvement of a number of Sudeten Germans in the persecutions in the Protectorate, but above all by Nazi plans for a "final solution" of the Czech problem. Beneš redrafted his resettlement blueprint in November 1943 in a "ten-point plan for the transfer of the German population," which he had first put forward during his negotiations with the Soviets in Moscow and then presented to the Foreign Office.[32] He proposed that Czechoslovakia decide through its own legislation on the question of citizenship for persons of German nationality and in this way identify those liable for transfer. Loss of citizenship, it was supposed, would primarily affect active Nazis, members of the Gestapo and representatives of the Nazi government in the Protectorate. Beneš ruled out any possibility of returning to pre-Munich special minority rights but stated that "minority citizens" would enjoy "all individual civic and democratic rights." The transfer would take place between 2–5 years after the end of the war, its political, economic and technical aspects would be duly planned, and it would be part of the overall "plan for reconstruction of the Republic." He explicitly envisaged not just the expulsion of the German population but also the arrival of Czechs from Vienna, thereby bringing into play the principle of population exchange. In addition, he proposed the "internal resettlement" of those Germans who would remain. In a memorandum entitled "Some of the Main Principles for the Future Status of the CSR," he returned to the question and conceded the possibility of an exchange of territory with Germany and Hungary and even went so far as to accept the possibility that after the transfer had been carried out, Czechoslovakia would not be averse to assenting to whatever arrangements might be stipulated for mi-

---

31   Smetana, *In the Shadow of Munich*, pp. 297–302.
32   TNA, FO 371/38945, C 1850, Memorandum delivered to the Foreign Office on 28 January 1944 by Nichols.

norities in European states at the peace conference.[33] This document, was presented to both the Soviets and the British, and, on 11 January 1944, was endorsed by the Czechoslovak government-in-exile.[34]

Preparations for the transfer were accelerated by the Czechoslovak commanders-in-chief. The discussions between Beneš and the military leadership in the second half of 1943 contain interesting material from the point of view of alternatives. In August 1943, General Neumann-Miroslav proposed "four variations on how to rid the country of around two million Germans and 400,000 Hungarians: Plan A – the resettlement of minorities agreed to by the Allies without territorial compensation; Plan B – a combination of transfer and cession of territory; Plan C – an exchange of populations with Germany and Hungary; and Plan D – the expulsion of minorities from Czechoslovakia during a "managed revolution."[35] After discussion with Beneš the commanders opted for a nationally homogenous state with minorities constituting 10 percent of the overall population at most and, for the time being at any rate, preferred the combination of territory cession (with 500,000 Germans) and transfer at a ratio of 1:3.

Although it might appear from post-war experience that transfer had already been adopted as communist policy from the time of Beneš's visit to Moscow in December 1943, in fact the leadership of the Communist Party of Czechoslovakia (CPCZ) initially reacted coolly to Beneš's transfer plan and put forward its own alternatives. On 21 December 1943, the CPCZ proposed that the German question be solved "as part of action taken to punish the perpetrators of the war and crimes against the Czechoslovak Republic, following the anti-fascist and anti-Nazi line."[36] Not surprisingly, the CPCZ approached the question with an eye to their own political interests, which meant, for example, taking a more conciliatory attitude to the German working-class, and they were keen to promote German Communists as "anti-fascists." The CPCZ stance was complicated by the legacy of its pre-war ideology and found it difficult to abandon the principle of "proletarian internationalism" overnight. Only when it became clear that in the strongly nationalist atmosphere of the post-war period they also stood to gain politically from the issue did the Com-

---

33   Hoover Institution Archives, Stanford University, Palo Alto, California (henceforth HIA Stanford), Eduard Táborský Collection, box 3.

34   Jan Němeček, Ivan Šťovíček, Helena Nováčková, Jan Kuklík, Jan Bílek, eds., *Zápisy ze schůzí československé vlády v Londýně* [Records from the Meetings of the Czechoslovak Government in London], Vol. IV/1, 1944 (Praha: Historický ústav AV ČR, 2014), pp. 85–115.

35   Vojenský ústřední archiv – Vojenský historický archiv [Central Military Archives – Historical Military Archive], Praha (henceforth VÚA-VHA), fund Štáb pro vybudování branné moci [Staff for the Build-up of Armed Forces], box 3, Meeting between Beneš and the Czechoslovak commanders-in-chief, 3 August 1943.

36   *Cesta ke květnu* [Road to May], Collection of Documents, Vol. I. (Praha: Nakladatelství Československé akademie věd, 1965), No. 3, p. 67.

munists begin to support the idea of transfer. Naturally enough, too, a fillip to their change of heart was official Soviet support for Beneš's transfer proposal.

On January 5 1944, State Secretary for Foreign Affairs, Hubert Ripka, spoke "informally" on the transfer of German and Hungarian minorities with William Baker from the Foreign Office Research Department.[37] Ripka himself expected a larger number of Sudeten Germans to be involved in the transfer and mentioned a figure of between two to 2.5 million. Only if such a transfer were agreed to by the Great Powers, would Czechoslovakia be prepared to make minor territorial concessions. Ripka was aware of the economic losses the transfer would cause but foresaw long-term advantages, especially the homogenous character of the Czechoslovak state that would result. For the Hungarian minority, he advocated a combination of transfer and population exchange together with small frontier modifications.

At the same time, Polish views were represented in their memorandum entitled "The Problem of Germany" prepared in October 1943 and "unofficially" handed to the Foreign Office a month later.[38] The memo referred to the problem of German minorities in the whole of Central Europe and their role as a "fifth column." The Polish government advocated the transfer of such minorities to "Reich territory," "wherever possible," and where such a course was not feasible, no concessions on minority autonomy should be considered. Furthermore, the Polish government rejected any renewal of the system of international minority protection. The memorandum also articulated Polish claims with regard to East Prussia and Western Silesia in order to "simplify" frontiers. Such a move, it was stressed, would weaken Prussia and thereby reduce its "poisoned ideologies" including militarism. The Poles still favoured the establishment of European confederations. There were, however, some doubts, too, on the Polish side about the transfer policy. An earlier memo concerning western frontiers by the Polish Minister, Marian Seyda, and former ambassador to Germany, Józef Lipski, in October 1942 worried that the transfer might not be acceptable to the Great Powers.[39]

Czechoslovak demands for removal of the German minority were formulated in final form in negotiations on the conditions of an Allied ceasefire with Germany. Beneš told British Ambassador Nichols on 23 May 1944 that apart from border questions the Czechoslovaks wanted the internationally-conducted transfer to be explicitly included in those conditions.[40]

---

37   TNA, FO 371/38928, C 643.
38   TNA, FO 371/34462, C 13881.
39   The memorandum was discussed by the Polish government-in-exile on 7 October 1942, before Sikorski's journey to the US. *Protokoły posiedzeń Rady Ministrów Rzeczypospolitej Polskiej* [Minutes of the Meetings of the Council of Ministers of the Polish Republic], Vol. V. (Kraków: Secesja, 2001), No. 135, pp. 26–31.
40   HIA Stanford, Táborský Collection, Diary by E. Táborský, record of 23 March 1944.

The government's proposal for an internationally-approved transfer was contained, alongside particulars on repatriation, retribution and property issues, in an *aide-mémoire* of 24 August 1944 on cease-fire conditions that was presented to the European Advisory Commission. On 7 November 1944 the Czechoslovak government debated a memorandum on the transfer which the Foreign Ministry intended to submit to the European Advisory Commission for detailed clarification of the principle set out in the *aide-mémoire* of 24 August 1944.

The draft of the memorandum was passed unanimously and sent to the European Advisory Commission on 23 November. In the text the Czechoslovaks requested that the allies accept into Germany those nationals who forfeited their right to Czechoslovak citizenship as a result of having accepted that of an enemy state. Czechoslovakia itself would keep 800,000 Germans and the remainder, some 1,600,000, would be transferred. In the case of Hungarians, an exchange of population was envisaged. At the same time the government expressed opposition to any plans to solve the German minority problem by cession of state territory. Nevertheless, as per instructions from Beneš on 7 February 1945, the Czechoslovak High Command prepared a contingency plan for the modification of Czechoslovak borders, which, together with areas designated "for annexation," also identified territory "for cession." This latter referred to a total of 1,790 km² with 340,000 inhabitants of German nationality in north-western Bohemia and other points.[41]

A report on negotiations with Ambassador Nichols and Foreign Minister Eden on what was known as the "border formula" and population transfer was presented to the Czechoslovak government on 1 December 1944. The British position had softened. It was now accepted that the Czechoslovak authorities would exercise full control within the pre-Munich boundaries. Moreover, a link between restored sovereignty in the affected areas and population transfer had been formed in Foreign Office minds at least since January 1944. A minute from John M. Troutbeck in July the same year noted that the re-establishment of the pre-Munich frontiers with minor adjustments appeared "so certain" that he did not feel the need to put forward any special arguments concerning a memorandum dealing with the eastern borders of Germany.[42]

The Polish government-in-exile showed a close interest in the Czechoslovak transfer plans during talks on a possible Czechoslovak-Polish confederation.[43] A similarity in the approach of both governments-in-exile to any

---

41   School of Slavonic and East European Studies, UCL, London (henceforth SSEES), Lisický Collection, sign. 4/1/2.
42   TNA, FO 371/39139, C 9093.
43   One instance among many others is the conversation between Edvard Beneš and the Polish ambassador to Britain, Edward Raczyński, on 23 February 1940. Institut Polski i Muzeum im. Gen. Sikorskiego, London, fund Ambasada Londyn, sign. A.12.49/CZ/IA.

such operation is evident from an *aide-mémoire* of 23 November 1942 on Polish war aims by Józef Lipski.[44] At the same time, a document was produced for the Polish Ministry of Foreign Affairs by Józef Winiewicz which contains statistical data "on the resettlement of Germans," based on possible locations for a new Polish western frontier and what was known as the "minimal line" involving a hypothetical resettlement of 3.3 million Germans. In addition, the Poles foresaw the resettlement of approximately 750,000 Germans living in what was pre-war Polish territory.[45] On 1 December 1942, a special memorandum on Polish claims against Germany was prepared, in which Poland demanded East Prussia, Danzig and parts of Silesia, and, in line with those claims, urged the Western Allies to confirm the policy of transfer "of certain sections of the German population."[46] This operation would be carried out in the framework of population exchange, mainly to facilitate the return of Polish workers in Germany. The Poles also predicted that part of the German population would flee before the end of the war.[47] The memorandum was accompanied with a special document on Polish western frontiers designating the Oder as "Poland's line of national security."[48]

Czechoslovak-Polish mutual support faded, however, after confederation plans were put into cold storage because of Soviet opposition to the project.[49] With the establishment of the so-called Lublin Committee and its recognition as the Polish interim government by Czechoslovakia, the issue of German population transfer was viewed differently by both exile leaderships, especially when the question of new Polish borders collided with Czechoslovak claims in areas such as Kladsko. Moreover, disputes concerning the Těšín territory complicated initial collaboration on the preparation of transfer plans.

The demands were submitted to the European Advisory Commission. Then on 5 September 1944 they were amended to include, as new "strategic" borders, not only East Prussia, Danzig and Upper Silesia but also "the territories between the Oder and the Polish-German frontiers from 1 September 1939." The cession of German territory would be connected to a transfer or perhaps an exchange of population. This was elaborated on further on 27 September 1944 when the Polish government called for the resettlement of Germans from Poland immediately after cessation of hostilities. This was

---

44   HIA Stanford, Collection Ministerswo spraw zagranicznych (MSZ) [Ministry of Foreign Affairs], box 617, folder 16.
45   Ibid., box 617, folder 13. The material was compiled on 25 June 1942.
46   TNA, FO 371/34396, C 3655.
47   Ibid.
48   TNA, FO 371/39139, C 9093.
49   Piotr S. Wandycz, *Czechoslovak-Polish Confederation* (Bloomington: Indiana University Publications, 1956), pp. 81–82.

based on "strategic" reasons and also on the assumption that coexistence of the Polish nation and a German population in a common state was not possible.[50] To buttress its case for transfer the Poles used both security and historical arguments.

German expulsion was also advocated by the Polish National Liberation Committee (*Polski Komitet Wyzwolenia Narodowego* – PKWN). In their first proclamation, dated July 22 1944, they set their sights on the incorporation of East Prussia, Pomerania and Silesia into a new Polish state that would have its frontier on the river Oder.[51] At the same time, committee members repeatedly referred to parts of Pomerania and Upper Silesia as "traditionally Polish areas." In a conversation with Mikołajczyk on 3 August 1944, Stalin offered to set Polish borders on the Oder, thus taking in the towns of Stettin and Breslau (Wrocław), as compensation for the loss of the eastern territories. The Chairman of the PKWN, Edward Osóbka-Morawski, on 29 August 1944, repeated the determination to fix Polish borders on the Oder and the Neisse. It was believed in the Foreign Office that such assertions were made with Soviet consent.[52] The proposed western boundaries put forward by the Polish government in London in December 1944 were more moderate and closer to the British standpoint but Stalin seized the opportunity to proffer more to the Lublin Committee.[53] Moreover, it was the Red Army which actually controlled the liberated territories.

As already mentioned, the decisive factor for implementation of the transfer as well as other possible courses of action was the attitude of the Great Powers. Great Britain in particular had been aware of the necessity for finding alternatives to inter-war minority policies from the very beginning of the war. The Royal Institute of Foreign Affairs held informal discussions on solutions to the European minority problem in early 1940 and established the Foreign Research and Press Service (FRPS) as a special analytical branch for the Foreign Office.[54] In May 1940 a group of FRPS experts prepared a report on national minorities in which transfer of population was seen as one remedy. The Greek-Turkish exchange was cited as an especially suitable model.[55]

In January 1942 the Foreign Office asked the FRPS to make a study of post-war territorial rectifications in Central and Eastern Europe. During

---

50 Piotr Lippóczy, Tadeusz Walichnowski, *Przesiedlenie ludności niemieckiej z Polski po II wojnie światowej w świetle dokumentów* [The Resettlement of the German Population from Poland after the Second World War in the Light of Documents] (Warszawa – Łodž: Państwowe Wydawnictwo Naukowe, 1982), No. 43, A – Theses, B – Memorandum, pp. 178–190.
51 Dziennik Urzędowy 1/1944, see note XY.
52 TNA, FO 371/39139, C 9093.
53 See TNA, FO 371/39139, C 17671.
54 TNA, FO 371/25234, W 9695, List of research topics of FRPS 22 August 1940.
55 SSEES, R.W. Seton Watson Collection, 13/1/1.

the visit of Anthony Eden to Moscow, it became clear that the Soviets were making preparations for discussions on the question and Stalin pressed for recognition of the new Soviet frontiers including those in the Polish eastern territories. In February 1942, the FRPS completed two reports that examined the viability of a Central European confederation and the transfer of minorities.[56] The authors focused particularly on the notion of a confederation that would serve as a buffer zone against any future German threat (and perhaps Soviet imperialism to boot)[57] and on German-Polish, German-Czech and Italian frontiers.

The first memorandum on the frontiers of the proposed confederation was prepared by John David Mabbott, fellow of St. John's College, Oxford. The transfer of the German minority was tied to frontier rectification, mainly to compensate Poland for losses in the east. It was thought that the Poles would demand "the departure of all Germans from territories ceded to Poland" and such a solution could be in the interest of the German population itself. Transfer was depicted as a security measure. Several alternatives were also discussed, differing in the extent of the territory ceded to Poland but not in principle. Cession and transfer were examined in terms of their economic, strategic and political implications. The total number of Germans who would be affected by the "eviction" was estimated at between three to 6.8 million depending on the size of the ceded territory and the rigour with which the ejection was enforced.

In the case of the Czech-German borders, one report stressed that if the areas acquired by Germany as a result of the Munich Agreement were returned to Czechoslovakia, the "confederation would be greatly strengthened." The ethnographic consequence of the pre-Munich frontiers, however, would mean the inclusion of approximately 3.3 million Germans in the state. In the event of Austria remaining with Germany, an alternative would be to transfer only Germans from Moravia and Silesia (approximately 800,000) or to combine transfer with cession of territory. With regard to Bohemia the memorandum mentioned a possible "territorial compromise." Cession of the mountainous areas and part of the land between Cheb and Karlovy Vary could reduce the number of Germans in the country by half a million and a further two to 2.5 million could be "evicted." The reasons behind such a decision were the pan-German, nationalistic orientation of the Sudeten Germans "in recent years." Mabbott referred to post-war anti-German animosity, especially as a result of Heydrich's policies. Indeed, "the departure" could be regarded as "the best service, which could be rendered to Germans themselves." Mabbott

56   TNA, FO 371/30930, C 2167.
57   See TNA, FO 371/32481, W 1823, Memorandum of 20 January 1942 by FRPS.

also expected a post-war exodus of refugees, which could reduce the number of Sudeten Germans by another 200,000.

A further possibility, it was suggested, might be an exchange of population between southern Moravia and Austria. An additional option would be to accord "limited" autonomous status to the Sudeten territories. However, the complete eviction of the Sudeten Germans "might be advocated in the interests of European security." On the other hand, the economic impact of such a measure would militate against its adoption. Transfer was also envisaged for Yugoslavia, with some 600,000 Germans with 50,000 or more in Slovenia, and also, together with population exchange, in connection with the problem of Italian-Austrian frontiers in the South Tyrol. The overall success of any British policy on the Central European confederation would depend on its contribution to collective security and how relations with the USSR might be affected.

The memorandum on frontier adjustment was accompanied by another on the transfer of minorities which stated that "evictions" of Germans would be imposed by the victorious Allied Powers and that a defeated Germany, in turmoil and the possible throes of revolution, would be in no position to refuse. Reference was made to the Greek-Turkish exchange and also to the "Hitlerite transfers." Questions of scale, means and time were seen as the main differences to the precedents mentioned. The first hurdle to be crossed would be selection and the merits of compulsory or voluntary transfer were discussed as well as the criteria to be used for classification. For Czechoslovakia, it was felt that language rather than religion would be the deciding factor.

The transfer, it was stipulated, would be orderly, gradual (over a span of five to 10 years) and under international control. Settlement of the evicted people in their new home, against a backdrop of a German population of 80 million and taking war losses into account, was not expected to cause any major problem, even if the number of expellees reached six million. The newcomers could be absorbed in agriculture, industry and public works. The cost of the resettlement of three million Germans was estimated at 40 million pounds. The main arguments against the move were the economic and social impairment of Poland and Czechoslovakia. On the other hand, both states "will pay no compensation for immovable property" of the Germans involved since this would be part of the reparations for war damage. It was stressed, however, that the analyses were merely speculative since final policy would depend on the course of the war. However, there was no doubting the "notorious dangers caused by German minorities" which created the contingency. Nonetheless, the final decision would be "difficult" and Mabbott foresaw that resentment in Germany against the territorial concessions would be fuelled by the millions of expelled people.

The reports influenced British policy in this field until 1944. On 2 March 1942, Frank Roberts stressed that the British were still not in a position to make any final decision on territorial questions in Central Europe but he supported the main thrust of the proposed territorial changes and transfer as a means to strengthen the notion of a Czechoslovak-Polish confederation and to weaken Germany. According to Roberts, Poland had to relinquish territory in the east "as the price for good relations with Russia" but was therefore eligible to "receive compensation in the West," even at the expense of the principles of the Atlantic Charter. Roberts also pointed out that "no German government will willingly accept any loss of territory and population" but that cession of land in East Prussia and much of Upper Silesia and the concomitant transfer was a "clear cut solution," which "will be in fact less dangerous than a compromise solution aiming at ethnographic justice."

As the war continued it became ever clearer that an internationally approved transfer of national minorities would be the most feasible way to solve the complex problems that beset Central Europe. The framework for international protection of minorities within national states had been shown to be ineffective during the inter-war period and there was no international consensus that might provide a basis for the eventual introduction of a similar or reformed system of safeguards. The cession of a large slice of territory inhabited by minorities, as had been applied at Munich, was unacceptable to the Czechoslovaks. After the proposed Czechoslovak-Polish confederation was put on hold, the British government gave its backing to the transfer policy in order to bolster the position of the national homogenous countries in Central Europe.

Reference has already been made to the close link between Czechoslovak-British negotiations on the non-validity of Munich and approval by the British War Cabinet of a "general principle of the transfer of German minorities" from Central and South-Eastern Europe based on the Anthony Eden memorandum of 2 July 1942 entitled "Anglo-Czechoslovak Relations."[58] This was the time when both sides were seeking a compromise formula for repudiation of the Munich Agreement. On 7 July Eden informed Beneš that the British favoured the principle of the post-war transfer of national minorities from the states of Central and South-East Europe.[59] Eden, referring to the Greek-Turkish and the Hitler transfers, stressed the necessity that the operation be conducted "in an orderly and peaceful manner."

Once Eden's proposal had been agreed upon by the War Cabinet, the memoranda on Central European frontiers and population transfer were cir-

---

58   TNA, Cabinet (CAB) 66/26, X/P 01406.
59   Ibid.

culated within other British government departments.[60] The FRPS was commissioned to give another expert opinion on the future of Germany and of Central and Eastern Europe with special regard to the question of borders and minorities.[61] On 29 June 1942 discussion between the FRPS and Lord Halifax along with other experts from the Foreign Office took place at Oxford. German population transfer was referred to in the context of the possible cession of East Prussia, Danzig (2.8 million) and Upper Silesia (up to 800,000). For Czechoslovakia, the restoration of the pre-Munich borders and the "eviction" of the bulk of its German population was seen as the most likely scenario. At the time, the Foreign Office still saw three possibilities: the re-establishment of independent national states, one large federative unit, or smaller regional confederations. Czechoslovakia, Poland, and Hungary were seen as constituting a possible "northern confederation," while a "southern confederation" would comprise Greece, Yugoslavia, Romania, and Bulgaria. Justification for the transfer was again provided by the potential security threat posed by the German population. The Foreign Office was of the opinion that the USSR would most likely keep the Polish eastern territories and thus the cession of East Prussia and Upper Silesia was regarded as a possible "compensation."

At the beginning of September 1942, a revised version of the policy paper on confederations was prepared by J. D. Mabbott.[62] In the case of Czechoslovakia Mabbott mentioned the special position of Slovakia because of its frontier with Hungary and also expressed concerns regarding socio-economic problems. The Foreign Office was asked to discuss "certain methods of minority protection," such as inclusion of minority clauses in any international agreement on confederation. Minority commissions like that on Upper Silesia during the inter-war period and the Estonian model of cultural autonomy were touched on.[63] Special consideration was envisaged for Jewish minorities.

The result was that the Foreign Office in 1943 again reviewed the possibility of minority protection within national states under the patronage of an international organization although this had proved ineffective between the wars. In addition, there was no international consensus for such a system even if reformed. The necessity for addressing the problem had already been mooted in a report on the International Bill of Rights prepared for the Foreign Office in June 1942. The British had no desire to renew the "old system" but, at the same time, wanted some means whereby a state which abused individual

60   TNA, FO 371/30390, C 2167.
61   TNA, FO 371/31500, U 276, List of topics, 14 June 1942.
62   Ibid.
63   TNA, FO 371/31500, U 1841.

or minority rights might be sanctioned. Minorities should be accorded full civil rights.[64] Another possibility was the setting up of permanent local agencies, acting under international auspices, for reporting minority mistreatment. Such a solution would require a network of international agreements and would link in with Roosevelt's four freedoms. In August 1943, a similar proposal to review international protection of minorities or to find a new system for those who would remain in re-established national states was formulated by P. B. Nichols after discussions with Beneš on minority questions.[65] A system of international minority protection was also evaluated in December 1943 from the legal point of view by the chief legal adviser to the Foreign Office, Sir William Malkin.[66] However, the Polish government-in-exile (and to a lesser extent the Czechoslovak) sharply rejected any "resuscitation" of minority treaties.[67] Influential British diplomats, too, voiced their disagreement. Frank Roberts, for example, in a minute dated 13 September 1942 wrote: "I think it is essential to do all we can to escape from the conception of minorities [...] those, who remain, will not be given minority rights." For such people he proposed "assimilation or integration within the state to which they will belong."[68] At the beginning of February 1944 he added that it was also highly unlikely that the US and the USSR would support "anything like" the protection guaranteed by the "Old League."[69]

The position of the Soviet government was taken into account. According to Nichols, "it was understood" that they (like the Americans) supported population transfer. This assumption was confirmed by John Balfour on 29 January 1944 when he informed Eden of the likelihood that the USSR "will support all means to reduce safety risks" and would therefore be ready to "remove" German minorities from the Balkans and Eastern Europe.[70] Balfour mentioned several possibilities: assimilation, population exchange, dispersal, and, the most radical option, short- or long-term unilateral transfer. It was thought this would have a special appeal for the Czechs and Poles. The Soviets were not expected to raise any objection to the transfer of the Hungarian minority in Slovakia. However, it was probable that they would want Big Three supervision over the minority policies of the small powers.

It is possible to conclude that Czechoslovakia and the validity of Munich led Britain to formulate its position on transfer, but the most salient factor for the other two Great Powers was the question of Polish borders. This is

---

64   TNA, FO 371/31500, U 1046, Memorandum by David Mitrany.
65   TNA, FO 371/39012, C 2212, Nichols dispatch of 20 August 1943.
66   TNA, FO 371/40477, U 999.
67   TNA, FO 371/39012, C 1002, F. Savery to the Foreign Office on 20 January 1944.
68   TNA, FO 371/31500, U 1841.
69   TNA, FO 371/40477, U 999.
70   TNA, FO 371/39012, C 2212.

especially evident in the case of the United States where the Czechoslovak situation played a far less important role. The transfer of the German population from both Czechoslovakia and Poland was discussed in detail by British and American diplomats in Washington on 19 March, 1943. The Foreign Office prepared a brief entitled "Transfers of Populations" and emphasized that such a policy could provide stability in post-war Europe, especially in the central regions.[71] William Strang informed R. Atherton that the British government had reached general agreement on the transfer of the German population and other minorities in the states of Central and South-Eastern Europe after the war where necessary or desirable.[72] Atherton concurred and found the idea interesting also in respect to the Japanese in Asia. Both men agreed, however, that there were serious economic and technical problems regarding transfer which needed further consultation. Although some British diplomats suggested that the USSR be advised of transfer plans, this was rejected because of diverging Soviet interests. On 16 April 1943, Frank Roberts wrote that the Soviet government was "ready to transfer millions of people without worrying about humanitarian considerations" and could possibly come up with a "very dangerous interpretation of such a principle."

It is, however, an undisputed fact that all three Great Powers were considering the transfer of German populations (mainly in terms of post-war frontiers) during the course of the Second World War, and confirmed their approval "in principle" in the case of Czechoslovakia and Poland, even though their conception of what would be achieved thereby differed as did their reasons for finally agreeing on a common policy for its implementation.

On 5 January 1943, Roberts recorded that Beneš was "extremely informally" aware of the War Cabinet's position on transfer.[73] The Foreign Office also "unofficially" informed the Polish ambassador.[74] At the same time, they did not want to give the Czechs and Poles a blank cheque on the minority question or make any firm commitments concerning frontiers. On 22 April 1943, Beneš was told that during his upcoming visit to the US he should proceed on the basis that the British had already consented to the principle of transfer.[75] Nevertheless, the specific details of how this might be carried out remained unclear and the British insisted that definitive sanction by the Great Powers would only come when a cease-fire with Germany was in place.

This policy was modified in October 1943 in the course of Cabinet discussions concerning the forthcoming talks between Foreign Ministers in Moscow. A confidential annex to the conclusions reached by the War Cabinet

---

71   TNA, FO 371/34396, C 3655.
72   TNA, FO 371/34396, C 3518.
73   TNA, FO 371/34396, C 416.
74   TNA, FO 371/34460, C 11013.
75   TNA, FO 371/34396, C 3665.

on 5 October on the basis of a report prepared by the Secretary of State on 27 September looked at possible post-war German frontiers.[76] Regarding Central Europe, the Cabinet confirmed in principle the idea of an independent Austria, the pre-Munich borders of Czechoslovakia (with small rectifications in the case of Cheb), and the cession of East Prussia, Danzig, and a considerable portion of Silesia to Poland, and, correspondingly, the "consequent" principle of transfer of populations.[77] This position was reflected in the Foreign Office brief for Eden for the conference in Moscow.[78]

During October 1943 the Foreign Office also proposed the setting up of an interdepartmental committee to deal with the political, financial, economic and technical aspects of the projected transfer.[79] According to the newly appointed adviser of the Foreign Office on Germany, J. M. Troutbeck, the British in 1943 were "committed to the principle but not to the method." The estimated transfer figures were still around three to 6.8 million Germans from Central Europe, with the assumption that a more moderate approach would be adopted by the Czechoslovak government. The number was therefore likely to be 4.5 million. However, other groups such as the *Volksdeutsche* already resettled by Hitler and German military and civil personnel stationed outside Germany had also to be taken into account.[80] Troutbeck maintained that the transfer should not be implemented "so brutally as to cause a strong movement of public sympathy for Germany either in this country or in the US" or to give rise to economic or social turmoil in Germany itself after the war.[81]

An Interdepartmental Committee on the Transfer of German Populations headed by J. M. Troutbeck was established. Its aim was to provide the Foreign Office and the War Cabinet with advice on British political, military and financial involvement in the transfer. The committee had to evaluate the territorial scale of the operation and propose measures to ensure that "the transfer is carried out without undue sufferings to the migrants and without serious economic dislocation both to Germany and to Poland and Czechoslovakia." They also had to assess whether the transfer would be compulsory or voluntary, draw up criteria for selection and examine property aspects. On 22 October 1943, J. D. Mabbott prepared a paper on the precedents for the proposed transfer which dealt mainly with lessons from the Greek-Turkish and the Greek-Bulgarian exchange of population as well as Hitler's

---

76   The memorandum was based on the recommendations of a committee on post-war settlement headed by C. Attlee. TNA, FO 371/34461, C 12122.
77   TNA, FO 371/34460, C 11296.
78   TNA, FO 371/34461, C 13589.
79   TNA, FO 371/34460, C 11013.
80   TNA, FO 371/34460, C 11013, Troutbeck's minute of 12 October 1943.
81   Ibid.

relocation of *Volksdeutsche*.[82] The fact that Greece with a population of 5.5 million was able to absorb 1.5 million expellees was stressed in favour of the German influx.[83] The following month, on 8 November, Troutbeck asked the British ambassador to the Polish government to find out "informally" what Polish plans were with regard to cession of German territory and population transfer and "how radical and ruthless do you suppose they will be in this respect?"[84] A similar letter was sent to Nichols to gauge developments in the Czechoslovak government.

The committee also looked at ways of settling the Czechoslovak-Hungarian, the Romanian-Hungarian, the Italian-Yugoslav, and the Romanian-Bulgarian disputes, again mostly in terms of population exchange and frontier rectification but eventual outcomes were difficult to predict. Eviction of Germans was also expected in post-war Yugoslavia. On 20 January 1944, the Foreign Office Research Department compiled a report on minority policies.[85] The paper identified "two extreme poles," that of full protection at one end and extermination on the other. The first was reflected in the inter-war system of protection under international law, by bilateral agreements and by the internal legal system of individual countries. Other points along the scale encompassed transfer, population exchange, and assimilation or a combination of transfer and assimilation. The alternatives to transfer (including the question of a new international Bill of Rights) were discussed mainly in respect of non-German minorities and international protection was not ruled out mainly because of the Jewish situation.[86] The Research Department advocated a revision of international minority protection as laid down in 1919. Analyzing plebiscites conducted after the First World War, the Interdepartmental Committee on the Transfer of German Populations submitted a report on 19 January 1944 which suggested that international commissions be established in the districts from which Germans were to be transferred and referred explicitly to Poland and the Sudeten areas of Czechoslovakia.

By the end of February 1944, the Foreign Office had concluded that Beneš's former moderate views on transfer had become more radical and that the Polish and Czechoslovak governments would cooperate closely in carrying out the proposed removals. On the other hand, the War Office considered the estimated numbers for transfer as too high since it seemed "probable that many of the Germans now residing in East Prussia, Poland and Upper Silesia

82   TNA, FO 371/34461, C 12352.
83   TNA, FO 371/34461, C 12443.
84   TNA, FO 371/34461, C 12764.
85   TNA, FO 371/34461; FO 371/39012, C 5224.
86   See TNA, FO 371/34461, C 5497, Special memorandum on Jewish minorities of 22 April 1944.

will have left by the time the transfer comes to be implemented [...]" because the area would be "over run" by the Soviets.[87]

For an understanding of British views on transfer the key document is the 12 May 1944 report of the Interdepartmental Committee. This opened by confirming that, like Czechoslovakia and Poland, Britain was committed in principle to population transfer and proceeded on the explicit assumption of a direct connection between the transfer of the German minority from a restored Czechoslovakia and that from "the new Polish territories" (including Allenstein, Oppeln Silesia, Danzig, part of Pomerania, and Brandenburg). Confirming the British War Cabinet resolution of 5 October 1943,[88] the report also envisaged the eventual removal of the German minority from Hungary, Romania, Yugoslavia, and Alsace Lorraine and drew attention to the economic and political problems associated with transfer. In points 12 and 13 of the "Conclusions on the General Subject" it was argued that a half-way measure would be the worst possible outcome and advised against international legal protection for the remaining un-transferred populations. Inevitably, the transfer would involve "very great human hardship" and should be conducted by the Allied occupation authorities, with the participation of Czechoslovak and Polish representatives. Point 18 in the Second Part of the "Recommendation for Action" is crucial. This specifically states that transferees will leave behind all moveable and immovable property apart from personal effects, that this property will be forfeit to the home state, and that it will probably be regarded as part of Germany's reparation payments. Point 8 in the same section asserts that all those who "at the present date" have German citizenship in accordance with German laws would be transferred. It was up to Czechoslovak and Polish legislators to stipulate exceptions. As far as the authors of the report were concerned, no other equally "practical" approach to a resolution of the problem existed. From a current perspective it may seem paradoxical that the committee feared that the home states might even try to prevent some persons from leaving.

The link between the estimated 5.5. million Germans liable for transfer (and the revised figure of 2.5 million) and Germany's projected borders with Poland and Czechoslovakia, with also a possible adjustment in the Egerland (Cheb) region, was confirmed in a Foreign Office memorandum of 7 July 1944 entitled Eastern German Frontiers. This was redrafted on 20 November and, along with a map of the areas involved, submitted to the Post-Hostilities Planning Committee.[89]

---

87   TNA, FO 371/34461, C 4688, Lt. Col. Arthur of the War Office to J. M. Troutbeck, 9 April 1944.
88   TNA, FO 371/34460, C 11296.
89   TNA, FO 371/39139, C 9093.

The first interesting item in this new document is that the number of Germans eligible for transfer has increased to between 7.6 and 10 million. However, officially Eden and Churchill repeatedly maintained in Parliament that the cession of former German territories to Poland would be decided only after the war and that no secret agreement had been concluded with Stalin in Teheran.[90] On the other hand, Churchill had already proclaimed on 22 May 1944 that Germany's borders were not guaranteed. Churchill was personally convinced that transfer of the German population from Czechoslovakia and Poland was the right decision, especially because of Polish western frontiers.[91] In a telegram to South African leader General Smuts on 30 October 1944, Churchill wrote: "It is of course intended to move all Germans out of the ceded territories back into Germany. The disentanglement of populations is an essential feature in all changes. Look what a success it has been between Turkey and Greece [...]."[92] Churchill's estimate of Germans in the Polish case was under six million and he spoke about "compensation" for Poland in East Prussia and Silesia for the loss of its eastern territory.

In November 1944 the Foreign Office Research Department prepared a new report on minority transfer which amended some aspects of the May 1944 document.[93] The relationship between transfer and the "inevitable" movement of millions of people because of the situation on the eastern front is emphasized and an even worse situation at the end of the war is predicted. The question of unilateral transfer or population exchange is once more considered. German minorities are again seen as a potential threat to European peace and as grounds for a renewed irredentism, and the precedents of Hitler's large-scale population transfers and the Greek-Turkish exchange are pointed out. The link between minority transfer and frontier rectification is stressed. Nor are counter-arguments overlooked. The main cause for the failure of the international system of minority protection was seen to lie in its operation and the strongest argument against transfer would be "the hardship and suffering for the people involved."[94]

Some questions were yet to be decided, such as whether selection for transfer would be optional or compulsory and the document referred to the methods applied in the earlier instances. The issue of the "remnants of minorities" was addressed using the example of Latvia and Estonia, where, despite the menace of "red terror," 20 percent of the German inhabitants opted

90   Ibid., C 9505, W. Churchill's reply to a question from MP Stokes, 18 July 1944.
91   Matthew Frank, *Expelling the Germans, British Opinion and Post-1945 Population Transfer in Context*, pp. 73 and following.
92   TNA, Dominion Office (DO) 35/2002. J. Smuts in his telegram to W. Churchill on 29 October 1944 was very cautious about changes to frontiers in Europe including Poland.
93   TNA, FO 371/39012, C 17689.
94   See "The Transfers of Population," in *The Times*, 16 February 1944.

to remain; in South Tyrol the number was even higher. The report also looked at difficulties that might arise with transport, food, accommodation, finance, and property, among others. It warned against the hardships that would result from badly-prepared transfers and urged that unnecessary human suffering be avoided. Because of insufficient available land, it was thought that the bulk of the resettled Germans would be absorbed into industry rather than agriculture. Use should be made, too, of public works.

In Appendix I, possible criteria for compulsory transfer were listed. These included race, language, religion, and membership of minority organizations. The possibility that the Czechoslovak and Polish states might enact their own legislation in this regard was mentioned. Appendix II dealt with the property rights of the transferred minorities, again using precedents from the past. The option of offsetting property against reparations was expressly touched on in the case of Allied states, specifically Poland and Czechoslovakia.

The Foreign Office Research Department also pointed out that the Jewish population did not fit into the minority schemes discussed and arguments were put forward as to why transfer was not suitable for them. Because of its general nature and the lack of a definitive statement on British policy, the document was considered suitable for circulation among various other government departments and to be passed on to the US State Department.

However, the question of the transfer of Germans from Poland was overshadowed by the more pressing issue of Polish-Soviet relations, in particular the fate of the Polish government-in-exile and its counterpart, the Polish National Liberation Committee (Lublin Committee), which had been transformed into the Soviet-backed provisional government. At Teheran, Churchill had undertaken to play the role of mediator between the Poles and the Soviets in discussions on common frontiers based on the Curzon line. This failed (mainly during Mikołajczyk's visit to Moscow, when he insisted that Lvov be part of Poland) and the Foreign Office was also unsuccessful in having the Curzon line accepted by the Soviet leadership as the border demarcation.[95]

The principle of population transfer conducted under international supervision was an important component of inter-Allied negotiations at the end of the war, especially in connection with decisions on the final form Polish western borders would take.[96] The US had reservations about plans to transfer the German minorities in Europe as early as the beginning of 1945. Roosevelt and the State Department repeatedly stressed that territorial changes (and the interconnected transfer of population) await a "general

95   TNA, FO 371/39421, C 17980, Draft brief for the Secretary of State on Polish-Soviet relations, 12 December 1944.
96   Anthony Polonsky, *The Great Powers and the Polish Question, 1941–45*, pp. 42–44.

post-war settlement."[97] They also viewed the situation in the broader context that the occupation authorities in Germany would have to contend with when all the displaced persons flooded into the country. It was felt that the peace and security of the continent as a whole should be taken into account. In December 1944, however, Roosevelt informed Stalin and Churchill that the US government had concluded that "the transfer of minorities in some cases is feasible and would contribute to the general security and tranquillity in the areas concerned." The US was prepared to support Poland in the resettlement of German nationals and to "join in assisting such transfers."[98] This was mentioned in connection with post-war Polish frontiers and Roosevelt pointed out that the policy had already been discussed by Eden during the Foreign Ministers' talks in Moscow. The Americans demanded that the final decision be taken at the next meeting of the Big Three.

The US also warned against the implementation of any "unilateral act of transfer of large groups," and supported the principle that such transfers must be undertaken only with international approval, under international supervision, and in stages. This was the view transmitted to the Czechoslovak government-in-exile by the *chargé d'affaires,* Rudolf Schoenfeld, on 31 January 1945 in response to a Czechoslovak memorandum of 23 November 1944, and it came with the added qualification that the US would make further investigations in the matter.

In line with its position, the US criticized the expulsions made in May and June 1945 and several times repeated its demand that transfer be carried out under the supervision of the Great Powers and on the basis of agreement between them. Britain took a similar stance, albeit with greater support for transfer. In a letter to Jan Masaryk on 27 January, and again on 8 March 1945, Ambassador Nichols acknowledged receipt of the Czechoslovak memorandum of 23 November 1944 and said he was studying its contents "with care and sympathy." However, since transfer was a task connected with an overall solution of the German question, Britain intended to discuss the matter with the other major allies first and appealed to the Czechoslovak authorities to exercise restraint in public pronouncements. The necessity for international agreement on transfers was also urged on Beneš by Churchill in their final talks on British soil on 25 February 1945.

The "wild transfer" in particular drew increasing condemnation from British politicians and sections of the general public. One definite factor here was the systematic and long-term propaganda campaign against transfer conducted largely by the German Social Democrats led by W. Jaksch. Some of the positions adopted by Jaksch, such as his arguments on ethnicity, de-

---

97   TNA FO 371/39420, C 17459, F. D. Roosevelt's personal telegram to W. Churchill, 17 December 1944.
98   Ibid.

mands for the establishment of minority rights according to the principles of American democracy, insistence that the transfer question be put off until the peace conference, and his stress on the economic losses and the practical difficulties of transfer are worthy of consideration. There are, however, no grounds to accept an idealized view of Jaksch. Indeed, a detailed analysis of the links between Jaksch's German nationalism and his socialist rhetoric,[99] and his demonization of the role of Beneš would be worth conducting. It must also be remembered that the Jaksch group was not the only mouthpiece for the German émigrés from Czechoslovakia, nor even the sole representative of Social Democratic currents among them. Moreover at the end of the war Jaksch offered neither the Czechs nor the British any viable alternatives to transfer (territorial autonomy was not an option, and still less the federalization of Central Europe). Furthermore, his claim that there had been strong anti-Nazi resistance in the Sudetenland proved unfounded, and so could not be used against the Czechoslovak-British agreement on the return of the entire pre-Munich state territory to Czechoslovak administration.

To sum up, in this chapter we have tried to demonstrate that the post-war transfer (expulsion) of the German population from Czechoslovakia and Poland to Germany should not be seen as an isolated problem in Central Europe. The crucial circumstance underlying the transfer was the decision reached by the wartime Allied coalition regarding national territories in the area. Especially relevant was the question of compensating Poland in the west for the loss of its eastern regions to the Soviet Union, although the British had initially seen transfer mainly in the context of redress for the 1938 Munich Agreement and as a solution for complex minority problems. In the case of the pre-Munich Czechoslovak frontiers and those of Poland on the Oder–Neisse line, the transfer was seen as a necessary step. In 1943–1944 the Foreign Office reached the conclusion that as far as Central Europe was concerned, it would be impossible to "resuscitate" the inter-war protection of national minorities and territorial autonomy was not considered an option.

On the other hand, border rectification, population exchange (around 240,000 people with Austria), and internal resettlement and assimilation of those remaining were still regarded as alternatives to the transfer (expulsion) of the German population from Czechoslovakia until the very end of Beneš's London exile.[100]

---

99 W. Jaksch demanded self-determination for the Sudeten Germans "in the spirit of socialism which brings nations together." HIA Stanford, Táborský Collection, box 8, Paper on Jaksch's guidelines for foreign policy, 15 February 1943.

100 VÚA-VHA, fund Studijní oddělení Hlavního velitelství [Research Department of the Main Headquarters], box 31, Record of conversation between E. Beneš and General F. Moravec, 7 January 1945.

The resettlement of the German minorities formed only one part of the overall post-war refugee problem and the repatriation of displaced persons. The argument for the removal of the possible threat posed by German minorities to the security of Central Europe and the avoidance of future conflict prevailed over humanitarian considerations. The most important factor, however, was the actual situation on the liberated territories themselves and the more radical policies put in train by the Polish provisional government and the Czechoslovak National Front government. In the case of Czechoslovakia, this marked a deviation from Beneš's avowed policies and a move closer to the wild expulsion during a "commanded revolution" as already envisaged in August 1943 by General Neumann-Miroslav.

CITIZENSHIP AND PROPERTY RIGHTS OF "OUR GERMANS": THE DEVELOPMENT BETWEEN 1943 AND 1945 OF THE LEGAL STATUS OF GERMANS IN POST-WAR CZECHOSLOVAKIA[1]

MATĚJ SPURNÝ

The development of plans for the expropriation and expulsion of Germans from Czechoslovakia can be interpreted as a history of the subversion of the liberal principles of citizenship and property rights. The context for this change was framed in more general contours than simply war and occupation. During the period after the First World War, the rights enshrined in property law had changed markedly throughout Europe. The example of the Soviet Union had shown that a political regime could drastically reduce and even abolish entitlement to individual property.

National Socialist Germany, in turn, demonstrated explicitly that the state could discriminate or privilege people in accordance with their membership of a political or ethnic group. Since the context of the German occupation of the Czech Lands, and National Socialist law, seems crucial, I would like, at first, to characterize the changes in citizenship and property law in the Sudetenland and in the Protectorate after 1938/39.

Next, I hope to show that among the Czech and Slovak political elite in London, in like manner, plans concerning the post-war citizenship and property of the German-speaking former Czechoslovak citizens seemed more feasible as hostilities drew to a close. The thesis put forward here is that the very radical solution based on ethnically-defined collective guilt was chosen as late as spring or summer 1945 and was not a direct reaction to "German brutality" against the backdrop of Lidice and Ležáky, as the popular narrative maintains. At the same time, I want to bring to light contradictions, and political instrumentality, in both the construction and application of ethnically-based inequitable legislation on the part of one segment of the population of the Czech Lands.

---

1   This paper reflects the findings of a joint project undertaken by the author together with Professor Dieter Gosewinkel. A larger article written by both researchers has been published in French in *Revue d´histoire contemporaine*, Vol. 61, No. 1, 2014, pp. 26–61.

THE END OF THE EQUALITY OF CITIZENS (1938–1939)

The division and subsequent complete breakup of the Czechoslovak Republic following the Munich Agreement of September 1938 put an end not only to the sovereignty of the Czechoslovak state but also to a principle that had shaped Czechoslovak law until 1938: the equality of citizens regardless of ethnic origin. From that point onwards, regulations governing German citizenship, which since 1933 had developed from an instituted rule of law into a political tool of racial segregation, came into effect in the hived-off Sudetenland.[2] A uniform citizenship was replaced by graduated classes of rights based on ethno-racial criteria and came into force in former Czechoslovakia. A discriminatory distinction was drawn between citizens of the Reich, who alone enjoyed full legal status,[3] and mere citizens, who, in accordance with the Nuremberg racial laws, were not of "German or kindred blood."

After the setting up of the Protectorate of Bohemia and Moravia in March 1939, ethno-racial selection standards regulating citizenship became more stringent. Only "German national inhabitants" of the Protectorate were classified as German Reich citizens, while those of "Czech nationality" were given the new, separate—and inferior—status of citizens of the Protectorate (not of the German Reich). The underlying principle of national (*völkisch*) segregation was that no member of the German nation (*Volkszugehöriger*) would be a mere citizen of the Protectorate. Czechs were thus granted a legal status lower than that of German citizens and in some respects were treated as foreigners by the German Reich.[4]

The property rights of Czech nationals, now reduced to "mere" citizens of the Protectorate, were subject to much greater restrictive and less predictable intervention by the German occupation authorities than those of citizens of German nationality (*Volksdeutsche*). Czech entrepreneurs and tradespeople with Protectorate citizenship were often pushed out of managerial positions in their companies and the firms transferred to German trusteeship.[5] On the other hand, many owners, particularly of medium-sized and smaller busi-

---

2   See Dieter Gosewinkel, *Einbürgern und Ausschliessen. Die Nationalisierung der Staatsangehörigkeit vom Deutschen Bund bis zur Bundesrepublik Deutschland*, 2nd edition (Göttingen: Vandenhoeck & Ruprecht, 2003), esp. pp. 393–420.

3   Verordnung zum Reichsbürgergesetz vom Reichsbürgergesetz, 14 November 1935, §3, 1.; see also Gosewinkel, *Einbürgern und Ausschliessen*, pp. 383–393.

4   Gosewinkel, *Einbürgern und Ausschliessen*, p. 402; Erlass des Führers vom 16. 3. 1939, Art. II, publ. in: Schmied, Erich; *Staatsangehörigkeit der Tschechoslowakei*, 2nd edition (Frankfurt am Main: Metzner, 1974), pp. 17.

5   Alice Teichova, *Wirtschaftsgeschichte der Tschechoslowakei, 1918–1980* (Wien – Köln – Graz: Böhlau, 1988), p. 72; Chad Bryant, *Making the Czechs German: Nationality and Nazi Rule in the Protectorate of Bohemia and Moravia*, dissertation thesis (Berkeley, CA: University of California, 1997), pp. 115, 311, 318.

nesses, did not lose their proprietorial status.[5] The full impact of National Socialist racial policy was reserved for Jews and their property. As mere "protected persons" (*Schutzangehörige*), their legal status was, in turn, inferior to that of "Protectorate citizens," and they were lumped together in a special category that no longer afforded any legal protection whatsoever—contrary to the euphemistic wording.[6]

THE SITUATION AFTER 1945

Czechoslovak plans to ethnicize access to citizenship and to collectively dispossess all members of certain national minorities, which were developed between 1943 and 1945 by the government-in-exile in London, were both a reaction to these changes and an adaptation of the measures enacted under National Socialist rule. It is therefore very interesting to note that a relatively protracted effort was made to uphold certain liberal norms concerning citizenship and property rights, at least in a rudimentary form, until the spring and summer of 1945 when they were finally abandoned on practical and ideological grounds.

Prominent among these principles was *the right of people to opt for the citizenship of their choice*, which had earlier been an essential element in the proposed reforms. The plans for granting citizenship in accordance with ethnic criteria developed by the London government-in-exile had assumed that at least those Germans who were not liable for criminal prosecution would have the right to choose Czechoslovak citizenship. Under this arrangement, the Czechoslovak state would have been obliged to examine each application individually and to state reasons for the decision reached. The Košice government programme of 5 April 1945 articulated the principle that any German who had not been active in National Socialist organizations would be allowed to reapply for Czechoslovak citizenship and that the state was required to judge every such request on its merits.[7] It was the decisive Decree No. 33 of 2 August 1945 that heralded a fundamental break with this position. Although the decree postulated that there could be exceptions to the rule by which German nationality was sufficient reason for deprivation of Czechoslovak citizenship, the onus of establishing grounds for exemption was on the person

---

6   Bryant, *Making the Czechs German*, pp. 112, 118; Diemut Majer, *"Fremdvölkische" im Dritten Reich: ein Beitrag zur nationalsozialistischen Rechtssetzung und Rechtspraxis in Verwaltung und Justiz unter besonderer Berücksichtigung der eingegliederten Ostgebiete und des Generalgouvernements* (Boppard am Rhein: Harald Boldt Verlag, 1981).

7   The so-called "Košice Statute," German version in: Fritz Peter Habel, ed., *Dokumente zur Sudetenfrage: unerledigte Geschichte. Veröffentlichung des Sudetendeutschen Archivs in München* (München: Langen Müller, 2003), pp. 506–507.

affected, and it was not incumbent on the state to examine each application on a one by one basis. The rationale behind this move was twofold and lay both in the practical impossibility of assessing millions of separate cases and in the ideological assertion of the collective guilt of all Germans.

A comparable development can be observed in the sweeping, ethnically-determined expropriation clause. Decisions had already been taken in London in 1943 and 1944 on the confiscation of at least some of the assets of Germans and Hungarians. However, proposals from early 1944 for regulating expropriation had still suggested that loss of non-agricultural assets at least should be incurred only by Germans who could be shown to have engaged in "activities directed against the state."[8] A memorandum of 23 November 1944 stressed that there was "no intention of confiscating the private assets of persons to be expelled unless on the grounds of a statutory penalty" and that compensation would be paid for relinquished immobile assets.[9] Even after the idea of collective expropriation by ethnic criteria had been accepted, policymakers still felt a strong need for a legal construction that would legitimize the procedure. The assets impounded in the territory of the Czechoslovak Republic could be held as security in a future international agreement. The explanatory protocol to the decree drafted (but not promulgated) in Prague in May 1945 after the end of the war in Europe emphasized that the sequestrated assets were to "be an integral element in the future settlement of war reparations."[10] At least until 1944, and to some extent even in the spring of 1945, confiscation without compensation was regarded as an extreme solution and one that would not be implemented on a large scale. It was not until, at the latest, the summer of 1945 that the link between expropriated assets and reparations vanished from further drafts of the confiscation decree. The history of this decree and the gradual disappearance of the principle of compensation for dispossession can be seen as one of the most striking examples of the subversion of a legal precept that had been crucial in Europe since the 19th century if not earlier.

In addition to the gradual decay of the formerly cherished principles of citizenship and property rights, post-war legislation was characterized by two other critical developments. The first concerned how the main criterion for the acquisition of citizenship and property rights in post-war Czechoslo-

---

8   Habel, *Dokumente zur Sudetenfrage*, pp. 494-495, Grundsatzpapier der Tschechoslowakischen (Exil-) Regierung für die Modalitäten des Abschubs der Sudetendeutschen, late May 1944.
9   Ibid., pp. 500-502, Memorandum of the Czechoslovak government-in-exile to the governments of the Allied Powers, 23 November 1944.
10 Karel Jech, ed., *Němci a Maďaři v dekretech prezidenta republiky: Studie a dokumenty 1940-1945* [Germans and Hungarians in the Decrees of the President of the Republic: Studies and Documents 1940-1945] (Praha, Ústav pro soudobé dějiny AV ČR, 2003), pp. 600-604, draft of an unpromulgated decree on the safeguarding of enemy assets of 24 May 1944.

vakia, *the concept of nationality,* was dealt with. Paradoxically, this concept, which determined the fate of millions of people, was not defined in the most important legislative texts such as the Citizenship Decree (No. 33). In internal government documents it was admitted that the absence of a definition of this key provision supporting the legal basis for expulsion was due to strategic considerations. The political actors were aware that they could never specify what constituted German nationality so unequivocally that it would apply to precisely those whom they wished to expel. They therefore sought to avoid a precise definition and in cases of doubt to leave the final decision on the matter to the Ministry of the Interior.[11] Such flexibility was felt to be necessary because, given the extremely mixed ethnic conditions in Czech border areas, it was not easy to distinguish Germans from Czechs in practice. It is one of the most remarkable incongruities of post-war legislation that, fully aware that "German" and "Czech" were not self-evident classifications, the authorities placed people of "German" and "Czech" nationality in two distinct categories with, correspondingly, completely different rights, without any clear definition of either term.

The second development that has so far attracted little attention is the special role played by agricultural property. In the case of the farming community, the determination to tie expropriation to ethnic criteria was even more uncompromising than in the case of non-agricultural property. Only those persons "who had participated actively in the struggle to preserve the integrity and achieve the liberation of the Czechoslovak Republic shall not be dispossessed of their agricultural assets."[12] This meant that even those Germans who were permitted to stay in Czechoslovakia and to keep their non-agricultural goods because they had "stayed true to the Czechoslovak Republic" would be deprived of their agricultural property if they had not actually participated in the armed struggle for the liberation of Czechoslovakia.[13]

This extreme ethnicization of agricultural property has to do with general questions pertaining to the Czech national historical narrative rather than the practical needs of the new legal order after the end of the Second World War. Since the 19th century, the Czech people had been defined above all as a nation of small farmers (in contrast to German large landowners and industrialists) and the sweeping confiscation of land that followed the Battle

---

11   Minister of the Interior, Václav Nosek, in: National Archives of the Czech Republic, Prague, 100/24, archival unit 1494, col. 137, record of the 30th meeting of the Czechoslovak government, 15 June 1945.

12   Drahomíra Palečková, *O konfiskaci nepřátelského majetku podle dekretu presidenta republiky ze dne 25. října 1945, čís. 108 Sb.* [On the Confiscation of Enemy Property on the Basis of the Decree of the President of the Republic, no. 108 of the Collection of Laws, of 25 October 1945] (Praha: Státní tiskárna, 1946), p. 43.

13   Ibid

of White Mountain in 1620 was held to be the primal national disaster. This played a fundamental role in preparing the first land reform undertaken after 1918, and there is abundant evidence that "redress for the White Mountain" was also the point of departure for the dispossession of German landowners after 1945. In this respect, therefore, it was also a question of completing the first land reform, which had essentially been directed against sizable land-owners from the nobility. In contrast to the situation after 1918, when aspira-tions to "redress the historical injustice suffered by the Czech people in the White Mountain period,"[14] were likewise referred to, after 1945 there were no longer legal obstacles at either the national or international level, with the result that "redress" could now be realized in radical terms.

CONCLUSION

The political upheaval that accompanied restoration of the Czechoslovak state can be interpreted as the culmination of the double ethnicization of two legal institutions: citizenship and property rights. In Bohemia before 1945, depri-vation of citizenship and dispossession as a result of ethnicity applied only to those persons defined as Jews by the National Socialist regime of occupation. In this context, the corresponding post-war attitude to German-speaking inhabitants can be seen as part of a continuing radicalization of society in the Czech Lands, both in legal terms and in regard to political practice.

The two ethnicization processes were interrelated in the sense that the criteria for withdrawal of citizenship and dispossession were similar. At the same time, the loss of both rights together did not occur as a matter of course. The nationalization of agricultural property in particular was as a rule more thorough and enduring than the rules on citizenship.

Whereas enjoyment of civil rights had to a certain degree depended on a person's mother tongue in the decades preceding the Second World War, by and large this applied less stringently than would later be the case; post-war legislation concerning people of German and Hungarian nationality in the re-established Czechoslovak Republic displayed aspects unprecedented at least in peacetime. They included, above all, the dispossession without com-pensation of entire national minorities. It was not until 1945 that the decision was made to confiscate without compensation the property of Germans who had not been subject to criminal prosecution. Another marked legal discon-tinuity, this time with the principles of citizenship, lay in the complete aboli-

---

14   Archiv Kanceláře presidenta republiky [Archive of the Office of the President of the Republic], Prague, KPR, Sg. D, Odpověď vlády na pozměňovací návrhy prezidenta republiky [Governmen-tal Reply to the Amendatory Proposal of the President of the Republic], 18 July 1945.

tion of the option for the German-speaking (and originally also Hungarian-speaking) population. That such an option clause for Germans not subject to criminal prosecution had still been provided for in the Košice government programme shows that, as with the question of expropriation without compensation, it had not been clear until the last moment whether this singular step would meet with international approval. The scruples about these issues that were still evident in the documents of the London government-in-exile reveal that the political actors involved were well aware that these two measures breached the framework of European legal development that had held since the 19th century.

THE CZECHOSLOVAK GOVERNMENT-IN-EXILE AND THE LEGACY OF POPULATION TRANSFERS: AN ANALYSIS OF THE ENGLISH LANGUAGE DISCOURSE

MARTIN D. BROWN

In comparison to the coverage granted the French, Polish and Yugoslav government-in-exile during the Second World War, the Czechoslovak government-in-exile, led by Dr Edvard Beneš, has had a more modest impact on English language histories.[1] There are two exceptions: the assassination of Reinhard Heydrich in 1942, and the forced removal[2] of the German-speaking populations[3] from the country after 1945.[4] Whereas our understanding of

---

1   Martin D. Brown, "Stanowisko Foreign Office wobec rzadów i komitetów na uchodzstwie w Wielkiej Brytanii podczas drugiej wojny swiatowej [Attitude of the Foreign Office to the Governments- and Committees-in-Exile in Great Britain during the Second World War]," in Radek Zurawski vel Grajewski, ed., *Rzady bez ziemi. Struktury wladzy na uchodzstwie* [Governments without Territories. Structures of Power in Exile] (Warszawa: Wydawnictwo DiG, 2014), pp. 329–48; Brown, *Dealing with Democrats. The British Foreign Office and the Czechoslovak Emigres in Great Britain, 1939–45* (Frankfurt am Main: Peter Lang, 2006), pp. 11–24; Vít Smetana, *In the Shadow of Munich: British Policy towards Czechoslovakia from the Endorsement to the Renunciation of the Munich Agreement (1938–1942)* (Prague: Karolinum Press, 2008), pp. 17–29.

2   For the purposes of this chapter, the phrase "forced migration/removals" is employed as an attempt at a "neutral" description of these events (see fn 6). See Alfred Rieber, "Repressive Population Transfers in Central, Eastern and South-Eastern Europe: A Historical Overview," in Alfred Rieber, ed., *Forced Migration in Central and Eastern Europe, 1939–1950* (Oxford: Oxford University Press, 2000), pp. 1–27; Alf Lüdtke, "Explaining Forced Migration," in Richard Bessel, Claudia B. Haake, *Removing Peoples: Forced Removal in the Modern World* (Oxford: Oxford University Press, 2009), pp. 16–22.

3   German-speaking population is here used in parallel with the Sudeten Germans of Czechoslovakia to denote the majority of the populations forcibly migrated, as opposed to the now commonly employed term "ethnic German." Given the history of the Bohemian Crown Lands, the implied association of the German-speaking population with Germany is at best tenuous if not misleading. This chapter focuses on the discourse surrounding events in Czechoslovakia, and not in Poland, Hungary or elsewhere. Eva Hahnová, *Sudetoněmecký problém: Obtížné loučení s minulostí* [The Sudeten German Problem: A Difficult Parting with the Past] (Ústí nad Labem: Albis International, 1999), pp. 60–81.

4   The two events are linked: the wave of violence which followed Heydrich's death, principally the obliteration of the village of Lidice, was later used in Czechoslovak propaganda to support and encourage the post-war removals of the German-speaking population. Some commentators have insinuated a connection between the assassination and these later events, suggesting Edvard Beneš intended the inevitable retribution to effectively end any possible post-war co-existence between the Czech and German-speaking communities. See R. M. Douglas, *Orderly and Humane: The Expulsion of the Germans after the Second World War* (New Haven, Conn. - London: Yale University Press, 2013), pp. 21–23; Jeremy King, *Budweisers into Czechs and Germans. A Local History of Bohemian Politics, 1848–1948* (Princeton: Princeton University Press, 2002), pp. 187–188. There is little evidence to support such supposition, but it is indicative of the tone of the discourse, cf. Brown, *Dealing with Democrats*, pp. 307–326.

Heydrich's life, career and death has been enhanced by recent works, the discourse surrounding the fate of Czechoslovakia's Sudeten German population remains more problematic.[5] Over the past 70 years rival historiographical interpretations of the forced removals have revolved around competing interpretations of the terms "expulsion" and "transfer."[6] While the majority of sources on this subject have been produced in either Czech or German, it has been English-language works that have greatly expanded the parameters of this public debate since 1989. Such works now refer to the "expulsion" of the Sudeten Germans and more recently to their "ethnic cleansing" (*avant le mot*) and genocide.[7] The term "transfer," as employed by the government-in-exile and the Allies, is rarely acknowledged as having any validity. George Orwell's seminal essay "Politics and the English Language" (1946) is partly to blame here, for in it he dismissed "transfer" as a euphemism.[8] While Orwell

---

5   Laurent Binet, *HHhH* (Paris: Grasset, 2009); Robert Gerwarth, *Hitler's Hangman: The Life of Heydrich* (London – New Haven, Conn.: Yale University Press, 2011); at the time of writing two new feature films about the assassination were in production, *Anthropoid* and *HHhH*.

6   Both terms are used in Article XII of the Potsdam Agreement of August 1945. At the time, "expulsion" referred to the "wild expulsions" of Sudeten Germans carried out across Czechoslovakia during the spring and summer of 1945, a period of disorganized, violent retribution. "Transfer" referred to the proposed organized removals to be carried out under international supervision and under the auspices of the Allied Control Commission that began in late 1945. Some 200,000 Sudeten Germans were given leave to remain, on political and other grounds, in Czechoslovakia after the transfers had been completed. For estimates of German speakers who remained in Czechoslovakia see, Karl Cordell and Stefan Wolff, "Ethnic Germans in Poland and the Czech Republic: A Comparative Evaluation," in *Nationalities Papers*, Vol. 33, No. 2 (June 2005), 255–276. It is important to note that these debates were primarily conducted in Czech and German and what little material was produced in English [principally Jaksch, *Europe's Road to Potsdam* and Luža, *The Transfer of the Sudeten Germans. A Study in Czech-German Relations*, published in 1963 and 1964 respectively and representing the rival interpretations] was often written by Czech or German speaking émigrés based in the West. As a result there are a number of terms in use, including: *Aussiedlung, odsun, divoký odsun, vertreibung, vyhnání* and *vysídlení, wilde vertreibungen*.

7   The linkage of these events to the term "ethnic cleansing" occurred post-1992 (see below): Robert M. Hayden, "Schindler's Fate: Genocide, Ethnic Cleansing, and Population Transfers," in *Slavic Review*, Vol. 55, No. 4 (Winter 1996), pp. 727–748; Donald Bloxham, "The Great Unweaving: The Removal of Peoples in Europe, 1875–1949," and Detlef Brandes, "National and International Planning of the 'Transfer' of Germans from Czechoslovakia and Poland," both in Bessel, Haake, eds., *Removing Peoples: Forced Removal in the Modern World*, pp. 167–207, 281–296; Alfred de Zayas, *A Terrible Revenge. The Ethnic Cleansing of the East European Germans, 1944–1950* (2nd ed., New York: Basingstoke, 2006); Jennifer Jackson Preece, "Ethnic Cleansing as an Instrument of Nation-State Creation: Changing State Practices and Evolving Legal Norms," in *Human Rights Quarterly*, Vol. 20, No. 4 (November 1998), pp. 817–842; Norman M. Naimark, *Fires of Hatred: Ethnic Cleansing in Twentieth Century Europe* (Cambridge, MA: Harvard University Press, 2001), pp. 3, 14; Steven Béla Várdy, T. Hunt Tooley, Agnes Huszar Vardy, eds., *Ethnic Cleansing in Twentieth-Century Europe* (Boulder: Social Science Monographs, 2003).

8   "[P]olitical language has to consist largely of euphemism, question-begging and sheer cloudy vagueness. [...] Millions of peasants are robbed of their farms and sent trudging along the roads with no more than they can carry: this is called transfer of population or rectification of frontiers [...]." George Orwell, "Politics and the English Language," in Peter Davison, ed., *The Complete Works of George Orwell, I Belong to the Left, 1945*, Vol. 17 (London: Secker & Warburg, 1998), p. 428;

undoubtedly had a point, his oft-repeated dictum ignores some key facts about the origins and development of the "transfer" concept.

This chapter will examine why the term "transfer" has been expunged from the English discourse and explain the current pre-eminence of the "ethnic cleansing" thesis. It will demonstrate that in its contemporary context "transfer" was not a euphemism, but rather a technical, legalistic term with a long, if controversial pedigree employed for the purposes of conducting international relations.[9] "Transfer" refers to a brutal method of imperial control imported into the European context. Yet it was legitimized by the Allied victors (and remains legally ratified[10]) and was substantially different from the forms of "ethnic cleansing" witnessed in the former Yugoslavia and Rwanda in the 1990s. This is not to reject completely the use of other terms, or to argue that one or other of these interpretations is wholly "right" or "wrong." Rather, it is to suggest that the current English discourse is flawed, and that any holistic understanding of the complex legacy of the policies of the government-in-exile on this issue should acknowledge and embrace this terminological dichotomy.

Increasingly accounts published in both the United Kingdom and the United States, for both general and specialized audiences, have begun to communicate this "ethnic cleansing" thesis to a global public. Collectively these accounts eschew a nuanced historical analysis of a complex discourse in favour of a narrowly conceptualized, geographically myopic, moralistic and sensationalist interpretation.[11] Such trends have coalesced into two re-

---

cf. Alfred-Maurice de Zayas, *The German Expellees: Victims in War and Peace* (Basingstoke: Macmillan, 1993), p. 34; Václav Havel (trans. Paul Wilson), *To the Castle and Back* (New York: Knopf, 2007), pp. 139–140.

9   These issues are usefully addressed in M. Frank's, *Expelling the Germans: British Public Opinion and Post-1945 Population Transfer in Context* (Oxford: Oxford University Press, 2008), pp. 1–12.

10   The question of the legality of the forced removals is much discussed, and while such acts would clearly be contrary to current International Law no judgement has yet found the transfers from Czechoslovakia to be illegal, irrespective of the morality of these actions. See fns. 30–31. Cf. Alfred-Maurice de Zayas, "The Legality of Mass Population Transfers: The German Experience 1945-48," in *East European Quarterly*, Vol. 12, No. 1 (1978), pp. 1–23; Douglas, *Orderly and Humane*, pp. 326–345.

11   The canon of work in English on the subject is broad and encompasses texts that range from the openly partisan and sensationalist, to the scrupulously researched and balanced. Nevertheless, the majority replicate the central tenets of the "expulsion"/"ethnic cleansing" thesis. These include a concentration on Edvard Beneš's role as the originator of the transfer plans, stressing the "rediscovered" nature of the subject, with less emphasis on the international Allied dimensions of decision making; some discussion of earlier incidents of forced population removals and little discussion of the "transfers" undertaken following the Munich Agreement in 1938; a focus on the "wild expulsions" of 1945, the associated violence in Brno or Ústí nad Labem, as well as the internment camps; identifying the German speakers as victims of collective punishment; discussion of the immorality or illegality of the transfer's and the associated decrees. These approaches also replicate the discourse conducted in Britain in the 1940s as the forced removals were being planned and executed. These features are especially apparent in work of the

cent high-profile texts by Anne Applebaum and Mary Heimann. These works present a narrative of the ethnic cleansing of Sudeten Germans triggered by resurgent "ethnic" nationalism that Beneš and the government-in-exile, with support from the Communists, duped the Allies into condoning.[12] In presenting this view, they ignore the long gestation of rival Czech-German nationalisms, comparisons with the use of population transfers elsewhere, and extensive discussions in Britain during the war over the utility of forced population removals, as well as the discussions over alternative post-war plans, such as the creation of European federations.[13]

propagandist Alfred de Zayas (cited above or below) and in Várdy et al., eds., *Ethnic Cleansing in Twentieth-Century Europe*, pp. 147–156, 474–484; cf. Hans Henning Hahn, Eva Hahn, "(Ne)patřičné poznámky k jednomu německému bestselleru. Alfred de Zayas o vyhnání Němců," in *Soudobé dějiny*, Vol. XVII, Nos.1–2 (2010), pp. 158–172; see also Otto von Habsburg, "Foreword," in Várdy et al., eds., *Ethnic Cleansing in Twentieth-Century Europe*, p. 5; Douglas, *Orderly and Humane*, pp. 1–6, 364–374; Benjamin Frommer, *National Cleansing. Retribution against Nazi Collaborators in Post-war Czechoslovakia* (Cambridge: Cambridge University Press, 2005), pp. 34–62; Hayden, "Schindler's Fate," p. 747; Norman Naimark argues the Poles had a rationale for their violent behaviour towards the German-speaking populations due to the brutality of the Nazi occupation while the Czechoslovaks did not as they suffered less under the occupation, Naimark, *Fires of Hatred*, p. 11. For references in the media [chronologically listed] see, Jolyon Jenkins, *The Sudeten Germans' Forgotten Fate*, BBC News, 7 February 2004, available at: http://news.bbc.co.uk/1/hi/world/europe/3466233.stm; R.M. Douglas, "The Expulsion Of The Germans: The Largest Forced Migration In History," in *The Huffington Post*, 25 June 2012, available at: http://www.huffingtonpost.com/rm-douglas/expulsion-germans-forced-migration_b_1625437.html; Douglas, "The Expulsion Of The Germans"; Colgate University professor R. M. Douglas discusses his book, 28 June 2012, available at: https://www.youtube.com/watch?v=V6UjtlHCXhA; Ondřej Horák, "Americký historik Benjamin Frommer se zamiloval do Čech. Vydal knihu o odsunu Němců," in *Online zprávy hospodářských novin* [Online news of an economic newspaper], 21 September 2010, available at: http://kultura.ihned.cz/c1-46520670; Peter Hitchens, "Orderly and Humane?," in *Daily Mail Blog*, 28 November 2012, available at: http://hitchensblog.mailonsunday.co.uk/2012/11/orderly-and--humane.html ; Paul Wilson, "Kicking the Germans Out of the East," in *New York Review of Books*, Vol. LX, No.9 (23 May – 5 June 2013), pp. 30–32; Director Peter Molloy, *1945: The Savage Peace*, broadcast on BBC 2 (24 May 2015), available at: http://www.bbc.co.uk/programmes/b05x30lb; as well as the relevant entries in *Wikipedia*: "Expulsion of Germans from Czechoslovakia," available at: https://en.wikipedia.org/wiki/Expulsion_of_Germans_from_Czechoslovakia; cf. Philipp Ther, *The Dark Side of the Nation-States. Ethnic Cleansing in Modern Europe* (New York: Berghahn Books, 2014), p. 8, 15, fn. 12.

12   Both Applebaum and Heimann reflect a far narrower version of the wider discourse, in line with their books' respective central theses, Anne Applebaum, *Iron Curtain. The Crushing of Eastern Europe 1944–56* (London: Allen Lane, 2012), pp. xxxvii, 124–135; Mary Heimann, *Czechoslovakia. The State that Failed* (New Haven, CT – London: Yale University Press, 2009), pp. 127–128, 140, 151, 155. Applebaum cites Heimann's work in her introduction.

13   A growing number of texts do make these comparisons explicit and include pre-20th century examples, which advocates of the "ethnic cleansing" thesis either reject, downplay or ignore: cf. Joanna De Groot, "Comparing Forced Removals," in Bessel & Haake, *Removing Peoples*, pp. 417–438; Mark Mazower, "Violence and the State in the Twentieth Century," *The American Historical Review*, Vol. 107, No. 4 (October 2002), 1158–1178; Panikos Panayi and Pippa Virdee, eds., *Refugees and the End of Empire: Imperial Collapse and Forced Migration in the Twentieth Century* (Basingstoke: Palgrave Macmillan, 2011); Philipp Ther, *The Dark Side of Nation-States. Ethnic Cleansing in Modern Europe* (New York – Oxford: Beghahn Books, 2014); Susan L. Woodward, "Genocide or Partition: Two Faces of the Same Coin?," in *Slavic Review*, Vol. 55, No. 4 (Winter, 1996), pp. 755–761.

While Applebaum's and Heiman's work does not reflect the entirety of the English language discourse (let alone the Czech or German), they borrow heavily from it and are wholly reliant upon it. Consequently we can make some broad generalizations about what they write, while acknowledging multiple other levels of scholarship on the subject. Alternative texts do address the issues listed above, but even these insist on labelling these events as a rediscovered history (it was never "lost" in Czech or German and has been widely discussed in English for over 20 years), stress "expulsion" and "ethnic cleansing" over "transfer," refer only tangentially to earlier population movements undertaken by the Nazi regime and others, focus narrowly on the events of the summer of 1945, identify the government-in-exile and Beneš as the sole originators of the transfer plans, and cite Article XIII of the Potsdam Conference.[14] As such they have adopted the politicized and polarized tone of the Czech–German Cold War discourse and projected it into the global public sphere. Less immediately apparent is why this restricted perspective has been taken. When the whole scope of English, Czech, and German literature on the subject is considered there are no "missing dimensions"; all the issues listed above have been thoroughly studied. This raises the question of whether these aspects have been accidently overlooked or intentionally ignored. The work of Applebaum and Heiman is thus emblematic of these analytical deficiencies and of the wider 70-year-old discourse.

After the Sudeten Germans were forcibly removed from Czechoslovakia and resettled in occupied Germany and Austria, parallel histories emerged, both of which claim to represent the "truth" about what happened.[15] Rival

---

14   Heimann claims it was Benjamin Frommer (2005) who was "[...] the first to bring the full horror of the 'transfer' to the attention of English-speaking readership [...]." See Heimann, *Czechoslovakia. The State that Failed*, p. 342-343, fn. 50, from: Benjamin Frommer, *National Cleansing. Retribution against Nazi Collaborators in Postwar Czechoslovakia* (Cambridge: Cambridge University Press, 2005), pp. 53-54. See also, Chad Byrant, *Prague in Black, Nazi Rule and Czech Nationalism* (Cambridge, Mas.: Harvard University Press, 2007), p. 210; Douglas, *Orderly and Humane*, pp. 2-4, 7-38, 93-129, 326-345, 348-362; Naimark, *Fires of Hatred*, pp.111-120.

15   A small selection of these include: Zdeněk Beneš & Václav Kural, eds., *Facing History. The Evolution of Czech-German Relations in the Czech Provinces, 1848-1948* (Prague: Gallery, 2002) pp. 210-233; Detlef Brandes, *Der Weg zur Vertreibung, 1938-1945. Pläne und Entscheidungen zum "Transfer" der Deutschen aus der Tschechoslowakei und aus Polen* (München: Oldenbourg, 2001), pp. 377-417; Byrant, *Prague in Black*, pp. 208-252; Frommer, *National Cleansing*, pp. 228-231; de Zayas, *A Terrible Revenge*, pp. 81-128; Eva and Hans Henning Hahn, *Die Vertreibung im deutschen Erinnern. Legenden, Mythos, Geschichte* (Paderborn: Schöningh, 2010); Hahnová, *Sudetoněmecký problém*, pp. 336-376; Radomír Luža, *The Transfer of the Sudeten Germans. A Study in Czech-German Relations, 1933-1962* (London: Routledge, 1964), pp. 277-292; Wenzel Jaksch, *Europe's Road to Potsdam* (London: Thames and Hudson, 1963), pp. 420-439; Josef Korbel, *Twentieth Century Czechoslovakia: The Meaning of its History* (New York: Columbia University Press, 1977), pp. 186-187; Tomáš Staněk, *Odsun Němců z Československa, 1945-1947* [The Transfer of Germans from Czechoslovakia, 1945-1947] (Praha: Naše vojsko, 1991).

mythological[16] interpretations were forged under the distorting influence of the adversarial politics of the Cold War. These contrasting versions of the past crystallized around two terms: "transfer" (which stressed the legality of this process and downplayed the associated violence) and "expulsion" (which rejected their validity, focused on the expellees as victims of collective punishment, and inflated the death toll). Both words refer to the same series of events, but their use indicates an adherence to differing politicized interpretations of what was presumed to have taken place.[17] During the Cold War these terms were divorced from their original contexts and, to put it crudely, "transfer" came to be associated with the left-wing version of history and the Czechoslovak state, and "expulsion" with a right-wing, anti-communist one aligned with the Sudeten German expellee organizations in West Germany. One notable aspect of this polemical debate was the argument over the associated death toll. Materials published in West Germany calculated over 250,000 deaths as a consequence of the removals (and some two million across the region). Radomír Luža, in a rare 1960s English-language work on the subject, challenged this total, but his recalculation was ignored until the late 1990s, when a far lower figure of around 30,000 emerged from official Czech-German discussions.[18] The figures remain the source of impassioned

16   Cyril Buffet, Beatrice Heuser, eds., *Haunted by History. Myths in International Relations* (Oxford: Berghahn Books, 1998), p. ix.

17   Martin D. Brown, "Forcible Population Transfers – A Flawed Legacy or an Unavoidable Necessity in Protracted Ethnic Conflicts? The Case of the Sudeten Germans," in *The Royal United Services Institute for Defence Studies Journal*, Vol. 148, No. 4 (August 2003), 81–87; Andrew Demshuk, *The Lost German East: Forced Migration and the Politics of Memory, 1945-1970* (New York – Cambridge: Cambridge University Press, 2012); Eva Hahn, Hans Henning Hahn, "'The Holocaustizing of the Transfer-Discourse:' Historical Revisionism or Old Wine in New Bottles?" in Michal Kopeček, ed., *Past in the Making. Historical Revisionism in Central Europe after 1989* (Budapest-New York: Central European University Press, 2008), pp. 39–58; Samuel Salzborn, "The German Myth of a Victim Nation: (Re-)presenting Germans as Victims in the New Debate on their Flight and Expulsion from Eastern Europe," in Helmut Schmitz, ed., *A Nation of Victims?: Representations of German Wartime Suffering from 1945 to the Present* (Amsterdam & New York: Rodopi, 2007), pp. 87–104; Bill Niven, "Implicit Equations in Constructions of German Suffering," in Ibid., pp. 105–123; Stuart Taberner, "Literary Representations in Contemporary German Fiction of the Expulsions of Germans from the East in 1945," in Ibid., pp. 223–246.

18   Společná německo-česká komise historiků [The Czech-German Joint Commission of Historians], *Konfliktní společenství, katastrofa, uvolnění: náčrt výkladu německo-českých dějin od 19. století* [The Conflicting Community, Catastrophe, Relaxation: an Outline of Presentation of German--Czech History since the 19th Century] (Praha: Ústav mezinárodních vztahů, 1996), pp. 29–30; For use of the higher totals see de Zayas, *Nemesis at Potsdam*, pp. 128–130; de Zayas, *The German Expellees*, p. 150; Niall Ferguson, *The War of the World. History's Age of Hatred* (London: Allen Lane, 2006), p. 584; Naimark, *Fires of Hatred*, pp. 119–120; Theodor Schieder, et al., eds., *Dokumentation der Vertreibung der Deutschen aus Ost-Mittel Europa*, 5 vols. (Bonn: Bundesministerium für Vertriebene, Flüchtlinge und Kriegsgeschädigte, 1953-1961); cf. Luža, *The Transfer of the Sudeten Germans*, pp. 293–230.

debate, and the huge disparity between the two totals is indicative of the gulf between these rival interpretations of the past.[19]

Importantly, this geographically myopic and polemical discourse was predominantly conducted in Czech and German, with little material (Luža being an exception) being communicated into English.[20] Exactly how this "expulsion" thesis was transmitted into English-language historiography is rarely considered in depth, and yet it is relatively easy to chart. One strand of this process can be traced back to the formation in the 1950s of various Sudeten German expellee organizations in West Germany, which began to formulate and disseminate their version of history via their own academic institutions with state support. [21] This history cast the German speakers as

---

19   See, the website of *Die Sudetendeutsche Landsmannschaft*: Missachtung ihres Selbstbestim-
      mungsrechtes – Die Tragik der Sudetendeutschen: http://www.sudeten.de/cms/?Historie:1919
      _-_1945#Opfer. Link no longer works.

20   Prior to the 1990s, English language references to the "expulsion" or "transfer" of the Sude-
      ten Germans were somewhat rare, giving rise to the "rediscovered history" thesis. Important-
      ly there had been extensive public debates in Britain as early as 1940 over the question of the
      utility and morality of "transfer" and possible alternatives, such as pan-European federations,
      see Martin D. Brown, "Desperackie lekarstwo. Brytyjskie Ministerstwo Spraw Zagranicznych,
      Wenzel Jaksch i kwestia sudetoniemiecka (pazdziernik 1938 – grudzien 1945)" ["Desperate
      Medicine. The British Foreign Office, Wenzel Jaksch and the Sudeten German Question (October
      1938 – December 1945)]," in *Przeglad Zachodni* [Western Survey], Vol. 327, No. 2 (2008), 45–70;
      Douglas, *Orderly and Humane*, pp. 85–94. For other references see A. De Zayas, *Nemesis at Pots-
      dam. The Anglo-Americans and the Expulsion of the Germans* (London: Routledge, 1979); Timothy
      Garton Ash, *The Uses of Adversity. Essays on the Fate of Central Europe* (Cambridge: Cambridge Uni-
      versity Press, 1989), p. 60, 167; Jaksch, *Europe's Road to Potsdam*; Luža, *The Transfer of the Sudeten
      Germans*; Victor S. Mamatey, Radomír Luža, eds., *A History of the Czechoslovak Republic, 1918–1948*
      (Princeton: Princeton University Press, 1973), pp. 416–427; M. J. Proudfoot, *European Refugees,
      1939–52. A Study in Forced Population Movement* (London: Faber and Faber, 1957); Hugh Seton Wat-
      son, *The East European Revolution* (London: Methuen, 1952), pp. 180, 360–361; Idem, "Conflict in
      Bohemia," in *The Times Literary Supplement*, No. 3936 (19 August 1977), p. 1001; Idem, "Introduc-
      tion," in Hubert Ripka, *Eastern Europe in the Post-war World* (London: Methuen, 1961), pp. viii–ix;
      Joseph B. Schechtman, *European Population Transfers* (Oxford: Oxford University Press, 1946);
      Idem, *Postwar Population Transfers in Europe 1945–1955* (Philadelphia: University or Pennsylvania
      Press, 1962).

21   Pertti Ahonen, *After the Expulsion. West Germany and Eastern Europe, 1945–1990* (Oxford: Oxford
      University Press, 2003); Ian Connor, *Refugees and Expellees in Post-War Germany* (Manchester:
      Manchester University Press, 2007); Ingo Haar, Michael Fahlbusch, eds., *German Scholars and
      Ethnic Cleansing, 1920–1945* (New York – Oxford, Berghahn Books, 2006), pp. vii–xviii, 1–21; Eva
      Hahn & Hans Henning Hahn, "Between 'Heimat' and 'Expulsion': The Construction of the Sude-
      ten German 'Volksgruppe' in Postwar Germany," in Eleonore C. M. Breuning, Jill Lewis, Gareth
      Pritchard, eds., *Power and the People. A Social History of Central European Politics, 1945–56* (Man-
      chester: Manchester University Press, 2005), pp. 79–95; Václav Houžvička, *Czechs and Germans
      1848–2004. The Sudeten Question and the Transformation of Central Europe* (Prague: Karolinum
      Press, 2015); Gilad Margalit, "The Foreign Policy of the German Sudeten Council and Hans-
      Christoph Seebohm, 1956–1964," in *Central European History*, Vol. 43, No. 3 (September 2010),
      pp. 464–483; Schieder, ed., *Dokumentation der Vertreibung der Deutschen aus Ost-Mittel Europa*.
      For an examination of the situation in Polish-German relations, see Jan M. Piskorski (trans.
      Andreas Warnecke), *Vertreibung und deutsch-polnische Geschichte: Eine Streitschrift* (Osnabrück,
      Fibre Verlag, 2005).

victims subject to an unjust collective punishment and inflated the death toll.[22] Understandably, such a perspective was rejected by the authorities in Czechoslovakia, who sought to justify the legislative basis for the removals and downplay the associated brutality.[23] Opposing theses were therefore adopted on either side of the Iron Curtain.[24] In 1951 the National Committee for a Free Europe (NCFE), a body created and funded by the American Central Intelligence Agency (CIA), encouraged anti-communist Czechoslovak émigrés in the west broadcasting on Radio Free Europe (RFE) to accept this emergent "expulsion" thesis, regardless of its veracity, in return for financing.[25] This first generation of Cold War emigrants, many of whom had been directly involved in the preparations for and removal of the Sudeten Germans, were reluctant, but the "expellee" version of history continued to be formulated and to find favour amongst anti-communist exiles.[26]

Conversely, a later generation of Czechoslovak dissidents willingly accepted this interpretation, which was directly opposed to the "transfer" thesis upheld by the communist authorities in Prague. The resulting discussions on the transfers (*diskuse o odsunu*) were sparked by a series of *samizdat* works and led many dissidents, most importantly Václav Havel, to accept the "expulsion thesis" outright, subsequently linking it to the communist takeover in 1948 - a perspective developed in conjunction with their own interests in a "totalitarian" and moralistic re-conception of the past.[27] (Havel and oth-

---

22   Ahonen, *After the Expulsion*, pp. 24–53, 92–200, 266–279; Mathias Beer, "Spannungsfeld von Politik und Zeitgeschichte. Das Großforschungsprojekt 'Dokumentation der Vertreibung der Deutschen aus Ost-Mitteleuropa,'" in *Vierteljahrshefte für Zeitgeschichte*, Vol. 46, No. 3 (1998), pp. 345–389; Martin D. Brown, Eva Hahn, "The Sudeten Dialogues," parts I and II, in *Central Europe Review*, Vol. 3, No. 16 (7 May 2001); Robert Moeller, *War Stories: The Search for a Usable Past in the Federal Republic of Germany* (Berkeley: University of California Press, 2001).

23   Bradley F. Abrams, *The Struggle for the Soul of the Nation: Czech Culture and the Rise of Communism* (Lanham, Md. - Oxford: Rowman & Littlefield, 2004), pp. 104–117, 156–177; Muriel Blaive, *Une déstalinisation manquée. Tchécoslovaquie 1956* (Brussels: Editions Complexe – IHTP, CNRS, 2005), pp. 133–138, 141–146; Frommer, *National Cleansing*, pp. 315–347.

24   This is not to suggest at all materials produced in Czech and German during the Cold War were simply propaganda, but rather that these early inclinations set the tone of the debate and continue to do so.

25   Francis D. Raška, "The Council of a Free Czechoslovakia, 1949–56," in *Acta Universitatis Carolinae - Studia Territorialia*, Vol. XII (2008), pp. 57–72, 68–69.

26   Houžvička, *Czechs and Germans*, pp. 362–368; Josef Josten, *Oh My Country* (London: Latimer House, 1949), pp. 60–62; Václav Houžvička, *Návraty sudetské otázky* [Comebacks of the Sudeten Question] (Praha: Karolinum, 2005), pp. 348–354; Frances Stonor Saunders, *Who Paid the Piper? The CIA and the Cultural Cold War* (London: Granta Books, 1999), pp. 130–132.

27   Applebaum, *Iron Curtain*, pp. 134–6; Bradley F. Adams, "Morality, Wisdom and Revision: The Czech Opposition of the 1970s and the Expulsion of the Sudeten Germans," in *East European Politics and Societies*, Vol. 9, No. 2 (1995), pp. 234–255; Bohumil Černý, Jan Křen, Václav Kural, Milan Otáhal, eds., *Češi, Němci, odsun. Diskuse nezávislých historiků* [Czechs, Germans, Transfer. A Discussion of Independent Historians] (Praha: Academia, 1990); Rudolf Hilf, *Němci a Češi: Sousedství ve střední Evropě, jeho význam a proměny* [Germans and Czechs: Neighbouring in Cen-

ers would later enshrine their perspectives into yet another state-approved version of "totalitarian" history.[28]) By the late 1970s, therefore, the two versions were well established, and the "expulsion thesis" began to be transmitted from German into English via the crusading propaganda work of Alfred Maurice de Zayas.[29]

With the collapse of the Soviet Bloc the "transfer" thesis lost some of its traction (but by no means all) and Havel, now President of the Republic, brought the "expulsion" thesis to the forefront of both the domestic and the foreign policy of Czechoslovakia (and of the Czech Republic after 1992). He also instigated attempts to bridge the gulf between these two state-sponsored interpretations.[30] However, efforts to "draw a line" under the subject faltered, while later negotiations over the Czech Republic's accession to the EU sparked yet more acrimonious disputes over the removals from both inside and outside the country.[31] Crucially, during these extensive discussions all three signatories of the Potsdam Agreement also restated their continued adherence to the terms of Article XII as part of the post-war settlement.[32]

---

tral Europe, its Importance and Metamorphoses] (Praha: Prago Media News, 1996), pp.183–202; Houžvička, *Czechs and Germans*, pp. 368–377.

28 It is interesting to note the overlap between those authors interested in promoting the "ethnic cleansing" thesis and the "totalitarian" school approach, especially as expressed in Applebaum's work: see Martin. D. Brown, "The Battle for History: Why Europe Should Resist the Temptation to Rewrite its Own Communist Past," in *EUROPP – European Politics and Policy, LSE*, 25 June 2015, available at: http://blogs.lse.ac.uk/europpblog/2015/06/25/the-battle-for-history-why-europe-should-resist-the-temptation-to-rewrite-its-own-communist-past/; Kristen Ghodsee, "Tale of 'Two Totalitarianisms': The Crisis of Capitalism and the Historical Memory of Communism," in *History of the Present: A Journal of Critical History*, Vol. 4, No. 2 (Fall 2014), pp. 115–142; George Soroka, "The Spotless Mind," in *Foreign Affairs* (14 July 2015), https://www.foreignaffairs.com/articles/europe/2015-07-14/spotless-mind.

29 De Zayas' work, which is openly and intentionally propagandistic, is widely cited and remains a key indication of the citing author's acceptance of the "expulsion" thesis. His perspective was also heavily influenced by the polemical debates in Britain in the 1940s, especially the writings of Victor Gollanz and F. A. Voight. See de Zayas, *Nemesis at Potsdam*, pp. xvii–xxiv, 103–124; Douglas, *Orderly and Humane*, pp. 343–344.

30 Havel, *To the Castle and Back*, pp. 139–140; Ladislav Holý, *The Little Czech and the Great Czech Nations: National Identity and the Post-Communist Transformation of Society* (Cambridge: Cambridge University Press, 1996), pp. 123–124; John Keane, *Václav Havel. A Political Tragedy in Six Acts* (London: Bloomsbury, 1999), pp. 467–472; Chad S. Peterson, *German Diplomacy in East Central Europe: Foreign Relations with the Czech Republic and Poland, 1990–1998*. Unpublished, Ph.D. thesis (London: London School of Economics, 2006), pp. 146–166; Michael Žantovský, *Havel: A Life* (London: Atlantic books, 2014), pp. 336, 372.

31 Timothy Burcher, *The Sudeten German Question and the Czechoslovak Relations Since 1989* (London: Royal United Services Institute for Defence Studies, 1996); Jürgen Tampke, *Czech-German Relations and the Politics of Central Europe from Bohemia to the EU* (Basingstoke: Palgrave Macmillan, 2003), pp. 143–155; A. Stroehlein, *Czechs and the Czech-German Declaration: The Failure of a New Approach to History* (Glasgow: University of Glasgow, 1998).

32 During negotiations over the Czech-German declaration (concluded in January 1997), and in response to suggestions the Czechs distance themselves from the "legality" of the Potsdam decisions, especially following comments by former Federal Foreign Minister Klaus Kinkel in the

Similar disagreements were still apparent during the Czech Republic's presidential elections in January 2013.[33] In response to these international developments, the Czech Republic and the EU recognized the continued legality of the presidential decrees (Beneš decrees) that had removed citizenship from the German speakers, sequestrated their property, and ratified their forced removal from the country.[34] Unlike the "ethnic cleansing" in Yugoslavia or Rwanda, the forced removals from Czechoslovakia, and its associated legislation, were internationally recognized as remaining "legal," irrespective of their morality.[35]

None of the above totally discredits either the "expulsion" or the "transfer" thesis, but it should be clearly acknowledged that both versions of the past were heavily politicized, and that they continue to be manipulated for political purposes. One of the most important consequences of these processes was that the "expulsion" thesis, as promoted by the "expellees" and by anti-communist Czechoslovaks, came to dominate western historiography.[36]

Frankfurter Allgemeine Zeitung (18 January 1996), the Czech Republic's Ministry of Foreign Affairs requested that the signatories clarify their positions, Britain, France, the United States of America, and the Russian Federation all responded: The note from the United States reads: "14 February 1996: The decisions made at Potsdam by the governments of the United States, United Kingdom, and the then-Soviet Union in July/August of 1945 were soundly based in international law. The Conference conclusions have been endorsed many times since in various multilateral and bilateral contexts. The Conference recognized that the transfer of the ethnic German population of Czechoslovakia had to be undertaken. Article XIII [sic, see fns. 38–45] of the Conference Report called for this relocation to be 'orderly and humane.' The conclusions of the Potsdam Conference are historical fact, and the United States is confident that no country wishes to call them in question. It would be inappropriate for the United States to comment on any current bilateral discussions under way between the Czech Republic and Germany." Dobroslav Matějka, ed., *Právní aspekty odsunu sudetských Němců* (Praha: Ústav mezinárodních vztahů, 1995), p. 103. The author would like to thank Ambassadors Jan Sechter and Jiří Šitler for their help in clarifying this issue.

33   Martin D. Brown, "History Is Too Important to Be Left to Politicians," in SSEES UCL Blog (10 July 2013), available at: http://blogs.ucl.ac.uk/ssees/2013/07/10/history-is-too-important-to-be-left-to-politicians/.

34   Ulf Bernitz, Jochen A. Frowein, Lord Kingsland, *Independent Legal Opinion on the Beneš Decrees and the Accession of the Czech Republic to the European Union*, DGIV working paper PE 323.374 (October 2002), available at: http://www.europarl.eu.int/studies/default_en.htm; Karel Jech, Karel Kaplan, eds., *Dekrety prezidenta republiky, 1940–45. Dokumenty* [Decrees of the President of the Republic. Documents], 2 vols. (Brno: Doplněk, 1995); Jan Kuklík, *Mýty a realita takzvaných Benešových dekretů* [Myths and Reality of the So-called Beneš Decrees] (Praha: Právnické a ekonomické nakladatelství a knihkupectví Bohumily Hořínkové a Jana Tuláčka, 2002); Emil Nagengast, "The Beneš Decrees and EU Enlargement," in *European Integration*, Vol. 25, No. 4 (December 2003), pp. 335–350.

35   See below for an examination of how the term "ethnic cleansing" entered the discourse.

36   Identifiable in the following: Applebaum, *Iron Curtain*, pp. 125–128; Michael Burleigh, *The Third Reich. A New History* (London: Macmillan, 2000), pp. 798–799; Norman Davies, *Europe: A History* (Oxford: Oxford University Press, 1996), pp. 1047, 1060; Douglas, *Orderly and Humane*, pp. 9–15, 36–38; Mark Cornwall, "Dr Edvard Benes and Czechoslovakia's German Minority, 1918–1943," in John Morrison, ed., *The Czech and Slovak Experience: Selected Papers from the Fourth World Congress for Soviet and East European Studies, Harrogate 1990* (Basingstoke – New York: Macmillan –

Western historians' presumed "rediscovery" of these forgotten events was largely based on the acceptance of a distorted and politicized discourse.[37] Demonstrating the influence of the "expulsion" thesis on English-language historiography is simple enough; a scan of the subjects discussed, as well as the bibliography, chronology and terminology employed will usually suffice.

One persistent inaccuracy is particularly emblematic of this dependency, and that is the suggestion that the "Orderly Transfer of German Populations" was sanctioned under Article XIII of the Potsdam Agreement of 1945.[38] In fact, it came under the terms of Article XII. This error is a consequence of the original release of the terms of the agreement in August 1945. At the time the Allies deliberately omitted several politically sensitive articles and reordered the numbering of the remaining sections, and as a result Article XII appeared as XIII.[39] The first published version differed from the agreement signed by the Allied leaders.[40] The complete text was belatedly released by

---

St. Martin's Press 1992), p. 188; R. Gerald Hughes, "Unfinished Business from Potsdam: Britain, West Germany, and the Oder-Neisse line, 1945–1962," in *The International History Review*, Vol. 27, No. 2 (June 2005), pp. 264–265, 285; Abby Innes, *Czechoslovakia: The Short Goodbye* (New Haven, CT – London: Yale University Press, 2001), p. 19; Heimann, *Czechoslovakia. The State that Failed*, pp. 150–161; Jeremy King, *Budweisers into Czechs and Germans. A Local History of Bohemian Politics, 1848–1948* (Princeton: Princeton University Press, 2002), pp. 189–198; Mark Mazower, *Dark Continent. Europe's Twentieth Century* (London: Allen Lane, 1998), pp. 220–221, fns. 12–13, p. 449; Timothy W. Ryback, "Dateline Sudetenland: Hostages to History," in *Foreign Policy*, No. 105 (Winter 1996–7), pp. 162–178.

37   Hahnová, *Sudetoněmecký problém*, pp. 23–59, 318–335; Houžvička, *Czechs and Germans*, pp. 443–466.
38   For a recent example see "Potsdam," by Michael Neiberg, review by Tony Barber, *Financial Times* (22 May 2015). When challenged over the use of Article XIII in his review Barber responded that as it was referenced in R. M. Douglas's book it must be correct. Dr Michael Neiberg confirmed that it was not. E-mail correspondence between the author and Barber and Neiberg, May 2015. See also Michael Neiberg, *Potsdam: The End of World War II and the Remaking of Europe* (New York: Basic Books, 2015).
39   American and German sources cite the correct wording of the paragraph of the Potsdam Agreement regarding the "Orderly Transfer of German Populations" but give the wrong number, listing it as Article XIII rather than Article XII. The Allies' published a censored version of the agreement in 1945, which omitted the original Article XIII dealing with the removal of oil equipment from Romania. American legal documents persisted in repeating this error, see Report of a Special Subcommittee of the Committee on the Judiciary, *Expellees and Refugees of German Ethnic Origin*, House of Representatives, 81st Congress, 2nd Session, Report No. 1841 (24 March 1950), Washington, D. C., pp. 5–8; "Report of Tripartite Conference of Berlin," in *The American Journal of International Law*, Vol. 39, No. 4 (October 1945), p. 256.
40   Cf. *The Times* (3 August 1945), this version had no article numbers; "United States, Great Britain, Soviet Union: Report of Tripartite Conference of Berlin," in *The American Journal of International Law*, Vol. 39, No. 4 (October, 1945), p. 256 – here it is listed as XIII; *Protocol of the Proceedings of the Berlin Conference* (His Majesty's Stationery Office, Cmd. 7087, Misc. No. 6 – 1947), p. 13 – the corrected final version, listed as XII. See also "Protocol of Proceedings of the Berlin Conference, July 17 – August 2, 1945. Department of State Press release, March 24, 1947," cited in Herbert Feis, *Between War and Peace. The Potsdam Conference* (Princeton, NJ: Princeton University Press, 1960), pp. 338–354; Luža, *The Transfer of the Sudeten Germans*, pp. 279–280. Applebaum cites the corrected version of the agreement, as XII, posted on Yale University's Law School's "Avalon" site: http://avalon.law.yale.edu/20th_century/decade17.asp; Applebaum, *Iron Curtain*, pp. 125, 521.

the American and British governments in early 1947 (by the USSR in 1955), in response to domestic pressure.[41] Documents published as part of the Foreign Relations United States (FRUS) series in 1960 also "appear" to replicate the same mistake, although a footnote clearly alerts the reader to the change in numbering.[42] German-language sources dealing with the expulsions have persistently referred ever since to "Article XIII," although historians referencing Potsdam in other fields do not.[43] While this error is not a major mistake as identical wording is quoted in both cases (and in the interests of full disclosure it is one that the current author has also made[44]), it is indicative of a lack of research triangulation and an uncritical reliance on secondary sources.[45]

Significantly, the "expulsion" thesis re-emerged into western historical discourse at around the same time as civil wars began in the former Yugoslavia in the 1990s. These two events coalesced and English-language sources began employing the phrase: "ethnic cleansing."[46] As might be ex-

---

41 *House of Commons Debates* (hereafter *HC Deb.*), 5th Series, Vol. 435, Cols. 833-835, 24 March 1947; The National Archives of the United Kingdom, London (henceforth TNA), Foreign Office files (henceforth FO) 371/55834, C 8892/2570/18, minute by B. Burrows in response to Lord Beveridge's written question from the House of Lords, 19 July 1946, C13890/2570/18, FO memorandum, 13 November 1946.

42 *Foreign Relations of the United States. Diplomatic Papers*, 1945, Vol. II, *The Conference of Berlin (the Potsdam Conference)* (Washington, D.C.: U.S. Government Printing Office, 1960), p. 1495.

43 Wenzel Jaksch, *Europas Weg Nach Potsdam. Schuld Und Schicksal Im Donaurum* (Stuttgart: Deutsche Verlags-Anstalt, 1958), p. 434; see also Feis above.

44 Brown, Hahn, "The Sudeten Dialogues," part I.

45 See Martin D. Brown, "The Diplomacy of Bitterness: Genesis of the Potsdam Decision to Expel Germans from Czechoslovakia," in *The Western Political Quarterly*, Vol. 11, No. 3 (September 1958), p. 624; de Zayas, *Nemesis at Potsdam*, pp. 86–89; Idem, *A Terrible Revenge*, p. 87; Douglas, *Orderly and Humane*, pp. 90–91; Hughes, "Unfinished Business from Potsdam," p. 264; Tony Judt, *Postwar. A History of Europe since 1945* (New York: The Penguin Press, 2005), p. 26; Mark Kramer, "Introduction," in Philipp Ther, Ana Siljak, eds., *Redrawing Nations: Ethnic Cleansing in East-Central Europe, 1944-1948* (Lanham, Md. – Oxford: Rowman & Littlefield, 2001), p. 30, fn. 24; Naimark, *Fires of Hatred*, p. 111; Jennifer Jackson Preece, "Ethnic Cleansing as an Instrument of Nation-State Creation: Changing State Practices and Evolving Legal Norms," in *Human Rights Quarterly*, Vol. 20, No. 4 (November 1998), p. 829; Malcolm Jarvis Proudfoot, *European Refugees, 1939-52. A Study in Forced Population Movement* (London: Faber and Faber, 1957), pp. 272–277; Joseph B. Schechtman, "Postwar Population Transfers in Europe: A Survey," in *The Review of Politics*, Vol. 15, No. 2 (April 1953), pp. 153–154; Staněk, *Odsun Němců z Československa*, pp. 90–92; Dariusz Stola, "Forced Migrations in Central European History," in *International Migration Review*, Vol. 26, No. 2 (Summer, 1992), p. 336; Tampke, *Czech-German Relations*, pp. 73, fn. 91; V. Walters, "On the Legal Construction of Ethnic Cleansing," in *Berkeley Electronic Press Legal Series*, paper 951(2006), available at: http://law.bepress.com/cgi/viewcontent.cgi?article=4600&context=expresso

46 The *Oxford English Dictionary* only added "ethnic cleansing" in 1992 and gives its earliest reference in English as 1991: "ethnic cleansing, n.," OED Online (June 2015), Oxford University Press, available at: http://www.oed.com/view/Entry/255528?redirectedFrom=Ethnic+Cleansing&. There are earlier references in other languages such as French, German, Romanian and Russian, see Vladimir Solonari, *Purifying the Nation: Population Exchange and Ethnic Cleansing in*

pected, the emergence of this novel term led to a scholarly discussion of its merits, definitions, and relation to the concept of genocide. Much of the debate revolved around the extent to which ethnic cleansing was an intrinsically modern concept caused by the dual effects of European nationalism and totalitarian ideology, as well as its utility in explaining earlier examples of forced population removals.[47] One of the earliest examples of its employment can be found in a 1993 *Foreign Affairs* article by Andrew Bell-Fialkoff (the same edition carried Samuel Huntington's "Clash of Civilisations") that referenced both the Nazi regime's pre-1945 and Czechoslovakia's post-1945 forced removal of populations as examples of the process.[48] In a later book-length publication, Bell-Fialkoff singled out the Czechoslovak example as a model case of successful population transfer.[49] Conversely, Eagle Glassheim later made a convincing argument that the period of the "wild expulsions" during the summer of 1945 does match the criteria of "ethnic cleansing." The evidence demonstrates that spontaneous murderous violence was perpetrated against the German-speaking population by a variety of state and sub-state groupings, and was widely encouraged by a variety of political figures, including Beneš and former members of the government-in-exile.[50] However, Glassheim concludes that the thesis is valid only if the wider pro-

---

Nazi-allied Romania (Washington, D.C: Woodrow Wilson Center Press, 2010), pp. xv–xvi; Ther, *The Dark Side of the Nation-States*, p. 4.

47   This is not to suggest that the term has no relevance or the debate no merit, but rather to question how relevant it is to the Czechoslovak case and whether its use owes more to academic fashion than established fact: Rogers Brubaker, David D. Laitin, "Ethnic and Nationalist Violence," in *Annual Review of Sociology*, Vol. 24 (1998), pp. 423–452; Carol S. Lilly, "Amoral Realism or Immoral Obfuscation?," in *Slavic Review*, Vol. 55, No. 4 (Winter, 1996), pp. 749–754; Drazen Petrovic, "Ethnic Cleansing – An Attempt at Methodology," in *European Journal of International Law*, Vol. 5, No. 3 (1994), pp. 342–359; Steve Smith, "Comment on Kershaw," in *Contemporary European History*, Vol. 14, No. 1 (February 2005), pp. 124–130. Niall Ferguson has attempted to argue that the entire twentieth century is best understood through the lens of ethnic conflict, Ferguson, *The War of the World*, pp. xxxiii–xli.

48   Andrew Bell-Fialkoff, "A Brief History of Ethnic Cleansing," in *Foreign Affairs*, Vol. 72, No. 3 (Summer 1993), pp. 110–121.

49   Andrew Bell-Fialkoff, *Ethnic Cleansing* (Basingstoke: Macmillan, 1996), pp. 215–243, 238.

50   Glassheim, "National Mythologies and Ethnic Cleansing," pp. 473–482; for details on the period see also Adrian von Arburg and Tomáš Staněk, "Organizované divoké odsuny? Úloha ústředních státních orgánů při provádění 'evakuace' německého obyvatelstva (květen až září 1945) [Organized Wild Transfers? The Role of Central State Authorities during Execution of 'Evacuations' of the German Population (May to September 1945]," part 1: "Předpoklady a vývoj do konce května 1945 [Preconditions and Development till the End of May 1945]," in *Soudobé dějiny* [Contemporary History], Vol. 12, No. 3–4 (2005), pp. 465–533; part 2: "Československá armáda vytváří 'hotové skutečnosti', vláda je před cizinou legitimizuje [The Czechoslovak Army Creates '*faits accompli*,' the Government Legitimates Them for Foreign Eyes]," in *Soudobé dějiny*, Vol. 13, No. 1–2 (2006), pp. 13–49; part 3: "Snaha vlády a civilních úřadů o řízení 'divokého odsunu,' [The Effort of the Government and Civilian Authorities to Manage the 'Wild Transfer']," in *Soudobé dějiny*, Vol. 13, No. 3–4 (2006), pp. 322–376.

cess of the organized "transfer" is ignored.[51] Herein lies the central problem with the use of "ethnic cleansing" to explain events in Czechoslovakia: the argument works only if we ignore or downplay the wider context beyond the summer of 1945 and the continued legality of the process.

Not all commentators agree with the term's use: Alfred Rieber argues that it lacks precision and has become a "weapon in propaganda wars,"[52] while Mark Mazower notes:

> "[...] the label "ethnic cleansing" has since turned into a means of attracting attention to and claiming significance for various more or less neglected episodes in the past. Yet the parallels with the Bosnian case are frequently less striking than the differences, and reveal the difficulty of making a hard and fast connection between organized violence, the homogenization of populations, and nation or state-building."[53]

Indeed, several problems can be identified in reference to the term's use in this case. First is the lack of a commonly employed definition. The definitions used vary dramatically, focusing on a dizzying array of factors and periods, resulting in a number of fuzzy, broad concepts.[54] Second is anachronism: while earlier examples of the use of the phrase "ethnic cleansing" can be found in various languages, these are sporadic, and only the Nazi regime rigorously employed the term.[55] The third problem relates to the pertinence

51 Glassheim, "National Mythologies and Ethnic Cleansing," p. 466.
52 Rieber, "Repressive Population Transfers in Central, Eastern and South-Eastern Europe: A Historical Overview," in *Forced Migration in Central and Eastern Europe*, p. 3.
53 Mazower, "Violence and the State in the Twentieth Century," p. 1163.
54 Bell-Fialkoff expands the term to cover all forcible population movements undertaken for ethnic, political or religious reasons across time, Bell-Fialkoff, *Ethnic Cleansing*, pp. 3–4, 40–49; Eagle Glassheim cites the United Nations' definition, UN Commission of Experts Established Pursuant to Security Council Resolution 780, *Final Report of the United Nations Commission of Experts Established Pursuant to Security Council Resolution 780* (1992): Annex Summaries and Conclusions, UN Doc. S/1994/ 674/Add.2 (Vol. 1), 28 December 1994, p. 17, in E. Glassheim, "National Mythologies and Ethnic Cleansing: The Expulsion of Czechoslovak Germans in 1945," in *Central European History*, Vol. 33, No. 4 (2000), pp. 465–466. Heimann uses ethnic and ethno-linguistic interchangeably and without definition, Heimann, *Czechoslovakia, the State that Failed*, pp. xxx, 2, 50, 66, 155, 158, 323. Michael Mann, relying on Naimark's work, stresses the modernity in concepts of ethnicity, but ignores the international dimension: "An ethnicity is a group that defines itself or is defined by others as sharing a common decent and culture. So ethnic cleansing is the removal by members of one such group of another such group from a locality they define as their own," Mann, *The Dark Side of Democracy*, p. 11, pp. 1–54; Norman Naimark links ethnic cleansing to genocide, on a sliding scale, and provides a very broad definition by citing R. G. Grillo, "Ethnicity arises in the interaction of groups. It exists in the boundaries between them," Naimark, *Fires of Hatred*, pp. 2–5, 108–122, 187, 189, 191–192. See also the discussion in David Wester Gerlach, *For Nation and Gain: Economy, Ethnicity and Politics in the Czech Borderlands, 1945–48*, Unpublished dissertation (Pittsburgh: University of Pittsburgh, 2007), pp. 5–12; Ther, *The Dark Side of the Nation-States*, pp. 1–8. Other authors such as Applebaum and Douglas provide no definition.
55 See Haar, Fahlbusch, eds., *German Scholars and Ethnic Cleansing*; Naimark, *Fires of Hatred*, pp. 4–5.

of employing a crude mono-dimensional differentiation of "ethnicity" to analyze the fluid nature of identity in the Czechoslovak context.[56] Fourth is the issue of legality: while they were demonstrably brutal, the "transfers" remain internationally recognized and approved, quite unlike the Yugoslav and Rwandan examples from the 1990s. Finally, there remains the issue of the total absence of the term's use in any of the Allied discussions leading up to the Potsdam Conference. None of these caveats precludes the use of the term "ethnic cleansing," but in the face of its ubiquitous and largely uncritical use, it is important to problematize and question its employment.

Significantly many English-language accounts, especially those of Applebaum and Heimann, which reject the concept of "transfer" also identify the origins of the plan to remove the Sudeten Germans solely with the Czechoslovak government-in-exile, and define it as an intrinsically modern expression of aggressive nationalism, therefore analogous to "ethnic cleansing" as per the 1990s debate.[57] As a result, the long gestation of the "transfer" process, and the role played by the British government and the other Allies in it, are downplayed or simply ignored, as is the fact that its employment predates Potsdam. So it is to a consideration of these issues that we must now turn.

The lengthy process that led to the wholesale "transfer" of the German-speaking minorities from Central Europe has been extensively researched and discussed, making the omission of this issue from many texts all the more conspicuous. Consequently there is no need to reiterate all the details here.[58] Nevertheless, by early 1945, as the Second World War drew to a close and before Czechoslovakia was liberated, the British government and their

---

56   Cf. Peter Demetz, *Prague in Danger: The Years of German Occupation, 1939–45: Memories and History, Terror and Resistance, Theatre and Jazz, Film and Poetry, Politics and War* (New York: Farrar, Straus & Giroux, 2008); Jan Křen, "Changes in Identity: Germans and Bohemia and Moravia in the Nineteenth and Twentieth Centuries," in M. Teich, *Bohemia in History* (Cambridge: Cambridge University Press, 1998), pp. 324–243; Elisabeth Wiskemann, *Czechs and Germans. A Study of the Struggle in the Historic Provinces of Bohemia and Moravia* (London: Oxford University Press, 1938), pp. 1–69.

57   Applebaum, *Iron Curtain*, p.128; Ahonen, *After the Expulsion*, pp. 1–2, 16–20; Bruce R. Berglund, "'All Germans are the Same': Czech and Sudeten German Exiles in Britain and the Transfer Plans," in *National Identities*, Vol. 2, No. 3 (2000), pp. 225–244; Mark Cornwall, "Beneš and Czechoslovakia's German Minority, 1918–1943," in Morrison, ed., *The Czech and Slovak Experience*, pp. 186–194; de Zayas, *The German Expellees*, pp. 27–31, 33; Douglas, *Orderly and Humane*, pp. 67–68; Glassheim, "National Mythologies and Ethnic Cleansing," pp. 470–472; Heimann, *Czechoslovakia. The State that Failed*, pp. 128, 160–161; Naimark, *Fires of Hatred*, pp. 108–116.

58   Beneš, Kural, eds., *Facing History*, pp. 116–191, 302–331; Brandes, *Der Weg zur Vertreibung*, pp. 171–206, 243–273, 290–314, 401–417; Brown, *Dealing with Democrats*, pp. 270–306; Douglas, *Orderly and Humane*, pp. 7–92; Luža, *The Transfer of the Sudeten Germans*, pp. 229–249; Karel Novotný, ed., *Edvard Beneš. Odsun Němců z Československa* [Edvard Beneš. The Transfer of Germans from Czechoslovakia] (Praha: Dita, 1996); Tampke, *Czech-German Relations*, pp. 73–94; Joseph B. Schechtman, *Postwar Population Transfers in Europe, 1945–1955* (Philadelphia: University of Pennsylvania Press, 1962), pp. 32–39, 55–79; Smetana, *In the Shadow of Munich*, pp. 273–302.

American, Czechoslovak, and Soviet Allies were in the process of agreeing to a "transfer" policy.[59] At the time this "desperate remedy"[60] had been accepted by all three members of the Grand Alliance as a *deus ex machina* solution to Central Europe's minority problems which was then perceived as having been among the war's main causes.[61] The Allies wanted definitive, legally negotiated solutions to Europe's frontier and minority problems, and they came to regard "population transfers" as the most expedient option on offer. Yet this policy had evolved over the course of the war, and various alternatives were considered. They eventually approved the forcible removal of the Sudeten Germans as part of an international settlement based on prior agreements with, and direct requests from, the Czechoslovak government-in-exile and others. So too, large numbers of German speakers were already on the move westward (along with millions of other displaced persons), encouraged by the collapsing Nazi regime to flee the approaching Red Army.[62] What was to follow was not simply an unexpected or arbitrary outbreak of ethnic nationalism, but rather a considered, brutal, and planned solution. It was a method which had been previously employed on numerous occasions, and the merits of which had already been much debated.[63]

Unquestionably the Czechoslovak government-in-exile provided the main impetus behind the execution of this solution, but this does not mean that it was originally their idea or that they developed it in isolation, as is so often suggested. Those texts that do attempt to trace the origins of "transfer" usually cite the Greco-Turkish "exchanges" of the 1920s as the model for what occurred,[64] yet this approach underestimates the longer-term genesis of these methods (and other far more murderous schemes) in European co-

---

59   TNA, FO 371/50658, U 3111/3/970, J. Masaryk to European Advisory Commission, 14 August 1945; FO 371/38946, C 16563/1347/12, P. Nichols to Foreign Office, Czechoslovak memorandum "The Problem of the German Minority in Czechoslovakia," 28 November 1944; FO 371/38946, C 16563/1347/12, Northern Department minutes, 3 to 12 December 1944, A. Eden to P. Nichols, 15 January 1945.

60   Archives of the Royal Institute of International Affairs (henceforth ARIIA) 20/11 J. D. Mabbott, unpublished study on "National Minorities," manuscript, 1940, section C, p. 5.

61   TNA, FO 371/24289, C 10776/2/12, W. Strang minute, 17 October 1940; Carlile A. Macartney, *National States and National Minorities* (London: Oxford University Press, 1934), pp. 421–422; Schechtman, *European Population Transfers*, 3–24, 451–479.

62   Eva Hahnová, "O antiruském stereotypu Goebbelsovy propagandy [On the Anti-Russian Stereotype of Goebbels' Propaganda]," in *Literární noviny* [Literary Newspaper] (2 March 2015), available at: http://www.literarky.cz/civilizace/89-civilizace/19398-0-antiruskem-stereotypu -goebbelsovy-propagandy; formatting in PDF of this URL; Alastair Noble, "The First Frontgau: East Prussia, July 1944," in *War in History*, Vol. 13, No. 2 (April 2006), pp. 208–210.

63   Brown, "Desperackie lekarstwo," pp. 64–69.

64   Frank, *Expelling the Germans*, pp. 16–25; Luža, *The Transfer of the Sudeten Germans*, pp. 249–251; Naimark, *Fires of Hatred*, pp. 110–111; Dimitri Pentzopoulous, *The Balkan Exchange of Minorities and its Impact on Greece* (London: Hurst, 2002), pp. 51–119.

lonialism.[65] The forcible removal and relocation of peoples also had numerous other antecedents; these included France's removal (*épuration*) of German speakers from Moselle and Alsace after 1918 as well as the British Peel Commission's consideration of the possibility of disentangling the Jewish and Arab communities in Mandatory Palestine.[66] The Third Reich, the Soviet Union, and the United States had also made frequent recourse to the obligatory re-settlement of peoples.[67]

The British Empire in particular had long experience of techniques required for the successful administration of subject populations, and these had frequently included the forcible relocation of recalcitrant natives. British (and English) methods had included the "plantation" of Protestants across Ireland and the later resettlement of rebellious Irish Catholics, as well as the forced removal of the Acadians from Nova Scotia in the mid-1700s, the Maasai in the early 1900s, the Chagossians in the 1960s, and even consideration of transfers in Northern Ireland in the 1970s.[68] Moreover, there

65 The strength of the connections between post-1945 population transfers and earlier colonial experiences is of course open to debate, but adherents of the ethnic cleaning thesis reject similarities to these earlier examples in order to focus on the modernity of the process, see Benjamin Lieberman, *Terrible Fate: Ethnic Cleansing in the Making of Modern Europe* (Chicago: Ivan R. Dee, 2006), pp. xii–xv; Mann, *Dark Side of Democracy*, pp. 34–54. See also Elazar Barkan, "Genocides of Indigenous Peoples: Rhetoric of Human Rights," and Isabel V. Hull, "Military Culture and the production of 'Final Solutions' in the Colonies: The Example of Wilhelminian Germany," both in Robert Gellately, Ben Kiernan, eds., *The Spectre of Genocide: Mass Murder in Historical Perspective* (Cambridge: Cambridge University Press, 2003), pp. 117–162; Mark Cocker, *Rivers of Blood, Rivers of Gold: Europe's Conflict with Tribal Peoples* (London: Pimlico, 1998), pp. 117–126, 150–153; Odd Arne Westad, *The Global Cold War. Third World Interventions and the Making of Our Times* (Cambridge: Cambridge University Press, 2005), pp. 396–397; Joseph Schechla, "The Ideological Roots of Population Transfer," in *Third World Quarterly*, Vol. 14, No. 2 (June 1993), pp. 239–275; Smith, "Comment on Kershaw," pp. 124–130.

66 Carolyn Grohmann, "From Lothringen to Lorraine: Expulsion and Voluntary Repatriation," in *Diplomacy and Statecraft*, Vol. 16, No. 3 (September 2005), pp. 571–587; Benny Morris, *The Birth of the Palestinian Refugee Problem Revisited* (Cambridge: Cambridge University Press, 2004), pp. 45–49, 56–57; Schechtman, *European Population Transfers*, pp. 454–460.

67 Frank, *Expelling the Germans*, pp. 29–38; Office of Population Research, "Transfers of Population in Europe," in *Population Index*, Vol. 6, No. 2 (April 1940), pp. 78–82; Terry Martin, "The Origins of Soviet Ethnic Cleansing," in *The Journal of Modern History*, Vol. 70, No. 4 (December 1998), pp. 813–861; Schechtman, *European Population Transfers*, pp. 27–353, 367–447.

68 TNA, Prime Minister's Office (PREM) 15/1010, Northern Ireland: Contingency Planning, Annex D – Possible Political Solutions, 23 July 1972, cited by M. Frank in author's response to Dr Alexander Clarkson, review of *Expelling the Germans: British Public Opinion and Post-1945 Population Transfer in Context*, (review No. 725), available at: http://www.history.ac.uk/reviews/review/725. See also Toby C. Barnard, *Cromwellian Ireland. English Government and Reform in Ireland, 1649–1660* (Oxford: Oxford University Press, 1975), pp. 10–11, 47, 74–75, 123; Nicholas p. Canny, *Making Ireland British, 1580–1650* (Oxford: Oxford University Press, 2001), pp. 121–242; John M. Faragher, *A Great and Noble Scheme. The Tragic Story of the Expulsion of the French Acadians from their American Homeland* (New York – London: W. W. Norton & Co., 2005), pp. 313–364; Lotte Hughes, *Moving the Maasai: A Colonial Misadventure* (Basingstoke: Palgrave Macmillan – St. Antony's College, 2006), pp. 23–58, 171–174; Mark Levene, *The Rise of the West and the Coming of Genocide. Genocide in the Age of the Nation-State*, Vol. II (London: I. B. Tauris, 2005), pp. 56–57; David Vine,

is evidence that the term "transfer" has its linguistic roots in these imperial "plantations." When the British first commissioned an investigation into the utility of "population transfers" in November 1939 (prior to any formal Czechoslovak proposals), it was revealingly titled "The Transplantation of Minorities."[69] Winston Churchill employed the same term in the House of Commons' debates in December 1944.[70] The origins of the term "transfer" emerged tangentially out of longstanding methods of imperial management and not solely out of modern Central European nationalism, as many claim.[71] Additionally, by 1939 the British government had already helped to pioneer the state-sponsored resettlement of peoples as part of the Munich Agreement, which explicitly used the term "transfer" seven years before the Potsdam meeting was even convened.

Under article seven of the Munich Agreement, which ceded control of regions of Czechoslovakia with a German-speaking majority (the "Sudetenland") to Nazi Germany, it was agreed that the signatories would facilitate "the transfer of population and settle questions of principle arising out of the said transfer."[72] This clause dealt with the tens of thousands of Czechoslovak citizens, both Czech and German speakers (thus not defined according to ethnicity), who had begun fleeing the border regions in the autumn of 1938 to evade the incoming Nazi administration.[73] When this mass movement of peoples was combined with earlier developments in refugee protection, as instigated by the League of Nations during the inter-war period, Neville

---

Island of Shame: The Secret History of the U.S. Military Base on Diego Garcia (Princeton, NJ: Princeton University Press, 2011).

69   ARIIA, Publications committee, agenda and minutes, 80th meeting, 19 November 1939.

70   Churchill's speech from 14 December 1944 is widely cited even though earlier British discussions over transfer are often not. In it he made reference to "disentanglement, expulsion, and transference," *HC Deb.*, 5th Series, Vol. 406, Col. 1484, 15 December 1944: de Zayas, *Nemesis at Potsdam*, pp. 82–83; Frank, *Expelling the Germans*, p. 95.

71   Cf. Bryant, *Prague in Black*, p. 211; Frank, *Expelling the Germans*, p. 16; Benjamin Fommer, "To Prosecute or Expel. Czechoslovak Retribution and the 'Transfer' of the Sudeten Germans," in Ther, Siljak, eds., *Redrawing Nations*, p. 222; Mann, *Dark Side of Democracy*, pp. 18–20, 34–54.

72   Llewellyn Woodward, et al., eds., *Documents on British Foreign Policy, 1919-1939* (henceforth *DBFP*), 3rd Series, Vol. 2, (London: His Majesty's Stationery Office, 1949), p. 628.

73   It should be noted that the flight of Czech and German speakers from the Sudetenland in 1938 was largely just that, they were not violently evicted in the same manner as German-speakers in 1945–1947. The exact numbers are disputed, these range from 92,000 to 800,000, and most fled the region as opposed to being forcibly removed; Imperial War Museum Archives, London (henceforth IWMA), Robert J. Stopford papers, RJS 04/14/1 2/1, unpublished manuscript, "Prague, 1938–1939, Part II," p. 6; Josef Bartoš, "Mnichov a československé pohraničí v roce 1938" [Munich and Czechoslovak Borderlands in 1938], in Karel Zelený, ed., *Vyhnání Čechů z pohraničí: vzpomínky* [The Expulsion of Czechs from the Borderland: Memories] (Praha: Ústav mezinárodních vztahů, 1998), pp. 16–18; Rick Fawn, Jiří Hochman, *The Historical Dictionary of the Czech State*, Historical Dictionaries of Europe, No. 72 (2nd ed., Toronto: Scarecrow Press, 2010), p. 163; Elisabeth Wiskemann, "Czechs and Germans after Munich," in *Foreign Affairs*, Vol. 17, No. 2 (January 1939), pp. 291–304.

Chamberlain's government found itself legally committed to assist with their resettlement.[74]

As bilateral discussions got underway, the government came under increasing pressure from a well-organized campaign, in the media and in political circles, to maximize these relief efforts. This lobby included journalists, Members of Parliament (MPs), and influential public figures motivated by what they perceived as the moral debt Britain owed to the Czechoslovaks because of Munich.[75] A voluntary organization called the British Committee for Refugees from Czecho-Slovakia (BCRC) was established in late October 1938.[76] Negotiations between British and Czechoslovak representatives culminated in the granting of a loan worth £8 million, and a cash gift (or "Gift Fund") of £4 million, to help with the resettlement of refugees from these border regions.[77] A British liaison officer, Robert Stopford, was dispatched to Prague to coordinate this process.[78] Between October 1938 and March 1939, the British authorities granted some 7,000 entry visas to refugees from post-Munich Czechoslovakia, assisted by the BCRC, nearly all of them German speakers and opposed to the Nazi regime.[79]

Some of these refugees were then resettled elsewhere in the British Commonwealth, specifically in Canada and Mandatory Palestine. At the same time, tens of thousands of Czech speakers from these border regions were resettled within the truncated, post-Munich, Czechoslovak state.[80] By

---

74 TNA, Cabinet files (hereafter CAB) 23/95 48(38), 3 October 1938; *HC Deb.*, 5th Series, Vol. 339, Cols. 462–464, 6 October 1938; Sir J. Hope-Simpson, *The Refugee Problem. Report of a Survey* (London: Oxford University Press, 1939), pp. 1–28, 191–261; Claudena M. Skran, *Refugees in Interwar Europe. The Emergence of a Regime* (Oxford: Oxford University Press, 1995), pp. 31–61, 71–73, 124–130, 205–214, 237–238.

75 TNA, CAB 23/95, 48(38), 3 October 1938, 49(38), 19 October 1938, 52(38), 2 November 1938, 55(38), 16 November 1938; 60(38), 21 December 1938; Treasury files (henceforth T) 160/1324 (Box 1), C 12975/11896/12 Memorandum by Sir John Hope Simpson, Chatham House, 20 October 1938; *HC Deb.*, 5th Series, Vol. 340, Col. 66, 1 November, Cols. 369–370, 379; Harold Nicholson, "After Munich," in *Nineteenth Century and After*, Vol. 124, No. 741 (October 1938), pp. 513–524.

76 TNA, Home Office files (henceforth HO) 294/39, The British Committee for Refugees from Czecho-Slovakia (hereafter BCRC), 1938–1939; HO 294/5, "History of Czech Refugee Trust Fund, 1939–1956"; *The Times*, 4 to 12 October 1938.

77 TNA, T 160/1324 (Box 1), C 13128/11896/1, Revised brief on refugees from Czechoslovakia by R. Makins, 31 October 1938; TNA, FO 371/22894, C 1128/3/12, Final text of Anglo-Czechoslovak agreement, 23 January 1939.

78 *HC Deb.*, 5th Series, Vol. 340, Cols. 77–79, 1 November 1938; Vol. 341, Cols. 1313–1317, 21 November 1938; Vol. 343, Cols. 25–26, 31 January 1939.

79 TNA, HO 294/44, R. Stopford memorandum "Situation of the British Fund for the Emigration of Refugees from Czecho-Slovakia, as at 13th May 1939," 19 May 1939; IWMA, RJS 04/14/1 2/1, "Prague, 1938–1939, Part II," p. 57.

80 TNA, CAB 23/96 49(38), 19 October 1938; CAB 23/99 27(39) 10 May 1939; HO 294/121–150 for a complete list of all the refugees' ultimate destinations; T 160 1324 (Box 1), C 713577/05/02, memorandum of meeting at the Dominions Office, 24 November 1938; (Box 2) C 15173/11896/12, minutes of meeting at the Dominions Office, 19 December 1938; Andrew Amstatter, *Tomslake. History of the Sudeten Germans in Canada* (Saanichton, B.C. – Seattle: Hancock House, 1978); Livia Rithkirchen,

using taxpayers' money to assist these refugees, the British authorities had assumed a financial and legal responsibility for their welfare.[81] In helping to remove both Czech- and German-speaking populations, the British government had unwittingly supported a rudimentary form of internationally sanctioned "population transfer" from the Sudetenland, and this is where the term employed at Potsdam originates.[82] British public support for the peoples forced from the Sudetenland in 1938 bears more than a passing resemblance to the later debates in Britain over the forcible removal of Sudeten Germans from Czechoslovakia in 1945, although this comparison and discussion of the Munich period are conspicuous by their absence from most sources.[83] These events also demonstrate that "transfer" cannot simply be dismissed as a euphemism or as a term developed by the Czechoslovaks to disguise "ethnic cleansing," but rather should be viewed as a term with a far longer history.

Indeed, as the Second World War began, the British government launched its own investigations into the potential utility of deporting populations, and commissioned the quasi-official Foreign Research and Press Service (FRPS) based at the Royal Institute for International Affairs (Chatham House), headed by Arnold Toynbee, to look into the matter.[84] These enquiries were carried out independently of the Czechoslovak émigrés, and long before Beneš first raised the issue with the Foreign Office or the government-in-exile was recognized. The process began with a research grant to Chatham House in September 1939 from the US-based Rockefeller Foundation. Part of this endowment was set aside for an examination into the aforementioned "Transplantation of Minorities."[85] This work was never carried out, but the FRPS undertook its own investigation into the issue. Written by Oxford academic John David Mabbott and entitled "The Transfer of Minorities," it was completed in late May 1940.[86] Not only did Mabbott suggest that forced deportations of

The Jews of Bohemia and Moravia: Facing the Holocaust (Lincoln – Jerusalem: University of Nebraska Press – Yad Vashem, 2005), pp. 77–82, 161–168.

81   TNA, CAB 23/100 37 (39) 12 July 1939.

82   Martin D. Brown, "A Munich Winter or a Prague Spring? The Evolution of British Policy toward the Sudeten Germans from October 1938 to September 1939," in Hans H. Hahn, ed., *Hundert Jahre sudetendeutsche Geschichte. Eine völkische Bewegung in drei Staaten* (Frankfurt am Main – New York: Lang, 2007), pp. 257–273.

83   There is no mention of these events to be found in Applebaum, de Zayas, Glassheim, Naimark, or Mann. Those who do mention it have little to say about the Czech and Slovak speaking refugees or "transfers," see Douglas, *Orderly and Humane*, pp. 14–15; Heimann, *Czechoslovakia*, pp. 92–94.

84   ARIIA 2/1/7a, Files on the formation of the FRPS and the Foreign Office Research Department (FORD), May 1938 to March 1943; HC Deb., 5th Series, Vol. 353, Cols. 1037–1040, 21 November 1939; McNeill, *Arnold J. Toynbee*, pp. 179–182. Cf. Douglas, *Orderly and Humane*, pp. 73–81.

85   ARIIA, Publications committee, agenda and minutes, 80th meeting, 19 November 1939.

86   The existence of these files was not revealed until the 1990s, R. W. Seton-Watson Archives, School of Slavonic and East European Studies, London (hereafter SEW), 13/1/1 J. D. Mabbott, "The Transfer of Minorities," 29 May 1940; Brandes, *Der Weg zur Vertreibung*, p. 20; Jan Rychlík, "Memorandum Britského královského institutu mezinárodních vztahů o transferu národnost-

populations were possible (highlighting that they had already been widely pioneered by the Third Reich, although omitting earlier British efforts), he also concluded that they were the most appropriate solution to a number of Central Europe's minority disputes.[87] In 1940 Mabbott's work had not yet been officially sanctioned. But, as Sir John Hope-Simpson of Chatham House later explained, it had been commissioned because of "a question asked by the Foreign Secretary. The study is thus confidential, but as you say it is immediately directed to 'influential quarters.'"[88] The evidence, such as it is, would imply that Lord Halifax had personally instigated the research.

The Foreign Office requested two further memoranda on the subject from Mabbott, and these were widely circulated within Whitehall.[89] As a result, the Foreign Office was well informed about the theory of "transfers" and the associated human costs that would accrue.[90] As Mabbott concluded in a related text:

"There can be little doubt that, however well conducted any such movement may be, it is fundamentally cruel and inhuman. [...] Only if nationalism returns in its most rabid forms or if for historical or other reasons there is no chance whatever of a co-operative spirit being achieved between majority and minority should such a *desperate remedy* be adopted [italics added]."[91]

The British authorities had no illusions, at any stage, about the "transfers" being "orderly and humane." By July 1942, the British Cabinet had decided that the above criteria had been met (at least "in principle"), in the case of the Sudeten Germans (and with an eye to resolving the complex issue of the frontier between Germany and Poland). It was a decision taken in the wake of the assassination of Heydrich and the retribution meted out on the towns of Lidice and Ležáky, events that were themselves used to stoke anti-German sentiments after the war. Equally important, we now know that Beneš acquired a copy of Mabbott's first memorandum, and similarities between it

ních menšin z roku 1940 [Memorandum of the British Royal Institute of International Affairs on the Transfer of National Minorities Dated 1940]," in *Český časopis historický* [Czech Historical Journal], Vol. 4, No. 91 (1993), pp. 612–631.

87 ARIIA, 20/1, J. D. Mabbott, unpublished study on "National Minorities," correspondence, 1940–1942. Confidential minutes of meetings held on 20 and 24 May 1940; SEW 13/1/1, Mabbott, "The Transfer of Minorities," pp. 1–3, 10–25.

88 ARIIA, 20/11, Hope Simpson to M. Cleeve, 15 June 1940.

89 TNA, FO 371/30930, C 2167/241/18, A. Toynbee to N. B. Ronald, Foreign Office, "Memoranda on Frontiers of European Confederations and the Transfer of German Populations," 12 February 1942, C 2167/241/18, Harrison minute, 2 March 1942, F. K. Roberts minute, 2 March 1942, Gladwyn Jebb to Toynbee, 10 August 1942; FO 371/39012, C 17689/184/62, J. D. Mabbott to Central Department, 14 December 1944.

90 FO 371/47085, N 3308/207/12, O. Harvey minute, 30 March 1945.

91 ARIIA, 20/11, J. D. Mabbott, unpublished "National Minorities" manuscript, section C, pp. 2, 5.

and the Czechoslovak government-in-exile's evolving "transfer" plans can be identified. A direct correlation between the two proposals has yet to be proven beyond a doubt, but it seems reasonable to suggest that Beneš used Mabbott's paper to help produce a credible policy that would be acceptable to the British authorities.[92]

The British government and its allies continued to examine the question of organized population "transfers" throughout the war in parallel to the Czechoslovak government-in-exile, and in conjunction with the possibility of establishing European federations. An Interdepartmental Committee on the Transfer of German Populations, headed by John Troutbeck, was established in December 1943 and submitted its report the following May. The committee also supported this solution to minority problems in Europe, and its recommendations drew heavily on Mabbott's work.[93] In July 1944 the Armistice and Post-war Committee chaired by the Deputy Prime Minister, Clement Attlee, examined Mabbott's report. They noted that "the amount of human suffering involved would be very great" and concluded that "transfers" should take place to enhance "peace and security" in the region.[94] It was with the establishment in late 1943 of the tripartite European Advisory Commission (EAC) – a body designed to deliberate plans for post-war reconstruction – that the "transfer" question became the focus of concerted Allied discussions and was finally acceded to in Potsdam.[95]

It should be made absolutely clear that the Foreign Office's involvement in the evolution of these "transfer" proposals was always peripheral to their eventual execution across Central Europe, and that the feasibility studies it commissioned did not automatically denote official British or Allied policy. Equally, possible Balkan, Central European and Danubian federations were also being discussed and, had these been enacted, they "may" have limited the scale of the transfers or possibly even prevented them from occurring.[96] That said, independent British consideration of the viability of "transfers"

92 Brown, *Dealing with Democrats*, pp. 271–281.

93 TNA, FO 371/34462, C14581/279/18, Minutes of 1st meeting of the Interdepartmental Committee on the Transfer of German Populations, 7 December 1943, 11 December 1943; FO 371/39092, C 5049/250/12, Minutes of 3rd and 4th meetings of committee, 11 April 1944, C 6391/220/18, final report of the committee, 13 May 1944, C 8654/220/18, War Cabinet Office "Transfer of German Populations" final draft, 26 June 1944.

94 TNA, CAB 123/235, Armistice and Postwar Committee, note for Deputy Prime Minister, C. Attlee, from Sir G. Laithwaite and Brigadier E. Jacob, 8 July 1944, agenda for meeting to be held on 20 July 1944.

95 TNA, FO 366/1331, X 12259/11509/503, On establishment of EAC, 1 December 1943; FO 371/50657, U 1021/3/70 Minutes of 7th EAC meeting with Czechoslovak representatives, 14 February 1945.

96 Neither of these alternatives is substantially discussed in the English language sources, instead they pursue a deterministic approach in which the forced removal is presented as the only outcome the Czechoslovak government-in-exile sought. Yet there exist a range of possible counter--factual alternatives.

was undertaken over an extended period, was influenced by British imperial experiences, was designed to "solve" Europe's minority problems, and developed in parallel to the Czechoslovak government-in-exile's schemes. Equally, the British authorities knew full well that the associated human costs would be extensive. Collectively the evidence demonstrates the centrality of an understanding of the term "transfer," as well as "expulsion" and "ethnic cleansing," to full comprehension of the historical context in which the forced removal of the German speakers of Czechoslovakia occurred. Unfortunately, such comprehension remains conspicuous by its absence from increasingly large parts of the English-language discourse, Applebaum and Heinmann being the most apparent examples.

On many levels the Czechoslovak government-in-exile proved reasonably successful in achieving most of its stated goals by the end of the war: Beneš and his colleagues returned to power in Prague, democracy was reinstated (albeit briefly), and the country's frontiers were restored.[97] The German-speaking minority, regarded as the cause of the country's dismemberment in 1938 and as enemies of the state, were removed under international agreement – achievements that stand in stark contrast to the fate of the Czechoslovaks' Polish colleagues and many other political organizations in exile. Yet this is not the narrative to be found in many English-languages histories today. Instead Beneš and his colleagues are accused of ethnic cleansing and genocide, and their fight for independence during the Second World War is recast as a toxic, immoral legacy. Viewed from the perspective of the 21st century, by which time the discourse had been thoroughly shaped by politicized state-sponsored accounts, it seems obvious that the forcible removal of the Sudeten Germans from Czechoslovakia was a vindictive collective punishment. However, such moralizing positions, as frequently taken by English-language sources, are anachronistic and obscure more than they reveal about the legacy of the government-in-exile and its policies. Tellingly, they offer no explanation of how the removals could have been avoided, what the credible alternatives were or quite how an "orderly and humane" outcome might have been achieved. This is not to ignore or attempt to justify the mayhem, murder, and violence meted out to German-speaking civilians and others, especially during the summer of 1945, or to downplay the trauma experienced by those forced from their homes during the subsequent organized "transfers," but rather to comprehend fully the historical context in which these events occurred.

"Transfer" was not a term designed to hide the reality of what was being proposed, and the Allies themselves had no illusions as to what it would actu-

---

97   Milan Hauner, "'We Must Push Eastwards!' The Challenges and Dilemmas of President Beneš after Munich,'" in *Journal of Contemporary History*, Vol. 44, No. 4 (October 2009), pp. 619–656.

ally entail. Rather, it was a process that emerged out of methods of imperial control, that had already been employed as part of the Munich Agreement, that had been repeatedly used by the Third Reich across its occupied territories, and that had been thoroughly considered by the Allies. As we have seen, the Czechoslovak government-in-exile and the Allies came to regard this "desperate remedy" as the most expedient solution on offer. Regardless of how cold-blooded and brutal the scheme might now appear, these "transfers" were designed to resolve Europe's minority problems and enhance regional security, and were couched in terms designed to reflect diplomatic niceties rather than objective truths. Although both the "wild expulsions" that took place during the summer of 1945 and the later organized "transfers" of the Sudeten Germans from Czechoslovakia were violent and brutal, they were part of an internationally sanctioned and supervised process, quite unlike the "ethnic cleansing" in Yugoslavia in the 1990s or the events in Rwanda in 1994. The fact that so many English-language sources now eschew any comprehensive explanation of the role of "transfers" in favour of the fashionable rhetoric of "ethnic cleansing" tells us little about the history of the events that took place after 1945 or about the historical legacy of Beneš's government-in-exile, but reveal a great deal about the resulting politicized discourse that has taken root over the intervening seven decades.

THE END OF THE INTERNATIONAL PROTECTION OF MINORITIES UNDER THE AUSPICES OF THE LEAGUE OF NATIONS[1]

RENÉ PETRÁŠ

Czechoslovakia between the two World Wars belonged to countries subject to the international protection of minorities applied within the League of Nations. The system of protection collapsed during the Second World War and the Czechoslovak exile contributed to its end.

Let us start with a brief description of the system for the protection of minorities and its impact upon Czechoslovakia.[2] Between the wars, this issue was of great importance for the republic. To indicate the legal context of that time it should be noted that the key Czechoslovak inter-war laws governing issues concerning national minorities within the state were drafted in compliance with the international treaty providing for minorities. Article Six of the Constitution should be mentioned, as well as the Language Act (*Jazykový zákon*) considered a key law by minorities. In addition, the respective clauses of the international treaty had precedence over national law, which was a concept scarcely comprehensible to most lawyers of the time. What was even more surprising was that almost identical obligations applied with respect to the whole of Central Europe and the Balkans.

A system for the international protection of minorities under the auspices of the League of Nations was in place. Minorities were entitled to raise their complaints at the international level; dozens of cases from Czechoslovakia were under consideration in Geneva, the seat of the League of Nations – in the 1920s 43 cases were submitted. The most frequent allegations by the German minority concerned the agricultural reform and its effect upon individual rights. There were also individual cases where, for instance, the state

---

1   This paper was drafted within the NAKI Project entitled "The legal status of minorities in practice and their development in long-term prospects" DF12P01OVV013 carried out at Charles University's Faculty of Law.

2   The author deals with this issue in many books and papers, such as René Petráš, *Menšiny v meziválečném Československu: Právní postavení národnostních menšin v první československé republice a jejich mezinárodněprávní ochrana* [Minorities in Inter-war Czechoslovakia: Legal Status of Ethnic and Language Minorities during the First Czechoslovak Republic and Their International Protection] (Praha: Karolinum, 2009); Idem, Práva národnostních menšin v justiční a správní praxi [Rights of Ethnic and Language Minorities in Judicial and Administrative Practice], in *Československé právo a právní věda v meziválečném období (1918–1939) a jejich místo ve střední Evropě 1* [Czechoslovak Law and Jurisprudence in the Inter-war Period (1918–1939) and Their Place in Central Europe] (Praha: Karolinum, 2010), pp. 485–514.

refused to award citizenship (Helene Neukirch) or a pension (the Lesonitzky case, which was quite embarrassing for Czechoslovakia), or where the state dismissed a civil servant (Johannes Löffler).[3]

The protection of minorities within the League of Nations may be perceived today as a common enough notion: the Czech Republic is subject to decisions made by the European Court of Human Rights in Strasbourg and has likewise to respect measures put in place by the Council of Europe, the UN and, naturally, the EU. However, at the beginning of the 20th century nothing like this existed. The international protection of minorities proclaimed by the League of Nations was quite a novelty within world politics and international law. Many countries including Czechoslovakia were compelled to accept international obligations to protect minorities at the Paris Peace Conference in 1919–1920,[4] although it was unclear at the time how the system would work.

The system for the protection of minorities, under the supervision of the League of Nations, the first international body set up to deal with political issues,[5] emerged after the First World War but it was built upon older traditions. These traditions differed from one another in many respects. Before 1919 the protection of minorities was not under the control of an independent (at least theoretically) organization but was the responsibility of states often directly involved in the question. From a more general perspective, minority protection dates back to the 17th century to the safeguarding of religious minorities.[6]

Certain aspects can be found in the Peace of Westphalia of 1648. However, the doctrine of international minority protection is generally considered to have started with the Peace of Oliva made between Poland and Sweden on 3 May 1660. The agreement included the ceding of Livonia to Sweden by Poland with the stipulation that in return Sweden would respect the rights of the Catholic inhabitants in the relinquished territory. Similar clauses, although with minor derogations, were incorporated into other treaties during the 17th and 18th centuries. It should be noted that the focus was not on the

---

3   Statistics in the book: Martin Scheuermann, *Minderheitenschutz contra Konfliktverhütung?* (Marburg: Herder Institut, 2000).

4   Harold W. V. Temperley, *A History of the Peace Conference of Paris V.* (London: Oxford University Press, 1921); M. O. Hudson, "The Protection of Minorities and Natives in Transferred Territories," in Charles Seymour, *What Really Happened at Paris* (New York: Charles Scribner, 1921), pp. 204-230; Christoph Gütermann, *Das Minderheitenschutzverfahren des Völkerbundes* (Berlin: Duncker Humblot 1979), pp. 17-29.

5   Jan Kuklík, René Petráš, *Nadnárodní integrace v Evropě* [Supranational Integration in Europe] (Luzern - Praha: Havlíček, 2007), pp. 62-104.

6   See e.g., G. E. Žvanija, *Meždunarodnopravovye garantii zaščity nacionalnych menšinstv* (Tbilisi: 1959); Patrick Thornberry, *International Law and the Rights of Minorities* (Oxford: Clarendon Press, 1992), pp. 25-37; Zdeněk Peška, "Historický vývoj mezinárodní menšinové ochrany před světovou válkou [Historical Development of International Minority Protection before the World War]," in *Zahraniční politika* [Foreign Policy], Vol. 2 (1929), pp. 1168-1182.

equality of a minority religious group but only on its tolerance usually in territories where state citizenship had changed.

Disparities in the legal position of various Christian denominations had disappeared in most European countries by the turn of the 18th and 19th centuries. As a result, the need to protect religious minorities, and if necessary to intervene on their behalf, gradually faded. However, in the 19th century, the significance of issues relating to ethnic and linguistic minorities began to increase. The year 1848 in particular is considered a turning point in Europe in this respect but religious differences still remained a thorny problem in many areas, most notably in the Balkans. With the Berlin Congress of 1878, which dealt with the collapse of the Ottoman Empire in Europe, the principle of minority protection was much further enhanced and refined.

The First World War, a few decades later, gave another substantial impulse to the development of minority protection. During the war several national movements became active and were inspired by the proclaimed right to self-determination. What soon became quite clear was that the new state frontiers would differ from those marking ethnic, language and religious borders; as a result, many new minorities emerged who were unwilling to resign themselves to their new status.

Despite different modes of creation, obligations with respect to minorities in the inter-war period, including those established in the late 1920s, resembled one another. These requirements can be divided into three parts. The first guaranteed certain basic rights, such as freedom and the protection of life, to all inhabitants of a state. The second contained provisions relating to the acquisition of citizenship, and this, in turn, was a pre-requisite for the third – and most important – section concerning the rights of citizens who differed from the majority in terms of race, language or religion, i.e., the rights of minorities proper.[7]

The first set of obligations relating to minorities was formed by peace treaties, which contained such undertakings, concluded during the Paris Peace Conference by the winning powers and the defeated states – Austria, Bulgaria, Hungary and Turkey. The second was composed of treaties regulating commercial transactions between the victorious powers and some of their allies – Poland, Czechoslovakia, the Kingdom of Serbs, Croats and Slovenes (after 1929 the Kingdom of Yugoslavia), Romania and Greece – in which

---

7   Harold W. V. Temperley, *A History of the Peace Conference of Paris V.* (London: Oxford University Press, 1921), pp. 112, 132–149; Pablo de Azcarate y Florez, *Protection of National Minorities* (New York: Carnegie Endowment for International Peace, 1967), pp. 7–8; Alois Hajn, ed., Problém ochrany menšin [The Problem of the Protection of Minorities] (Praha: Orbis, 1923), pp. 25–26, 237–256; Peter Mosný, "Československý menšinový problém v medzinárodných zmluvách po prvej svetovej vojne [The Czechoslovak Minority Problem in International Treaties after the First World War]," in *Právněhistorické studie* [Studies of Legal History], No. 31 (1990), pp. 152–153.

minority protection was set out in detail. The third was in the form of declarations on the protection of minorities made by some states before the Council of the League of Nations at the beginning of the 1920s as a pre-requisite
to joining the organization; the countries in question were Albania, Finland
(with regard to the Aland Islands), Latvia, Lithuania, Estonia and later also
Iraq (1932). The fourth but separate group comprised mutual (usually bilateral) treaties on the protection of minorities, and on other issues, entered
into by many, primarily neighbouring, states. The main significance of the
various agreements was that some legal statutes, specifying commitments
contained in the first three categories and, to a lesser extent, the fourth, were
placed under the supervision of the League of Nations. Thus a system of safeguards had been put in place under the tutelage of the League of Nations,
particularly the Minorities Department of its Secretariat in Geneva.[8]

In many countries the effectiveness of this system for minority protection was rather limited; however, in states, such as Czechoslovakia, where
complications arising from minority conflicts were imminent, governments
tended to agree with the rulings of the League of Nations at any price in order
to avoid a potential international dispute. At times the conspicuous concessions made by diplomats were concealed by individual governments so as to
avoid provoking nationalists in the majority community. This fact was well
understood by officials in the Minorities Department of the League of Nations'
Secretariat: they always preferred confidentially negotiated compromises to
an open airing of grievances which might give rise to public outcry and stir
up extreme emotions among nationalists from both sides of the divide.

The Czechoslovak Republic, for example, was successful in avoiding overt
consideration of complaints during the whole inter-war period, although
one case in 1936 was a narrow squeak when a German submission alleging
restrictions in public procurement with respect to armament supplies was
filed. When studying historical documents deposited in the Archives of the
Ministry of Foreign Affairs in Prague, the funds of the Second Section – the
League of Nations,[9] one can clearly see a grotesque disparity in the public and
private approach to minority affairs. On the one hand, there are the cautious
and confidential negotiations of diplomats fearful of conveying any grounds
for constitutional change. On the other, there are the official, self-confident

---

8   See René Petráš, "Mezinárodněprávní ochrana menšin po první světové válce [International Le-
gal Protection of Minorities after the First World War]," in *Historický obzor* [Historical Horizon],
Vol. 11, No. 1–2 (2000), pp. 31–40; Idem, "Mezinárodněprávní ochrana menšin [International
Legal Protection of Minorities]," in *Mnichovská dohoda* [The Munich Agreement] (Praha: Karo-
linum, 2004), pp. 363–371; in Slovakia particularly papers by Bohumila Ferenčuhová and Peter
Mosný.
9   Archiv ministerstva zahraničí, Praha [The Archive of the Ministry of Foreign Affairs in Prague],
II. sekce SN [the Funds of the Second Section – the League of Nations].

declarations by state representatives denying, until 1937, any threat minorities might pose to the very existence of the state.

A failure to take this essential difference into account has led some historians to underestimate the question of international minority protection. Indeed, it is surprising in this context what some states have acquiesced to regarding the situation of their minority. The case of minority schools in Albania, for instance, has been considered a precedent in international practice until today. The Albanian authorities closed private schools, which the relatively small number of children from the Greek community in the country were completely dependent on for their education. As a result, the League of Nations forbade the measure to apply to private Greek schools. This case is seen as the beginning of so-called positive discrimination in favour of minorities.[10]

A still legally disputed issue is when the inter-war system for the protection of minorities actually ended. The prevailing opinion suggests it was with the demise of the League of Nations, which to all intents and purposes ceased to function in 1939 although it was not until 1946 that its affairs were formally wound up. This was the year when, apparently, the force of treaties protecting minorities connected with the League of Nations terminated according to the principle of *"clausula rebus sic stantibus."* This term is interpreted as implying that the obligations contained in international treaties are no longer binding when a fundamental change of circumstances has occurred. Adherence to the provisions of such treaties, governing the status of minorities, continued to apply only in the case of Greece and Turkey, and also that of the Finnish Aland Islands.[11]

However, views on the question are far from unanimous; what is particularly contentious is determining when the system ceased to function.[12] The UNO (replacing the former League of Nations) has, for its part, put the principle of human rights protection in the topmost position, i.e., preference has been given to the rights of the individual over collective and group rights, and this is also the position when it comes to the protection of national minorities. This priority can be seen in the General Declaration of Human Rights adopted in 1948 which contains no single provision dealing with national

---

10   See http://www.icj-cij.org/pcij. Very important, too, for example is "Access to German Minority Schools in Upper Silesia." The main definition of minorities is in the "Greco-Bulgarian Communities" case.

11   René Petráš, *Cizinci ve vlastní zemi* [Strangers in their Own Country] (Praha: Auditorium, 2012), pp. 104–109.

12   Francesco Capotorti, *Study on the Rights of Persons Belonging to Ethnic, Religious and Linguistic Minorities* (New York: United Nations, 1979), p. 27; Patrick Thornberry, *International Law and the Rights of Minorities* (Oxford: Clarendon Press, 1992), pp. 113–117; Natan Lerner, "The Evolution of Minority Rights in International Law," in *Peoples and Minorities in International Law* (Dordrecht – London: Martinus Nijhoff, 1993), p. 86.

minorities.[13] As late as 1950 the UN officially refused to take over the minority obligations from the period of the League of Nations. The UN Secretariat declared that the force of the obligations had lapsed and that the UN had no responsibility in the matter.[14]

International statutory minority responsibilities might therefore seem to have been in effect until the end of 1950. During the Second World War, however, the governments-in-exile of Czechoslovakia and Poland vehemently refused to accept their continuing force. In practice, the system for the protection of minorities stopped operating when the activities of the League of Nations were frozen in 1939. Initially, this appeared a form of hibernation, but it soon became clear that the chances of reviving the system were minimal. It should be noted in this context that the Czechoslovak exile, and Edvard Beneš in particular, played an important role in the process. The Polish government-in-exile adamantly maintained that it would not uphold the treaty. The refusal by Beneš seems to have been even more influential: in January 1942 he designated the system of protection as broken without any chance of restoration.[15]

With the start of the Second World War, the system in place for the protection of minorities ceased to work. After the defeat of France in 1940, most of the European continent was under the sway of German and Russian totalitarian regimes, which meant in effect that minority protection advocacy was largely irrelevant. As the end of hostilities drew near, however, solutions to this sensitive issue were gradually tabled for consideration.

Perhaps surprisingly, but no doubt logically, Czechoslovakia played a significant part in the process. Only a few member states of the victorious alliance had obligations regarding minorities in the decades between the two World Wars. Those that did now faced complex political conditions in their homelands due primarily to the conflict between left- and right-wing forces, which in the case of Poland, Yugoslavia and Greece, led to civil war. Traditionally, Czechoslovakia had been numbered among those countries which exerted the greatest influence on the international minority protection agenda. Indeed, hardly any politician had more experience in the area than Edvard Beneš. In his capacity as Foreign Minister of the fledgling Czechoslovak Republic, Beneš had had an impact on the formulation of commitments regarding minorities during the Paris Peace Conference in 1919.

---

13   *Minderheiten – und Volksgruppenrechte in Theorie und Praxis* (Bonn: Verlag Wissenschaft und Politik, 1993), pp. 29 and elsewhere. Felix Ermacora, *Nationalitätenkonflikt und Volksgruppenrecht* (München: Bayerischen Landeszentrale für politische Bildungsarbeit, 1978), pp. 107 and elsewhere.
14   René Petráš, Helena Petrův, Harald Scheu, eds., *Menšiny a právo v České republice* [Minorities and Law in the Czech Republic] (Praha: Auditorium, 2009), pp. 75–78, 478–479.
15   Carlile A. Macartney, *National States and National Minorities* (2nd ed., New York: Russell, 1968), p. 505.

New approaches by the Powers to the question of minority protection were evident, most conspicuously in the case of the United Kingdom. Britain in the inter-war period had insisted on the enforcement of minority rights as a guarantee of peace; but this attitude underwent a radical change. In the first years of the Second World War, London had considered making territorial concessions regarding Czechoslovakia for the benefit of Germany. However, as a result of the increasing brutality of the Nazi terror, Whitehall's stance became more uncompromising. British politicians, it would appear, were influenced in this regard by their talks with Beneš. In 1940, the first reports drafted by the experts emerged; they emphasized that the system of minority protection had contributed to the destabilization of Europe and, as a result, to the outbreak of war. The studies referred to forced transfers in the past, particularly that between Greece and Turkey in 1923, which was originally thought to have furthered the establishment of peaceful relations.[16]

Political realism seems to have been the main inducement behind the new approach by the Powers, which subsequently led to agreement on the mass transfers of Germans in Central Europe. The prevailing opinion was that the key states involved – Poland and Czechoslovakia – would undoubtedly refuse to resume their commitments towards minorities after the War. This was certainly the case, particularly with regard to Poland, which actually renounced its obligations as early as 1934. The situation was critical and raised concerns that wild mass banishment or even annihilation of Germans might win out over organized transfers. Such a process, which would have been out of the control of the Powers, could have easily destabilized the whole of Europe. Indeed, attempts by the Powers to enforce minority protection might well have the opposite effect to that intended. It should be noted that at the end of the Second World War several massacres of minorities did in fact occur, especially in Poland and Yugoslavia, with a few also perpetrated in Czechoslovakia.[17]

In terms of international politics, the issue was essentially disposed of during the Paris Peace Conference in 1946. Hungary sought to introduce the question of minority obligations in her dispute with Czechoslovakia but the attempt met with rejection.[18] The authorities in Budapest had documents and arguments prepared, based on the existence of international norms establishing the rights of minorities. Czechoslovakia in reply maintained that

16   Jan Rychlík, "Memorandum Britského královského institutu mezinárodních vztahů o transferu národnostních menšin z r. 1940 [Memorandum of the British Royal Institute of International Affairs on the Transfer of National Minorities of 1940]," in *Český časopis historický* [Czech Historical Journal], Vol. 91, No. 4 (1993), pp. 612–631.
17   René Petráš, *Cizinci ve vlastní zemi*, pp. 152–159, 234.
18   Karel Kaplan, *Československo v poválečné Evropě* [Czechoslovakia in Post-War Europe] (Praha: Karolinum, 2004), p. 124.

the question of minority protection had been exploited by those opposed to the Republic and had been one of the reasons for the destabilization of Central Europe. Budapest found that, unlike the situation after the First World War, the Great Powers were unwilling to make any explicit provisions for the rights of minorities, or undertake to enforce the extensive regulations already existing, particularly in connection with Czechoslovakia, an allied country.[19]

The issue of international minority protection remained formally unresolved until 1950 when the UN officially discounted the notion of any inherited obligations in the area from the inter-war period. At the Paris Conference in 1946, however, it had already been clear that essentially the Great Powers were not interested in the topic. Pleas based on relevant inter-war minority treaties were usually ignored. Therefore, it may be claimed that the Paris Peace Conference of 1946 marked the *de facto* end of minority obligations originally adopted, ironically enough, during the Paris Peace Conference of 1919–1920.

19   René Petráš, *Menšiny v komunistickém Československu* [Minorities in Communist Czechoslovakia] (Praha: Eurolex Bohemia, 2007), pp. 99–102, 367–371. On the issue of the Constitution 1948, see René Petráš, "Constitutional Development in Czechoslovakia in the 1960s and Problems of Ethnicity," in *Czech Law between Europeanization and Globalization* (Prague: Karolinum Press, 2010), pp. 60–68.

IV. PROPAGANDA AND EDUCATION IN WAR-TIME BRITAIN

BRUCE LOCKHART, BRITISH POLITICAL WARFARE AND OCCUPIED EUROPE

RICHARD OVERY

In 1952, Robert Bruce Lockhart wrote that "Nothing in my life has affected me so deeply as the tragedy of the unfortunate Czechoslovaks."[1] The relationship Bruce Lockhart established with the Czechs was nevertheless an unusual one. The son of a Scottish headmaster, he joined the Foreign Office, was sent to Russia in 1918 where he was famously accused of plotting to assassinate Lenin, and eventually ended up as a junior diplomat in the British Embassy in Prague in the 1920s. He stayed in the Czechoslovak capital for five years before moving to Britain as a journalist specializing in the affairs of Eastern Europe. He had all the likes and dislikes typical of an upper middle-class British background. He enjoyed fishing, rugby and good wine, and carried with him a lifelong hostility to Communism (which he regarded as "more dangerous than Nazism"). But, that said, he believed that the Czechs had much in common with the Lowland Scots from whom he was descended: "They were a fine people, hard-working, highly-educated, rational, efficient."[2] His own books and papers suggest a man who was tolerant (to a degree), humane and upright, all virtues that manifested themselves in his dealings with Czechoslovakia.

Although he had retired from public life by 1938, the growing international crisis prompted the government to try to recruit Lockhart for a new political intelligence organization, in which his specialist knowledge of Eastern Europe, directly threatened by German ambitions for territorial expansion, could be mobilized to secure greater cooperation with Russia and a better understanding of the issues at stake. He accepted a position in the Political Intelligence Department of the Foreign Office offered him by Rex Leeper, head of the Foreign Office News Department, on 28 September 1938, the day the convening of an international conference to resolve the Sudeten German crisis was agreed.[3] This marked Lockhart's entry into a conflict in which he was closely involved until the end of the war in August 1945. Building on their experiences in the First World War, the Foreign Office and the Cabinet believed that good political intelligence was essential in helping to

---

1 Robert Bruce Lockhart, *My Europe* (London: Putnam, 1952), p. 87.
2 Ibid., p. 92.
3 Robert Bruce Lockhart, *Comes the Reckoning* (London: Putnam, 1947), pp. 10–13.

frame government initiatives and long-term political strategy, but it would take several years more before inter-departmental squabbles finally ceased and the setting up of an organization dedicated to achieving this end was approved. As a distinct form of warfare in its own right, it had no counterpart among the other major combatant powers in the Second World War.

Lockhart's area of expertise in the new Intelligence Department was changed during 1939 to Central Europe and the Balkans because of his experience there in the 1920s. In September 1939, he became Liaison Officer to the Czechoslovak leaders in Britain who had arrived in the wake of their truncated country being occupied and broken up by the Germans in March 1939. In December 1939, Lockhart was attached to the new Czechoslovak National Committee and in July 1940 became the British representative to the Provisional Czechoslovak government, by which time he had been seconded by the Foreign Office to join SOE under the Minister of Economic Warfare, Hugh Dalton, as an expert on Czechoslovak affairs. He found the work uncongenial, though he enjoyed his close contacts with prominent Czech exiles, particularly his friend Jan Masaryk and the Czechoslovak leader, Edvard Beneš. Much of his time was spent compiling detailed reports on the Czech economy, or statistical data on the occupied state, which seemed scarcely relevant. In December 1940, he complained to Dalton that he had "a wider, longer and more varied personal knowledge of European countries and leading personalities than most people," and asked to be given more challenging responsibilities.[4] His major ambition was to get the British government to recognize the Czechoslovak Provisional government as a national government-in-exile with full diplomatic honours. The Czechoslovak émigrés were understandably anxious to be given formal status. Masaryk asked Lockhart if the Czechoslovak airmen who had died fighting for the RAF should be regarded as only "provisionally dead."[5] Lockhart devoted a lot of time to lobbying in support of the Czechoslovak claim, which was finally acknowledged by Churchill's government on 18 July 1941, spurred on by the possible problems Soviet recognition the same month might pose.

Whether Lockhart's request for a more challenging role had been taken on board by the government, or whether he was generally considered to have the necessary experience and diplomatic tact, he was invited in July 1941 to chair a new executive agency serving an inter-ministerial committee which was to coordinate British overseas propaganda. The objective was to try to reduce duplication of effort among different ministries, which resulted in

4   The National Archives, London (henceforth TNA), FO 800/868, Lockhart to Dalton, 19 December 1940, Dalton to Lockhart, 22 December 1940.
5   Lockhart, *Comes the Reckoning*, pp. 118–119.

heated arguments about jurisdiction and responsibility.[6] By the summer of 1941, propaganda was dominated by two organizations, the Ministry of Information now run by Churchill's protégé, Brendan Bracken, which was responsible for "overt" propaganda, and the propaganda wing of the Ministry of Economic Warfare (SO1), controlled by Hugh Dalton, which covered "covert" or black propaganda. Both ministers were members of the new inter-ministerial committee. They were based in different locations, the Ministry of Information in London University Senate House, while the MEW, under the direction of Rex Leeper, was sited at Woburn in Bedfordshire 50 miles from London. Propaganda was also disseminated by the BBC which was expected to coordinate its broadcasts with the Ministry of Information but often failed to do so.[7] Lockhart was keen to involve the Foreign Office more fully so that he could move from rural isolation near Woburn to the centre of foreign affairs in London. As chair of the new executive committee he was also made a Deputy Under-Secretary at the Foreign Office as its spokesman for the propaganda effort, while the Foreign Minister, Anthony Eden, chaired the inter-ministerial triumvirate set up in July 1941.

Lockhart later wrote that he considered the establishment of his organization for political warfare "a thoroughly bad compromise" and deprecated his own appointment for a task for which he felt himself to be unfit and which meant he would have to "leave my Czechs."[8] The establishment of a joint organization for European political warfare did not end the wrangling between Bracken, Dalton and the BBC, and Lockhart found himself at the centre of a hegemonic storm that blew over only when Dalton was removed from the Ministry of Economic Warfare in February 1942 and the SO1 department was forced to collaborate with the London committee. Bracken became *de facto* master of what was now called the Political Warfare Executive (PWE), and Lockhart was appointed Director-General of the organization, with offices based in the BBC's Bush House building in Aldwych. The Executive was formally responsible for coordinating all European propaganda and political warfare and the inter-ministerial committee was abolished. This did not end the bureaucratic arguments entirely and it took time for the PWE to establish a working team. Lockhart found the work strenuous and the political arguments tedious and he suffered long periods of illness. He relied on

---

6   Michael Stenton, *Radio London and Resistance in Occupied Europe: British Political Warfare 1939-1943* (Oxford: Oxford University Press, 2000), pp. 23–28. See too David Garnett, *The Secret History of PWE: The Political Warfare Executive 1939-1945* (London: St. Ermin's Press, 2002), pp. 13–80 for a detailed history of the establishment of political warfare from 1939 to the summer of 1941. This reproduces Garnett's original report, written in or shortly after 1945.

7   Details can be found in Andrew Boyle, *Poor, Dear Brendan: The Quest for Brendan Bracken* (London: Hutchinson, 1974), pp. 270–3.

8   Lockhart, *Comes the Reckoning*, p. 117.

effective colleagues in the executive: Brigadier Dallas Brooks, who acted as an unofficial deputy and liaison with the Chiefs of Staff; Ivone Kirkpatrick, who as Bracken's appointee controlled the European side of the BBC; and the left-wing journalist Ritchie Calder, who was made Director of Plans and Propaganda Campaigns in August 1942, and also on occasion acted as Lockhart's deputy (though perhaps because of his political views, Calder was left out entirely from Lockhart's memoir of the war years).[9] Years later, Lockhart concluded that the personnel of the PWE were not "an easy team."

DEFINING POLITICAL WARFARE

There was no general consensus on exactly what the tasks of the PWE were, or on the precise definition of political warfare. In his memoirs, Bruce Lockhart defined it as "every form of overt and covert attack which can be called political," but this covered a wide range of possibilities, in terms both of policy and of operations.[10] The confusion was institutionalized in the physical separation of black propaganda, controlled from Woburn in the Bedfordshire countryside, and "white" propaganda and political warfare based with Lockhart in Bush House, in central London. Lockhart also recognized the persistent tension between the desire of the PWE officials to make foreign policy by propaganda and the insistence of the Foreign Office that propaganda should follow policy rather than seek to lead it.

The effort to define what was meant by political warfare began as soon as the original committee had been set up in the summer of 1941. Lockhart himself seems to have contributed little to the debate. Ritchie Calder played perhaps the largest part in getting the PWE team to define the nature of what they were doing. He saw little difference, as he told Rex Leeper at Woburn, between secret and open propaganda because in total war it all served the same purpose: "all propaganda, directed to the enemy or the people under enemy domination, is, in its ultimate analysis, subversive – aimed at producing disruption."[11] Calder instead defined political warfare as a two-pronged strategy of "morale making" and "morale breaking," the first directed at the occupied populations to encourage them to resist, the second aimed at the German people to discourage their war effort.[12] He argued strongly for politi-

---

9   Stenton, *Radio London*, pp. 37–9; Boyle, *Poor, Dear Brendan*, pp. 281–3, 286–9; Lockhart, *Comes the Reckoning*, pp. 151–4.
10   Lockhart, *Comes the Reckoning*, p. 155.
11   TNA, FO 898/305, Ritchie Calder to Rex Leeper, encl. memorandum "Operational Propaganda as Part of Political Warfare," 26 August 1941, p. 1.
12   TNA, FO 898/313, Ritchie Calder memorandum, "Bombing (Military, Economic and Morale Objectives)," March 1942, pp. 1–5, "Notes for Morale Bombing," 18 August 1941.

cal warfare to be integrated into the general strategic picture on the grounds that in total war there were in effect five fighting services, rather than three: "Military, Naval, Air, Economic, Political." He regretted the failure of the military planners to recognize what he called "the fundamental principle of cooperation" and the military usefulness of instilling either fear or hope in the populations of the war zone.[13] His idea that either breaking or sustaining morale was the key element of political warfare seems to have been generally accepted in the Executive. A long memorandum drafted in October 1941 by Rae Smith listed seven possible political objectives of which "build up morale" and "break down morale" were the first. But Smith was very attracted to modern psychological theory, particularly the work of the Swiss psychoanalyst, Carl Jung, and, more than Calder, hoped that the "power of suggestion" could be mobilized against the "subconscious mind" of the enemy. In November 1941, he added to the growing pile of definitions the concept of "psychopathic warfare," creating hypochondria or neuroses in the enemy using manipulative psychology.[14]

The debates through the second half of 1941 resulted in the drafting of a "Central Plan of Political Warfare" which was submitted to the Standing Ministerial Committee and approved on 6 January 1942. The starting-point of the plan was to direct all political energy to the defeat of Germany. Italy was regarded as a political target only to the extent that it could be separated from the German alliance. In this case it was assumed that "the natural disposition of the Italian people" coupled with economic crisis and defeat had already created the conditions in which an effective political warfare campaign could quickly drive Italy out of the war. Political warfare against the German satellite states in Eastern Europe was intended to drive a wedge between the Axis allies, while the political offensive against the German people themselves was to communicate the idea that Allied victory was "inevitable but not intolerable." The occupied states in the West were to be encouraged to find ways to "injure and undermine" the enemy in their midst.[15] In general this remained the agenda for political warfare over the course of most of the war period.

In May 1942, Bruce Lockhart was invited by the British Chiefs of Staff to attend one of their regular meetings so that he could explain what his Executive understood to be its purpose. Lockhart did not exaggerate the claims of his organization; its object was by a variety of means to destroy enemy morale and at the same time to sustain the resistance of the estimated 200 million people "under Germany's heel." After that Lockhart could not help

---

13 TNA, FO 898/24, Calder to Leeper, 26 September 1941, comments on the Joint Planning Staff paper "The Planning of Political Warfare," 23 September 1941.
14 TNA, FO 898/305, memorandum by Rae Smith for Leeper, "Some Notes on the Employment of Political Warfare," 30 October 1941, pp. 1–2, Smith to Leeper, 7 November 1941.
15 Ibid., PWE "Central Plan of Political Warfare for Europe," 6 January 1942, pp. 1–2.

returning to his Czechs. He argued that revolutionary activity was difficult with modern methods of physical control, but suggested that the Czechs were an educated and loyal people, who had developed a well-planned resistance compared with other occupied territories. Even here Lockhart understood the limits of any British appeal to dissenting activity and told the Chiefs of Staff that military successes were the key to raising the flag of European resistance: "Best facts are victories; best figures dead Germans."[16] The Chiefs of Staff broadly approved the programme and encouraged the PWE to stimulate resistance movements wherever they could and to conduct a propaganda campaign of "go slow" in the occupied territories as a form of passive resistance. [17]

This was the closest that the PWE organization came to achieving the degree of integration with Britain's overall strategy that Calder and others desired. It led on to a series of political initiatives designed to encourage all forms of resistance but the possibility of active opposition or sabotage remained the preserve of SOE and its separate organization. As the Allies began to take the strategic initiative, PWE found opportunities to collaborate with their American opposite numbers, the Psychological Warfare Branch (PWB), which was much more closely integrated with the American military effort. PWE officials joined the Branch in the Mediterranean where they collaborated on propaganda initiatives towards Italy in 1943. In preparations for the Allied invasion of France in 1944, a London Political Warfare Coordinating Committee was set up with representatives from the American Office of War Information, the Ministry of Information (PWE) and the American European Theater of Operations, but its role was largely to act as a clearing-house for ideas on propaganda while the real work in preparation for D-Day was undertaken at General Eisenhower's headquarters.[18] In October 1943, Brooks complained to Bracken that too much planning was now done independently in the different campaign theatres, but it was a trend difficult to reverse. PWE now had representatives at the Supreme Headquarters (SHAEF) where they conducted a campaign together with the Americans under General Robert McClure, head of the Political Warfare Division, an organization which relied less and less on what Bruce Lockhart and his team were doing in Bush House.[19]

---

16 TNA, FO 800/868, minutes written by Bruce Lockhart from meeting with the Chiefs of Staff, 28 May 1942.
17 Lockhart, *Comes the Reckoning*, pp. 182–3.
18 Daniel Lerner, *Psychological Warfare Against Nazi Germany: The Sykewar Campaign, D-Day to VE-Day* (Cambridge, MA: MIT Press, 1971), pp. 48–54. On setting up the committee see TNA, FO 898/372, Lockhart to Eden, 9 September 1943 and Robert Sherwood to Wallace Carroll (Director OWI), 5 September 1943.
19 TNA, FO 898/24, Brooks to Bracken, 24 October 1943.

A more fruitful area for the PWE in 1942–1943 was collaboration with the British Air Ministry. This came about not only because Bomber Command had responsibility for carrying and distributing the leaflets and newspapers designed by the political warfare agencies, but because from early on in its existence PWE officials had recognized the close links between bombing and propaganda. This was a connection that Air Chief Marshal Arthur Harris, Commander-in-Chief of Bomber Command from February 1942, did not entirely relish. He regarded the dissemination of what he described derogatorily as "pieces of bumph" to be a waste of his precious resources of airmen and aircraft.[20] The driving force once again behind the effort to link bombing and political warfare was not Lockhart, but Calder. The argument in favour of collaboration between bombing and political warfare was confined largely to the bombing of occupied Europe, which in 1941 and 1942 absorbed a considerable amount of Bomber Command's operational effort. For PWE, bombing had the advantage that it could demonstrate to occupied populations that Britain was still serious about the war against Germany, while leaflets dropped at the same time could drive home the message that working for the German war effort was dangerous now that the bombing offensive was speeding up and liberation coming a step nearer.[21]

By spring 1942, Calder claimed to have secured cooperation with the Air Ministry on a plan to integrate propaganda and bombing, chiefly against France, though the actual extent of the collaboration is not entirely clear.[22] In April 1942, Leeper asked Anthony Eden to get Cabinet approval for an increased bomber offensive against occupied Europe so that political warfare could be run in harness with bombing operations, and from the spring of 1942 the existing restrictions on attacking targets in occupied Europe were gradually removed.[23] PWE grasped at every piece of intelligence information from Europe to demonstrate that bombing had just the effects they hoped for in "bracing morale" among the occupied populations, though the longer the bombing continued and the heavier the casualties, the more difficult it was to conduct a political campaign to persuade allies that liberation was coming closer or that bombing was a worthwhile manifestation of Allied determination.[24] The link neverthe-

---

20   Lockhart, *Comes the Reckoning*, p. 171.
21   TNA, FO 898/313, Calder memorandum, "RAF and Morale-Making in Occupied Countries," 25 August 1941, "Notes for Morale Bombing," 18 August 1941.
22   TNA, FO 898/311, PWE memorandum, "Psychological Aspects of Bombing Policy during the Spring and Summer," 14 April 1942, Note by Richard Crossman for Anthony Eden, "Note on Proposal to Publish a List of RAF Targets over Germany," April 1942.
23   Ibid., Leeper to Eden, 13 April 1942. See too the discussion in Richard Overy, *The Bombing War: Europe 1939–1945* (London: Allen Lane, 2013), pp. 553–6.
24   On "bracing morale" see TNA, FO 898/311, Richard Crossman, note for Eden, April 1942, PWE memorandum, "Suggestions for Propaganda Basis to Maximise the Effect of RAF Attacks upon Targets outside Germany," March 1942.

less remained a close one throughout the war and was exploited more widely against the German home population by 1944. In July 1944, the PWE official Richard Crossman, now Deputy Director of Eisenhower's Political Warfare Division at SHAEF, argued for a close match between political aims for Germany and the pattern of strategic raids: "Allied air power is the one manifest demonstration to the German civilian of Allied material superiority and of the Allied determination to smash the German war machine." Crossman thought that propaganda should emphasize that the bombing would only end if the German people could begin "actively assisting in the destruction of the war machine which has brought all the evils upon them."[25] By November 1944, PWE supported the heaviest possible bombing of Germany to try to engender a fear in the German people greater than their fear of the Gestapo and the SS.[26]

CONDUCTING POLITICAL WARFARE

The best-known form of British political warfare was the radio broadcast. The decision to base the PWE organization at Bush House was to ensure that it was close to the heart of the BBC's European broadcasting unit. An early appointment by the then Minister of Information, Duff Cooper, of a Foreign Office representative to the BBC, Ivone Kirkpatrick, was designed to ensure that the BBC's foreign political propaganda could be integrated with the wider propaganda effort. Kirkpatrick became a member of the PWE in order to forge a personal link between the BBC European service and the organization for political warfare.[27] The broadcasting project promoted some rivalry and hostility between the professional broadcasters and those whose job it was to decide on the political message, but under Bracken as Minister of Information, the BBC officials found themselves compelled to accept direction from Lockhart's executive and the bevy of experts recruited for their knowledge about the different regions of occupied and unoccupied Europe. Broadcast propaganda was a gigantic undertaking. The BBC broadcast 160,000 words a day in 23 different languages, of which roughly one-fifth was targeted at Germany.

The second medium was the air-dropped leaflet or newssheet. This, too, was a prodigious effort. Over the course of the war 1.4 billion pieces of propaganda were dropped by air across Europe, 95 million pieces by balloon.

---

25 TNA, FO 898/340, memorandum by Richard Crossman, "Suggested Amendments to 'Propaganda to Germany,'" 5 July 1944.
26 TNA, FO 898/306, PWE "Political Warfare against Germany: The Next Phase," 14 November 1944, pp. 1–2.
27 Boyle, *Poor, Dear Brendan*, pp. 275, 281; more generally on links with the BBC see Stenton, *Radio London*, pp. 25–6, 33–36.

The chief target was Germany, where 757 million (50 per cent) were dropped; France received 676 million (it was close enough for regular air drops) but distant Czechoslovakia only 3.6 million, prompting Czech complaints about their neglect.[28] The pattern of distribution depended on geography, and more distant targets in Eastern and Central Europe could not be reached early in the war. When they could be reached by Lancaster or Mosquito aircraft, the priority was for bombing raids rather than leaflet drops. Great efforts were made to ensure that the leaflets reached their intended target area, and intelligence sources were scoured to see whether the leaflets had arrived where they should and what possible impact they were having. Given the prevailing weather conditions in Northern and Central Europe it was difficult to be certain that the propaganda would reach the hands it was destined for. PWE received approving letters from Switzerland lauding the British propaganda effort, but it was not an official destination.

Indeed, the leaflet-dropping balloon was the most unpredictable method of conveying propaganda. Experiments were carried out in England in 1940 to see whether balloon distribution would work. Postcards in different colours were dropped by balloon asking anyone who picked one up to send it, post free, back to the Air Ministry with details of where it had been found. In 1941 a special balloon unit was set up, codenamed "M," sending 200 balloons a night over France, the Low Countries and Western Germany. The balloons were made of rubberised fabric, were three metres wide and could carry a four-kilo load. A slow-burning wick was timed so that the string holding the leaflets would be burnt through at just the right moment and the load released. Dropped from 15,000 feet, the leaflets took an hour to reach the ground. Research soon revealed that the winds were too capricious for sending material to Germany, and the campaign was confined to France, Belgium and the Netherlands. Further investigation found that few of the leaflets destined for the Low Countries ever arrived and in February 1942 the PWE decided to suspend the balloon campaign as too unreliable.[29]

The campaigns of broadcasting and leafleting included not only the dissemination of news about the war, or propaganda contesting the claims of the enemy, but involved a number of defined political projects that continued across much of the war period. One of the first was the effort to incite what came to be called a "Peasants' Revolt" in the rural areas of occupied Europe.[30]

---

28   Leaflet figures from TNA, FO 898/457, "Annual Dissemination of Leaflets by Aircraft and Balloons, 1939–1945"; TNA, FO 898/318, Dr. Vojacek to PWE, 11 January 1943, Dr. Vojacek to PWE, 19 February 1943.

29   TNA, FO 898/460, memorandum by Capt. p. Ryder "'M' Unit," 7 October 1941, PWE to Ryder, 23 February 1942.

30   For details of the whole campaign see Charles Cruickshank, *The Fourth Arm: Psychological Warfare 1938–1945* (London: Davis-Poynter, 1977), pp. 113–21.

After an initial series of broadcasts in late 1940, a more concerted effort was mounted from 1941 with a dedicated "Peasant Programme" aimed not at the German countryside but at the farmers in occupied countries, who it was hoped might expand the black market and frustrate German plans to exploit foreign food resources.[31] Those responsible for the peasant programme recognized that any appeal to the peasantry had to recognize that peasants were "predominantly individualist and self-centred," and that any encouragement for them to resist the occupying power would work only to the extent that they saw some benefit to themselves.[32] In 1942, Lockhart criticized the current political propaganda directed at the farming community because it emphasized too much that Britain had become almost self-sufficient and that abundant food was going to flow in from the United States. These facts, he thought, would alarm the peasantry in occupied countries with the prospect that they would have no markets left after the war. Instead he recommended keeping quiet about Allied food supplies and emphasizing the revival of European agriculture after the war, perhaps more aware than his colleagues of European realities.[33]

There were advantages as well as problems in targeting the peasantry. Calculations were made to show that there was an inverse ratio between the number of radios owned and the size of the rural population. In Eastern and South-Eastern Europe some three-quarters of the population lived in the countryside, in Western Europe around one-third; but in Western Europe almost the whole population had access to a radio, while in Eastern and South-Eastern Europe radio ownership was negligible. It was decided that those most likely to have radios would be given "informative talks," while distant rural populations would get only "short slogans."[34] On the other hand, it was realized that peasants were good potential listeners because their radios were less likely to be jammed by German counter-measures, and there were no inquisitive neighbours as there were in towns. It also allowed PWE to send programmes very early in the morning when farmers rose for work, and a broadcast titled "Dawn Peasants" became a PWE project in 1942.[35] By this time more elaborate plans had been formulated to encourage a widespread "peasants' revolt" on the unproven assumption that "nine peasants out of ten are 'agin the government.'" One suggestion was the establishment of what

---

31   TNA, FO 898/338, memorandum by W. Klatt (PWE), "Ten Months of BBC German Peasant Propaganda," 23 September 1941.
32   Ibid., memorandum by W. Klatt, "What Do the European Peasants Signify in Regard to Britain's Political Warfare?" 25 October 1941, p. 3, Klatt to Calder, 6 September 1941.
33   Ibid., PWE minute by Bruce Lockhart, "Special Directive on Food and Agriculture," 1 August 1942.
34   Ibid., Klatt memorandum "What Do the European Peasants Signify," Appendix 1, Tables 1 and 2.
35   TNA, FO 898/338, PWE memorandum "The Peasant in Western Europe," 5 April 1943, David Garnett to Calder, 10 July 1942, "Dawn Peasants."

was called a "Green International" for orchestrating passive resistance to German occupation which might well have devastating results: "If the peasants do not cooperate, the war machine of the National Socialist dictators will one day just cease to function."[36] There was a good deal of fantasy in these speculations but peasant propaganda remained a major priority for PWE. On 23 October 1942 Bruce Lockhart finally approved a plan of action for rural propaganda which ran down to the last year of the war.[37]

A second important project was the appeal to those European workers forced to labour for the German war effort either in their own country or, as the war went on, as an exile workforce in Germany. This project was given the title "Trojan Horse" (since many of the foreign workers were inside the German walls) and it was sustained right until the end of the war. The initiative for the programme came from Calder who presented a paper in January 1942 suggesting that the propaganda used so far to try to dissuade workers in occupied countries from taking up employment in Germany should be replaced by the idea of sending "an 'Expeditionary Force' into German factories," where the foreign workers would try to undermine German support for the war effort from within. Calder's aim was to create solidarity between workers of all nationalities and to increase German mistrust of the factory workforce.[38] The immediate reaction at PWE was unenthusiastic. A note penned probably by Lockhart himself argued that it was inconsistent policy to now suggest that workers should go to Germany after all: "Our line so far has been to distinguish as black sheep those workers who went to Germany; it will be difficult to say that among them there may also be some heroic white sheep."[39] In May 1942, a PWE sub-committee on Propaganda Bearing on Germany's Manpower Crisis concluded that nothing would be gained for the moment from encouraging fraternization between German and foreign workers, since the latter almost certainly hated the former. Labour propaganda continued to focus on declining living standards in Germany.[40]

The strategy changed once it became evident how many foreign workers were being forcibly transferred to Germany by the efforts of the newly-appointed Reich Plenipotentiary for Labour Supply, Fritz Sauckel. By 1944 PWE had remarkably accurate figures on the total number of conscripted foreign workers and prisoners-of-war in the German economy; the aggregate number of foreign workers was estimated at 6.5 million, the number of POWs and

---

36   Ibid., Major J. Baker White to Calder, "The Peasant Revolt: A Thesis of One Aspect of Political Warfare," 13 February 1942, p, 1, Appendix 1, p. 2.

37   Cruickshank, *Fourth Arm*, pp. 118–20.

38   TNA, FO 898/340, minutes of meeting at SOE headquarters, 3 January 1942, p. 1.

39   Ibid., PWE minute "Foreign Labour in Germany," 4 January 1942.

40   Ibid., PWE sub-committee on Propaganda Bearing on Germany's Manpower Shortage, Interim Report, 12 May 1942, pp. 1–2.

concentration camp labour at just over two million, both figures close to the reality.[41] In the late summer of 1943, PWE and SOE planned to try to infiltrate into the forced labour transports from Western Europe a number of "Trojan Horse missions" whose task would be to encourage dissent and sabotage in German factories. A report compiled by an agent on the attitude of Belgian forced labourers showed a considerable willingness to go slow at the expense of the German war effort, but the workers lacked direction and a common objective.[42] PWE drew up a "General Directive for Foreign Workers Going to Germany" in March 1944 and communicated this to the Belgian Embassy. The instructions were now designed to spread discontent among German workers in contact with foreigners by playing on the relentless bombing, the hopeless nature of the German war effort and the widespread evidence of demoralization: "Spreading slogan 'Schluss' (To hell with it all!) by asking what it really means and why it is scrawled up on so many walls, lavatories, etc." After that, the Trojan horses were to encourage German workers in subtle ways to engage in all forms of malingering, go-slow and passive resistance.[43]

The confidence of the political warriors in the possibility of using foreign workers to foment unrest or even revolution in Germany was a product of little more than impressionistic intelligence and wishful thinking on the real state of the labour force in the Reich. In March 1944, Patrick Gordon-Walker, later a Labour government minister, drafted a strategy document on "Harnessing the Trojan Horse." Foreign workers, he claimed, "constitute a unique revolutionary force" with an explosive, though brief revolutionary potential, since their desire was not to transform Germany but simply to return home – "a revolution without social content." Gordon-Walker favoured controlling this force rather than allowing it to be dissipated in "premature and uncoordinated acts"; the timing of any upheaval, he thought, should be designed to help Allied military operations.[44] This suggestion became policy at Eisenhower's supreme headquarters when the Political Warfare Division began to plan ways of coordinating propaganda and operations. Foreign workers were to be a force for passive resistance inside Germany until the right moment came to begin more active resistance. In July 1944, after the successful invasion of France by Allied armies, PWD shifted its strategy as the right moment apparently approached: "Foreign Workers: These are to be induced to think

---

41   TNA, FO 898/340, SHAEF Political Warfare Division, "Plan for Psychological Warfare against Foreign Workers in Germany," 31 May 1944, Appendix A and B. On actual figures for foreign workers in Germany see Ulrich Herbert, *Fremdarbeiter: Politik und Praxis des "Ausländer-Einsatzes" in der Kriegswirtschaft des Dritten Reiches* (Berlin: Dietz Verlag, 1985), p. XY.

42   TNA, FO 898/340, Harman (PWE) to Calder, 19 August 1943, Ministry of Information to Lt. Ides Floor (Belgian Embassy), 24 November 1943.

43   Ibid., General Directive for Foreign Workers Going to Germany, Appendix B of draft mission, 4 March 1944.

44   TNA, FO 898/340, Patrick Gordon-Walker, "Harnessing the Trojan Horse," 31 March 1944, pp. 1–2.

of themselves as, and to build themselves up into, a disciplined army, ready to act when the word is given and not before."[45] This ambition was sadly removed from the reality of life for the forced labourers in Germany, whose revolutionary potential, if it ever existed, was stamped out by a harsh regime of discipline and exemplary punishment.

The "Trojan Horse" campaign highlighted one of the central purposes of the PWE organization, as set out by Lockhart to the Chiefs-of-Staff, that somehow properly-directed propaganda would stimulate serious social unrest against the National Socialist "New Order," both in the occupied population and among a putative anti-Hitler constituency inside Germany itself. Lockhart himself believed that the Czech people would play a critical part in this political upheaval. In notes written up after discussions with President Beneš in October 1941, Lockhart asserted his conviction that "the Czechs will play a leading part in the synchronized national revolt which we wish to arouse in Europe [...]," a view that he continued to assert over the coming years.[46] In November 1942, he forwarded intelligence reports to the Foreign Office on Czech resistance to prove his point. One report indicated that anti-German feeling was as strong and universal as ever: "Everyone has a hidden knife or a selected candlestick and club for the Germans." Another report confirmed that the Czechs hated the Germans immeasurably and "show their hatred whenever they can."[47] Lockhart shared the view of the "Trojan Horse" advocates that timing was of the essence in stimulating an anti-German revolt across Europe. In his meeting with the Chiefs of Staff in May 1942, Lockhart pointed out how delicate the question of timing was: "We should not try to provoke a premature revolt which might be easily crushed. We must not allow the Allies to wait until the last minute when we have won the war [...]."[48]

The Czech example clearly showed the limitations of the PWE expectation that somehow British political propaganda would create the conditions for national revolt. The intelligence evidence was in this case unambiguous in the view that however much the Czechs hated the Germans, there were powerful constraints on active resistance. "Active opposition is today impossible [...] an open revolt has no sense, and people feel that it is better to wait and not to make useless sacrifices," concluded one of the reports Lockhart sent to the Foreign Office.[49] Beneš warned Lockhart that the chief enemies

45   Ibid., SHAEF, PWD "Plan for Psychological Warfare against Foreign Workers in Germany," 31 May 1944, SHAEF, PWD memorandum "Propaganda to Germany: The Final Phase," 4 July 1944.

46   TNA, FO 800/872, Bruce Lockhart, "Summary of Recent Conversations with President Beneš and M. Maisky," October 1941, p. 9.

47   TNA, FO 898/879, Lockhart to William Strang (FO), 21 November 1942, encl. three intelligence reports on the Protectorate of Bohemia and Moravia.

48   TNA, FO 800/868, Lockhart's minutes of the meeting of the Chiefs of Staff, 28 May 1942, p. 3.

49   TNA, FO 800/879, Lockhart to Strang (FO), 21 November 1942.

of popular resistance were apathy and resignation. The information office of the Czech foreign ministry-in-exile warned Lockhart in November 1942 that Allied political propaganda was mentally "twenty thousand miles" from European realities since it had been completely unable to prevent millions of non-Germans, voluntarily or involuntarily, from working, fighting and dying for the German cause.[50] This must have been galling criticism for Lockhart, who took pride in the fact that he understood the nature of Central European concerns, and had campaigned to get the British government to abrogate the Munich Agreement of 1938 and to accept the restoration of the Sudetenland to a liberated Czechoslovakia, both of which the Foreign Office was wary of promising.

The Czech case was just one example of the belief that propaganda could produce a definite political and military advantage to the Allies. Throughout the last years of the war the British intelligence system searched avidly for signs of an impending social and political crisis in Germany. By the autumn of 1943 the Joint Intelligence Committee, which supplied the British War Cabinet with regular evaluations of the political situation in Europe, concluded that conditions in Germany were similar to the conditions Germany had faced in 1918 on the eve of the German collapse. For the next year political intelligence regularly reported that bombing, defeats and declining living standards might push German society to the limits, even though there was a wealth of intelligence assessment, particularly from the recently-founded American Office of Strategic Services, which suggested that there was little evidence of a social or political breakdown, and strong reasons why German dissenters did not want to take the blame for Germany's defeat.[51] The attraction of the more sanguine outlook to those generating the intelligence reports, however, is clear. It is what the Allies wanted to hear because they hoped it might shorten the war and save Allied lives. Moreover, the focus on creating conditions of rebellion in Germany and German-occupied Europe gave the whole political warfare structure its credibility, since this is what Lockhart and his team had promised. In March 1942, Dallas Brooks, one of the founder members of the PWE, drew up a plan for political warfare which suggested that wherever Allied forces decided to establish a bridgehead in Continental Europe, "it would be possible to raise a major revolt."[52] As late as

---

50   Beneš comment in TNA, FO 800/872, "Summary of Conversations," October 1941, p. 10; criticism of Allied policy in TNA, FO 800/879, Dr. Jan Kraus to Lockhart, 10 November 1942, pp. 2–3.
51   See Richard Overy, "The 'Weak Link'? The Perception of the German Working-Class by RAF Bomber Command, 1940–1945," in *Labour History Review*, Vol. 77, No. 1 (2012), pp. 1–33.
52   TNA, FO 898/306, Dallas Brooks memorandum, "Plan of Political Warfare for the Spring and Summer of 1942."

November 1944, the PWE policy was still trying to encourage panic conditions in Germany in order to make "continuance of the war impossible."[53]

There were nevertheless further problems to confront in advocating popular rebellion. Those who ran the political warfare programme were aware that a social crisis was likely to favour Communism and to turn populations, after the outbreak of the German-Soviet war in June 1941, towards the Soviet Union as the country evidently fighting to the full against the German enemy. The PWE organization itself was divided politically between a number of prominent, if moderate, left-wing officials and others, including Bruce Lockhart, who were strongly opposed to Communism and Socialism in all their many guises. The message to be sent to potential resisters had therefore to be gauged carefully. Desmond Morton, Churchill's intelligence adviser and a member of the PWE board, wrote to Lockhart in November 1941 highlighting the need to understand all the different "isms" of the extreme left ("Marxism, Leninism, Trotskyism, Bukharinism, Communism" – though interestingly not Stalinism) in order to find a way to combat the propaganda of the international communist movement. "The problem," wrote Morton, "is how to maintain enthusiasm for our Russian Allies without creating it for 'Communism.'" He suggested treating Russian history, art and culture in the propaganda but avoiding Russian politics.[54]

This balance was difficult to maintain and in Yugoslavia broke down altogether in favour of supporting Tito. In his relations with Beneš, Lockhart was less convinced than the Czech president that the Soviet Union had no designs on Eastern Europe after the war but Beneš insisted that he was basing his whole policy on the argument that the Soviet Union had "no expansionist programme in Europe."[55] On the whole, the PWE had to accept this line rather than risk alienating a communist ally that Lockhart distrusted. In April 1944, Dallas Brooks observed in a PWE minute that propaganda would have to be coordinated with the Soviet Union as the Red Army approached the Balkans to avoid any hint of Allied disunity or to give the impression that Britain was "bidding against Russia."[56] But a month later Eden complained to Orme Sargent, Deputy Permanent Secretary at the Foreign Office, that PWE propaganda was "boosting the Russians" and ought to cease. Lockhart rejected the idea that his organization had been boosting anything other than the British position.[57] Intelligence sources were already warning that a communist or Bolshevik mentality was developing among the hungry and bombed popu-

---

53   Ibid., PWE "Political Warfare against Germany: The Next Phase," 14 November 1944, pp. 1–2.
54   TNA, FO 800/868, Morton to Lockhart, 15 Nov 1941, Morton to Lord Swinton, 11 November 1941.
55   TNA, FO 800/873, record of meeting between John Wheeler-Bennett (Lockhart's assistant) and President Beneš, 5 July 1943.
56   TNA, FO 898/24, minute, Brigadier Brooks paper, April 1944.
57   TNA, FO 800/868, Sargent to Lockhart, 3 May 1944; Lockhart to Sargent, 4 May 1944.

lations in Europe, which threatened to hamper efforts to win the liberated peoples over to a post-war model more consistent with Western war aims and with British political propaganda.[58]

"THE HOT-AIR ARM"?

At the end of the war, the head of the British Joint Intelligence Committee, Victor Cavendish Bentinck, suggested that it was "doubtful if [political warfare] shortened the (recent) war by one hour."[59] This was a harsh judgement, which the PWE hoped to contest, but Bruce Lockhart himself was aware of the limitations of his organization. When he addressed officers preparing for Operation Torch in November 1942 he introduced his remarks with the comment that he represented the "hot-air arm." Self-deprecating this may have been, but in his memoirs he concluded that political warfare had been a "necessary evil," but not one that contributed very much to the wider strategy of the war.[60] Critics at the time and since regarded Bruce Lockhart as a rather ineffective chairman of the organization, and with the creation of the SHAEF Political Warfare Division, of which the former PWE official Richard Crossman was Deputy Director, the London organization under Lockhart played a declining role.[61] Lockhart's deputies were certainly talented, but many of them were in his judgement "prima donnas" who understood little of the workings of the Whitehall machinery and thought they could use their talents to direct policy rather than to execute it. When it was suggested to the Joint Planning Committee of the British Chiefs of Staff that the PWE draft a report on morale in Europe in spring 1942, the idea was rejected. The PWE was regarded as "wild and irresponsible."[62]

British political warfare was always trapped between ambition and reality. The officials understood the purpose of propaganda well enough, which was neither to overstate a case nor to mislead the reader or listener, while maintaining credibility. Yet time and again the propaganda encouraged false optimism or exaggerated the capacity of the recipients to engage in acts of dissent or resistance, however minor. In Germany and Italy picking up a leaflet was a crime. In Italy after German occupation in 1943, Field Marshal Kesselring, Commander-in-Chief, ordered the death penalty for handling enemy propaganda. The political warfare offensive to be successful depended

58   See Overy, "The 'Weak Link'?"
59   TNA, FO 898/420, PWE memorandum, "Suggested Enquiry into the Effects of British Political Warfare against Germany," 12 July 1945.
60   Lockhart, *Comes the Reckoning*, p. 198.
61   Lerner, *Psychological Warfare*, p. 48, 52–4; Cruickshank, *Fourth Arm*, pp. 183–5.
62   Lockhart, *Comes the Reckoning*, pp. 155–6.

critically on the evidence of Allied military achievements. In an essay written shortly after the end of the war, Richard Crossman concluded that psychological warfare was only effective "when it has become clear to the enemy that outright victory is impossible." Based on his experience at SHAEF, he came to realize that there had to be a strict coordination between the strategy of political warfare and military strategy.[63] Yet for too much of the war period the PWE was poorly integrated with the system for directing the military side of the war.

The limitations of political warfare were evident to those who conducted it because much of the political intelligence fed through from Europe indicated how restricted the real possibilities of resistance were in the terms hoped for in London. The PWE chafed at the bit to try to get populations in occupied Europe to move from a position in which "they feel the right way" to "the stage of doing." The campaign in 1941 to use the "V" for victory sign as a way to weld together a broader base for resistance created, according to Calder, "a sentiment but not a movement." That campaign, he concluded, was "like an orchestra continually tuning up but never being given a piece to play; and like an orchestra tuning up, has created discord." This might well stand as a more general epitaph for the whole political warfare campaign.[64] Throughout the war political warfare remained a large and cumbersome organization, with much responsibility relegated to the departments responsible for particular countries or regions and limited prospects for effective coordination. In some cases, of course, resistance did play a part in challenging Axis occupation. Yet in France and Yugoslavia and Greece the impulse came from within those communities as an expression of their anti-German and anti-Italian armed struggle, while British political warfare followed as much as it precipitated the actual conditions of resistance. In almost all these cases what the resistance wanted was active material assistance rather than encouraging pieces of political advice or information.

In August 1945, Bruce Lockhart resigned from his position as Director of the Political Warfare Executive to be succeeded by Brig. General Kenneth Strong. In his memoirs, he reflected on what his organization had achieved. He acknowledged the contemporary evidence that propaganda seemed to have affected the German people little, but still maintained that political warfare had had "a very considerable effect in sapping and undermining the efficiency of the Nazi war-machine." Of the effects on the occupied territories, he concluded that it did more "to sustain British influence in Europe than any

63   Richard Crossman, "Supplementary Essay," in Lerner, *Psychological Warfare*, p. 346.
64   TNA, FO 898/305, memorandum for Brigadier Brooks, 9 September 1941, memorandum by Ritchie Calder for Leeper, 26 August 1941, "Operational Propaganda as Part of Political Warfare," pp. 4–5.

other single factor."[65] This effort had been another of the special campaigns orchestrated by the PWE, the "Projection of Britain," which began in 1942 and continued into 1945. Lockhart himself thought the projection was naïve in holding that any rebellion fomented in Europe would result in a "pale pink affair of the British socialist type," but the propaganda message about the British way of life focused not on its political import but, as Ritchie Calder put it, on "a form of common life which offers greater opportunities to humanity than any other."[66] Lockhart echoed these sentiments in the conclusion to his memoirs of life served with the PWE: "I saw the future in Europe, not as a battle for frontiers and strategic vantage points, but as a political contest between two ways of life."[67] Ironically his "unfortunate Czechoslovaks" ended up under Soviet control, while the majority of those enemies that political warfare had fought against so unremittingly became a part of the democratic world.[68]

---

65   Lockhart, *Comes the Reckoning*, pp. 372–3.
66   TNA, FO 898/413, Calder to Lockhart, 13 August 1942.
67   Lockhart, *Comes the Reckoning*, p. 374.
68   Idem, *My Europe*, p. 87.

"ANYTHING THAT IS DEAR TO THEIR HEARTS": CZECHOSLOVAK HISTORY AND CULTURE IN THE LONDON BROADCASTS, 1939–1945

ERICA HARRISON

The Czechoslovak government-in-exile in London broadcast regularly to their homeland throughout the Second World War and made frequent use of cultural and historical themes in their transmissions. As one of the many groups of European exiles that had gathered in London following Nazi Germany's early military successes across the continent, the Czechoslovaks assembled around former President, Edvard Beneš, were able to maintain contact with their people and promote their cause over the radio. While their hosts at the British Broadcasting Corporation (BBC) understood that cultural programming could be effective in attracting listeners in occupied Europe, for the Czechoslovak exiles culture was not just a facilitator for propaganda but also a key component of it.

The BBC began broadcasting in Czech on 8 September 1939 and the Corporation's Czechoslovak Section continued to expand throughout the war. Following the provisional recognition of the Czechoslovak government-in-exile by the British government in July 1940, the Czechoslovak Ministry of Foreign Affairs in London began to collaborate with the BBC's Czechoslovak Section in the production of a new daily programme entitled *Hovory s domovem* [Conversations with the homeland]. The relationship between the two parties was described by one BBC commentator as "harmonious," and even the BBC's Controller of European Services Ivone Kirkpatrick (who was generally critical of the corporation's obligation to work with exile governments) conceded that, "we have less trouble with the Czechoslovaks than with any other allies."[1] In 1943, following the pattern of negotiations with other European exiles, *Hovory s domovem* was renamed *Hlas svobodné republiky* [Voice of the free Republic] as the Czechoslovak government-in-exile, fully recognized by Britain since July 1941, were freed from any obligation to follow British propaganda directives (although they still remained subject to British censorship requirements). The exiles received greater and greater amounts of broadcasting time as the war progressed and these broadcasts constituted the strongest connection

---

1   BBC Written Archives Centre, Caversham (henceforth BBC WAC), E2/10, "Report on broadcasting by foreign Governments resident in London, the Greek Government and the Fighting French," undated, "Allied Broadcasting," memorandum from Kirkpatrick to Minister of Information, 30 November 1942.

between the London Czechoslovaks and their listeners at home. They were therefore the primary means of propaganda for the exiles.

The principal aim of the propaganda produced by the Czechoslovak government-in-exile both for home and international audiences was the projection of a single, united Czechoslovak state that they could be held to represent. By 1939, the population of what had been Czechoslovakia was divided across several European states and the Allies offered no guarantee that the country would be recreated in the event of their victory. As self-declared representatives of the unified pre-1938 republic, the government-in-exile in London worked to promote a Czechoslovak identity which drew on the cultural heritage of both the First Republic and the Czech National Revival, and which reminded listeners of the cultural and historical ties that they shared. The use of cultural elements within their broadcasts was a means to simultaneously counter German attempts to discredit Czechoslovak culture, unify the divided home population, and promote the image of a cultured, independent Czechoslovak nation to an international audience.

To modern listeners, the dominance of Czech elements within the examples of Czechoslovak culture presented in the broadcasts is obvious. For the programme makers however, emphasizing any distinction between Czech and Slovak culture would have been counter-productive. While political talks and historical arguments for home audiences did distinguish between these groups, differences were rarely addressed in cultural programming which sought to be unifying and emotive. While most of the writers, composers and other cultural figures celebrated within the broadcasts were identified as Czech, it should also be noted that many such programmes were made in an effort to rebut German propaganda within the Protectorate and therefore logically had a Czech focus. Distinctly Slovak cultural contributions were limited to the occasional poem or folk song and were rarely analyzed and discussed in the way that Czech works were. Generally, the personages depicted were celebrated as heroes of "the nation," without any distinction being made and the terms "Czech" and "Czechoslovak" were often used interchangeably in a way that they were not in political broadcasting.

The deployment of culture for propaganda purposes had been accepted well before the Second World War and the circumstances of the German occupation of the Czech Lands were particularly conducive to its use. The first Czechoslovak President, Tomáš Garrigue Masaryk, had written about the importance of culture in making effective propaganda in the 1920s, arguing that a propagandist could not rely simply on enthusiastically stating his case when attempting to convince his audience. Warning that, "political agitation often puts people off or fails to win them over," Masaryk advised would-be propagandists accordingly:

"There is one important lesson in the psychology of propaganda: Do not think that people are won over to a political programme solely and principally by having its various
points energetically and enthusiastically laid out to them – the thing is to catch their
attention by any means, perhaps indirectly. Talk about art, about literature and so on,
about whatever the other person is interested in and you will win him."[2]

For Masaryk then, the affinity that people felt for cultural subjects provided the perfect means for winning the audience's attention and preparing
their ears for the required propaganda message. In the context of the occupied Protectorate, where censorship and the imposition of German cultural
dominance had outlawed many works of Czech literature and culture, this
was likely to carry even more weight.

The BBC had also recognized the value of using cultural and historical
elements in their broadcasts in their efforts to win the loyalty of listeners.
A European Intelligence report from a correspondent of the BBC Overseas
Intelligence Department in early 1940 proposed the use of more cultural material in the broadcasts to Czechoslovakia, explaining that, "Only those who
know the people well and who have experienced the pleasure they receive
from hearing anything that is dear to their hearts being broadcasted from
London or Paris, will fully understand the value of this suggestion."[3] By offering the "pleasure" of being able to hear references to familiar and popular
works of Czechoslovak culture, the BBC could win the attention of a wider
audience for its news and for the government-in-exile's political output. A fa-
miliarity with and a love for the national cultural classics were an assumed
characteristic of all Czechoslovaks, without regard to class or profession. The
Czechoslovaks had a reputation in Britain for being highly educated and government speakers had confidence in the cultural education of their listeners.[4]
In response to the attempts of the Protectorate authorities to separate the
"workers" from "the intelligentsia," Jan Masaryk responded scathingly that,
"For us, the intelligentsia means workers, farmers, professors, priests, office
workers and teachers; we are an intelligent nation that cannot be divided."[5]

The interpretation of Czechoslovak history and culture that was presented in the wartime broadcasts from London was principally characterized
by its distinction from all things German. Increasingly, the understanding

2   Tomáš Masaryk, *Světová revoluce: za války a ve válce, 1914–1918* [The World Revolution: during
    War and at War, 1914–1918] (Praha: Čin a Orbis, 1925), p. 100.
3   Asa Briggs, *The History of Broadcasting in the United Kingdom Volume III: The War of Word*, (Oxford:
    Oxford University Press, 1970), pp. 162–3.
4   National Archives of the Czech Republic, Prague, Ministerstvo vnitra Londýn, box 271, 2-82-10,
    Tisk-rozhlas 1944, "Zpráva o poměru anglického veřejného mínění k Československu [Report on
    the Attitude of English Public Opinion towards Czechoslovakia]," October 1940 – March 1941.
5   Jan Masaryk, *Volá Londýn* [London Calling] (Praha: Panorama, 1990), p. 145.

of what it was to be Czechoslovak came to be defined by its opposition to that which was perceived to be German and this definition by opposition was not unprecedented. Narratives of the history of the Czech Lands and Slovakia had previously been viewed as a struggle against, respectively, German and Magyar aggression and it was not difficult to extend this theory to include this latest conflict. In a discussion of the German strategy of "total war," President Beneš maintained that this represented nothing new for the Germans and stated that, "In our history we have been occupied, enslaved and ravaged several times by our German neighbours."[6] Foreign Minister Jan Masaryk was rather more exact in his claim, recorded during a speech to Czechoslovak pilots in Britain during the war, stating that their nation had suffered at the hands of the Germans every 25 years.[7]

The German authorities in the Protectorate were also looking back into Czech history and their reinterpretation of the legacy of certain individuals drew responses from London. Historical figures such as St Václav and Jan Amos Komenský were lauded by the Germans for their supposed support for unity with Germany but rebuttal from the exiles came quickly. Early in 1941, in answer to claims that Komenský had recommended that the Czechs should unify with the Germans for protection, one government speaker offered to help the Protectorate authorities with their history: "Yes, Komenský did preach humanism, love for your neighbour and love between nations. And it was that same Germanic darkness, anger and hatred of reformation that drove him from his homeland, just as Wilhelmine Germany chased out Masaryk and Nazi Germany did Beneš."[8]

When Protectorate propaganda emphasized the influence of German writers and musicians on their Czech counterparts in order to bolster Nazi claims that much of Czech culture was merely derivative of German culture, a debate on the matter was broadcast from London. Several speakers assured one another than no Czech was deceived by this pathetic attempt at Germanization before an extract of Dvořák's Slavonic Dances was played and the announcers concluded that this music represented a certain "Czech truth" that was both "ungermanized and ungermanizable," predicting that "it will win out in the end."[9] True Czechoslovak culture, as presented in these broadcasts, was impervious to this German assault and beyond German understanding. The cultural artefacts that were chosen to represent the pinnacle of the na-

---

6   Edvard Beneš, *Šest let exilu a druhé světové války: Řeči, projevy a dokumenty z r. 1938-1945*, [Six Years of Exile and the Second World War: Talks, Speeches, and Documents from the Years 1938–1945] (London: Týdeník Čechoslovák, 1945), p. 250.
7   Czech Radio Archive, Prague [henceforth CRA], BBC Wartime Recordings [working title], 0462-0463, "S čs. stíhací perutí [With the Czechoslovak Fighter Squadron]."
8   CRA, LN Z 1941 – 5, "News Commentary", 5 January 1941.
9   CRA, LN Z 1941 – 5, "Czechoslovak Programme," 4 March 1941.

tion's achievement – her language, her literature and her music – were presented as being incomprehensible to the Germans. Anything that was truly Czech could not be understood by a German: they could not play Czech music, they could not read Czech books and, crucially, they could not speak Czech.

Nineteenth-century Czech nationalism had previously tied the fate of the nation to the fate of the Czech language and the symbolic importance of the language that had been established then continued to be upheld in the wartime broadcasts.[10] Prokop Drtina, a regular broadcaster, said that by imposing the German language on the Czechs, the Germans had robbed the people, "of that which is dearest and most sacred to the nation – its language, its mother tongue."[11] Minister Jaroslav Stránský, another regular broadcaster who often discussed more philosophical topics, also spoke on the subject of language. He criticized the German understanding of nationhood which limited itself to *Blut und Boden*, blood and land, maintaining that the most important factor for the Czechoslovak nation was language. According to Stránský, Czechs understood that a language was "the soul of the nation [...] part of every one of us. We say 'our language' but we are more hers than she is ours." For him, language was not merely a means of communication, it was "the wisdom, experience, feeling, taste and humour of countless generations [...] the inexhaustible treasure of the nation." Stránský argued that it was the duty of the nation to retain this connection with their language in the face of German opposition, and to ignore the Protectorate press and radio as they reproduced their translations "from bad German into bad Czech."[12] Anything said in Czech in support of Germany was judged to be bad Czech, contaminated by a German mentality, even when it was written by native speakers. When condemning the Protectorate press in a speech in 1941, Prokop Drtina dismissed it as being "written in Czech but thought up in German."[13]

As an important spiritual treasure of the nation, the Czech language became something reserved for those who deserved it and enemies of the nation were deemed unworthy. Speaking in October 1942, Jan Masaryk wanted to address Nazi Secretary of State for the Protectorate Karl Hermann Frank in one of his broadcasts but refused to do so in Czech: "For the guy who christened Masaryk Embankment Heydrich Embankment and simultaneously allowed innocent women and children to be imprisoned, I believe Czech is too good. I will not speak with Frank in the language of Hus, Palacký and

---

10   Chad Bryant, "The Language of Resistance? Czech Jokes and Joke-telling under Nazi Occupation, 1943–45," in *Journal of Contemporary History*, Vol. 41, No. 1 (2006), pp. 140–141.

11   CRA, LN Z 1941 – 5, "Czechoslovak Programme," 23 February 1941.

12   CRA, LN Z 1941 – 8, "Czechoslovak Programme," 8 August 1941.

13   Prokop Drtina, *A nyní promluví Pavel Svatý: Londýnské rozhlasové epištoly z let 1940–1945* [And Now, Pavel Svatý Will Speak: London Radio Epistles from the Years 1940–1945] (Praha: Vladimír Žikeš, 1945), p. 144.

Čapek."[14] For Masaryk, Czech listeners are, however, intrinsically linked to the Czech language and he ends his broadcast with these words:

> "And now, a word of good night to you all, you dear, sacred and innocent ones, whether you are already in Terezín or a concentration camp. I thank you in our sweet mother tongue. I think of you in Czech, I pray for you in Czech and in the name of all free Czechoslovaks, I thank you in Czech."[15]

Writers, as masters of the language, were frequently celebrated within the broadcasts. In response to a speech made by Goebbels at a gathering of cultural workers, the government programme reported that the Reich's Propaganda Minister had "sacrificed himself so much that he recently read a few Czech books and watched a few Czech films." "Which books were they?" the programme asked, "We doubt that he would read Palacký, Neruda, Masaryk or Čapek. If his brain, ravaged by Nazi nihilism, was at all capable of understanding the great works that the small Czech nation has given the world, works filled with a deep humanity, Dr Goebbels would never be able to lower himself to the superficiality of his speech to Czech cultural workers." The announcer suggested that the anti-Semitic magazine *Štít národa* [Shield of the nation] was probably the greatest work of Czech literature that Goebbels would ever understand and concluded that it was this move against high culture that had caused the Germans to lose their humanity: "It is just that kind of literature, which has mutated Germany into a nation of monsters."[16] Czechoslovak literature, on the other hand, could be proud of great writers such as those mentioned above and great characters, such as Božena Němcová's *Grandmother*. In one of his early broadcasts from London, Jan Masaryk told listeners he was going home to read *Grandmother* again, commenting, "A nation that has such grandmothers can never be wiped out – God bless them!"[17]

Czech music was felt to be just as incomprehensible to German ears as the Czech language. Speaking in 1944, Jan Masaryk was disgusted to hear that Germans in the Protectorate were celebrating the 120th anniversary of the birth of Bedřich Smetana, and felt that their performance of *Z českých luhů a hájů* was so bad as to seem almost deliberately poor. "I can imagine though," he added, "that, for the German *Horst Wessel Lied* generation, playing Smetana is difficult. Smetana – pure, clear, Slavic, optimistic and unyielding in the face of suffering – is the absolute antithesis of everything the former so-called Germany has done, is doing and will continue to do for a little while

---

14   Masaryk, *Volá Londýn*, p. 145.
15   Ibid., p. 147.
16   CRA, LN Z 1940 – 3, "Czechoslovak Programme," 7 December 1940.
17   Masaryk, *Volá Londýn*, p. 32.

yet." He then suggested that love of great Czech music should inspire listeners to greater acts in defence of the nation, predicting that, over the next few months, "Czechs and Slovaks will show, must show, the world that they are worthy of Bedřich Smetana."[18]

Other speakers drew hope from the work of Czech composers and remarked on the power of music to affect foreign listeners, as well as those whose nation it represented. In a programme entitled "Czech Music in England," the narrator noted the admiration on the faces of the British audience when they heard a Czech trio's performance of a piece by Josef Suk and suggested that the music was capable of winning people over to the Czechoslovak cause. "This music was born in Bohemia," he commented, "The freedom of the nation that gave the world that music is worth fighting for." Later, after a performance of a Dvořák piece, he claimed that listening to Czech music abroad was quite different to hearing it at home and described the effect it had on the exiled listener in very emotive terms:

> "It is like returning. It is as if your home has come back to you. As if you were hearing the rustling of our forests. As if all the waters of our country were flowing towards you, as if they all mixed within you in great faith and certainty [...]. Just listen [...]. Who could still doubt, having heard such music? Its strength, its timelessness, its triumphant certainty [...]."[19]

This programme suggested that music could serve as effective propaganda all by itself, filling Czechoslovak listeners with patriotic feeling while simultaneously convincing listeners from other nations of the worthiness of that state. Just as the announcer credited Suk with winning over the audience at the concert, so too did Drtina suggest in another programme that Antonín Dvořák was an effective propagandist because his work was not limited by any constraint of language. Dvořák had written music "in his mother tongue," leaving a legacy of works in which, "he spoke Czech, but he was speaking a language that is understood in England and America as well as in Kralupy."[20]

Dvořák's popularity abroad made him a frequent subject of Czechoslovak propaganda intended for international audiences and this also caused programme-makers to re-examine him from a Czechoslovak perspective. In a Czech-language programme made to mark the 100th anniversary of Dvořák's birth in 1941, the announcer suggested to listeners that:

---

18   Ibid., p. 203.
19   CRA, BBC Wartime Recordings, 0101, "Česká hudba v Anglii [Czech Music in England]."
20   Drtina, *A nyní promluví Pavel Svatý*, pp. 169–170.

"The fact that we are celebrating this important anniversary in the midst of a cruel war, in which the free existence of our country is at stake, allows us to hear something different in Dvořák's music and to understand his life anew. The most important question for us today is 'What does Dvořák mean for his nation?'"[21]

The narrator then went on to tell the story of Dvořák taking his place in the Austrian House of Deputies, only to then fill his pockets with government-issue pencils and take them home to compose with because he could do more for the nation with his music than by any political action. The theme of the political power of culture is pronounced here as Dvořák's work is given as an example of cultural achievements working to advance the international profile of the nation. The narrator explains that Dvořák's membership of the House of Deputies was only lifelong while his music was eternal and, when stealing the pencils, the composer knew that "the music he would write with them would resound and speak for his country long after even the most celebrated speech given in the House of Deputies had mouldered into oblivion." Dvořák's credentials as a patriotically-motivated cultural producer are then confirmed in a quote from a letter he wrote to his publisher. The composer proclaimed that, "An artist also has a homeland in which he simply must have strong faith and for which his heart beats passionately. We must hope that nations which are represented by their art will never be eliminated, however small they may be."[22]

The desire to use cultural references in propaganda is logical. When speaking to a national audience, programme makers can use the attachment listeners feel to certain familiar cultural works to encourage them to associate with a political idea, in this case that of the rejection of the German occupation and loyalty to the government-in-exile. For the benefit of an international audience, Czechoslovak cultural works and the people behind them could be presented as positive ambassadors for their nation and the inherently Czechoslovak nature of these works emphasized in the hope that the Allies would come to respect the Czechoslovak nation as culturally (and, by extension, politically) valid in its own right. German censorship within the Protectorate forbade listening to foreign radio but programme makers used the promise of hearing something comfortingly familiar being broadcast from London to tempt people to defy the German laws and tune in. Great cultural works of the past were then upheld as aspirational patriotic examples as programme makers sought to encourage a feeling of national unity. By reminding listeners at home of the music and culture that they held dear to their hearts – and the fact that they were being denied

21   CRA, BBC Wartime Recordings, 029–030, "Antonín Dvořák."
22   Ibid.

it by the occupying Germans – programme makers sought to heighten the loyalty of listeners to the Czechoslovak identity they were promoting. By defining this cultural identity in opposition to all that the occupiers signified and promoting themselves as its true representatives, the Czechoslovak broadcasters in London mobilized culture for their own campaign of political warfare.

WALKING ON EGG-SHELLS: THE CZECHOSLOVAK EXILES AND ANTI-SEMITISM IN OCCUPIED EUROPE DURING THE SECOND WORLD WAR

JAN LÁNÍČEK

In late June 1942, at the peak of the deportations of the Czech and Slovak Jews from the Protectorate and Slovakia to ghettos and death camps, the famous journalist Josef Kodíček addressed the issue of Nazi anti-Semitism over the air waves of the Czechoslovak BBC Service in London: "It is obvious that Nazi anti-Semitism which originally was only a coldly calculated weapon of agitation, has in the course of time become complete madness, an attempt to throw the guilt for all the unhappiness into which Hitler has led the world on to someone visible and powerless."[2]

Wartime BBC broadcasts from Britain to occupied Europe should not be viewed as normal radio speeches commenting on events of the war.[3] The radio waves were one of the "other" weapons of the war — a tactical propaganda weapon to support the ideology and politics of each side in the conflict, with the intention of influencing the population living under Nazi rule as well as in the Allied countries. Nazi anti-Jewish policies were an inseparable part of that conflict because the destruction of European Jewry was one of the main objectives of the Nazi political and military campaign.[4] This, however, does not mean that the Allies ascribed the same importance to the persecution of Jews as did the Nazis and thus the BBC's broadcasting of information about the massacres needs to be seen in relation to the propaganda aims of the

1   This article was written as part of the grant project GAČR 13–15989P "The Czechs, Slovaks and Jews: Together but Apart, 1938–1989." An earlier version of this article was published as Jan Láníček, "The Czechoslovak Service of the BBC and the Jews during World War II," in *Yad Vashem Studies*, Vol. 38, No. 2 (2010), pp. 123–153. This version was significantly refined and supplemented. The author would like to thank *Yad Vashem Studies* for permission to reprint parts of the original article in this volume.

2   Archiv Českého rozhlasu [Archive of the Czech Radio] (henceforth AČR), BBC 1939–1945, box 14, broadcast on 26 June 1942, read by Josef Kodíček.

3   For the way the BBC treated Jewish themes during the war see: Jeremy D. Harris, "Broadcasting the Massacres. An Analysis of the BBC's Contemporary Coverage of the Holocaust," in *Yad Vashem Studies*, Vol. XXV (1996), pp. 65–98; Jean Seaton, "The BBC and the Holocaust," in *European Journal of Communication*, Vol. 2 (1987), pp. 53–80.

4   See Jeffrey Herf, *The Jewish Enemy: Nazi Propaganda during World War II and the Holocaust* (Cambridge, MA: Harvard University Press, 2006); Gerhard Weinberg, *Germany, Hitler and World War II: Essays in Modern German and World History* (Cambridge: Cambridge University Press, 1995), pp. 217–244; David Welch, *The Third Reich. Politics and Propaganda* (London – New York: Routledge, 1993).

Allies, including those of the Czechoslovak government-in-exile, officially established in London on 21 July 1940.[5] As part of the Czechoslovak exiles' struggle against the German occupier, and Czech and Slovak collaborators, they were allowed by the British government to address the people in their homeland via the BBC. One of the topics that inevitably came up was German harassment of the population, including Jews, and also the issue of local anti-Semitism, or rather the alleged non-existence of indigenous anti-Semitism. When analyzing the content of Czechoslovak broadcasting on the BBC, one becomes aware of the instrumentalization of the situation in occupied Europe.

This chapter examines wartime speeches dealing with the persecution of Jews aired by Czechoslovak politicians in exile. However, other issues also need to be addressed here. The exiles' use of the BBC services calls for investigation in the light of various complex factors that had an influence on the decision-making process of the émigré politicians. The study also moves on to an examination of the broadcasts themselves. The complex situation the politicians faced during their British exile is explained and also why broadcasts dealing with the Holocaust took the final form in which they were aired.[6]

The BBC broadcasts were the main means the Czechoslovak exiles had for communication with the broad masses at home, with men and women who very often risked their own and their family members' lives to listen to the radio. These broadcasts emanated from a political élite without a country, and without regular contact with the people they purported to represent. They were shaped by a mix of mutually competing pressures. The government-in-exile's intention was to influence the population at home. Simultaneously, the broadcasts themselves were inspired by reports coming from there. These reports were meant to reveal the actual mood and demands of the population, but necessarily represented those of the resistance leaders who were in charge of informing the exiles. To put it simply, the government's efforts to mould public opinion at home reflected the content and tone of the messages forwarded to them by the Czechoslovak underground movement.

---

5   There were also other governments-in-exile, including the Belgian, Czechoslovak, Dutch, French (National Committee), Greek, Luxembourg, Norwegian, Polish, and Yugoslav. See also Jan Láníček, "Governments-in-Exile and the Jews during and after the Second World War," in Jan Láníček, James Jordan, eds., *Governments-in-Exile and the Jews during the Second World War* (London: Vallentine Mitchell, 2013), pp. 69–88.

6   Transcripts of the BBC Czechoslovak Service between the summer of 1940 and the end of the war are used as the main source in this article. In all probability the first months from the beginning of the war are missing. However, the indications we have show that the broadcasts before late 1940 did not deal in any significant manner with Jewish issues (consult the *Daily News Bulletin* and archival sources of exiled Jewish politicians). We also have no recordings of the speeches dealing with Jewish matters; unfortunately, this deprives us of one dimension that is significant for an evaluation of the broadcasts, the tone of the speeches.

The information broadcast usually became public knowledge in London as well.[7] Various activists and journalists in Britain and the United States often drew on the broadcasts dealing with Jewish issues. Also, the Czechoslovak exiles occasionally published the radio talks in their official publications.[8] It cannot be ruled out that some of these were intended not only to inform people at home, but also to enhance the exiles' image in the West. The minor Allies wished to be seen as adherents to the democratic tradition, to democratic ideals, and as an integral part of the war between the forces of light, as the Allies wanted to be identified, and of darkness, the evil power of the Nazis. In addition, since the BBC was a British government agency, British censorship and the Corporation's own unwritten laws inevitably affected its European Service, too.[9] The Czechoslovak government consequently had to carefully weigh every broadcast. They needed to comply with British demands *as well as* to stay in line with their policy towards the people at home, whilst, at the same time, keeping in mind their own ideological precepts.

A JEWISH THREAT?

Anti-Semitism was a major theme in Nazi and collaborationist propaganda across the whole of occupied Europe. Accusations that the Jews had been ruling the world and were seeking to re-establish their mastery with the help of their Bolshevik and plutocratic allies, or slaves, regularly appeared in speeches by Nazi ideologues, among others Adolf Hitler, Joseph Goebbels, Alfred Rosenberg and Julius Streicher.[10] Similarly, throughout the war these widely shared tropes concerning Jewish world domination were employed against the representatives of the Czechoslovak exiles in London.

The German authorities assumed total control of the public media in the Protectorate and used their grip to spread Nazi ideology, including anti-Semitism, among Czechs. The collaborationist press played a key role in those efforts. In the first two years, an influential grouping of activist journalists (Vladimír Krychtálek, Karel Lažnovský, Emanuel Vajtauer, contributors to the vitriolic anti-Semitic weekly *Arijský boj* [Aryan Struggle], Rudolf Novák,

---

7   For example, a broadcast by Juraj Slávik on 9 February 1944, was published by Arnošt (Ernest) Frischer, a member of the State Council. See London Metropolitan Archives (henceforth LMA), Board of Deputies (henceforth BoD), Acc3121/E/03/510. For the reaction of British Jewish organizations to Ripka's broadcast on 18 September 1941, see *We Think of You* (London: HaMacabbi, 1941).

8   "The Fate of European Jews: Oswieczim and Birkenau, a Document," in *Central European Observer*, 21 July 1944, p. 226.

9   Láníček, "The Czechoslovak Service of the BBC and the Jews during World War II," pp. 131–133.

10 For further details see Herf, *The Jewish Enemy: Nazi Propaganda during World War II and the Holocaust*.

and others) adopted a strongly pro-German slant in their writings and colluded intensively with the Nazi authorities.[11] The collaborationist wing became even more prominent when in January 1942 the leader of the group, the former colonel of the Czechoslovak army, Emanuel Moravec, was appointed Minister of Education and National Enlightenment.[12]

During the war, topics deemed suitable for publication in the Protectorate press were discussed at regular meetings of Czech journalists with officials from the *Reichsprotektor's* office. Newspapers were entirely under the control of German agencies and later also came under the supervision of Moravec's ministry.[13] Jewish themes regularly appeared on the agenda at the consultation meetings, chaired by Wolfgang Wolfram von Wolmar from the "Group Press" (*Gruppe Presse*) of the *Reichsprotektor* Office, and the collaborationist press frequently attacked Jews in its pages.[14] In the eyes of German officials, the role of the press was, by and large, to enlighten the Czechs, a majority of whom continued to reject Nazi racist ideology, and to persuade them that supporting Jews was not in their interests.[15]

According to von Wolmar, the task of the Czech press was to combat whispering propaganda. At the same time, it should propagate Nazi ideology and educate Czech people in the true spirit of the new order. One of the issues to be tackled was the so-called Jewish question. Von Wolmar lamented that the Czech people still did not fully comprehend this delicate problem. There was a lot of compassion towards the Jews in the Czech Lands, but the Czechs ought to be aware, von Wolmar threatened, that the duration and economic situation of the Czech nation was contingent on their attitude towards the Jews.[16] They ought to be aware that there was no space in the new Europe for people who were "fraternizing" with the Jews. The duty of the press

11   Jan Cebe, Jakub Končelík, "Novinářský aktivismus: protektorátní kolaborantská žurnalistika a její hlavní představitelé z řad šéfredaktorů českého legálního tisku [Journalistic Activism: Collaborationist Journalism in the Protectorate and Its Major Representatives amongst Editors-in-Chief of the Czech Legal Press]," in *Sborník Národního muzea v Praze* [Anthology of the National Museum in Prague], Vol. 53, No. 1–4 (2008), pp. 39–48; Milotová, Jaroslava, "Die Protektoratspresse und die 'Judenfrage,'" in *Theresienstädter Studien und Dokumente*, 1996, pp. 153–184.

12   Jiří Pernes, *Až na dno zrady. Emanuel Moravec* [To the Very Bottom of Treachery. Emanuel Moravec] (Praha: Themis, 1997).

13   Cebe, Končelík, "Novinářský aktivismus: protektorátní kolaborantská žurnalistika a její hlavní představitelé z řad šéfredaktorů českého legálního tisku," p. 40.

14   Pavel Večeřa, "Židé a antisemitismus na stránkách vybraných českých deníků v letech 1939–1945 [Jews and Anti-Semitism on the Pages of Selected Czech Dailies in the Years 1939–1945]," in *Média a realita 2002. Sborník prací Katedry mediálních studií a žurnalistiky FSS* [Media and Reality 2002. Anthology of Papers of the Department of Media Studies and Journalism of the Faculty of Social Studies] (Brno: Masarykova univerzita, 2003), pp. 103–120.

15   Jan Gebhart, Barbara Köpplová, eds., *Řízení legálního tisku v Protektorátu Čechy a Morava* [Managing the Legal Press in the Protectorate of Bohemia and Moravia] (Praha: Klementinum, 2010, CD-ROM), see for example, meetings on 26 January, 18 and 25 October and 15 November 1940.

16   Ibid., press meeting on 18 October 1940.

was to manipulate Czech public opinion in such a way that any subsequent legislation, limiting the position of Jews in the society, was perceived not as an imposition by the authorities, but rather as an expression of the will of the people and as a public necessity.[17] The press was assigned the mission of persuading Czechs that the solution to the Jewish question was not only in the German interest, but that the whole world was getting rid of a tangible danger and would eventually become a safer place.[18]

The Czech public was constantly bombarded with articles that portrayed the malicious influence of Jews in the world and in particular in the pre-war Masaryk republic. Regardless of this comprehensive press campaign, von Wolmar kept complaining about a lack on the Czech side of any understanding of Nazi racial ideology. Concurrently, the Nazis had no illusions about what they labelled Czech pro-Jewish sentiments and frequently ascribed them to the expression of Czech anti-Germanism. Simply put, the compassion shown to the segregated Jews by Czechs was a way of conveying anti-German sentiments. Although the post-Munich republic had witnessed a rise in local anti-Semitism, Czechs were allegedly cured of this disease by the German occupation, when any continuation of anti-Semitism was largely perceived as sympathizing with the German overlord.[19]

Another chance for Protectorate propaganda to isolate the Jews from the Czech people was offered in the autumn of 1941 with the arrival in Prague of Reinhard Heydrich as Deputy *Reichsprotektor* and the radicalization of German occupation policies in the Protectorate thereafter. At press briefings from early 1941, von Wolmar had repeatedly stressed his concern at the whispering propaganda in the Protectorate and the role of Jews in spreading unconfirmed news and stirring up anti-German feelings among Czechs. The activist journalists were advised to warn their compatriots about the possible repercussions of being led astray by Jews. Their task was to depict the situation in such a manner that any crackdown by the Nazi authorities in the Protectorate would be perceived as a response to Czech opposition, which was instigated by Jews and their helpers, both in the Protectorate and in London. The Jews were to be blamed for leading the Czech people to catastrophe.[20]

As a consequence, the motif that linked the official Czechoslovak exiled representation in London with the Jews emerged. Nazi propaganda painted

---

17   Ibid., press meeting on 25 October 1940.
18   Ibid., press meeting on 31 October 1940.
19   Jan Láníček, *Czechs, Slovaks and the Jews: 1938–1948: Beyond Idealisation and Condemnation* (Basingstoke: Palgrave Macmillan, 2013), pp. 16–21; Miroslav Kárný, "Czech Society and the 'Final Solution,'" in David Bankier, Israel Gutman, eds., *Nazi Europe and the Final Solution* (Jerusalem: Yad Vashem, 2003), pp. 309–326.
20   Gebhart, Köpplová, eds., *Řízení legálního tisku v Protektorátu Čechy a Morava,* press meeting on 7 February 1941.

Allied war efforts against the Axis as being inspired by international Jewish circles; essentially the western "plutocratic" Allies were in thrall to the Jewish capitalists and financiers. After 22 June 1941 and the outbreak of the German-Soviet War, the spectre of Jewish bolshevism and barbarity re-entered Nazi discourse. Together with the major Allied Powers, and also the so-called minor Allies, the governments-in-exile were presented as being directed by Jewish puppeteers. The Beneš government was overtly trumpeting its allegiance to the ideals of the first Czechoslovak president, Tomáš Garrigue Masaryk, for many "the idol of the Jews." Masaryk's son, Jan, also widely known for his contacts with Jewish politicians, as well as Beneš himself and others, such as Jaroslav Stránský and Hubert Ripka, could easily be fitted into this suppositious Jewish network.

The connection made between the Czechoslovak government-in-exile and Jewish interests became eventually one of the main features of Protectorate collaborationist propaganda. In February 1941, for example, Krychtálek described the Beneš exile administration as full of Jews (notably members of the State Council, Julius Friedman and Julius Fürth, as well as Minister of State – later Minister of Justice – Jaroslav Stránský). The Beneš government's struggle for the liberation of their homeland was presented as waging a war on behalf of the Jews both for their money and in their interests. Protectorate journalists not only searched for "Jews" among the exile politicians themselves but also among their relatives. Jewish family members were "revealed" in the case of Bohumil Laušman, a member of the State Council and a prominent Social Democrat, and Hubert Ripka, Minister of State and war-time head of exile propaganda, who allegedly divorced an Aryan just to marry a Jewish lady. They also commonly referred to President Beneš as a "White Jew," a term used for non-Jews "fraternizing" with Jews,[21] and Foreign Minister, Jan Masaryk, was labelled a Jew-lover and a Jewish *Mischling*. The collaborators followed developments among the émigrés and frequently took their cue from them. In his reaction to the Jewish Telegraphic Agency (JTA) report about Czechoslovak Zionist demands for representation in the exile parliament, Krychtálek depicted Beneš and "his gang" as living on Jewish money that would one day have to be paid back by the Czechs. If the Allies won, Krychtálek predicted that the Czech people would be enslaved by

---

21   Peter Richard Pinard, "Alois Kříž a cyklus rozhlasových relací 'Co víte o Židech a zednářích?,'" in *Terezínské studie a dokumenty* [The Terezín Studies and Documents], 2005, p. 218. For another example of the Protectorate propaganda attacking the exiles on Jewish issues, see for instance, Central Zionist Archives (henceforth CZA), A320/25, *Moravské noviny* [Moravian Daily], 24 August 1944.

"Jewish bloodthirsty hyenas." He concluded that the whole allied world was in bondage to the Jews.[22]

This did not pass unnoticed in London where Beneš complained that he was being attacked daily by Protectorate propaganda as being under Jewish influence.[23] In fact the notion existed in exile political circles that the Jewish presence was too prominent among them. After returning from one of his stays in the United States, Jan Masaryk for instance expressed amazement about what he perceived as the Judaization (*užidovštění*) of the Czechoslovak Foreign Ministry while he was abroad and thought this might cause trouble for the exiles.[24] The source of Masaryk's concerns should probably be sought directly in his anxiety lest this staple of Protectorate propaganda be substantiated.[25]

The exiles were aware of what was being promulgated about them and their information was corroborated by reports from the Czech and Slovak underground. These suggested the rise of anti-Semitic sentiments among the home population, as well as deep-seated prejudices, thus testifying to the effectiveness of Nazi propaganda.[26]

There is also evidence to show that some elements of the Czech underground movement did not approve of the publicity given to the Nazi per-

---

22   Archiv Ústavu Tomáše Garrigua Masaryka [Archive of the Institute of Tomáš Garrigue Masaryk] (henceforth AÚTGM), Sbírka [Collection] 38, Vladimír Klecanda, file 172, *Večer* [The Evening], 22 February 1941.

23   United States Holocaust Memorial Museum (henceforth USHMM), WJC-L, C2/96, interview with the President of the Czechoslovakian Republic, Dr Beneš, 17 April 1941, minutes prepared by Noah Barou and Sydney Silverman.

24   Jana Čechurová, Jan Kuklík, Jaroslav Čechura, Jan Němeček, eds., *Válečné deníky Jana Opočenského* [War Diaries of Jan Opočenský] (Praha: Karolinum, 2001), p. 229, diary entry for 15 August 1942. Masaryk returned to London after nine months in the US. During a talk with Ladislav Karel Feierabend, the Czechoslovak Minister of Finance, Masaryk mentioned his surprise at the growth and size of the Foreign Ministry's administration and its "Judaization." Opočenský was a historian by profession and was involved in the formation of the Czechoslovak exile administration. He was Feierabend's housemate while in London, and his personal diaries offer a unique insight into the internal life of the Czechoslovak exile during the Second World War.

25   Similarly, Renée Poznanski in her case study of Free French Jewish policy confirms that Nazi propaganda caused Gaullists to be cautious when dealing with Jewish issues on the BBC. Renée Poznanski, "French Public Opinion and the Jews during World War II: Assumptions of the Clandestine Press," in Beate Kosmala and Feliks Tych, eds., *Facing the Nazi Genocide: Non-Jews and Jews in Europe* (Berlin: Metropol, 2004), pp. 134–135. Michael R. Marrus and Robert O. Paxton, *Vichy France and the Jews* (New York: Basic Books, 1981), pp. 189–190. Likewise, David Engel suggests that Polish exiles during the war carefully weighed any public declaration on behalf of the Jews. Information received in London documented a negative perception of Jews in occupied Poland. The Sikorski government thus did not want to stand out as a defender of Jewish interests and thereby leave itself open to attacks from Nazi propaganda. David Engel, *In the Shadow of Auschwitz: The Polish Government-in-Exile and the Jews, 1939–1942* (Chapel Hill: The University of North Carolina Press, 1987), esp. pp. 62–64; David Engel, *Facing a Holocaust: The Polish Government-in-Exile and the Jews, 1943–1945* (Chapel Hill: The University of North Carolina Press, 1993).

26   Láníček, *Czechs, Slovaks and the Jews: 1938–1948*, pp. 16–41.

secution of Jews in BBC transmissions and were irritated by broadcasts in which sympathy for the Jews was expressed. The Czechoslovak exiles took this development seriously and carefully tried to avoid giving Protectorate propaganda any pretext that could possibly exacerbate such tendencies. Although Jewish affairs were hardly a major theme in the BBC Czechoslovak broadcasts, talks in which Jews were mentioned still provoked ambiguous responses at home. For example, Hubert Ripka, Minister of State in the Foreign Ministry and the man in charge of its information department, maintained that during the war the exiles were criticized for radio appeals to help Jews.[27] Masaryk, a case in point, received letters castigating him for such requests. Indeed, one writer claimed that a broadcast by Masaryk in support of the Jews incited resentment among the Czech people.[28]

The exiles soon realized the difficulties of combating the accusation that they were serving the interests of the Jews. In response to the February 1941 article by Krychtálek mentioned earlier, the Czechoslovak BBC presenters issued a rebuttal. Although we do not have the text of the broadcast, we know that it made an unfavourable impression on Czechoslovak Jewish exiles in London who subsequently complained to Minister Ripka, thus emphasizing that there were several factors the exiles had to consider when preparing their counter-propaganda campaign.[29] After reading the text of the broadcast, Ripka expressed his displeasure to Josef Korbel, the head of Czechoslovak broadcasting – again, unfortunately for us, without making any particular comments that would help to acquaint us with the text.[30] The only certainty is that the broadcast gave the impression of being an apology and an attempt to explain that the Czech exiles were not as Jewish-oriented as Protectorate propaganda claimed. According to Ripka, this was not how anti-Semitism should be fought. However, it seems that no better way could be found and the exiles did not return to the subject for the rest of the war but rather focused on general statements condemning Nazi anti-Semitism *per se*. In June 1942, when informing listeners in the Protectorate about the first mass murders of Jews

---

27   Marie Bulínová, ed., *Československo a Izrael v letech 1945–1956. Dokumenty* [Czechoslovakia and Israel in the Years 1945–1956. Documents] (Praha: Ústav pro soudobé dějiny AV ČR, 1993), p. 23. Minutes of the 62nd government meeting, 2 October 1945.

28   National Archive of the Czech Republic, Prague (henceforth NA), Archive of Hubert Ripka (henceforth AHR), 1-50-49, Czechoslovak Foreign Ministry to the Chancellery of the President, Ministry of National Defence, Ministry of the Interior and Council of Ministers, 24 January 1944.

29   Archiv Ministerstva zahraničních věcí [Archive of the Ministry of Foreign Affairs], Prague (henceforth AMZV), Londýnský archiv [London Archive] (henceforth LA), 1939–45, box 511, Lev Zelmanovits to Ripka, 13 March 1941.

30   Ibid., Lev Zelmanovits to Ripka, 13 March 1941 – Ripka's note on the letter. See also ibid., Ripka to Zelmanovits, 27 March 1941, Drtina to Ripka, 31 March 1941.

in Eastern Europe (according to the report prepared by the Jewish Social-democratic group Bund in Poland, 700,000 Jews had already been murdered), Josef Kodíček continued as follows:

"The Czechoslovak lands have also been defiled and are being defiled by the bestialities of Hitler's anti-Semitism. Hitler's plan is clear. As always he is concerned in the first place with robbery. This has already been carried out. Now he is concerned by means of anti-Semitism to disintegrate the moral balance and good sense of the Czech nation. Hence he has launched an anti-Semite propaganda whose madness and perverted nature surpasses even the darkest times of the persecution of witches. The Jews, they say, are responsible for the war in which, in fact, he attacked the world. Humanity is a cunning Jewish invention. The murders which he is carrying out are, he says, committed by Jews. The desire of nations for freedom and democracy is said to be a Jewish intrigue. Capitalism is a Jewish weapon, Communism, too, is a Jewish weapon. Liberalism is a husk of Jewry. A progressive spirit is an expression of Jewish unrest. Conservatism is also a product of the Jews. England is in the service of the Jews. Roosevelt is really Rosenfeld. The Chinese are serving the Jews. Christianity is an offshoot of Jewish philosophy [...] National-Socialism alone is said to be a purely Aryan-Nordic-German invention. For that the Jews have no responsibility."[31]

Nevertheless, whereas ordinary members of the Czechoslovak BBC staff on several occasions brought up the topic of anti-Semitism or relayed news about the suffering of Jews under the Nazis, the situation was more complex in the case of the main exile representatives. Indeed, those Czechoslovak politicians who did raise the question were carefully selected. President Beneš never referred to the Jews in his talks on the BBC. When pressed by a group of the Czech-Jewish assimilationists in London to do so, he declined, citing "reasons of higher interests."[32] Almost no allusion to the Jewish plight can be found in the addresses presented by popular exile spokesmen such as Prokop Drtina[33] and Jaroslav Stránský.[34] In the latter's case, the reason may have been his alleged Jewish descent, constantly harped on by Protectorate journalists.[35] Generally speaking, there were very rarely Jews among the speakers, and when there were, their Jewish origin was not mentioned. Even

31   AČR, BBC 1939–1945, box 14, broadcast 26 June 1942, read by Josef Kodíček.
32   NA, Ministerstvo vnitra – Londýn [Ministry of the Interior – London] (henceforth MV-L), box 255, 2-63-1, Report on the meeting of the Association of Czech Jews, 15 May 1942.
33   Prokop Drtina, *A nyní promluví Pavel Svatý: Londýnské rozhlasové epištoly Dr Prokopa Drtiny z let 1940–1945* [And Now Pavel Svatý Will Speak. The Radio Epistles of Dr Prokop Drtina from the Years 1940–1945] (Praha: Vladimír Žikeš, 1945).
34   Jaroslav Stránský, *Hovory k domovu* [Talks to the Homeland] (Praha: Fr. Borový, 1946).
35   Walter Jacobi, *Země zaslíbená* [The Promised Land], pp. 156–158. For example, there is the reaction of Protectorate propaganda to Stránský's speech on the eve of T. G. Masaryk's birthday, where he – with reference to Masaryk – asked Czechs to help Jews. Dalibor Krčmář, "Walter Jacobi.

Masaryk, whose positive attitude toward Jews has been repeatedly praised, seldom dealt expressly with Jewish matters. Ignacy Schwarzbart, a Zionist in the Polish National Council, drawing on a discussion he had with Masaryk, asserted that Masaryk, as Foreign Minister, was not able to deliver a speech condemning the branding of Jews in the Protectorate with the Star of David in September 1941 (see below). We can argue about Masaryk's motive but the explanation most probably lies in the significance he attached to his political position. In any event, the speech was read by Minister Ripka.[36] On another occasion, shortly after the end of the war, Pavel Tigrid (originally Schönfeld) and his colleagues from the Czechoslovak Service of the BBC were discouraged by Ripka from revealing their real names as opposed to pseudonyms during their last broadcasts.[37] At issue, as Ripka saw it, was the fact that most of the broadcasters had Jewish-sounding names and hence could possibly confirm, for people at home, the story that transmissions from London were solely in the hands of the Jews.

These concerns were amplified by Protectorate propaganda efforts to link the Nazi persecution of Czechs with the resistance activities that were allegedly stimulated by the exiles and thus directly or indirectly by the Jews. Indeed, all the misfortunes suffered by the Czech nation following the first imposition of martial law after Heydrich's arrival in Prague, and again after his assassination in May 1942, were blamed on the Czechoslovak exiles and their Jewish masters.[38] Several key events allowed the activist journalists to bolster these charges. In September 1941, the London exiles demonstrated their influence over people at home by supporting the organized boycott of the Protectorate press, which was accused of working on behalf of the German occupier and spreading Nazi propaganda. The campaign was extremely successful and the daily sale of the major Protectorate newspapers decreased

---

'Vysloveně intelektuální typ' v čele protektorátního SD [Walter Jacobi. An 'utterly intellectual type' heading the Protectorate SD]," in *Terezínské listy* [The Terezín Papers], Vol. 39 (2011), pp. 28–53.

36   Yad Vashem Archives (henceforth YVA), M.2/765 and the Polish version M.2/749, Schwarzbart's diary, 6 October 1941. The descriptions of this story differ somewhat in the Polish and English versions of Schwarzbart's diaries. The Polish version mentions only that Masaryk told Schwarzbart that the broadcast had been his idea, but Ripka gave the speech. In the English version, Schwarzbart further developed the story and added Masaryk's explanation that he, as Foreign Minister, could not read the speech. The fact is that the English version is only a translation made by Schwarzbart in the late 1950s. This notwithstanding, the issue remains that Masaryk, well-known for his pro-Jewish sympathies, made the first direct speech on their behalf, over the BBC, only in December 1942.

37   Pavel Tigrid, *Kapesní průvodce inteligentní ženy po vlastním osudu* [The Pocket Guide of an Intelligent Woman through Her Fate] (Praha: Odeon, 1990), p. 219.

38   Similarly, Czech journalists were informed in February 1941 about a situation in the Netherlands where incitement by Jews and sources in London led to public unrest and, consequently, to a crackdown by the police and armed forces, with many ordinary Dutch people suffering. 28 February 1941.

in the week of 14–21 September 1941 by 50–70 per cent.[39] The successful boy-cott unsettled the Protectorate authorities and according to some authors eventually contributed to the dismissal of Konstantin von Neurath and the appointment of Heydrich as Deputy *Reichsprotektor*.[40]

Concurrently, the Protectorate authorities were further disquieted by incidents that accompanied the compulsory branding of Jews in the Protectorate with the Star of David, ordered on 1 September 1941 and made compulsory 17 days later. On the same day, 18 September 1941, the BBC Czechoslovak Service transmitted a speech that for the first time attacked the persecution of Jews in the Protectorate, directly addressed the beleaguered minority and asked Czechs to support the Jews, now publicly segregated from their non-Jewish compatriots. It is noteworthy that although the exiles made other speeches during the war that dealt with Nazi persecution of the Jews, none matched the tone and compassion of this address. Minister of State, Ripka, was asked to deliver the broadcast and addressed his audience as follows:

"So Hitler has forced the Jews in our country, too, always to appear in public with a special Jewish distinguishing mark by which they should be easily distinguished from others. Thus it is to be made easier for the Nazi mob and the rabble of Vlajka and of Tuka and Mach to hurl themselves on the wretched defenceless Jews whenever they wish. It was not sufficient for these barbarians to rob and plunder the Jews, cruelly to persecute them and sadistically to torture them; no, over and above this they now expose them by publicly distinguishing them from others to daily insults and brutal caprice. [...]

If the Jewish distinguishing mark is now being introduced into our lands we wish to tell you, Czech and Slovak friends, that we believe you will do nothing for which you will have to be ashamed one day. We are convinced that you do not forget your honourable privilege in belonging to the nation of Masaryk.

This spiritual and political leader used every opportunity offered to him to educate the people to a European and world spirit. The Hilsner affair roused his conscience and he openly took up his position against the superstition of ritual murder which was intended to bring about and to work up base anti-Semitic passions. Thanks to the heroic struggle which Masaryk then carried on, our intelligentsia and our people became possessed with disgust for anti-Semitism and cast out the degrading, uncultured, barbarous, biological racial teachings from their emotional background. This process of spiritual and moral regeneration contributed considerably to the Czechs' individual and national consciousness: it was generally recognized that those members of the na-

---

39   Jan Gebhart, Jan Kuklík, *Velké dějiny zemí Koruny české* [The History of the Lands of the Czech Crown – the Big Series], Vol. XVb, 1938–1945 (Praha – Litomyšl: Paseka, 2007), pp. 34–35.
40   Ibid., p. 36.

tion who were racially of Jewish origin could be just as good patriots and decent people or otherwise as could those belonging to any other racial origin.

We here are well informed about everything that is happening at home. Therefore, we also know well how everyone has behaved and is behaving towards the Jews. It fills us with justified pride when we can announce to the civilized world that our people behave towards the persecuted Jews with Christian sympathy and profoundly human understanding for their cruel hardships. We are happy that the German anti-Semites are joined only by a handful of rascals who speak Czech and Slovak but have sold their souls to their slave-drivers.

Czechoslovak Jews, we think of you with sincere sympathy in these days. We know of your sufferings and we carefully assemble all the data about the way in which you are persecuted and the people who persecute you. We know that they are driving you out of the towns, that they are restoring the ghetto, that they imprison you in concentration camps and torture you there to death [...].

We know everything, even the details. We cannot help you for the present. But we tell the world about your sufferings and we assure you that they will not be forgotten.

To-day they wish to designate you publicly by a mark of shame. But the yellow Star of David is a sign of honour which all decent people will respect [...].

Jewish friends, do not hide your Jewish character, be proud of it – you cannot be discriminated against in any other way than all men are: the deep irreconcilable difference rests only in whether a man is worthy or unworthy, humane or inhumane. In these times of bitter trial strengthen your minds in faith in the victory of justice. To-day victory is already certain and it is no longer in the far distant future. You will live to see the day of liberation and just retribution."[41]

This speech was one of the most outspoken examples of the exiles publicly expressing their sympathy for the persecuted Jews, and remained so for over a year. In December 1942, the Allied information campaign confirmed the available news about the "Final Solution" to the Jewish question and Minister Masaryk raised the subject in his radio broadcast.[42] Even then there was allegedly an instruction to the BBC Czechoslovak Service that the Jews should not be addressed directly by the broadcasters.[43] Ripka's speech seems to have been an exception.

The German administration in the Protectorate anxiously followed events in September 1941. The public labelling of Jews in the Protectorate led to the most serious acts of defiance on their behalf displayed by the Czech population during the whole war. Nazi agencies complained that Czechs were

---

41   Hubert Ripka, *We Think of You* (London: Maccabbi, 1941).
42   AČR, BBC 1939–1945, box 50, broadcast by Jan Masaryk, 9 December 1942. For further details see Jan Láníček, "Czechoslovakia and the Allied Declaration of 17 December 1942," manuscript submitted to *Yad Vashem Publishers*.
43   CZA, A280/33, Ernest Frischer to Joseph Linton, 21 April 1944.

demonstratively greeting the branded Jews in the streets, and were offering compassion to the persecuted minority. In one chocolate factory in Moravia, employees came to work several days before the introduction of the law with Stars of David attached to their clothes. Von Wolmar furiously asserted that this incident brought such shameful disgrace on the Czech nation that the press should not even mention it.[44] Conversely, newspapers were asked to emphasize to the public that any Czech seen fraternizing with Jews would be treated as a non-Aryan, with all the limitations in daily life that would result thereby. This warning was to be publicized by all possible means. Von Wolmar also referred to the broadcast by Ripka, "who in one of the broadcasts from London considered it necessary to call the Jews his brothers."[45] Von Wolmar advised journalists to exploit the broadcast in the daily press and provided them with quotes from Ripka's speech. Every expression of sympathy with Jews was to be sharply condemned. Furthermore, and more dangerously as far as the exiles were concerned, the German authorities perceived commiseration with Jews in the Protectorate as being instigated by the London-based exiles. Any subsequent punishment of Czechs, whether for boycotting the Protectorate press or showing compassion towards Jews, could be blamed on the exiles. Hence, too, the subsequent crackdown by Heydrich was portrayed as unavoidable because of the émigrés- and Jewish-inspired acts of defiance.

On 4 February 1942, in a speech to Nazi officials in Prague, Heydrich returned to the difficulties the authorities had faced in September 1941. In his view, the Protectorate had been on the verge of an overt revolt and the situation was saved at the last possible minute. The government-in-exile had clearly been in contact with resistance groups in the Protectorate and the people were blindly following orders from London, as could be seen for example in their response to decrees concerning Jews.[46] Only his timely appearance on the scene, the suppression of all treacherous activities by the introduction of martial law and the execution of Czech patriots and resistance leaders removed the threat.

According to Heydrich's interpretation therefore, his arrival and the terror directed against Czechs that resulted were triggered by the extensive collaboration of the Protectorate population with the exiles. Similarly, SD reports, compiled in late September and October 1941 asserted that ordinary Czechs felt bitterness towards the exiles for leading them astray and causing

---

44 Gebhart, Köpplová, eds., *Řízení legálního tisku v Protektorátu Čechy a Morava*, press meeting on 19 September 1941.
45 Ibid., press meeting on 19 September 1941.
46 Miroslav Kárný, Jaroslava Milotová, Margita Kárná, eds., *Protektorátní politika Reinharda Heydricha* [The Policy of Reinhard Heydrich in the Protectorate] (Praha: TEPS, 1991), document 61, 4 February 1942, pp. 214–215.

havoc in their lives from their place of safety in Britain.[47] Furthermore, they accused the Jews of initiating a whispering campaign, which had allegedly helped to stir up Czech dissent. This theme also appeared in Protectorate propaganda.[48] An issue that future historians will have to unravel is how far Czech resentment against the exiles at this particular point in the war, and Nazi propaganda stories concerning Jewish influence over the London-based government, impacted on the Jewish position in the Protectorate. From the perspective of Protectorate Jewry, the period between September 1941 and late 1942 represented a time of heightened persecution, manifested particularly in deportations to ghettos and camps in the east. Cases of overt Czech sympathy with the plight of the Jews, similar to that expressed in September 1941, were not repeated until the very end of the war. Even more significantly, the number of Jews who survived the war by hiding in the Protectorate was very low, especially in comparison with neighbouring countries, including Germany.[49] In this respect, the timing of the deportations was crucial for Jews in deciding whether to "submerge" and avoid the transport or to obey the peremptory order. Several issues were at play here, including the willingness of Jews to risk the lives of those who would be doing the concealing. At the same time, the offer had to come from the "Aryan," non-Jewish side.

Apart from the decision of individual non-Jews to endanger their own and family members' lives, it might be argued that a directive or request from a moral authority, such as the government-in-exile, could have persuaded ordinary Czechs to offer hideouts to Jews. Yet after the Nazi crackdown in autumn 1941 and for most of 1942, the Czechoslovak BBC Service evinced apparent ambiguity on Jewish matters. This was exactly the time when the majority of Czech Jews were being sent to Terezín (Theresienstadt) and further east. Although the BBC Czechoslovak Service occasionally broadcast information about the massacres of Jews in Eastern Europe, the Czechoslovak government-in-exile avoided the topic of how Jews were faring in the Protectorate

---

47   Dalibor Krčmář, "Mimořádné zpravodajství protektorátního SD o reakcích obyvatel na události z 27. a 28. září 1941 [Extraordinary reports by the Protectorate SD on reactions of the population to the events of 27 and 28 September 1941]," in *Terezínské listy*, Vol. 40 (2012), pp. 27–28.

48   NA, Fund Německé státní ministerstvo pro Čechy a Moravu [German State Ministry for Bohemia and Moravia], 110-5-29, Situational report from Kladno (211/41), 3 October 1941, Situational report by the Prague SD-Dienstelle, 226/41, 6 October 1941.

49   It is estimated that by 30 September 1944, there were 844 Jews in the Protectorate who were in custody, or whose whereabouts were unknown, see YVA, 0.7CZ/99, a statistical report prepared on 18 September 1945. See also Chad Bryant, *Prague in Black. Nazi Rule and Czech Nationalism* (Cambridge, MA: Harvard University Press, 2007), p. 151. Bryant notes, with reference to H. G. Adler, that only 424 Jews survived in hiding in the Protectorate. Adler's figures were sharply criticized by Miroslav Kárný, who argued that the number had to be higher and that Adler's estimate had been influenced by his anti-Czech bias, see: Miroslav Kárný, *"Konečné řešení". Genocida českých židů v německé protektorátní politice* ["The Final Solution." The Genocide of Czech Jews in the German Protectorate Politics] (Praha: Academia, 1991), p. 113 and p. 149, footnote 156.

and did not ask their fellow-Czechs at home to support the doomed deportees, although, significantly, this was not the case with Slovakia. This silence was broken only in late 1942 when the United Nations finally admitted knowing about the Nazi extermination campaign against the Jews.[50] Why the leading exiles did not raise the issue earlier is a matter for speculation, but the impact of the terror unleashed by the Nazis in the Protectorate in late 1941 and the ways in which the Nazi persecution was "justified" would undoubtedly have been a contributing factor. The exiles did not want to be perceived as leading the Czech people to destruction because of the Jews.

"OUR NATION WILL ENTER THE NEW EPOCH UNSTAINED AND CLEAN"[51]

When dealing with the Czechoslovak government-in-exile's response to the Holocaust, we have to first differentiate between the events that took place in the Protectorate of Bohemia and Moravia, and in Slovakia. While the Protectorate was under Nazi occupation, Slovakia was independent, ruled by people who were seen by the exiles as traitors to the unified state and collaborators with the Germans. In the Protectorate, considerable obstacles hindered dealings with the Czech authorities. The President, Emil Hácha, today sometimes labelled a symbol of collaboration, had been lawfully elected to office before the occupation. In the first years of the war, both he and Prime Minister Alois Eliáš were in contact with the resistance movement and also with the exiles. Even later, from late 1941 onwards, when Hácha and the new government were cooperating with the Nazis in excoriating the exiles, Minister Ripka, the head of the exiles' propaganda section, advised restraint in the approach to Hácha. Generally speaking, he maintained, it was not advisable to attack the Protectorate authorities.[52] For diplomatic reasons, Hácha and his government were to be condemned only for the specific measures they took. The situation with regard to the Slovak government, on the other hand, was different: Tiso and Tuka were to be reviled on all fronts. There were no misgivings about the propaganda tools and methods to be employed. Moreover, in connection with Slovakia only, the Advisory Committee on Czechoslovak broadcasting recommended raising the issue of Jewish persecution. BBC transmissions to Slovakia therefore constitute a unique case study, which will be dealt with separately.

---

50 See Láníček, "Czechoslovakia and the Allied Declaration of 17 December 1942."
51 AČR, BBC 1939–1945, box 29, broadcast by Hubert Ripka, 5 January 1944.
52 NA, MV-L, box 271, Minutes of the Advisory Council to the Czechoslovak broadcasting section, 9 July 1942.

Although no requests were made to shelter Jews, the Czechoslovak exiles in their broadcasts to the Protectorate repeatedly asked their compatriots to offer solace or help to Jews whenever possible. However, the negative reports from the home underground on the issue had left their mark. Thus, assisting the Jews was not portrayed as fundamentally an altruistic deed. In March 1943, for instance, the exiled Justice Minister, Jaroslav Stránský, addressed people at home on the eve of the birthday of the first president of the republic, Tomáš Garrigue Masaryk, in the following manner:

> "Among you alone the Germans have tortured and tortured to death tens of thousands of these human beings without the merest semblance of any guilt, simply because they were born of Jewish fathers and mothers — on the European continent these victims go into millions [...]. Not many of the castaways from this wretched ship have remained among you — all the help and relief that you grant them will be for your honor and glory in the world. And it will be put to the credit also of our own national cause. [Tomáš Garrigue] Masaryk's world popularity from which our cause profited so abundantly during the First World War was originally founded on the valiant campaign against the ritual superstition and against the injustice committed against a single insignificant and poor Jewish fellow-citizen. In this way, too, therefore help in whatever way you can, help and you will be helped."[53]

Stránský's plea is couched in such a way as to make clear that assistance extended to the stricken people would actually be in the national interest. In time, the charity would be reciprocated and in the long run the Czechs would benefit as well. The belief about Jewish efficacy in international affairs hung in the background of Stránský's broadcast.[54]

Since the time of Tomáš Garrigue Masaryk, the Czechoslovak government shared the view that Jewish influence on public opinion in the United States was considerable[55] and that the eyes of the world were watching how Czechs treated Jews in the Protectorate. Czech decency towards the persecuted Jews would redound to their credit and generate support for their own political struggle, their fight for the Czechoslovak Republic against foreign oppression as had happened during the First World War. The exiles considered it important therefore to *explain* to the Czechs why they should help the Jews.

The Czechoslovak leaders in London were keen to sustain the notion of Czech uniqueness. The ideal of Czechoslovak democracy and fair treatment

---

53   AČR, BBC 1939–1945, box 19, broadcast by Jaroslav Stránský, 6 March 1943.
54   For a description of these concerns, see for example: NA, MV-L, box 255, file 2–63–2, "A Report by the Association of Czech Jews," 15 May 1942.
55   For Masaryk's views, cf. Karel Čapek, *Talks with T. G. Masaryk* (North Haven, CT: Catbird Press, 1995), pp. 167–168, 192–3.

of minorities was fostered.[56] Providing succour to the Jews in the Protectorate would strengthen these democratic values and thus further the cause of
restoration of the state.

On the other hand, the negative perception of Jews living in Bohemia and
Moravia held by the resistance at home had to be taken into account in preparing the BBC broadcasts. For instance, the exiles avoided making any political
commitments concerning the Jews' post-war position. They also made no effort
to change accepted stereotypes of Jews among people in the Protectorate, such
as that regarding German-speaking Jews, who had often been resented by the
Czech population and this feeling further increased during the war.[57] Minister
Masaryk once raised the topic of German-speaking Jews in Czechoslovakia on
the BBC, only to stress that the Jews themselves now realized their previous
mistake.[58] Masaryk asked Czechs to overlook Jewish reliance on German as
a means of communication.[59] But he did not actually say that condemning the
Jews for such behaviour was wrong. As expressed by Masaryk, the Jews were in
a desperate situation and were still using German in the vain hope that it might
save their lives. Consequently, the Czechs should treat them benevolently.[60]

Nonetheless, Masaryk did not tackle the erroneous assumptions under-
pinning the accusations. The Jews did not use German because they sym-
pathized with the Germans (much less the Nazis) or because they wanted
to Germanize the Czechs. Rather the linguistic pattern emerged because of
historical developments in the Czech Lands and the position of Jews within
the community, which created a way of life that could not be easily altered.
Masaryk, however, had assimilated the underground's perception of Jewish
attachment to German national and cultural identity that was part of Czech
discourse from the second half of the 19th century.[61]

There were other features of the Czechoslovak broadcasts, too, that need
to be considered here. We can characterize the broadcasts to the Protectorate by closely analyzing one particular address. On 17 December, 1942, Ripka
commented on the Allies' declaration acknowledging their awareness of the
Nazi extermination campaign against the Jews. The broadcast started with

---

56   For the history of pre-war efforts to spread the myth of democratic Czechoslovakia, see Andrea
     Orzoff, *Battle for the Castle: The Myth of Czechoslovakia in Europe, 1914-1948* (Oxford: Oxford Uni-
     versity Press, 2009).
57   Láníček, *Czechs, Slovaks and the Jews: 1938-1948*, pp. 21–31; see also for example, Karel B. Palkovský,
     Londýnské epištoly [The London Epistles] (Praha: Václav Petr, 1946), p. 169.
58   AČR, BBC 1939–1945, box 25, broadcast by Jan Masaryk, 29 September 1943, 7:45 p.m.
59   Ibid.
60   Ibid. See also AÚTGM, Klecanda Collection, file 177, the broadcast about Alois Kříž, an inveterate
     anti-Semitic broadcaster in the Protectorate, 5 December 1944.
61   Michal Frankl, *"Emancipace od židů". Český antisemitismus na konci 19. století* ["Emancipation from
     Jews." Czech Anti-Semitism at the End of the 19th Century] (Praha – Litomyšl: Paseka, 2007),
     pp. 36–46.

a detailed description of the crimes committed in furtherance of this objective, confirming that news on what is now called the Holocaust had found its way to the BBC. It also provided estimates of the number of Jews who had already been murdered by the Nazis:

"The joint declaration of the Governments of the United Nations which you have just heard [it was read earlier — J. L.] is only a moderate expression of the horror and disgust with which civilized mankind is moved today. For the horrors committed against the Jewish population of Europe cannot be portrayed in an official declaration. The history of mankind is not without its shadows. But what is now being carried out by Hitler's regime against innocent and defenceless people, this slaughter that goes into hundreds of thousands and perhaps millions, this torture by hunger, extermination by gas and electric current, these massacres of old men, women, invalids, and children, are the most shameful defilement of the name of man. It has been reserved for Hitlerite Germany to win this darkest record of vileness and barbarism. [...]

[T]he present anti-Jewish madness is nothing but the expression of a pathological demon who is driven to fury by the very conception of humanity. In anti-Jewish massacres on this scale there is, it is true, method but there no longer appears from them any normal human feeling. Only one thing is clearly evident in them: the fear of defeat of Hitler and his regime."[62]

It cannot therefore be claimed that the persecution of Jews was overlooked by the *Voice of the Free Republic*. Very detailed information was indeed broadcast, especially around 17 December 1942.[63] At issue, however, is the way in which the information was relayed. It was in fact German persecution of Czechs that played the most prominent part. For example, in December 1942 listeners were told: "Hecatombs of death are covering the Czech land, currents of blood are irrigating it day after day."[64] In light of the reports describing feelings at home and the mind-set of the exiles themselves, a link to the German extermination programme against other people and nations was always made and highlighted: "[A]fter Jews (and together with them), Poles, Russians, Czechs, Yugoslavs will be butchered. The Nordic consciousness is supposed to steel itself with the view of the murder of Jews, not to shake when the turn of the others will come."[65] The persecution of Jews was not a unique phenomenon in its own right. Jewish victimization, though stressed as a crime unparalleled in the annals of history, was still presented only as a prelude to the annihilation of other nations.

---

62   AČR, BBC 1939–1945, box 17, broadcast by Hubert Ripka, 17 December 1942.
63   See ibid., box 17.
64   Ibid., box 17, broadcast on 11 December 1942, 6:45 p.m.
65   Ibid., box 17, broadcast on 15 December 1942, 6:45 p.m.

Indeed at times the Jews were even relegated to the background. As noted by Ivan Petruščák, a member of the Czechoslovak State Council, on 25 June 1944: "The Germans on their way as conquerors of Europe annihilated millions of innocent people, Slavs, Frenchmen, Belgians, Greeks, Norwegians, and Jews."[66] Ripka returned to the theme in his broadcast on 17 December 1942:

> "[N]othing may be able to save [the Nazis] any longer. And therefore they proceed to the realization of their program of nihilists and desperadoes: to drag the rest of the world into destruction with them. [...] The German nation, already burdened by so much guilt, is to share in a crime which history will never be able to forget. And all that is in Hitler's reach is to share his fate of confusion, destruction, death. The massacres of the Jews are only a dress rehearsal for massacres of the other enslaved nations. Some of them, such as the Czechoslovak nation, he still needs. But when his situation is still more hopeless he will spare none who are within the reach of his power. This is the political importance of the campaign of extermination against the Jews and of this you must be aware."[67]

Czechoslovak perceptions of the Nazi occupation of their country led them to underscore the political importance of the Nazi extermination drive against the Jews. Above all, the interest of the nation, of the republic was the first priority. An evaluation of the exiles' ranking of objectives hence explains why some critical features of the Jewish situation did not receive significant attention on the BBC. For example, the first wave of deportations from the Protectorate — apart from the October 1939 Nisko Operation — in mid-October 1941 coincided with an escalation of persecution of Czechs following Heydrich's arrival in Prague. Resistance leaders, including Prime Minister Eliáš, were imprisoned, hundreds of people were shot and martial law was declared in the Protectorate. The events of late September and October 1941 received considerable BBC coverage.[68] Such was not the case with the first deportations of Jews.

This state of affairs was repeated in June 1942. The Bund Report, mentioned earlier, arrived in London exactly at the time when the Germans were avenging the assassination of Heydrich by the brutal oppression of Czechs and the razing of the town of Lidice. The BBC Polish Service drew attention to the Bund Report on 2 June 1942.[69] The Czechs, and others using the BBC frequencies, referred to it in their communiqués only in late June after

---

66   Ibid., box 33, broadcast by Ivan Petruščák, 25 June 1944.
67   Ibid., box 17, broadcast by Hubert Ripka, 17 December 1942.
68   Ibid., box 9, broadcasts from October 1941.
69   Yehuda Bauer, "When Did They Know?" in Michael R. Marrus, ed., *The Nazi Holocaust: Historical Articles on the Destruction of the European Jews – Bystanders to the Holocaust* (Westport: Meckler, 1989), Vol. 8.1, p. 53.

the British press had published the report.[70] Significant for the comparison of Czech and Jewish persecution was a planned speech by the Minister of the Interior in the exile government, Juraj Slávik. His talk dealing with the suffering and deportation of Slovak Jews was originally scheduled to air on 11 June 1942 (according to some sources as early as 1 June 1942). This was postponed for four days, most likely because of the events in Lidice.[71]

Let us now focus on another feature of Ripka's December 1942 broadcast that deserves further attention. Ripka depicted anti-Semitism as something German, or Nazi, but definitely not Czech, and as a phenomenon that could have no appeal for Czech people. Other speakers on the BBC Czechoslovak Service also distanced the Czechs from Nazi anti-Semitism. This differentiation was not couched in the form of pleas to the Czech people to avoid participation in Jewish persecution. Rather it found expression in a terminology of self-assurance, of self-congratulation, of doing the right thing, thus keeping the "myth" of Czech decency, even exceptionality, alive. The role of Czech collaborators in the Final Solution was scarcely mentioned and without emphasis.[72] Even the existence of Czech fascists cast no aspersions on the Czechs as a whole. This message was undoubtedly directed at audiences in the West as well as in the occupied country:

"Vain have been Hitler's attempts to infect with spiritual poison the nations which he has enslaved. The French, Dutch, Polish peoples, and among the first also the Czech people, have shown themselves to be immune to the plague which was to seize them and then disrupt them. The escutcheon of the Czech people is pure and nothing has happened on Czech initiative that might dishonour the good name of the Czechs. [...]

Czechoslovak people: the Czechoslovak government has signed the declaration of the United Nations in the knowledge that it is thus defending not only the cause of humanity and justice but the sincerest interests of the Czechoslovak nation. It is convinced that it is thus expressing your innermost conviction. [...] It has many times been stressed in the Nazi program that the aim of Hitlerism is to eradicate the Czechoslovak nation from Central Europe. [...]

Bear in mind that when [the Nazis] will be still more threatened, they will do everything also to fulfil their anti-Czech and anti-Slovak programme. Be prepared for this and be prepared with fighting determination. And realize that the future of

---

70   Churchill Archives Centre, Churchill College, Cambridge, NERI, 1/1/2, European Service directives for 25 June 25, 26, 27 and 30 June 1942.

71   AČR, BBC 1939–1945, box 14, broadcast by Juraj Slávik, 15 June 1942 (originally scheduled to be aired on 11 June 1942). One source even suggests that the speech was originally planned for 1 June 1942. The assassination of Heydrich took place on 27 May 1942, and this might have been the reason for the postponement of the broadcast until 11 June and later to 15 June. See Hoover Institution Archives, Stanford – Palo Alto, California (henceforth HIA), Juraj Slávik Papers, 18:4.

72   AÚTGM, Klecanda Collection, file 177, broadcast on 5 December 1944 about Alois Kříž.

the Czechoslovak nation is safeguarded only by loyalty to the ideals of the President-Liberator [Masaryk] and by unshakeable solidarity with all suffering and fighting nations.

And solidarity with the suffering, tortured and slaughtered Jews is today a sacred duty of every decent man. We, obedient to the voice of our national tradition, have always fulfilled this duty and shall continue to fulfil it to the end with fervency of heart and with the profoundest inspiration of soul."[73]

Broadcasts to the Protectorate alluding to the Nazi persecution of Jews followed the same documented pattern. The description of concrete events was juxtaposed with a link to the destiny of other nations and concluded by stressing Czech decency and non-involvement in the extermination campaign. On 16 July 1944, for instance, Ripka broadcast very detailed information about the Auschwitz Protocols, a comprehensive report on the Auschwitz death camp, prepared by two Slovak Jews (Walter Rosenberg and Alfred Wetzler) who had escaped from there in April 1944. In his speech the minister outlined the most important facts and described in detail the killing machinery employed. He refrained, however, from mentioning one of the most salient features of the report: the overall number of Jews killed in the Auschwitz concentration camp complex.[74] The second part of the talk was designed to show the Czech people the broader dimension of Nazi political thinking and how the Jewish fate tied in with that planned for other nations.[75] The destruction of European Jewry was never presented in its own singularity.

The situation with Jewish persecution in Slovakia was different. The anti-Semitism of the Slovak government figured prominently in the BBC Czechoslovak broadcasts and became another tool to support the exiles' political programme for a refurbished unified state of Czechs and Slovaks.

"SLOVAK PEOPLE ... YOUR HEART IS CLEAR AS CRYSTAL"

Broadcasts to semi-independent Slovakia on the topic differed significantly. The mainstream Slovak political opposition, starting in 1943, was willing to seal a new pact with the Czechs in order to avoid the unconditional defeat

73   AČR, BBC 1939–1945, box 17, broadcast by Hubert Ripka, 17 December 1942.
74   The National Archives of the United Kingdom, London (henceforth TNA), Foreign Office (henceforth FO) 371/42809, Ripka to the British Ambassador Philip Nichols, 4 July 1944. In this letter, Ripka expressed the view that the overall number of Jews killed in Auschwitz, as stated in the report, might be exaggerated. It might be that the number 1,765,000 was seen as unrealistic by the minister and hence he avoided mentioning it in the broadcast.
75   AČR, BBC 1939–1945, box 34, broadcast by Ripka, 16 July 1944.

of Slovakia.[76] However, the Slovak resistance fighters, although by and large respecting Beneš as president and leader in dealings with foreign concerns, firmly declared their resolve to settle the internal affairs of Slovakia on their own. Hence the exiles' political position *vis-à-vis* Slovakia was very weak. With regard to the Jews, in contrast with the Czech Lands, anti-Semitic sentiments had always been more pronounced in Slovakia even before the war.[77] The Slovak government cooperated (with the help of a considerable segment of the population it must be said) in the Final Solution. The Tiso-Tuka government's policy of "cleansing" Slovak society of Jews and the instalment of the "new and just" order was in many ways approved even by the opposition forces and by the Slovak people. The anti-Jewish sentiments were borne out in underground reports sent to London.[78] Contemporary historiography reveals that the Slovak population altered their views on this hounding of Jews when confronted with the reality of deportations in 1942.[79] However, London had no information on this change in Slovak attitude. Nor did the modification of Slovak views mean they favoured the return of the Jews. The dispatches that reached London confirmed that the Slovak population did not want to allow the Jews to regain their pre-war social status, which had been, in their opinion, unjustified and disproportionate.[80]

There was, however, another international implication the government-in-exile had to consider when deciding on the content of broadcasts to Slovakia. During a government session in June 1943, Minister of the Interior Slávik presented a message received from the Slovak underground.[81] This expressed

76 Jaroslav Hrbek, Vít Smetana et al., *Draze zaplacená svoboda: Osvobození Československa, 1944–1945* [Dearly Paid Freedom: The Liberation of Czechoslovakia, 1944–1945] (Praha: Paseka, 2009), p. 235.

77 For historiography, see Gila Fatranová, "Historický pohľad na vzťahy slovenského a židovského obyvateľstva [Historical view at the relations of the Slovak and Jewish population]," in *Acta Judaica Slovaca*, Vol. 4 (1998), pp. 9–37; Eduard Nižnanský, *Holokaust na Slovensku* [Holocaust in Slovakia], Vol. 7, *Vzťah slovenskej majority a židovskej minority (náčrt problému). Dokumenty* [Relationhip of the Slovak majority with the Jewish minority (an outline of the problem). Documents] (Bratislava: Nadácia Milana Šimečku, 2005); Ivan Kamenec, "Changes in the Attitude of the Slovak Population to the So-Called 'Solution to the Jewish Question' during the Period 1938–1945," in David Bankier and Israel Gutman, eds., *Nazi Europe and the Final Solution* (Jerusalem: Yad Vashem, 2003), pp. 327–338.

78 NA, AHR, 1-50-56c, report from Slovakia, 26 June 1944 (sent 23 June 1944); Dezider Tóth, ed., *Zápisky generála Rudolfa Viesta (Exil 1939–1944)* [Notes of General Rudolf Viest (Exile 1939–1944)] (Bratislava: Ministerstvo obrany, 2002), p. 200, the Viest diary entry, 22 April 1943.

79 Kamenec, "Changes in the Attitude of the Slovak Population," pp. 334–336.

80 NA, AHR, 1-50-56c, 26 June 1944, report from Slovakia. Similar remarks were made by the Communist member of the Slovak National Council, Laco Novomeský, during his stay in London in October 1944. See Vilém Prečan, "Delegace SNR v Londýně (říjen – listopad 1944). Nové dokumenty [The delegation of the Slovak National Council in London (October – November 1944). New documents]," in *Česko-slovenská historická ročenka* [Czecho-Slovak Historical Yearbook] (Brno: Masarykova univerzita, 1999), pp. 221–222.

81 AÚTGM, EB-II, box 182, minutes of the Czechoslovak government session, 25 June 1943.

strong negative sentiments towards Jews and warned the government-in-exile to be careful when publicly airing Jewish issues concerning Slovakia. The Slovak people, it was claimed, did not want to listen to the subject.[82] The report further suggested that the Jews in Slovakia had been supporting Hungarian irredentism. The Slovak Jews, together with Jews in the United States, were allegedly pressing the Americans to back the Hungarian position in post-war negotiations (the Hungarians had occupied southern Slovakia in November 1938). The Slovak government's persecution of Jews and their relative security in Hungary played a role in this development.[83] Although Slávik did not accept that a pro-Hungarian Jewish lobby existed in the United States, he thought that for international purposes it was important to show that the Slovaks were decent people and not guilty of the crimes committed by their Quisling government. This was of great significance for the image of the Czechoslovaks.[84] Slávik deemed it necessary, in the interests of the Czechoslovak resistance movement, to play down any tarnishing of the wider Slovak population. In his broadcast on 18 December 1942, the minister highlighted that the messages coming from Slovakia advised the exiles to avoid mentioning the persecution of the Jews when addressing the home audience, but continued:

"However, we know that the Slovak people do not agree and that they could never approve this fury and murder. Evangelical bishops resolutely protested against the brutal fury against Jews and the Slovak people not only showed respect, but also helped the victims of this bloody regime."[85]

Thus Slávik addressed the situation in Slovakia by making the point that though the people there did not want to hear about the Jewish persecution, nevertheless, they had no part in its functioning. They were, *in fact*, helping the Jews. Indeed, exonerating the Slovak people was the main feature of broadcasts to Slovakia. In June 1942, at the peak of the deportations of Slovak Jews to Poland, Slávik spoke to his audience in Slovakia:

"Slovak kinsmen, the crimes of your traitors and unworthy leaders must appear in a quite new and even more frightful light [...]. [T]he God-fearing Slovak people will avenge its shame and disgrace, [...] it will make order with the traitors and diabolic evil-doers [...]. The whole world is shocked at the cruelty and the un-Christian vengeful rage with which the executioners under Mach and Tuka are running amok. Revenge

---

82   Ibid.
83   Ibid.
84   Ibid.
85   HIA, Juraj Slávik Papers, box 29, file 3, BBC Special Late Night Czechoslovak News, by Dr Juraj Slávik and Dr Ivo Ducháček, 18 December 1942.

and hate are their law. And, at the same time, disgusting Pharisees, they boast of their Christianity. You yourselves see every day how they are shaming and distorting the doctrine of Christ. Only look at what they are doing to the Jews. Sano Mach publicly boasts that by September he will drive 90,000 Jews from Slovakia. He envies the dubious fame of Herod. In cruelty and mercilessness he wishes to surpass his master, the monster Hitler. He is a disgusting vengeful lackey who wishes to curry favour with his commander and master. He even boasts, moreover, that he is doing it without pressure and at the commandment of his own black soul. The newspapers of a neutral country, which trembles before the Nazi danger, Sweden, venture to give expression to their horror at the fact that in no country, not excluding even Nazi Germany, is the Jewish question settled in such an inhuman fashion as in Slovakia."[86]

Slávik's intention was to distinguish between the actions of the Slovak government and the feelings of the ordinary Slovak citizen. The persecution of Jews was portrayed as a crime committed by the "traitorous leaders" of the Slovak state. Slovak government policies, the outrages against Jews among them, threatened the reputation of the Slovaks in world opinion.[87] The danger was that by publicizing information about the situation in Slovakia, the image of the Czechoslovaks as a whole might be harmed. As stated by Viktor Fischl, an exile Foreign ministry official, the British did not differentiate between Czechs and Slovaks.[88] The Slovaks as well as the Czechs had to appear as decent people in the eyes of the international community.

While the cooperation of the general Slovak population in the Final Solution did not find its way into the broadcasts, the Tiso government's persecution of Jews was castigated regularly. The Slovak government's collaboration in Nazi extermination plans allowed the exiles to attack them on humanitarian grounds. Pavel Macháček, Chairman of the Czechoslovak State Council, addressed the issue in late August 1942: "How much misery and suffering have these Jewish fellow citizens of ours suffered, how many of them have paid with their lives – Slovak history will speak of this bestiality and sadism of a so-called Catholic government with the greatest shame. These deeds, however, are so horrible and frightful that we are compelled to raise our voice in protest against them in the interests of the good name of the Slovaks and in the interest of Catholicism."[89] This consideration caused a higher number of programmes dealing with the Jews to be broadcast to Slovakia than to the Protectorate. The exiles sought to demonstrate that the Slovak population was different from those who represented them — such figures as President

---

86   AČR, BBC 1939– 1945, box 14, broadcast by Juraj Slávik, 15 June 1942 (originally scheduled to be aired on 11 June 1942).
87   HIA, Eduard Táborský Papers, box 3, Beneš's message to Slovakia, 20 March 1943.
88   NA, AHR, 1–46–6–10, a note by Viktor Fischl, 5 June 1942.
89   AČR, BBC 1939–1945, box XY, broadcast by Pavel Macháček, 31 August 1942.

Josef Tiso, Prime Minister Vojtěch Tuka, and the Minister of the Interior, Alexander Mach. The message proclaimed by the exile government was that when the Czechoslovak Republic was re-established and Slovakia again became an integral part of the unified state, the democratic spirit would once more rule throughout the whole country:

"It is unbelievable that they can boast in Slovakia of the fact that they are driving people from place to place, even old men, women and children, that they are imprisoning them, goading them like wild beasts, depriving them of shelter and property and of all legal protection, that they are driving them into a foreign land, just as in the twilight of antiquity wild hordes of cruel warriors drove their slaves into the woods or in front of the hooves of their horses [...].

The Slovak people has never been inhuman and cruel and it has always had a profound faith in God. Today, dear kinsmen, show your Christianity and your love for your neighbour to those who are suffering most. Carry each other's burden and thus fulfil Christ's law. And to your rulers with hearts of stone, it would be well to remind [them] of Christ's saying: 'Judge not that you be not judged.' They do not only judge, they torment and torture, but they will not escape the just judgment and retribution which they deserve. But in tormented Slovakia cruelty and fury will pass into oblivion. Again we shall be guided not by the example of Nero and Caligula, not by the laws of Hitler and Mach, but by Christ's love and by the humanist principles of Masaryk. Czechoslovak unity will be further consolidated and cemented by the inhuman bestialities, unexampled in history, that are being committed by the monsters who murder even women and children. The brotherhood of the Czechs and Slovaks will again be the foundation of a happy life for future free generations."[90]

The main theme of these pronouncements was to underline Czech and Slovak adherence to liberal democracy, tolerance, and the ideals of Masaryk democracy. The broadcasts would show the Slovak people and the world that the rulers in Slovakia were foreign to the Slovaks' own national tradition and to Christianity, which they claimed to represent:[91]

"Slovak people, to you I address myself, to you whose soul I know is undefiled and whose heart is clear as crystal – do not support the rulers imposed upon you by the pagan Hitler in their Herod-like deeds. Know that whoever supports anti-Semitism supports Nazism and thus the rule of the so-called German race over all nations, in particular over us Slavs. Know that it is the anti-Jewish poison which has destroyed Europe and which to-day forms the core of Nazism. The more anti-Semitism rages the

90   AČR, BBC 1939–1945, box 14, broadcast by Juraj Slávik, 15 June 1942 (originally scheduled to be aired on 11 June 1942).
91   Jozef Tiso, the President of the Slovak Republic, was a priest and the Catholic Church played an important role in the regime.

more will Nazism celebrate its orgies, Nazism whose main task is to destroy Christianity and exterminate the Slavs."[92]

Nevertheless, we need to return to the effect that the reports from the Slovak underground had on the exiles' broadcasts. Prompted by the information they contained, Slávik, for instance, used his BBC air time to stress that the exiles understood the negative perception of Jews among some Slovaks. The minister had no wish to contradict the sentiments of the Slovak people:

"There are bad Jews as there are bad Christians. We know that there were Jews who did not become reconciled to a Slovak life. There are good and bad Jews as there are good and bad Christians. But inhumanity and barbarism, medieval torture and atrocities are an offence to Christianity."[93]

The exiles did not want to be perceived as siding with the Jews regardless of previous Jewish "behaviour" towards Czechs and Slovaks. A clear division was made between political and humanitarian issues. The Slovaks were called on to support the Jews in the name of humanity and in their broadcasts the exiles focused on cases when ordinary people and clerics had helped Jews.[94] However, this did not mean that the Jews would be accepted into mainstream society with no preconditions. Slávik's discourse suggested that in the future Jews would need to be "reconciled to a Slovak life." The exiles were aware that the situation in Slovakia represented a threat to their immediate status in Britain and later, after the war had ended, at home. The Beneš government realized that their position in Slovakia was by no means assured and that there was still a lurking danger that the leaders of the Slovak resistance movement, among them many Communists, might reject the exiles' authority. It was important for the government-in-exile therefore to hold the full recognition of the Slovak people and to avoid handing any potential opposition leadership a pretext that could lead to independence tendencies.

For example, it was not worth jeopardizing the exiles' homecoming to Slovakia by touching on Jewish restitution, an issue that was clouded and tangled by Slovak "Aryanization." Both Slávik and Masaryk in their broadcasts repeatedly informed the Slovaks that all belongings stolen from Jews would be restored to their rightful owners.[95] The central Czechoslovak government, however, never applied this precept in practice in post-war Slovakia and it even took more than a year after the war to get Slovak agreement

92   AČR, BBC 1939–1945, box XY, broadcast by Pavel Macháček, 31 August 1942.
93   Ibid., box 14, Juraj Slávik broadcast, 15 June 1942 (originally scheduled to be aired on 11 June 1942).
94   Ibid., box 31, broadcasts by Vladimír Clementis, 28 March and 1 April 1944.
95   LMA, BoD, Acc3121/E/03/510, broadcast by Juraj Slávik, 9 February 1944; AČR, BBC 1939–1945, box 50, broadcast by Jan Masaryk, 9 December 1942.

on legislation that would make the return of such property possible. At the same time, enforcement of the new law was piecemeal and dilatory,[96] with little will on the part of the authorities to test how those who had profited from Aryanization might react, among them many active members of the post-war Slovak governing parties.

Other governments-in-exile, too, attempted to gloss over the record of their citizens and presented their behaviour towards the Jews during the war in a diametrically different manner from that in the intelligence reports received from the subjugated homelands. The Polish government-in-exile repeatedly altered the content of messages concerning anti-Jewish sentiments in Nazi-controlled Poland. In February 1940, for example, a courier from the Polish underground state, Jan Karski, reached the Polish government-in-exile, then still in France. He prepared a comprehensive appraisal, including a description of Polish-Jewish relations, which he drew in dark colours, highlighting especially Polish resentment against Jews, caused partly by their alleged collaboration with the Soviet occupiers. The Polish government was aware that such an unvarnished statement of facts would do no good to their reputation among the Allies and asked Karski to compose another, this time a censored version, of his findings. Karski complied and it was this second version, with the previous controversial comments omitted and painting a rosy picture of Polish-Jewish coexistence, which was shared with western governments.[97]

CONCLUSION

Political considerations played an enormous role in the decision-making process concerning the content and tenor of wartime BBC broadcasts. Nazi anti-Semitic policies and the involvement of some among the local population in Jewish persecution was a topic that the Czechoslovak exiles could not avoid in their communiqués to their occupied homeland. But the initial response to exile transmissions in the early years of the war and the existence of a Protectorate propaganda campaign depicting the exiles' alleged collaboration with Jewish groups affected the content and form of the broadcasts that followed. This influence can be seen in the selection of speakers, the themes

96 For the development of post-war Slovakia, see articles by Yeshayahu A. Jelinek, for example: "The Communist Party of Slovakia and the Jews: Ten Years (1938–1948)," in *East Central Europe*, Vol. 2 (1978), pp. 186–202; "Židia na Slovensku 1945-1949 [Jews in Slovakia 1945-1949]," in Idem, ed., *Židia na Slovensku v 19. a 20. storočí* [Jews in Slovakia in the 19th and 20th centuries], Vol. II (Bratislava: Judaica Slovaca, 2000), pp. 79–96.
97 Jan Láníček, "Governments-in-exile and the Jews during and after the Second World War," pp. 82–83.

presented, and especially in the prolonged silence on the situation of Jews by the exiled politicians, which lasted from September 1941 until late 1942. The last two features were, to a certain degree, swayed by apprehension about how people at home would react if Jewish matters featured too prominently. This disquiet later coloured the tone of the broadcasts reporting on Jewish persecution, or which asked Czechs and Slovaks to aid and shelter Jews. Moreover, it should be pointed out that references to the oppression of the Jews did not stand alone but were always linked to reports of similar Nazi plans for other peoples.

The BBC broadcasts were shaped by a complex of interacting factors. The reports sent by the home underground movement and the government-in-exile's own diplomatic strategies changed the rules of the game. The Czechoslovaks wanted to be seen as a democratic nation, a people who adhered to democratic and humanitarian principles. It was therefore sought to distance the people in the Czech Lands and in Slovakia from the anti-Jewish persecution conducted by the Nazis and the Slovak government. The role of Protectorate collaborators in the Holocaust was almost entirely suppressed. In the case of the Slovaks, their behaviour was whitewashed in order not to harm the Czechoslovak diplomatic struggle abroad.

Yet, it should be added that there was no intention on the part of the exiles to downplay the horror of the Nazi extermination campaign against the Jews. However, the main thrust of the programmes transmitted, among a number of competing priorities, was directed at the Nazi attack on the Republic, which was always seen as the foremost item on the Czechoslovak agenda. Nonetheless, political considerations notwithstanding, the exiled Czechoslovaks did on several occasions broadcast news and commentaries on the persecution of the Jews and it cannot be claimed that the Holocaust was totally ignored. The fact that most of the broadcasts carried broader messages and subtexts which regularly overshadowed or diluted news about the plight of the Jews was a result of the political complexities the exiles had to face.

TRUTH CONQUERS... POLITICAL PAMPHLETS OF THE CZECH AND SLOVAK OPPOSITION VERSUS EDVARD BENEŠ AND THE CZECHOSLOVAK GOVERNMENT-IN-EXILE

DUŠAN SEGEŠ

In recent decades, scholarship on the subject of political emigration from Czechoslovakia after 1938 and during the Second World War, has made immense progress. This finding is true both for the activities of the Czechoslovak government-in-exile (and the Czechoslovak National Committee, its predecessor) and for the political activities of politicians, army officials, journalists, etc., who were in opposition to the government and to Edvard Beneš.[1] From the point of view of political programmes, ambitions and motivations, this very heterogeneous collection of individuals and political groupings, such as the Czecho-Slovak National Council (1939–1940), the Czech National Union and the Slovak National Union (1943), the Czech National Council (1944–1945) and the Slovak National Council (1944), is referred to as the "anti-Beneš" opposition. It is worth mentioning that in the most comprehensive monograph on this topic to-date, which was written by Jan Kuklík and Jan Němeček and titled *"Proti Benešovi!"* ["Against Beneš!"], one of the criteria for the classification of particular politicians as "anti-Benešists" were their

---

1 Jan Němeček, *Od spojenectví k roztržce. Vztahy československé a polské exilové reprezentace 1939–1945* [From Alliance to Rift. Relations between the Czechoslovak and Polish Exile Representations 1939–1945] (Praha: Academia, 2003); Toman Brod, *Osudový omyl Edvarda Beneše 1939–1948. Československá cesta do sovětského područí* [Fateful Mistake of Edvard Beneš 1939–1948. Czechoslovakia's Road to the Soviet Thrall] (Praha: Academia, 2002); Jiří Friedl, *Na jedné frontě. Vztahy československé a polské armády (Polskie Siły Zbrojne) za druhé světové války* [On a Single Front. Relations of the Czechoslovak and Polish army (Polskie Siły Zbrojne) during the Second World War] (Praha: Ústav pro soudobé dějiny AV ČR, 2005); Marek Kazimierz Kamiński, *Edvard Beneš kontra gen. Władysław Sikorski. Polityka władz czechosłowackich na emigracji wobec rządu polskiego na uchodźstwie 1939–1943* [Edvard Beneš versus General Władysław Sikorski. The Policy of the Czechoslovak Governments-in-Exile towards the Polish Government-in-Exile 1939–1943] (Warszawa: Neriton, 2005); Martin D. Brown, *Jak se jedná s demokraty. Britské ministerstvo zahraničí a československá emigrace ve Velké Britanii 1939–1945* (Praha – Plzeň: Beta-Dobrovský Ševčík, 2008), originally published as *Dealing with Democrats. The British Foreign Office and the Czechoslovak Émigrés in Great Britain, 1939 to 1945* (Frankfurt am Main: Peter Lang Verlag, 2006); Vít Smetana, *In the Shadow of Munich. British Policy towards Czechoslovakia from the Endorsement to the Renunciation of the Munich Agreement (1938–1942)* (Prague: Karolinum Press, 2008); not to mention the editions of series of documents issued in the Czech Republic, such as several volumes of *Dokumenty československé zahraniční politiky* [Documents of Czechoslovak Foreign Policy], edited by Jan Němeček, Jan Kuklík, Helena Otáhalová and Ivan Šťovíček.

"several mainly propagandistically oriented publications released during the Second World War."[2]

Two factors have crucial importance in the analysis of Czechoslovak exile politics, especially at the first stage of the Second World War: legitimacy and interpersonal relations.

I consider it appropriate to broaden our horizons, while stressing the importance of the very complex issue of political exiles and exile politics, by using some theoretical frameworks and approaches. Max Weber's concept of legitimacy is one. Weber stressed the necessity for stable government to maintain a sustainable level of "pure legitimacy," the legal authority of the institute of political governance. In the case of a government-in-exile that is divorced from control over its state apparatus, ideas of "pure legitimacy" become important. Beneš and the Czechoslovak government made symbolic gestures designed to gain support from the Americans, British, and Soviets. This rhetoric and symbolism had a dual effect; it was not only projecting an (false) image of Czechoslovak national unity to the Allied Powers, but it was also self-justifying the rule of Czechoslovak émigrés in Great Britain amongst themselves. By pre-empting labels such as "national committee," "national council," and "government-in-exile," and by continuing to employ state symbols, flags, familiar slogans, hymns, uniforms, national attributes, and the like, the Czechoslovak as well as other exile groups and their leaders encourage prospective contributors to think of their organization as having national stature and authority.[3] However, as Vít Smetana argues, the recognition of a Czechoslovak government and Edvard Beneš as head of the Czechoslovak liberation movement (as president) constituted a serious problem, since Beneš's legitimacy was questionable from the legal point of view. Unlike the situation with other governments-in-exile residing in London, Beneš's claim "was not based on continuity, but on a legal construction […]. Therefore the recognition came only at the moment, when the balance of advantage switched in favour of meeting Beneš's request."[4] This moment came in July 1940, when the Provisional Czechoslovak government was recognized by the British government (full diplomatic recognition did not come until July 1941).

---

2   Jan Kuklík, Jan Němeček, *Proti Benešovi! Česká a slovenská protibenešovská opozice v Londýně 1939–1945* [Against Beneš! The Czech and Slovak Anti-Beneš Opposition in London 1939–1945] (Praha: Karolinum, 2004), pp. 10–11.

3   Yossi Shain, *The Frontier of Loyalty. Political Exiles in the Age of the Nation-State* (Middletown: Wesleyan University Press, 1989), p. 59.

4   Smetana, *In the Shadow of Munich*, p. 198; for more information on this topic see e.g., Jan Kuklík, "The Recognition of the Czechoslovak Government in Exile and its International Status 1939–1942," in *Prague Papers on the History of International Relations*, Vol. 1 (1997), pp. 173–205; Jan Kuklík, Jan Němeček, "Repudiation of the Munich Agreement during the Second World War as Seen from the Czechoslovak Perspective," in *The Disintegration of Czechoslovakia in the End of 1930s. Policy in the Central Europe* (Prague: Institute of History, 2009), pp. 97–122.

The second factor significantly influencing wartime politics was interpersonal relations – in the case of Czechoslovak, Polish and other émigrés, these relations were additionally determined by the very specific circumstances of being forced to act abroad, in exile. Josef Korbel, the Czechoslovak diplomat and father of the former Secretary of State of the United States of America, Madeleine Albright, gives a striking personal account:

"Political émigrés are strange people. Uprooted from their national environment and deprived of a political base, they struggle among themselves for power. Often they cover their personal ambitions with high-sounding patriotic pronouncements; they dream and scheme, enter into constantly shifting coalitions and, in search of security, frequently find themselves with very strange bedfellows indeed. They must do all this not only without embarrassing the host country in its domestic or foreign affairs, but also without ever losing sight of their ultimate goal of returning home and resuming positions of leadership."[5]

Voices of discord and political opposition played an integral part in the Czechoslovak exile during the whole of the Second World War. When using terms like "opposition," "anti-Beneš," and so on, however, one has to bear in mind the very specific émigré situation. No proper critical explication was forthcoming from the independent media. Neither were there democratic elections nor the mechanisms of a parliamentary system other than the State Council, which was a quasi-parliament consisting of members appointed by President Beneš.

The threat posed by Czech and Slovak political opposition differed at various stages of the war. The risks were more serious from the first stage of the war until 1941 when Beneš and the Czechoslovak National Committee were struggling for full international recognition as official representatives of Czechoslovakia. Especially in France in 1939/1940, it was absolutely impossible to reach a compromise in order to create a unified Czechoslovak front because of conflict among the émigrés. The diary of Jaromír Smutný, Chief of the President's Cabinet, presents a very sad and dark picture. He noted:

"we live in an atmosphere of constant, general and persistent mistrust, struggle, conflict, controversy competition for authority, in a war of all against all [...]. Only in criticizing other people, always in a malicious way, can we agree."[6]

---

5   Josef Korbel, *Twentienth Century Czechoslovakia* (New York: Columbia University Press, 1977), p. 185.

6   Milada Červinková, Libuše Otáhalová, eds., *Dokumenty z historie československé politiky 1939–1943. Acta Occupationis Bohemiae et Moraviae* [Documents from the History of Czechoslovak Politics 1939–1943], Vol. I, *Vztahy mezinárodní diplomacie k politice československé emigrace na západě* [At-

In democratic regimes, political controversies and criticism constitute an integral component of everyday politics. There is hardly any doubt that silencing a political opponent by using methods such as denunciation (based on false or unverified evidence) is undemocratic. The National Committee under Beneš's non-formal leadership and the Czechoslovak Secret Service headed by Colonel František Moravec did not hesitate to employ all possible means to eliminate their strongest political opponents: after the fall of France, in July 1940, almost all the members of Milan Hodža's Czecho-Slovak National Council were interned by the British authorities after arrival in the United Kingdom.[7] They were held under deportation and detention orders by the Home Secretary on the advice of the British MI5, which had no independent records on them. MI5's recommendation for the internment of six Czechoslovaks (Robert Hildprandt, Karel Locher, Vladimír Borin-Ležák, Peter Prídavok, František Schwarz and Josef Waldmüller-Leśniewski) was based on two allegations by a "Czech counter-espionage officer": they were portrayed to a greater or lesser degree as being under German influence (or even agents of the Gestapo), or as constituting a serious threat to the unity of the present Czecho-Slovak national effort led by Beneš.[8] Accusations made by the Czechoslovak *Deuxième* Bureau forwarded to the War Office and MI5 that the internees were pro-Nazi sympathizers were without foundation.[9] As Frank Kenyon Roberts, the head of the Central Department of the Foreign Office, noted: "After a good deal of research nothing really serious could be

---

titudes of International Diplomacy towards Policy of Czechoslovak Emigration in the West] (Praha: Academia, 1966), p. 91, diary entry by Smutný from 22 March 1940.

7   The internment of former members of the Czecho-Slovak National Council (further C-SNC) was described in detail by Kuklík and Němeček, although I cannot agree with their viewpoint that the internment itself was a purely British affair. See Kuklík, Němeček, *Proti Benešovi!*, pp. 369–382; Detlef Brandes, *Großbritanien und seine osteuropäischen Alliierten 1939-1943. Die Regierungen Polens, der Tschechoslowakei und Jugoslawiens im Londoner Exil vom Kriegsausbruch bis zur Konferenz von Teheran* (Munich: Oldenbourg, 1988), p. 88. The direct involvement of the Czchoslovak Secret Service in accusations against the former C-SNC members and their subsequent internment in Britain is confirmed in an undated report by J. Slávik handed over to the archive of the Ministry of the Interior on leaving the post of Minister in 1945. See Národní archiv České republiky [The National Archives of the Czech Republic], Prague (henceforth NA, Prague), Collections Ministerstvo vnitra – Londýn [Ministry of the Interior – London], box 105, signature 2-7-1.

8   The National Archives, London (henceforth TNA), Foreign Office (henceforth FO) 371/24292, C 8774/8067/12, letter by an MI5 officer signed G. D. White to Hopkinson from the Foreign Office, 10 August 1940. It is also worth mentioning that on the British side it was Robert Bruce Lockhart who made some recommendations to the Foreign Office in 1940 that Czechoslovak internees should be released from internment. See TNA, London, FO 371/24292, C 8774/8067/12, minute by F. K. Roberts, 14. August 1940.

9   In the above-mentioned letter from MI5 to the FO, Locher was characterized as a "man [who] collaborated with the Fascists in Czecho-Slovakia. On this account he is now considered entirely pro-German and a great danger to the Czecho-Slovak interest." Schwarz was described as "a Czech Fascist" and considered "to be pro-Nazi on account of his Fascist associations and is regarded as an enemy agent." Ibid.

pinned on to any of these gentlemen, with the possible exception of Mr. Bo-
rin-Lezak."[10]

Colonel Moravec was in fact Beneš's "hatchet man," who took responsibility for getting political opponents off the President's back in situations where
it would be inappropriate for Beneš to do so himself.[11] If Moravec's testimony
can be credited, it was Beneš who demanded that opposition members in the
Czecho-Slovak National Council should be arrested by the British authorities
in the summer of 1940 and asked Moravec to arrange matters.[12]

On the other hand, the Czechoslovak Provisional government intervened
several times at a ministerial level at the Home Office on behalf of Czechoslovak citizens who were arrested by the British, asking for their release from
the detention camps.[13] I would argue that the methods used by Czechoslovak
officials had a strong impact on the activities of Czech and Slovak "renegades"
who were even more belligerent and radical after release from the camps,
where they had spent several months, some even more than a year.[14]

When observing the wartime activities of the Czech and Slovak opposition, one is reminded of a committee at cross purposes. Viewed ironically,
Beneš might be seen as eventually the only effective chairperson who could

---

10   TNA, FO 371/30843, C 3337, minute by F. K. Roberts written in the file "Subversive activities of
     Mr. Karel Locher," 3 April 1942.

11   Jiří Šolc, *Po boku prezidenta. Generál František Moravec a jeho zpravodajská služba ve světle archivních
     dokumentů* [At the President's Side. General František Moravec and His Intelligence Service in
     the Light of Archival Documents] (Praha: Naše vojsko, 2007), p. 152.

12   As Moravec wrote in his memoirs, Beneš was indignant at the activities of "three right-wing
     politicians" (unfortunately, Moravec gives no detailed record) and told Moravec, he wished to
     silence them during the negotiations with the British government on recognition of the Czecho-
     slovak Provisional government. Beneš asked the Colonel if there was any possibility of having
     them remanded in custody. "I said I would try to arrange it. The British authorities co-operated
     with us and all three gentlemen were arrested. Beneš was deeply satisfied and thanked me for
     my help in such a precarious situation that was so important for our nation." František Moravec,
     Špión, jemuž nevěřili [A Spy That Was Not Trusted] (Praha: Rozmluvy, 1990), p. 236. Originally
     published as *Master of Spies* (New York: Doubleday, 1975). One has to take into account that these
     memoirs were written in Washington in 1966, and were strongly influenced by Moravec's disil-
     lusionment with Beneš's behavior, especially after 1945.

13   TNA, FO 371/24292, C 8774/8067/12, letter of the Czechoslovak Ministry of Foreign Affairs to
     Frank K. Roberts, 23 October 1940, on behalf of Dr. Moses Simon. Simon was released on July
     1940.

14   After being moved to the Lingfield military internment camp, the six Czechoslovak internees
     threatened to go on hunger strike and demanded to be heard by an MI5 officer. The officer who
     interviewed them formed the opinion that the internees should be regarded as at least genuine
     opponents of the Beneš regime and *not persons likely to be in German pay* [highlighted by D.S.].
     When the British officer questioned them concerning the attitude they would take to the Beneš
     government if, on review, it was decided they could be released, each gave an undertaking that
     he would refrain from all open opposition to the Beneš national government since, albeit mis-
     takenly in their view, it had been recognized by the British government. "They remained quite
     firm, however," the British officer maintained, "in stating that they would endeavour to obtain
     a hearing for their views in British circles and would, if it were possible, proceed to the U.S.A."
     TNA, FO 371/24292, C 8774/8067/12.

coordinate the politically active, dissatisfied exiles from Czechoslovakia, among whom there was no one coherent, homogeneous group but rather a broad spectrum of different individuals representing a variety of political and social aspirations. On the left were the Social Democrats around Rudolf Bechyně and the newspaper *Nová Svoboda* [New Freedom], as well as the Czechoslovak Communists in London and the Soviet Union. On the right were the military, represented by General Lev Prchala, and financial interests grouped around such figures as Josef Malík, former Director of the National Bank of Czechoslovakia. In addition, there were those acting on behalf of the Slovaks and other national minorities, such as the anti-Nazi Sudeten Germans led by Wenzel Jaksch.

Owing to personal animosities and fundamental political differences, co-operation between these individuals and groups was limited. The "unity" they sought to manifest was confined either to resolutions on post-war settlement, issued by organizations such as the Slovak and Czech National Union (subsequently renamed Council) headed by Peter Prídavok and General Lev Prchala, or cooperation in various federalist committees, most under the auspices of Poles, such as the Independent Central European Federal Association (ICEFA) and the Czech-Polish-Slovak Club. Other examples of *ad hoc* collaboration can be seen in the main outburst of attacks against Beneš and Czechoslovak foreign policy in December 1943, during the Slovak Uprising in 1944, and again in 1945 when Beneš and the Czechoslovak government moved to liberated Czechoslovakia.

"ANTI-BENEŠ" PAMPHLETS

The pamphlets were part of a campaign by opponents of Beneš and the Czechoslovak government-in-exile. Although every brochure published in Britain was scrutinized by the censors, the censorship was relatively liberal. The leaflets were distributed among Czechoslovak citizens throughout the United Kingdom and also in other areas of the world, especially the US and the Middle East, where a section of the Czechoslovak armed forces were stationed until 1943.

It is hardly surprising that most of these materials were published by the former members of the Czecho-Slovak National Council who had been interned by the British authorities in 1940. The majority were printed in 1942–1943.

In January 1942, General Prchala, Ferdinand Kahánek (who had died in Romania in 1940) and, indirectly, Osuský were attacked by Beneš's nephew Bohuš, editor of the officially sponsored weekly newspaper *Čechoslovák*. In a rather sensational article entitled "Do posledního roku" [Into the last year],

Bohuš Beneš, writing under the pseudonym "Tenax," described the political activities of these "dissidents" of the time as selfish and unpatriotic:

"There were numerous attempts to create a schism and to set up an opposition within our liberation movement. In two cases, Poland and France, all the complications were solved for us by events, just as President [Edvard Beneš – D. S.] had confidently and patiently predicted. In Paris, all our difficulties – far more serious than the pitiful attempts to create a 'separate Liberation movement' in Poland – were exacerbated by those French politicians who bore the blame for Munich, but matters were settled for us by Adolf Hitler in his crushing of France."[15]

This item caused a stir in Czech and Slovak opposition émigré circles. In the succeeding months of 1942, a series of pamphlets by Karel Locher, František Schwarz, Štefan Osuský and Vladimír Borin-Ležák, were published in response.

Locher's pamphlet *Naše akce* [Our campaign] starts with: "Mr. Tenax is in an advantageous position [...]. He knows that some of his opponents are already dead – like Dr. Ferdinand Kahánek – so they cannot answer. He knows that others cannot do so either because they were, or still are, in prison and internment camps, where they were put thanks to the care of some operatives of "our action" [...]. The gentlemen started the attack. We answer."[16] Circulation of *Naše akce* reached a remarkable 2,525 copies. Locher calls "our action," meaning the liberation movement, a "totally undemocratic personal dictatorship by Dr. E. Beneš," self-appointed president and dictator. Locher claimed that there was no democratic Czechoslovak institution abroad representing the people at home; in his view there was neither government nor parliament, only a "dictatorially appointed Czechoslovak government" and an equally "dictatorially appointed State Council," along with hundreds of civil servants, announcers and bodyguards. At the end of his critique, Locher extolled the merits of General Prchala and Š. Osuský.

The Czechoslovak government responded immediately. In a letter to State Secretary Herbert Morrison, Minister Juraj Slávik sent a list of members of the Czecho-Slovak National Council (which was incorrect, since the council had discontinued its activities in the summer of 1940) accusing them of "sub-

---

15 In Czech, the article reads as follows: "Měli jsme několik pokusů o rozkol a utvoření oposice uvnitř naší akce. Ve dvou případech, v Polsku a ve Francii, všechny komplikace za nás vyřídily události, tak jak to president od počátku akce s jistotou a trpělivostí předpovídal. Kahánkovština a *prchalovština* [highlighted by D. S.] zhasla v Polsku s beckovským režimem dříve, než se rozrostla ve skutečný rozkol. V Paříži všechny naše obtíže – mnohem závažnější, než ubohé pokusy o „separátní odboj" v Polsku – zneužívané francouzskými politiky, kteří s sebou nesou vinu za Mnichov, za nás vyřídil Adolf Hitler tím, že rozdrtil Francii!" *Čechoslovák*, 2 January 1942, p. 1.
16 Karel Locher, *Naše akce* [Our Action], (London: published by Karel Locher – 32 Elvaston Place, 1942).

versive activities." He devoted particular attention to Locher's pamphlet and insisted that the author had eluded wartime censorship and thus committed a penal offence. Slávik went further, alleging that Locher had also cast aspersions on the British Crown and the British government: President Beneš and the Czechoslovak government had been recognized by the British, so "any person defaming this measure in the abusive terms adopted by Locher, indirectly vilifies a measure taken by His Majesty's government." Slávik goes on to state that if it is ascertained that Locher's views, which he terms calumnies, false allegations and abusive attacks, are shared by persons within the reach of Czechoslovak military law, proceedings will be taken against them. Finally, he expressed the hope that the British authorities would in due course after investigating all the available material, proceed against such persons so as to render impossible any further subversive activities by them on the territory of Great Britain.[17] The Foreign Office was informed of Slávik's letter by their envoy, Philip Nichols, who spoke with Hubert Ripka, State Minister in the Czechoslovak Foreign Ministry, and Edvard Beneš before Slávik's letter had been forwarded to the Home Office. Both Ripka and Beneš expressed the view that Locher's pamphlet was criminal rather than political in character[18]; and, further, that Locher's action was contrary to the conditions of his release from internment. Beneš personally maintained that if Locher were to ignore any warning that might be issued by the British authorities, he should be returned to captivity without more ado. The Foreign Office, however, was struck by Slávik's *modus operandi*[19] and did not recommend that any special action be taken against him, explaining that the present moment was not an appropriate time for helping the Czechoslovak government in any heresy-hunting against political opponents.[20]

State Secretary Morrison informed Anthony Eden of Slávik's letter but expressed the Home Office opinion that the pamphlet and the other activities in question did not provide a basis for criminal proceedings against Locher since attacks are made against British ministers similar to those made by Locher against the Czechoslovak government and it would not be possible under British law for Locher to be prosecuted. A second question raised by Morrison was whether the British government should amend Defence Regu-

---

17   TNA, FO 371/30843, C 4093, letter by Minister Slávik to Secretary H. Morrison, 24 March 1942.

18   TNA, FO 371/30843, C 3337, letter by Philip Nichols to R. Makins, 27 March 1942.

19   It was considered by the Foreign Office as rather odd to worry the Home Office, since it would have been normal for the Czechoslovak government to take the matter up with either the Foreign Office or Envoy Nichols.

20   Ibid., letter by F. K. Roberts to A. Newsam from the Home Office, 3 April 1942. In a minute dated 3 April 1942, Roberts expressed the opinion that in view of Czechoslovak internal squabbles, as instanced by Osuský's dismissal, "feeling is obviously high among the Czechs and Slovaks, and we must be careful not to aid and abet heresy hunting on the part of the Czechoslovak government." Ibid.

lation 39A so as to make it an offence to attempt to suborn personnel serving in any of the Allied forces from lawful duty.[21]

Eden agreed with Morrison's suggestion that it would be inadvisable to "make any attempt to meet Dr. Slavik's request." When it came to verbal attacks on a head of state, remedy in such cases was either through civil or criminal libel proceedings and Eden felt it would not be in British, or indeed Beneš's interest, to pursue any such course, since it would only give "a great deal of undesirable publicity to a handful of relatively unimportant Czechoslovak malcontents." With regard to the second issue, Eden thought there would be every advantage in changing Defence Regulation 39A.[22]

Consideration of the emergency regulation came as a result of Slávik's warning that circulation of Locher's pamphlet *Naše akce* could have an adverse effect on unity within Czechoslovak civil and military circles.[23] This apprehension was reinforced by a report from the head of counter-intelligence in the Czechoslovak Secret Service, Lieutenant-Colonel Josef Bartík, who informed the Home Office that the opposition was about to issue a second edition of Locher's pamphlet to be distributed among the Czechoslovak Air Force in particular. In Lt.-Col. Bartík's view, the activities of the Czech and Slovak opposition constituted a "menace to the discipline and efficiency of the Czechoslovak military units in Great Britain" and also had a detrimental effect on the Czechoslovak struggle at home and abroad.

On 15 May 1942, Slávik attended a meeting at the Home Office which F. Roberts from the Foreign Office also joined. Slávik repeated his previous arguments. The Attorney General, who was also present, informed him of the British tradition of freedom of opinion and the press and refused to take any action against Locher. This was not what Slávik and the Czechoslovak government had expected. Indeed, all that Slávik could salvage from his efforts was a vague promise to amend Defence Regulation 39A.[24]

In spring 1942, František Schwarz published a pamphlet called *Doktor Beneš o vojně před válkou i za ní* [Doctor Beneš on military conflict before and during the war].[25] He drew attention to the "confident and patient predictions" of E. Beneš mentioned in the *Čechoslovák* article and referred to the false prophecies made by Beneš concerning the end of the Second World War, maintaining that they would severely damage the Czechoslovak liberation movement and indeed Beneš himself when the time came. It is interesting

---

21 TNA, FO 371/30843, C 4093, letter by H. Morrison to A. Eden, 16 April 1942.
22 Ibid., letter by A. Eden to H. Morrison, 29 April 1942.
23 TNA, FO 371/30843, C 3337, letter by Philip Nichols to R. Makins, 27 March 1942.
24 TNA, FO 371/30843, C 10362.
25 František Schwarz, *Dr. Beneš o vojně před válkou i za ní. Boj za právo* [Dr. Beneš on War before the War and After. A Struggle for Justice] (sine loco: published by František Schwarz, undated).

to note, that the printing and distribution of Schwarz's pamphlet was under-taken by Karel Locher.[26]

In this case too, the Czechoslovak government reacted promptly. This time around, however, there was a procedural distinction in that the Foreign Office was contacted first. State Minister Ripka informed Envoy Nichols in a seven-page letter (more work for British officials no doubt pleased to receive additional reading material!) about the pamphlet and its author whom he described as "a member of a Fascist Party in Czechoslovakia." Ripka claimed that some of the arguments put forward by Schwarz were identical to those employed in Nazi propaganda in the Protectorate and that his attacks on E. Beneš constituted a crime, which in wartime under Czechoslovak law would incur the severest penalty. In the name of the Czechoslovak government, Ripka expressed his regret that at a time when official Czechoslovak printed material was subject to restrictions resulting from shortage of paper, publications of a definitely harmful character from the political and military point of view receive a supply sufficient for their needs.[27]

British reactions to the complaints followed the same line as that concerning the Locher pamphlet. The only good news for the Czechoslovaks was that Secretary Morrison decided, with Foreign Office approval, to seek Cabinet authority for extending the scope of Defence Regulation 39A to encompass the armed forces of Allied governments. However, the Home Secretary was very sceptical about allegations of pro-Nazi sympathies among opposition members of the so-called Czecho-Slovak National Council. He suggested that Slávik arrange for collaboration between the Czechoslovak and British security services in order to examine the charges and assured the Czechoslovak minister that if the British were satisfied that substantive evidence existed of pro-Nazi sympathies or doings on the part of any member of the Czecho-Slovak National Council, the British government would "not hesitate to take the most drastic action against the persons responsible for such activities."[28] To put it simply, the Czechoslovak government once again achieved very little.

Technically, there was a legislative gap in the United Kingdom regarding censorship of pamphlets and the press. The relevant Interdepartmental Committee dealt only with postal and telegraph censorship. On a practical level this meant that the democratic principle of freedom of expression entailed

26 Archiv bezpečnostních složek [Archive of the Security Services], Prague (henceforth ABS, Prague; former Archive of the Czech Ministry of the Interior), signature 305-112-6, František Schwarz, *Moje politická činnost za druhé světové války* [My Political Activity during the Second World War] (manuscript), pp. 31–32.

27 TNA, FO 371/30843, C 10914, letter by H. Ripka to Philip Nichols, 9 September 1942.

28 NA, Prague, Collection Ministerstvo vnitra – Londýn [Ministry of the Interior – London], box 105, signature 2–7–5, letter by H. Morrison to J. Slávik, 3 November 1942; TNA, FO 371/30843, C 10914.

the risk that harmful opinions might be propagated. Nevertheless, there was a very effective tool at hand to hinder undesirable publications, the paper restrictions imposed by the Ministry of Supply's Paper Control Order No. 48 of September 1942. The non-availability of paper was a censorship tool that could be resorted to if necessary. However, the "anti-Beneš" opposition was only partially affected by this order.[29]

Without paper, the anti-Beneš opposition would be severely hampered in disseminating their criticism but because of attitudes at the Foreign Office, this ploy was not employed extensively against Czech and Slovak political opposition pamphlets published in Britain. According to Foreign Office minutes, when the opinion was voiced that the authorities should have recourse to the Paper Control Order to stop such embarrassing publicists as Locher, F. K. Roberts replied that there were printers ready to help out in such instances.[30] Similarly, Peter Prídavok's Open Letter to Foreign Secretary A. Eden from January 1944, described in more detail below, drew the response that there was no legal way to halt supplies of paper for occasional publications, such as the Open Letter of the Slovak National Council, and even if there were, Prídavok would in any case be able to get enough paper by one means or another.[31]

In the editorial by Bohuš Beneš, mentioned earlier, General Prchala was accused of subversive activities and attempts to disrupt the Czechoslovak liberation movement. Osuský filed a libel suit against B. Beneš and the *Čechoslovák* newspaper for the attacks on him and Prchala. Osuský argued, that his and Prchala's actions were not aimed at creating disunity in the Czechoslovak liberation movement since no such organized movement existed until the creation of the Czechoslovak National Committee on 16 November 1939. Osuský further stressed that a schism could be created only in an established, recognized institution.

Osuský's immediate reaction to the press attack, however, and which led to his dismissal from the Czechoslovak government and the State Council by Edvard Beneš in March 1942, was his pamphlet *Pravda víťazí* [Truth conquers].[32] Formerly Czechoslovak ambassador to France and particularly active in Paris after the outbreak of war, Štefan Osuský was a prominent

---

29 See Kuklík, Němeček, *Proti Benešovi!*, pp. 407–408.

30 When the opinion was expressed during an FO debate that an embarrassing publicist such as Locher should be stopped by using the paper shortage ruse, F. K. Roberts asserted that there were printers ready to help out in such cases. TNA, FO 371/30843, C 3337, minute by F. K. Roberts, 17 April 1942.

31 TNA, FO 371/38930, C 4525, minute by Fanny Gatehouse from the Central Department of the FO, 19 April 1944.

32 Štefan Osuský, "*Pravda víťazí*" (*Pohľad do zrkadla druhého odboja*) / "*Truth Conquers*" (*A Glance into the Mirror of the Second Resistance*), Vol. 1 of the edition "Pravda" (London: Lowe and Brydone

figure and a highly-respected diplomat. His position was therefore different from that of General Prchala. In 1942, after an altercation with fellow ministers, including Hubert Ripka, Juraj Slávik, and Sergej Ingr among others, who criticized him for the disastrous evacuation of Czechoslovak citizens and soldiers from France in 1940, Osuský was dismissed from his ministerial post by Beneš. Although concisely characterized as a "conductor without an orchestra," Osuský's dissent was considered especially dangerous because of his relatively high prestige in British political circles. Indeed, Foreign Affairs official Ivo Ducháček was not wrong in stating that Osuský's opposition to Beneš was one of the major controversies which divided Czechoslovak exiles during the Second World War.

The title of this chapter is derived from Osuský's pamphlet *Pravda víťazí!* which first appeared in London in 1942 as the first of a series with the emblematic title "Pravda – the Truth." In 1943, it was translated into English and published in the US with the somewhat bizarre title, *"Truth Conquers" (A Glance into the Mirror of the Second Resistance).*[33]

Osuský explains the expression as follows: "In democratic countries reigns the motto: 'Truth Conquers' (Pravda vítězí)! In dictatorship and totalitarian regimes, however the motto: 'Truth to the conqueror' (Pravda vítězi)!"[34]

Osuský was an exponent of the so-called ambassadorial concept, a theory which maintains that Czechoslovak diplomats who remained at their posts after the breakup of the country were more credible representatives of state continuity than a president who had voluntarily quit his office in 1938. Osuský argued with a touch of irony that if after 15 March 1939, he had waited until Monsignor Jan Šrámek and Beneš had propounded their belief in the legal continuity of the Czechoslovak Republic, then he would not have preserved the Czechoslovak Embassy in Paris nor signed the French-Czechoslovak agreement on the reconstruction of the Czechoslovak army on 2 October 1939. In his critique of the Czechoslovak political regime in exile, Osuský went much further than other opponents by maintaining that Beneš's notion of president was in a fact a "Führer" concept, thus, for all intents and purposes, calling Beneš the Hitler of Czechoslovakia. Osuský also made the point that the Czechoslovak government and State Council could decide to regard Dr. Beneš as the legal President of Czechoslovakia but this did not mean that Beneš thereby signified the legal continuity of the Czechoslovak Republic. The government and State Council decision had only political propaganda value.

Printers Ltd., 1942). Second edition: *"Truth Conquers" (A Glance into the Mirror of the Second Revolution)* (New York: Jednota Press, 1943).

33   It should actually be called "Truth Prevails."

34   Štefan Osuský, *"Truth Conquers,"* p. 10.

Osuský published other pamphlets such as *Řízená demokracie při práci* [Controlled democracy at work] printed in 1942,[35] and *Beneš a Slovensko* [Beneš and Slovakia],[36] which criticized the Czechoslovak political leadership from various perspectives. Nevertheless, neither he nor any of the other disaffected émigrés could ever seriously contest or bring into question Edvard Beneš as president of the Czechoslovak Republic in exile.

LIBEL ACTION BY GENERAL PRCHALA AND ŠTEFAN OSUSKÝ AGAINST BOHUŠ BENEŠ AND UNWIN BROTHERS LIMITED

The Czechoslovak government feared that a public hearing of Prchala's and Osuský's action might damage Edvard Beneš's reputation and give adverse publicity to the internal squabbles which had attended the Czech and Slovak emigration, especially in 1939. As one Foreign Office official noted, "a good deal of public washing of Czechoslovak dirty linen will be inevitable if this case is heard in the court."[37] In the Foreign Office, the opinion prevailed that documents produced by Prchala against B. Beneš might lead to a raking over of old issues which could "do little credit to Czechoslovak leaders, especially President Beneš and General Ingr, or to the Czechoslovak cause as a whole." General Prchala, who had formed the Legion of Czechs and Slovaks in Poland before September 1939, emerged as a "difficult but apparently patriotic figure whose chief crime seems to have been that he established excellent relations with the Poles at a time when Czechoslovak-Polish relations generally were strained." However, it was considered that no strong case for a hearing *in camera* (behind closed doors) existed.[38]

The libel action was postponed several times at the request of the defendants and Bohuš Beneš was conveniently ensured diplomatic immunity by being appointed Consul General of Czechoslovakia in San Francisco. The proceedings finally took place on 12–13 October 1943 at the Royal Courts of Justice.[39] One could say humorously that thanks to the loaded words *"kahánkovština"* and *"prchalovština"* and the linguistic explanation provided, the High Court received a free lesson in the Czech language. The legal defence of the doctrine of Czechoslovakism by the barrister Sergeant Sullivan and his denial that the

35 Štefan Osuský, *Řízená demokracie při práci* [Controlled Democracy in Action], 2nd volume of the edition "Pravda [Truth]" (London: The Continental Publishers and Distributors, 1942).

36 Štefan Osuský, *Beneš a Slovensko* [Beneš and Slovakia], 4th volume of the edition "Pravda" (London: The Continental Publishers and Distributors, 1943).

37 TNA, FO 371/30826, C 10643.

38 TNA, FO 371/30826, C 10643, letter by F. K. Roberts to Philip Nichols, 29 November 1942.

39 For a detailed description see Kuklík, Němeček, *Proti Benešovi!*, pp. 411–430; Slavomír Michálek, *Diplomat Štefan Osuský (1889–1973)* (Bratislava: Veda, 1999), pp. 163–166.

article referred to General Prchala (!) or that the word *"prchalovština"* was defamatory were hardly convincing.[40] The attempt by Bohuš Beneš, and indirectly his uncle Edvard and the government-in-exile, to criminalize General Prchala and depict him as an obedient servant of a "reactionary" Poland led by Colonel Józef Beck, failed. Nor is it surprising that a representative from the Polish Ministry of Information, who attended the hearing, expressed his unhappiness with the affair to an official from the Czechoslovak Foreign Ministry: "I note with sadness how Poland is dragged before the English courts by Czech lawyers."[41]

In the case of Osuský, it was announced that the parties had agreed to an order staying the proceedings. The defendants denied that the article referred to Osuský and Barrister Sullivan stated that they extremely regretted that it should have been misunderstood by anybody as so doing. Justice Croom-Johnson said there was not a scintilla of evidence that the article was ever intended to refer to Osuský, who had always proven himself to be a patriotic and courageous man of scrupulous honour.[42]

As for General Prchala's action, Justice Croom-Johnson held that the article was in fact defamatory of General Prchala because it suggested that he was doing something hostile to the Czechoslovak liberation movement. This was as loathsome a suggestion to make of a patriot, the judge maintained, as

---

40 The following is a transcript of the libel action Prchala vs. Beneš:
"Question by Mr. Croom-Johnson: The statement in this document [the article of B. Beneš – D. S.] is Kahánkovština a prchalovština zhasla v Polsku [...]. Do you object to the expression 'ština' following your name? Answer Prchala: Yes, My Lord. Q[uestion].: [...] What does the use of your name with that addition of 'ština' after it convey to your mind? A[nswer].: Only what is harmful and bad. Q.: in other words... A.: Evil. [...]Sergeant Sullivan: I have to submit first on behalf of the Defendants that this action, of the Plaintiff's own evidence, must be dismissed. First, before I get to the plea of fair comment, I must respectfully submit there is no libel here. You have not got the whole article but you have sufficient before you... Mr. Justice Croom-Johnson: Which branch of the problem that I have to face are you submitting that upon at the moment, the capacity of the words to be defamatory or their being defamatory in fact?
Sergeant Sullivan: The capacity of the words to be defamatory in this context. They are not capable of a defamatory meaning. Alternatively, if capable of a defamatory meaning, they are not defamatory of the Plaintiff in his personal capacity...all that they [the words – D. S.] mean is Kahanekism and Prchalaism and they are stated in the context. 'Kahánek and Prchala nuisance' is how they have translated it. It certainly means not nuisance...If you take 'Kahanekism and Prchalaism dies off in Poland with the Beck regime,' all that means is Kahanekism was the scheme and theory propounded by Kahánek and Prchalaism was the movement and scheme and policy advocated by General Prchala. We have stated that they died off in Poland with the Beck regime before they grew into a real schism." The High Court of Justice, King's Bench Division, Royal Court of Justice, Wednesday, 13 October 1943, Second Day, pp. 6–7. Copy held by TNA, FO 371/38932, C 288.
41 Quoted in Němeček, *Od spojenectví k roztržce*, p. 255.
42 Hoover Institution Archives, Stanford University, Collections Poland – Ministerstwo Spraw Zagranicznych [Ministry of Foreign Affairs], Series No. 3, Political reports, box 16, folder No. 8, General, Press report by Reuters, 14 October 1943.

to say of an Englishmen that he was a fifth columnist, and he awarded Prchala £150 libel damages.[43]

It is not surprising that this legal decision provided Prchala with further ammunition in his struggle with Edvard Beneš. In the so-called Open Letter from the Czech National Union in London, which he headed, to Anthony Eden dated 20 January 1944, Prchala argued that Beneš was not the legal president of Czechoslovakia. Thus "the Treaty of friendship, mutual help, and post-war co-operation between the USSR and the Czechoslovak Republic agreed in Moscow on 12 December 1943 [...] is null and void and does not bind the Czech nation in any way," and the inhabitants of Czecho-Slovakia "cannot today be bound by international treaties concluded by unauthorized negotiators." In Annex 5 of the Open Letter there are numerous extracts from the evidence that underline both Prchala's "extremely distinguished army career with plenty of active fighting" and Beneš's position as a private person, a former president, who resigned his position just after Munich.[44] When Prchala and Locher received no reply to a request for a meeting with the Foreign Office, and were at a loss as to what the snag might be, they sought an interview with the Metropolitan Police as a matter of urgency. This took place on 2 February 1944, with Locher very anxious not to embarrass the British government. He and Prchala were informed that the Open Letter was not a direct concern of the police, but they were advised to refrain from any hasty action.[45] In a secret MI5 report to the Foreign Office, Borin-Ležák and Locher were described as "only too well known to us as indefatigable agitators against the Beneš government ever since their regrettable escape from France in June 1940." Furthermore, the writer goes on, stronger than any ideological bond "is their fanatical hatred of Dr. Beneš, which would appear to be pathological rather than political in its nature."[46]

The pamphlets and press articles by the Czech and Slovak opposition, directed primarily against Edvard Beneš, continued to cause serious concern to

43   Ibid.
44   Ibid, box 42, folder 24, Open letter from the Czech National Union in London to H. M. Secretary of State for Foreign Affairs, The Rt. Hon. Anthony Eden, London, 20 January 1944, signed by General Lev Prchala, Vladimír Ležák-Borin, Karel Locher, Josef Kratochvíl, Robert Hildprandt and Ludmila Balnarová.
45   TNA, FO 371/38929, C 1873, report by the Metropolitan Police, Special Branch, 3 February 1944. A copy of the report was sent by the Home Office to the Foreign Office on 8 February 1944. The answer by W. D. Allen from the Central Department of the Foreign Office to the Home Office dated 14 February 1944 is self-explanatory: "We have received the Open Letters addressed to the Foreign Secretary by the Czech National Union and the Slovak National Council, which are referred to in this report. We propose to ignore them." See also Kuklík, Němeček, *Proti Benešovi!*, pp. 430–431.
46   TNA, FO 371/38929, C 3481, letter by W. D. Robson-Scott to W. D. Allen, No. L.271/1489/E.5.L., 16 March 1944.

the Czechoslovak authorities. In October 1943, Vladimír Ležák-Borin, former Secretary of the Czecho-Slovak National Council, published a tract with the self-explanatory title *Curious History of a Nation that Never Existed*, challenging the concept of Czechoslovakism and arguing in favour of two independent national states, Bohemia and Slovakia, that would take their place as separate members of the Central European Union that had to be created after the war.

The Czechoslovak government's reaction to these activities included secret agent shadowing of their opponents and the buying up of a substantial number of the pamphlets. At the same time, complaints to the British authorities about the dissidents continued. In a confidential letter to Herbert Morrison, the Secretary of State for Home Affairs, dated 1 March 1943, titled "Czecho-Slovak National Council – its subversive activities – request for proceedings," Slávik again drew Morrison's attention to Peter Prídavok, František Schwarz, Vladimír Borin-Ležák, Karel Locher, and General Lev Prchala who, he claimed, "do not represent any section of the Czechoslovak nation and have no rights to act on his behalf," but are merely a small assortment of individuals who take no part in the struggle for liberation. Slávik was especially incensed by the fact that they "live in very easy circumstances and spend a good deal of money on publishing pamphlets and leaflets which abuse the president of the Czechoslovak Republic and members of the government in a most insulting manner." Slávik was further annoyed by the fact that they were doing so because being on British soil they could escape prosecution by the Czechoslovak authorities, although, significantly, their actions did not constitute a crime under Czechoslovak law either. The irate Czechoslovak minister added that the Czech and Slovak perpetrators of the offences were drawing on some unknown financial resources.[47] In this case, "unknown" meant of Polish origin.

Although it could be proved that there were direct links between the Polish government and the Czech and Slovak opposition in the United Kingdom, the British authorities took no measures to stop further activities by the anti-Beneš opposition. Foreign Office reaction in the case of Peter Prídavok was typical. Prídavok, a former member of Hodža's Czecho-Slovak National Council, caused several difficulties for the Czechoslovak government after his release from internment in 1941. He wrote a number of articles for the *Catholic Herald* in which, for example, he described Edvard Beneš as "strongly anti-Catholic" and referred to him as "a very active freemason."[48] In 1943, he published the pamphlet *A Good Word to Slovaks Worthy of It*, first printed in

---

47 NA, Prague, Collection Ministerstvo vnitra – Londýn [Ministry of the Interior – London], box 107, signature 2-7-35/3.

48 "Dr. Benes' record," in *Catholic Herald*, 18 July 1941, p. 1.

Slovak in the American newspaper *Slovák v Amerike* [A Slovak in America],[49] which sharply criticized the notion of Czechoslovakism and its main protagonists, most notably Beneš, and also prominent Slovaks such as Štefan Osuský and Milan Hodža, who at this time and until his death in 1944 was politically active in the United States.[50] Both according to Prídavok were "not worthy" of trust. Citing the popular nationalist motto, "I am Slovak – who is more?" Prídavok portrayed the Slovaks as a nation in their own right and concluded that Slovakia had to be an equal and full-fledged partner of a postwar Central European federation.

In 1943, a leaflet by P. Prídavok titled *Slovákom v Anglicku* [To the Slovaks in England] was distributed among soldiers of the Czechoslovak armed forces stationed in Britain. He was also behind a memorandum from Slovak soldiers of the Czechoslovak Independent Armoured Brigade to the Polish Minister of Defence requesting their transfer to the Polish armed forces in the West.[51] The final straw, however, was Prídavok's Open Letter to the Foreign Secretary A. Eden dated January 1944, in which he, in his capacity as Chairman of the Slovak National Council, described the Czechoslovak government as unconstitutional and self-appointed. Further, he declared that "neither Dr. Edvard Beneš, nor any other person in his services, nor any person or organization aiming at the reconstruction of Czecho-Slovakia, can act in the name of the Slovak nation who had for 20 years experienced from the Czecho-Slovak government under Dr. Beneš's leadership nothing but falsehood, deceit, misrule and corruption."[52]

The Czechoslovak Foreign Ministry informed Envoy Nichols about Prídavok's conduct and asked what the British authorities could do to stop him.[53]

---

49   Peter Prídavok, "Dobré slovo Slovákom súcim na slovo [A Good Word to Slovaks Worthy of It]," in: *Slovák v Amerike* [Slovak in America] (New York, 8 April 1943), pp. 3, 6–7; Peter Prídavok, *A Good Word To Slovaks Worthy Of It*, foreword and translation by Philip James Anthony (Middletown, PA: Jednota Press, 1943).

50   For a detailed historical analysis of Hodža's activities in the United States during the Second World War see Pavol Lukáč, "Politická činnosť Milana Hodžu v emigrácii v USA a reakcie na jeho federalistické plány [Political Activity of Milan Hodža in Emigration in the USA and the Reactions to His Federalist Plans]," in *Historický časopis* [Historical Journal], Vol. 51, No. 4 (2003), pp. 605–626.

51   For a detailed account see Dušan Segeš, "Memorandum slovenských vojakov 1. Československej samostatnej obrnenej brigády vo Veľkej Británii pre poľského ministra národnej obrany z roku 1943 (Slovensko-poľské vojenské kontakty za 2. svetovej vojny) [Memorandum of Slovak Soldiers of the 1st Independent Armoured Brigade in Great Britain for the Polish Minister of Defence from the Year 1943 (Slovak-Polish Military Contacts during the Second World War)]," in *Vojenská história* [Military History], Vol. 12, No. 4 (2008), pp. 35–62.

52   Open Letter from The Slovak National Council, 7, Wilton Crescent, London, S.W.1, to His Britannic Majesty's Secretary of State for Foreign Affairs, The Rt. Hon. Anthony Eden, London, January 1944. A fragment from the Open Letter was published under the title "Slovak National Council Formed" in the *Catholic Herald*, 11 February 1944, p. 6.

53   TNA, FO 371/38930, C 4525, letter by H. Ripka to Philip Nichols, 31 March 1944.

In a letter to Nichols, F. K. Roberts outlined the position of the Foreign Office to any measures that might be taken. He referred to a meeting on 27 January 1944, at the Home Office, where the possibility of action against Prídavok was discussed. According to Roberts, depriving Prídavok and his associates of the requisite supply of paper was out of the question. With regard to Prídavok's subversive activities among Czechoslovak soldiers in Britain, the charge of suborning Slovak members of the force from their allegiance to the Czechoslovak government was considered insufficient grounds for action to be taken.[54]

At the same time, there was no let-up in Prídavok's endeavours. In April 1944, he addressed a complaint to the Secretary of War, James Grigg, claiming that hundreds of Slovak nationals serving in "Mr. Edvard Beneš's units" are "constantly bullied and persecuted by their Czech officers for no other reason than expressing their national feelings."[55]

Further letters by H. Ripka from the Czechoslovak Foreign Ministry to the British Foreign Office on Prídavok's "subversive activities" still brought no results. A breakthrough, however, came in July 1944, when a warrant to search Prídavok's flat, which was also the seat of the Slovak National Council, was executed by the Special Branch of the Metropolitan Police and Captain Buzzard from the War Office. Prídavok admitted using the Polish diplomatic bag to communicate with Karol Sidor, the Envoy of the Slovak Republic to the Vatican, and also acknowledged that he had received payments from the Polish government.[56]

Since I have already published a detailed analysis of correspondence between the Foreign Office and the Czechoslovak government, and the reactions of the Home Office and the War Office in connection with Peter Prídavok's activities,[57] I will confine myself here to simply agreeing with Martin D. Brown's conclusion that the Foreign Office swept the whole Prídavok-affair under the carpet.[58] No action was taken against him and he carried on as before. The Foreign Office did, however, advise the British ambassador to the Polish government to inform the Polish Foreign Minister, Tadeusz Romer, that it is "a folly of the Poles dabbling in third rate Central European intrigue [...] which achieves nothing for them and puts them in an extremely dangerous position." It was considered rather "galling" that

54   Ibid., draft of a letter by F. K. Roberts to Philip Nichols, 21 April 1944.
55   TNA, FO 371/38930, C 5981, letter by the Slovak National Council to J. Grigg, 4 April 1944.
56   TNA, FO 371/38930, C 10923, letter by W. E. Hinchley Cooke from the War Office to T. Atkinson, Director of Public Prosecutions, 16 August 1944.
57   Dušan Segeš, "Casus Peter Prídavok," in Peter Sokolovič, ed., *Slovenská republika 1939–1945 očami mladých historikov* [Slovak Republic in the Eyes of Young Historians], Vol. 7, *Perzekúcie na Slovensku v rokoch 1938–1945* [The Persecutions in Slovakia in the Years 1938–1945] (Bratislava: Ústav Pamäti Národa, 2008), pp. 80–108.
58   Brown, *Jak se jedná s demokraty*, p. 144.

British money was used to support Prídavok, but, it was added, "there is no particular hurry about this."[59]

CONCLUSION

The activities of the Czech and Slovak opposition in Great Britain (not to mention the Czechoslovak Communists residing in Moscow, who represent a very important and still under-researched topic from the point of view of political and social developments in Czechoslovakia after liberation from Nazi-occupation) were not limited to pamphlets and press articles. As the end of the war approached, the number of political malcontents from Czechoslovakia living in London increased. The Czechoslovak authorities took special pains to eliminate the anti-Beneš pamphlets and activities which they feared could have an undesirable impact on the fragile unity of the Czechoslovak movement. Suppressive and retaliatory measures were made on two levels. Firstly, the Czechoslovak Ministry of the Interior bought up or otherwise gathered the pamphlets and brochures and then destroyed them. The irony of such a strategy was, of course, that in so doing, the Czechoslovak government was indirectly financing their adversaries from its own budget. Secondly, with their constant complaints and requests for intervention against the "renegades" to the British authorities, they added to the workload of already over-burdened departments, especially at the Foreign Office and the Home Office. This led among other things to a re-evaluation of existing British legislation, particularly the Defence (General) Regulations, related to punishments for subversive activities or acts (pre-eminently Defence Regulation 39A), and initiated an exchange of correspondence between the Foreign Office and the Home Secretary as to whether Defence Regulation 39A should be amended so as to make it an offence for any person to attempt to seduce from their duty personnel serving in any (not only those included under National Service Acts) of the Allied Forces.[60]

In general it can be said that despite maximal effort in seeking action against politically active Slovaks and Czechs who criticized Beneš and representatives of the Czechoslovak state-in-exile, very little was actually achieved from the British authorities. The Foreign Office took up the Czechoslovak demands with the Home Office, MI5 and the War Office, and in replies

---

59 TNA, FO 371/38930, C 11009, letter by G. W. Harrison to Ambassador O. O'Malley, 9 September 1944.
60 This finally led to the Amendment to Defence Regulation 39A in 1942. TNA, FO 371/32251, C 6893. The first extension of the Defence Regulation 39A was discussed in 1940. See the House of Commons debate on 9 May 1940, available at: http://hansard.millbanksystems.com/commons/1940/may/09/government-proposals#S5CV0360P0_19400509_HOC_136

to the Czechoslovak Foreign Ministry, was in most cases very restrained. The Foreign Office refused to get involved in Czechoslovak government "heresy hunts"[61] and was reluctant to instigate criminal proceedings against authors of pamphlets, such as Locher and Schwarz. Examining the "minutes" of some Foreign Office officials, one gets the impression that they were irritated by the numerous requests for intervention. A lot of time and energy had to be devoted to the internal problems of the Czechoslovak émigrés to the detriment of other issues that were more important in terms of the British war effort.

The agenda of the Czechoslovak political opposition was dominated by two major concerns: the legitimacy of Edvard Beneš as President of the republic and the continuity of the pre-Munich constitutional order. Czech and Slovak dissenters took full advantage of liberal legislation in the United Kingdom, especially with regard to freedom of opinion and the press, and these were fully exploited during the inter-war and Second World War periods for anti-Czechoslovak government and anti-Beneš polemic. On the other hand, the impact of the politically disaffected on émigré circles was relatively slight. After the diplomatic recognition of the Czechoslovak government in 1940/1941, it was impossible for the "anti-Benešites" to create any kind of internationally-accepted organizational base for their activities. None of the pamphlets, resolutions, or open letters to Foreign Secretary Eden by Peter Prídavok, head of the Slovak National Council, or his counterpart, General Prchala, from the Czech National Union were nothing more than nuisance value to the Czechoslovak government and at no stage were a serious menace its existence.

Regarding the activities of the Czech and Slovak opposition, one can ask if there was a viable alternative to the Beneš government-in-exile. An answer to this hypothetical question can be found in Churchill's letter to Stalin dated 12 May 1943, wherein he states that should recognition be taken away from Beneš, "we should not get anyone good in his place."[62] Far from his occupied homeland, Beneš eventually regained power not by democratic means but through the only course open to the political exile: behind the scenes manoeuvring, cultivating friends in high places, arguments coated in semi-legal logic, and, above all, hope and perseverance.

Most of the wartime anti-Benešites did not return to Czechoslovakia from Great Britain in 1945. One exception was František Schwarz, author

---

61 TNA, FO 371/38930, C 11099, minute by F. K. Roberts on the activities of p. Prídavok, 2 September 1944.

62 *Korespondence předsedy rady ministrů SSSR s prezidenty USA a ministerskými předsedy Velké Británie za Velké vlastenecké války 1941–1945* [Correspondence of the Chairman of the Council of Ministers of the USSR with the Presidents of the US and prime ministers of Great Britain during the Great Patriotic War 1941–1945] (Praha: Svoboda – Naše vojsko, 1981).

of the pamphlet *Doctor Beneš on Military Conflict before and during the War*. In October 1945, a warrant for his arrest for subversive action against the Czechoslovak liberation movement abroad had been issued by the Czechoslovak Ministry of the Interior and he was taken into custody on arrival in Prague in April 1946. Testimony gained during his interrogation incriminated Locher, Borin-Ležák, Prchala and Prídavok.[63] All, however, continued their political agitation in London and their attacks against Beneš and the Czechoslovak government in bulletins such as the *Czech Press Service* or *Centropress* became even sharper. Members of the so-called Czecho-Slovak National Council were monitored by the Czechoslovak secret service from 1945. In 1946, the Czechoslovak Ministry of the Interior filed charges against Locher and Borin-Ležák for crimes committed in violation of the Law for the Protection of the Republic, the Retribution decree, and the law of the land.[64]

The activities of the anti-Benešites also reveal how domestic political issues can get caught up in international intrigue, at least unofficially, as was the case with the Czechoslovak opposition in the person of Milan Hodža, Lev Prchala and Peter Prídavok in their transactions with the Polish government-in-exile, and with the French government in 1939–40.

This study is the outcome of the Vega-grant No. 2/0142/16 *Changes, transformations and replacements of Slovak political, cultural and intellectual elites in the years 1938–1958*, that is realised by the Institute of History of the Slovak Academy of Sciences.

63   See the interrogation protocols in: ABS, Prague, signature 305–112–6.
64   ABS, Prague, signature 305–354–1, Charge against V. Borin-Ležák and K. Locher, 8 August 1946.

LOOKING FOR FRENCH, ANGLOPHILE OR SOVIET INSPIRATION? THE DIPLOMATIC STRUGGLE FOR THE POST-WAR ORIENTATION OF CZECHOSLOVAK EDUCATION AND CULTURE

DOUBRAVKA OLŠÁKOVÁ

The fate of culture, science and education during the war period did not belong among the key issues discussed by the governments-in-exile; in fact, this topic was very rarely given much attention. However, sharing the same level of intensity as discussions on post-war political arrangements, discussions about the future direction of culture reflected different priorities on the international orientation of the post-war state. Governments-in-exile represent in this sense a sort of unique laboratory where discussions on the future orientation of culture and education are influenced by the presence of numerous governments-in-exile and representatives of international organizations and institutions. Proposals on particular measures therefore very often reflect not only the internal political situation and debate, but also the determination of many countries to maintain their cultural influence as well as to strengthen that of the region in general.[1] Czechoslovakia was no exception to this during the Second World War, but rather the contrary was the case. This was so because of the country's geographical position, with the result that the Czechoslovak conception of post-war culture and education found a central place on the agenda of the cultural attachés of the Great Powers.

The aim of the chapter is to briefly outline the discussions regarding the notions of Czechoslovak post-war education and science. In the first part of the chapter, attention is paid to the initial discussions about science, education, and culture in exile and also to the major personalities and the circumstances responsible for launching the debate. The question to be answered is whether and to what extent this was a priority of the government-in-exile or whether, and again to what extent, it resulted from the pressure and initiative of Czechoslovak intellectuals who had found asylum in Great Britain and the USSR. The second part of the chapter focuses on the debates that took

---

1   As for cultural diplomacy, cf.: Thomas A. Breslin, *Beyond Pain: The Role of Pleasure and Culture in the Making of Foreign Affairs* [online] (Westport, CT: Praeger, 2002); Glenn E. Schweitzer, *Scientists, Engineers, and Track-Two Diplomacy: A Half-Century of U.S.-Russian Interacademy Cooperation* [online] (Washington, D.C.: National Academies Press, 2004), available at: http://site.ebrary.com/lib/natl/Doc?id=10051602 (accssed 23 October 2017); Eliška Tomalová, *Kulturní diplomacie: francouzská zkušenost* [Cultural Diplomacy: The French Experience] (Praha: Ústav mezinárodních vztahů, 2008).

place in 1944 when, in addition to military developments, the attention of Czechoslovak exile politicians turned to such issues as the post-war order in Europe; hand in hand with which the question of the establishment of a new cultural and scientific orientation for Czechoslovakia arose. Ideas that had not been considered important in previous years began to appear on the political agenda and in the discussions of the government-in-exile.

The future of Czechoslovak education and culture was discussed in London and in Moscow in late 1943 and in 1944. It is not surprising that underlying concepts did not differ in terms of general principles but rather in the international orientation of the post-war Czechoslovakia they envisioned. In this context, not two, but three different directions were at play, namely, the British, the French, and the Soviet. The basic tenets which were adopted both in London and in Moscow were denazification, democratization, and de-Germanization.

In 1945, in the last stage of preparation for post-war arrangements, pressure to influence the external orientation of the cultural and scientific policy of the new Czechoslovakia peaked. The notions and topics discussed in these negotiations can be compared with the eventual outcome. Undoubtedly, much to the surprise of the Czechoslovak government-in-exile representatives, a proposal, about which only a few individuals with communist leanings had any specific knowledge, was adopted. However, this result can be assessed in the context of the political priorities and internal pressures of particular lobby groups.

TWO IN ONE: THE MINISTRY OF THE INTERIOR AND THE MINISTRY OF EDUCATION

In November 1942, Juraj Slávik, a Slovak politician and member of the Slovak Agrarian Party in inter-war Czechoslovakia, became Minister of Education in the Czechoslovak government-in-exile in London.[2] This man, who later, in 1946, was appointed the first Czechoslovak post-war ambassador to the US, seemed a good candidate. It soon became clear, however, that he was a better diplomat and politician than Minister of Education.

The problem with his appointment to the post lay in the fact that he was a professional diplomat who had worked as Czechoslovak ambassador in Warsaw during the inter-war period[3] and because of his loyal attitude to-

2 Slavomír Michálek et al., *Juraj Slávik Neresnický: Od politiky cez diplomaciu po exil (1890–1969)* [Juraj Slávik Neresnický: From Politics through Diplomacy to Exile (1890–1969)] (Bratislava: Prodama, 2006).

3 Juraj Slávik, *Moja pamäť – živá kniha: Moje poslanie vo Varšave 1936–1937* [My Memory – a Live Book: My Mission in Warsaw 1936–1937] (Bratislava: Veda, 2010).

wards Beneš he was always pretty much in line when it came to filling new posts. Edvard Beneš had already taken him into account when the Czechoslovak National Committee was being established in Paris in the autumn of 1939. His name also featured in Beneš's proposal on the National Council, a sort of "emergency parliamentary corps overseas," whose design was conceived in April 1940.[4] However, the position of Juraj Slávik became most significant after the relocation of the National Committee to London. On 22 July 1940, he was appointed Minister of the Interior of the government-in-exile by President Beneš and retained this post until the liberation of Czechoslovakia.

The position of Juraj Slávik in Czechoslovak exile was crucial for the Czechs. As one of the devoted few who showed loyalty to Beneš and his conception of the Czechoslovak nation, his stance put him in opposition to his Slovak colleagues, Milan Hodža and Štefan Osuský. Being Slovak, Juraj Slávik was of great value to Beneš; however, when one looks at his career, it is clearly evident that he was also an able politician who worked his way up from local politics to the highest levels of diplomatic and domestic political circles. For this reason, J. Slávik was already extremely busy at the time of his work within the Czechoslovak National Committee in Paris. Even though he was officially assigned management of social and health affairs, in fact his remit had a very wide scope: ranging from the care of Czechoslovak citizens abroad to the organization of the free time of Czechoslovak soldiers. Moreover, as Slávik stated in his correspondence, as former Czechoslovak ambassador to Poland he was also in charge of contacts with the Polish government-in-exile and other associated bodies.[5] After being appointed Minister of the Interior, although he had officially resigned from the ambassadorial post, in fact he remained active in the area.

---

4   Kuklík, Jan, *Vznik Československého národního výboru a Prozatímního státního zřízení ČSR v emigraci v letech 1939–1940* [The Creation of the Czechoslovak National Committee and the Provisional Constitutional Order of the Czechoslovak Republic in Exile 1939–1940] (Praha: Karolinum, 1996), p. 89. Cf. also: Detlef Brandes, *Exil v Londýně 1939–1943: Velká Británie a její spojenci Československo, Polsko a Jugoslávie mezi Mnichovem a Teheránem* [Exile in London 1939–1943: Great Britain and Its Allies Czechoslovakia, Poland and Yugoslavia between Munich and Teheran] (Praha: Karolinum, 2003), pp. 35, 68.

5   Michálek et al., *Juraj Slávik Neresnický*, p. 213. Cf. also: Jan Němeček, Jan Kuklík, Helena Nováčková, Ivan Šťovíček, eds., *Dokumenty československé zahraniční politiky* [Documents of the Czechoslovak Foreign Policy], Vol. B/1, *Od rozpadu Česko-Slovenska do uznání československé prozatímní vlády 1939–1940 (16. březen 1939 – 15. červen 1940)* [From the Break-up of Czecho-Slovakia to the Recognition of the Czechoslovak Provisional Government 1939–1940 (16 March 1939 – 15 June 1940)] (Praha: Ústav mezinárodních vztahů, 2002); Jan Kuklík, Jan Němeček, Helena Nováčková, eds., *Dokumenty československé zahraniční politiky* [Documents of Czechoslovak Foreign Policy], Vol. B/1 – Appendix, *Zápisy ze zasedání Československého národního výboru 1939–1940* [Memos from the Meetings of the Czechoslovak National Committee 1939–1940] (Praha: Ústav mezinárodních vztahů, 1999).

The appointment of Juraj Slávik to the Ministry of Education on 14 November 1942 resulted in the first major political crisis of the government-in-exile and also in pressure from workers in education and public awareness to establish an independent department. Among the major critics of the right-wing orientation of the government-in-exile were, among others, Václav Patzak, one of the leading members of the Petition Committee Faithful Forever (*Petiční výbor Věrni zůstaneme*), who was head of the Workers Academy, the social-democratic educational institute for workers in inter-war Czechoslovakia. Patzak had a wide knowledge and sophisticated understanding of extramural and extracurricular education and research at the time.[6] It is quite possible that he secretly thought of himself as a suitable candidate for the ministerial post, a conclusion that can be reached from a perusal of correspondence from the period. He had the requisite qualifications and appropriate affiliation to a leftist party: in the years 1925–1939 he belonged among the key figures of the Czechoslovak Ministry of Education, while from 1940 to 1945 he was one of the prominent exile personalities in the area of education, which was managed by the Ministry of the Interior. However, after the then Minister of the Interior, Juraj Slávik, was confirmed as administrator of educational affairs with no real change taking place, the tension between Václav Patzak, head of the Education Department, and Deputy Chairman of the State Council František Uhlíř escalated to such an extent that Patzak was forced to leave his post in the spring of 1943. It was only at that stage that a fundamental reorganization of the special education department occurred.

This was also a time when major political turmoil arose within the Czechoslovak exile, mainly because of the increased influence of the Communist Party.[7] The new situation illustrated the problematic effect political parties could have on the international orientation of post-war education: J. Slávik became unacceptable to leftist leaders and his authority in the government-in-exile in London led to numerous disputes with the Communists and the Social Democrats.[8] He managed to defend himself successfully, however, and maintained the position entrusted to him; his adversary, the Social Democrat Václav Patzak, whose sympathies lay with the Communist Party, was the one who had to vacate the field. Patzak's departure apparently alleviated the tense atmosphere at the exile Ministry of the Interior, especially in the

6   Václav Patzak, Jaroslav Kříž, eds., *Čtyřicet let výchovné práce Dělnické akademie: 1896–1936* [Forty Years of Educational Work of the Workers' Academy: 1896–1936] (Praha: Dělnická akademie, 1936).

7   Michálek et al., *Juraj Slávik Neresnický*, p. 222.

8   Ibid.

area of education, where because of ongoing political differences numerous administrative problems accumulated in the long term.[9]

On 21 August 1943, nine months after the official appointment of Juraj Slávik as head of education, a special department for education and public instruction was established in London. Its members were nominated by various relevant associations, such as associations of university professors, the advisory board of the film censor, and the like. At the international level, they collaborated with the Central and Eastern European Planning Board and, in the area of politics, cooperated with the Conference of Allied Ministers of Education. Both of these groups played, both during the war and especially in the aftermath, a crucial role in assessing the concept and aims of international cultural and scientific organizations. The influence they came to exert on the national and cultural policies of individual states should not be underestimated. Indeed, it was here that personalities whose ideas received a favourable hearing in the liberated countries after the war came together.

The main goal of the department was to prepare presidential decrees on the adjustment of education, culture, science and research in post-war Czechoslovakia. Such a programme, it was thought, would primarily show a comprehensive grasp of the issues involved and set general principles to be followed in the post-war period. These expectations, however, were not met and the plan, as originally conceived, was never fully adopted. Rather, it took the form of various regulations.

GENERAL PRINCIPLES

In autumn 1943, the Research Department for Educational and Public Awareness Affairs (*Studijní oddělení pro věci školské a osvětové*) was made responsible for drafting the decrees and legal measures that would define the basic principles of post-war education. The texts of these legal documents were to be prepared both by the Cultural Council and by particular commissions within the Study Department. They were divided into: 1) a Commission for National, Secondary, and Vocational Schools and Popular Education, 2) a Commission for Tertiary Education, 3) a Public Enlightenment Commission, 4) a Commission for Religious Affairs, 5) a Commission for International Cultural Relations. Above all, the composition of the last commission is worth mentioning in detail since its members included, among others, the following prominent personalities who significantly influenced the orientation of Czechoslovak post-war culture: Opočenský, Klecanda, Císař, Kunoši, Berger,

---

9   Cf. Jana Čechurová, Jan Kuklík, Jaroslav Čechura, Jan Němeček, eds., *Válečné deníky Jana Opočenského* [War Diaries of Jan Opočenský] (Praha: Karolinum, 2001), p. 46.

Clementis, Patzak, Hník, Odložilík, Bruegel, Weatherallová, Goldstücker.[10] Their aim was to focus on the following topics, which were to be implemented in the form of decrees: a decree on transitional measures, a decree on the establishment of educational centres, a decree on the restoration and reform of tertiary education and the abolition of all German schools on the territory of the Republic, a decree on the facilities of universities and research institutes, a decree on the establishment of educational chambers, a decree on mandatory youth service, a decree on copyright, a decree on films (in collaboration with the Film Advisory and Censorship Committee), a decree on national planning and research, and a proposal to ensure the dispatch of "obligatory copies of major Czechoslovak publications for three world libraries in London, Moscow and Washington."[11]

The biggest problems arose in the case of minority education. The final draft was worked out by František Uhlíř of the Research Department for Educational and Public Awareness on 18 February 1944.[12] The draft defined the starting point for post-war education and culture as the situation that existed prior to October 1938.[13] On the one hand, the main aim was to resume teaching and make education accessible to all schoolchildren and university students, while, on the other, municipal authorities would be given the right to close all non-national – i.e. foreign-language schools.

The denazification issue was the key element in the final draft. It included the immediate dissolution of all German-language universities in Czechoslovakia. Moreover, denazification was closely connected with de-Germanization, which concerned itself mainly with the many primary and secondary schools among the so-called "minority schools." The decree, however, was not in opposition to the Sixth Head of the Constitutional Charter, which guaranteed the protection of national, religious and ethnic minorities. Yet, while the protection of religious and racial minorities was to be preserved, the protection of national minorities was to be suspended by this decree until minority issues as such had been sorted out. In fact, this statement meant that the provisions governing education in other than the Czech or Slovak language would be abolished. An exception was of course the Russian language, which was preserved as a teaching language in particular with regard to Carpathian Ruthenia.

10 National Archives of the Czech Republic, Prague (henceforth NA), personal papers Václav Patzak, box 5, sign. 38-13, Correspondence, Report of the Research Department for Educational and Public Awareness Affairs, pp. 3-5.

11 Ibid., pp. 41-50.

12 NA, personal papers Václav Patzak, box 5, sign. 38-13, Educational Commission - confidential, fol. 30-39.

13 Ibid., Correspondence, Constitutional Decree of the President of the Republic, pp. 15-26.

The final draft of the decree which was completed in the late spring of 1944 was never adopted. Members of the different committees had not been able to come to an agreement on a general principle that would define the approach to minority education and its renewal after the Second World War. While the representatives of teachers and professors recommended an immediate dissolution of all German schools, the Ministry was against this proposal because the issue of minority education also depended on the possible post-war transfer of the German population.

The Ministry therefore objected to the view adopted by the professors, writing in a confidential analysis dated 24 April 1944: "The Germans and Hungarians will probably disappear from our homeland, at least for the most part; that means that their schools will also disappear because there will not be students or teachers. But if they remained in our country as a result of some sinister international interference, we would have to cancel the proposed constitutional decree and allow them their schools, which would mean an embarrassing defeat."[14]

Other decree proposals examined in detail the establishment of relationships in post-war education and drew mainly on internal discussions that were held at the Ministry of the Interior. Only the proposal regulating minority schools directly addressed the question of multiculturalism.

If we were to seek a unifying premise on which these proposals were based, it would no doubt be that of democratization, denazification and de-Germanization (de-Hungarianization in the case of Slovakia). All three notions were present in all of the proposals and they would become the main pillars of educational policy in post-war Czechoslovakia. One other subject – the international orientation of Czechoslovak education – was, however, at least as important as the three principles.

When looking at individual aspects of these proposals, we become aware of the extent London and British society influenced ministry officers – above all Juraj Slávik, whose anglophile orientation was becoming increasingly prominent. Despite President Beneš's proclaimed shift towards the Soviet Union, a great number of planned changes in education – including details of structure and particulars of decision-making in education bodies – were inspired by British examples and by British education.

The proof of this considerable move towards a British and broadly Anglophone orientation is found in the proposal for a special measure suggested by the department. It states that a copy of all books that would be published in Czechoslovakia should be sent to three international libraries: the National Library in London, the Library of Congress in Washington, and the National Library in Moscow. This surprising detail shows that the inter-war tendency

---

14   Ibid., Educational Commission, fol. 13–14.

towards France and the French education and cultural system was to be abandoned and replaced by an axis consisting of Great Britain, the United States,
and the Soviet Union.

In terms of the power factors at play in implementing this approach,
one cannot help thinking that during the discussions on the new post-war
orientation of the Czechoslovak state in culture and education, those who advocated a post-war orientation towards the USSR, within the boundaries outlined by Beneš and his government, were defeated. Sharp conflicts between
the leadership of the government-in-exile and the head of the Education
Department, whose ambition was no doubt to be Minister of Education in
the government-in-exile, led to a consolidation of the position of the National
Socialists and pushed out leftist attitudes. Orientation towards the USSR was
indeed part of the post-war plan, but in this context it should be seen only
as statements to this effect. In fact, the pressure exerted in London by the
representatives of France and the US on the post-war pro-Western orientation of Czechoslovak education was very strong. In addition, the creation of
a global "education organization" at the end of the war as part of the United
Nations, was likewise discussed as a possible outcome. On top of that, in the
summer of 1944, the possibility that America, Britain and Russia could reach
agreement on the framework of this major project still seemed an entirely
realistic possibility.[15]

The question arises as to how much Czechoslovak diplomats let themselves be lulled by these big promises and also to what extent they underestimated the fact that in preventing left-wing politicians from discussing the
final concept of Czechoslovak orientation, they had already condemned the
proposal to failure almost as soon as it came into being. The fact remains,
however, that on the list of presidential decrees that were agreed and which
came into force after the war, we find only a few that had been worked out
in London. The issue of foreign-language tertiary education that was dealt
with in the original decree, together with minority primary and secondary
schools, was quite comprehensively addressed.[16] In addition, the president
paid great attention to the question of emoluments, the training of teachers, and educational research.[17] From this it is clear that the new regime was

---

15   Čechurová et al., eds., *Válečné deníky Jana Opočenského*, p. 360.
16   To be more precise, these were the Decree of the President on the Abolition of the German Uni-
      versity in Prague (Decree No, 122/1945 Coll., in force from 18 October 1945), Decree of the Presi-
      dent on the Abolition of German Technical Universities in Prague and Brno (Decree No. 123/1945
      Coll., in force from 18 October 1945).
17   The question of emoluments was settled by the Decree of the President amending and supple-
      menting the Salary Act of 24 June 1926, No. 103 Coll.; as for university professors and assistants,
      it was Decree No. 73/1945 Coll., in force from 6 September 1945 to 1 April 1950. Other issues were
      modified by the Decree of the President on Educating the Teaching Staff (Decree No. 132/1945
      Coll., in force from 27 October 1945 to 7 May 1953) and Decree of the President establishing the

well aware of the need for re-education, entitlements, and the emphasis that would be placed on the upbringing and education of post-war generations. Decrees regulating film, and its role in education, were also issued.[18] Other topics, however, such as those of copyright, and pedagogical staff, were completely neglected.

LA FRANCE IS BACK

The declarative orientation towards the Eastern ally, which defined the new post-war Czechoslovak policy, was confirmed by presidential decrees and regulations relating to post-war education and culture. One such decree, which was among the last to be adopted, was that on the Establishment of the College of Political and Social Studies in Prague (Decree No. 140/1945 Coll., valid from 26 October 1945 to 4 November 1949). The inspiration for this college was not a Soviet institute or college, but the French *École Libre des Sciences Politiques* (today's Sciences Po), which served – and indeed still serves – as a prestigious state university for state administration and diplomacy. Moreover, Edvard Beneš himself studied at this institution in Paris in the years 1904–1906. Moving outside the line of Soviet orientation is surprising only in the context of the proclamations of the government-in-exile in general. At the same time, it must be borne in mind that French diplomatic pressure to maintain cultural influence in Central Europe was very intense.

The great majority of documents from the Education Department consist of internal memos from the Czechoslovak government-in-exile; foreign diplomats may therefore not have been aware of their content or indeed their existence. However, the new post-war international orientation of Czechoslovakia had already become widely known. Apparently it was this that activated French diplomats, aware as they were from meetings with President Beneš, that France was losing one of its greatest supporters and loyal allies in Central Europe.

In 1943–1944, French diplomats and Czech Francophiles still hoped to renew the special relationship France had with Czechoslovakia. A Czechoslovak-French declaration which called the Munich treaty *"nuls et non avenus"* and mentioned *"la politique traditionnelle d'amitiée et d'alliance"* was eventually

---

Jan Amos Comenius Research Institute for Education (Decree No. 133/1945 Coll., in force until today).

18   Decree of the President on Measures in the Field of Film (Decree No. 50/1950 Coll., in force from 11 August 1945 till today) and Decree of the President on Awareness State Care (Decree No. 130/1950 Coll.).

signed in London on 22 August 1944.[19] Beneš was a pragmatic Francophile and therefore did not oppose the idea. The diplomatic correspondence, however, shows that he warned the French that they could not count on the same level of official support as before the Second World War.[20]

French diplomacy therefore decided to take the first – and rather interesting – step towards successfully reinstating French influence in post-war Czechoslovakia: they nominated as members of the French repatriation mission scientists and cultural diplomats who had actively participated in the activities of the French Institute in Prague before the war.[21] Jean Prunet, the former head of the Scientific Department of the French Institute in Prague, was appointed head of the mission.[22] French diplomats in London were fully convinced that this appointment together with that of his colleagues would be seen as proof of the continuity of Czechoslovak-French relations. It should be noted that their position in inter-war Czechoslovakia was indeed very prominent and they were very influential (as testified to, for example, by their relationship with Škoda directors and engineers) and privileged (compared to, say, the Rockefeller Foundation or the American Institute).

A renewal of French influence in Czechoslovakia was not, however, viewed favourably by the Soviets. In 1944 when the French delegates applied for transit through the recently liberated countries of Romania and Bulgaria, the Soviets refused to grant visas to all members of the French repatriation mission and, at the same time, began to obstruct the whole process of accreditation.[23] They argued that these officials did not have diplomatic status within the hierarchy of the French Ministry of Foreign Affairs.

The French government then decided to promote the former members of the French Institute in Prague and granted them diplomatic status. Soviet reaction was swift: the Soviet ambassador in London protested against this procedure and informed the Czechoslovak Minister of Foreign Affairs, Jan Masaryk, in person about "problematic" conduct on the part of the French diplomatic service.[24] His words met with understanding. And since at the time the French lobby were trying to gain Czechoslovak support, it became clear that the situation required a delicate balancing act on the part of the Czechoslovak government. Finally, it was decided to make an official protest

19 Jan Němeček, Helena Nováčková, Ivan Šťovíček, Jan Kuklík, eds., *Československo-francouzské vztahy v diplomatických jednáních (1940–1945)* [Czechoslovak-French Relations in Diplomatic Negotiations (1940–1945)] (Praha: HÚ AV ČR – SÚA – Karolinum, 2005), Nos. 269–273, pp. 395–401.
20 Ibid., Nos. 60–61, pp. 118–120.
21 Jiří Hnilica, *Francouzský institut v Praze 1920–1951: Mezi vzděláním a propagandou* [The French Institute in Prague 1920–1951: Between Education and Propaganda] (Praha: Karolinum, 2009).
22 Archives du Ministère des Affaires étrangères, Paris, Series Z Europe, 1944–49, Tchécoslovaquie, No. 1, box 1, fol. 14–15, fol. 22–27.
23 Ibid., fol. 43–44.
24 Ibid., fol. 84–85.

against the composition of the French repatriation mission on the grounds that, according to an international agreement between Czechoslovakia and France in November 1943, France was obliged to consult the Czechoslovaks on the nomination of each member. This condition was apparently not formally fulfilled since the French diplomats had merely discussed the matter with the Czechoslovak government informally. French diplomats in London were aghast.

Among the community of foreign diplomats in London, the news spread like wildfire. The French moves, however, had also been supported by Czechoslovak diplomats, as is clear from the diplomatic archives and notes of Jan Opočenský. As early as 11 April 1945, Jan Masaryk dispatched a telegram to Zdeněk Nejedlý in Košice about sending a Czechoslovak delegation to Paris for negotiations on the renewal of the Czechoslovak-French cultural agreement.[25] At the same time, other negotiations took place in parallel, this time outside the official framework of diplomatic circles. For example, on 13 April 1945 Hubert Ripka, Paul Vaucher, Marcel Aymonin and Louis Goldberger (Gross) met for lunch. This group included some very special French historians and scientists who were actively involved in various commissions throughout the Second World War. In this case, the coupling element was the Historical Commission of E. Barker.[26] Jan Opočenský, a member of the same commission, noted on this date: "Friday. Lunch with Ripka, Vaucher, Aymonin and Gross. Ripka to negotiate something in Paris. Apparently, his point is to counterbalance Russia's cultural influence. Russia's political influence in our country will be so great that just culturally will be able to do something. Therefore, it is necessary that the French send their best people to us."[27]

The problem was that the strong personalities appointed to the French repatriation mission were seen as jeopardizing the future orientation of Czechoslovakia. Only a week later, on 20 April 1945, Jean Prunet decided to write a letter to the French ambassador in London. He stated that he was shocked by the Czechoslovaks and their conduct, since he had been, after all, the leading figure in international cooperation between France and Czechoslovakia. His person, he wrote, was blackened in the eyes of the Czechoslovak government when the Soviets emphasized his relationship with the Škoda

25 Němeček et al., eds., *Československo-francouzské vztahy v diplomatických jednáních 1940-1945*, pp. 464-465.

26 Louis Goldberger (alias Gross), of French origin, was a member of a special Commission for Periodicals and Journals of the Conference of the Allied Ministers of Education and of the Commission of E. Barker. However, he also worked for the secret service. Marcel Aymonin was a member of staff of the French Institute in Prague; he worked as a policy officer at the French Ministry of Information between 1939 and 1940, headed by Alfred Fischell at the time. Paul Vaucher was a French historian who became head of the Association of Allied Professors during the war.

27 Čechurová et al., eds., *Válečné deníky Jana Opočenského*, p. 411.

industry and his close relations with the former director of the firm. In this context, he mentioned other Czechoslovak factories which had strong French participation as well. Jean Prunet had been denounced by the Soviets as "a representative of French imperialist interests in Central Europe and a representative of a bourgeois regime."[28]

In the end, France succumbed to the pressure and modified the composition of the French repatriation mission. Yet, despite an official declaration from presidents De Gaulle and Beneš on the future of Czech-French relations,[29] the hope of fruitful future cooperation between the two countries seemed endangered by Soviet diplomatic moves.

SURPRISING OUTCOME

Eventually, the only general outline of the education policy to be pursued was drawn up by Zdeněk Nejedlý in Moscow. He was not subject to the same demands from lobby groups and was therefore probably better able to keep sufficient distance and allow for various details to be resolved later.

Zdeněk Nejedlý, an important representative of the Czechoslovak Communist exile in Moscow, was the sole author of paragraph 15 of the Košice government programme which was adopted by the new Czechoslovak government on 5 April 1945. According to some historians, his was the only general outline of education and cultural policy that could be taken on board without objections.

Such an outcome had the effect of at least occasioning surprise for the group working in London on post-war education and culture, if not indeed outright shock. From the reports, which were available in London at the time about Nejedlý's activities in Moscow, there had been no indication that the Communist leaders stationed there had decided to develop their own ideas on the subject. Smutný, for example, reported in early 1944 to London circles on Nejedlý, whom he characterized as an "old man" who was completely removed from politics and who concentrated fully on cooperation with Russian scientists. A similar view was expressed in the reports of other politicians who returned from a visit to Moscow.[30]

Compared to presidential decrees prepared in London, Nejedlý's document is much more general – and superficial. It defines the same three principles: denazification (that is, purges in all schools, universities, and cultural

28   Ibid., fol. 96–98.
29   Němeček et al., eds., *Československo-francouzské vztahy v diplomatických jednáních 1940–1945*, No. 334, pp. 471–472.
30   Ibid., Nos. 212, 214, pp. 325, 327.

bodies), democratization (i.e., the re-opening and the provision of improved accessibility for all Czech and Slovak schools, universities and cultural institutions), and de-Germanization. To quote from the above mentioned government programme: "All German and Hungarian schools in Czech and Slovak cities will be closed, including the German University in Prague and the German Technical University in Brno, which proved to be the worst fascist and Hitlerian nests in our homeland." It goes on to state that all German-language schools will remain closed until the "German question" is resolved.

This *communiqué* was unanimously adopted. It was formulated so as to clearly imply that it was a transitional, provisory solution and merely the first step in the drawing up of the future plan, possibly based on the London decree on education, which would be issued later.

What was different, however, was the open and outright acceptance of the Soviet paradigm without any reference to British, American, or French influence. The key term included in the programme was the "ideological revision" of Czechoslovak cultural policy. According to the document, cultural policy was to focus on reinforcing the Slavonic orientation of Czechoslovakia, erase all anti-Soviet notions from schools and textbooks, and make Russian the first foreign language of post-war Czechoslovak generations.

While for pro-leftist intellectuals, such as Václav Patzak, the project for new Czechoslovakia represented the actual implementation of their previous dreams, other members of the London exile perceived Nejedlý's work in Czechoslovak education and culture very differently. Jan Opočenský, in April 1945, for example, noted after a discussion with an official of the Ministry of Education, Bohumil Vančura: "One has great fear of Nejedlý if one is not exclusively oriented to the East. Furthermore, one has fear of what Patzak will make of the work of the Study Department."[31]

Gradually, however, it became clear that London diplomatic circles had greatly underestimated Nejedlý. The new minister of the Košice government, Zdeněk Nejedlý, openly asserted that "we have to decide for Eastern culture"[32] and first impressions from his office at the Ministry of Education in Prague also gave rise to fright among former members of the London Exile: "[...] at Minister Nejedlý['s office] with all the Czech-Russian inscriptions it looks the same as in a Russian province."[33] On the other hand, it seems that the actual physical appearance of Minister Nejedlý again lulled them back to complacency: "He is hunched as a result of his age and I do not know if he

---

31 Čechurová et al., eds., *Válečné deníky Jana Opočenského*, p. 409. Cf. also: Milada Sekyrková, ed., *Otakar Odložilík. Deníky z let 1924–1948* [Otakar Odložilík. Diaries from the Years 1924–1948] (Praha: Výzkumné centrum pro dějiny vědy, 2002–2003), p. 481.

32 Čechurová et al., eds., *Válečné deníky Jana Opočenského*, p. 419.

33 Ibid.

will last."[34]Appearances can be deceptive, though, and Zdeněk Nejedlý died in the early 1960s, 17 years after the end of the war.[35]

What the diplomats in London failed to achieve was to be enforced in a somewhat roundabout way through the contacts and personalities of a specific group from the Conference of Allied Ministers of Education. The efforts of this very interesting circle were realized eventually by the signing of the Czechoslovak-French Agreement on Scientific, Literary and Cultural Cooperation, even though the debate on its wording took the whole of 1945. Negotiations were held not only between the Czechoslovak and the French, but it was also found necessary to involve the new Minister of Education Zdeněk Nejedlý, a supporter of the Communist Party, who spent the Second World War with the communist leadership in Moscow.[36]

---

34 Ibid.
35 Jan Opočenský died in 1969, Zdeněk Nejedlý in 1962.
36 Cf. Jiří Křesťan, *Zdeněk Nejedlý: Politik a vědec v osamění* [Zdeněk Nejedlý: A Lonely Politician and Academician] (Praha: Paseka, 2012).

ABOUT THE CONTRIBUTORS AND EDITORS

Detlef Brandes is a professor of history. He has held teaching and research positions at several institutes and universities in Germany and abroad. He received an honorary doctorate from Charles University in Prague in 2001. He is the author of the following monographs: *Die Tschechen unter deutschem Protektorat 1939-1945* in 2 vols. (München – Wien, 1969, 1975), *Großbritannien und seine osteuropäischen Alliierten 1939-1943* (München, 1988), *Der Weg zur Vertreibung 1938-1945* (München, 2001, 2005), *Die Sudetendeutschen im Krisenjahr 1938* (München, 2008), *"Umvolkung, Umsiedlung, rassische Bestandsaufnahme". NS-"Volkstumspolitik" in den böhmischen Ländern* (München, 2012) – all of the monographs were also published in Czech. He also published: *Von den Zaren adoptiert: Die deutschen Kolonisten und die Balkansiedler in Neurussland und Bessarabien 1751-1914* (München, 1993) and, with Andrej Savin: *Die Sibiriendeutschen im Sowjetstaat 1919-1938* (Essen, 2001).

Martin David Brown is an associate professor of international history and an associate dean for research at Richmond, the American International University in London. He is a fellow of the Royal Historical Society and a member of the New Diplomatic History Network. He is the author of *Dealing with Democrats. The British Foreign Office's Relations with the Czechoslovak Émigrés in Great Britain, 1939-1945* (Frankfurt am Main, 2006), which was also translated into Czech (Praha, 2008). Together with professors Mikuláš Teich (Cambridge) and Dušan Kováč (Bratislava), he co-edited the book *Slovakia in History* (Cambridge, 2011). He is currently researching British foreign policy during the era of détente leading up to the Helsinki Final Act of 1975.

Kathleen Geaney is a young Czech-Irish historian. In her work, she primarily deals with European neutral states during the Second World War and political immigration from the West to the East during the Cold War.

Erica Harrison completed her doctoral dissertation (*Radio and the Performance of Government: Broadcasting by the Czechoslovaks in Exile in London, 1939-1945*) as part of a collaborative project between the University of Bristol and the Czech Radio, also producing a new archival catalogue of wartime recordings for the Czech Radio archive in Prague. An overview of the project was published in a special issue of *Media History*, Vol. 21, No. 4 (2015). Her research interests focus on Central and Eastern Europe (in particular Czechoslovakia 1918-1948), the Czechoslovak exile government, propaganda, and the medium of radio. She is currently working in the social and public sector and developing her dissertation into a monograph.

Albert Kersten is an emeritus professor of Leyden University. His main areas of interest are Dutch foreign policy, history of European integration since 1945 and history of diplomacy. Together with Ad Manning, he published *Documenten betreffende de Buitenlandse Politiek van Nederland 1940-1945* [Documents concerning the Foreign Policy of the Netherlands 1940-1945] in 6 volumes. In 1996-2002 he was a member of a research group commissioned by the Dutch government to deal with the massacre of Srebrenica in 1996: *Srebrenica. Een "veilig" gebied* [Srebrenica. A "Safe" Area] (Amsterdam, 2002). His most recent book is *Luns. Een politieke biografie* [Joseph Luns. A Political Biography] (Amsterdam, 2010).

Chantal Kesteloot holds a Ph.D. in contemporary history at Université libre de Bruxelles. Since 1992, she has been a member of the permanent team of the Centre for Historical Research and Documentation on War and Contemporary Society (CegeSoma - www.cegesoma.be), she is currently in charge of the sector of public history. Her main areas of interest are the history of Brussels, memory of the war and Belgian history, issues of nationalism and national identities. She is a corresponding secretary of the International Federation for Public History. Her latest publications include: "De la séparation administrative au nationalisme belge: la quête identitaire du mouvement wallon à la faveur de la Grande Guerre," in Sylvain Gregori & Jean-Paul Pellegrinetti (eds.), *Minorités, identités régionales et nationales en guerre 1914-1918* (Rennes, 2017) or, with Bruno Benvido, *Bruxelles, ville occupée, 1914-1918*, La Renaissance du Livre (Bruxelles, 2016).

Jan Kuklík is a professor of legal history at the Faculty of Law, Charles University in Prague. The main topics of his research include Czechoslovak law and diplomacy during the Second World War, international protection of minorities, restitution of Jewish property after 1945, and the development of Czechoslovak socialist law. He is the author of numerous books, e.g. *Mýty a realita tzv. "Benešových dekretů"* [Myths and Realities of the So-called "Beneš Decrees"] (Praha, 2002), *Do poslední pence. Československo-britská jednání o majetkoprávních a finančních otázkách 1938-1982* [To the Last Penny. Czechoslovak-British Negotiations on Property Rights and Financial Issues 1938–1982] (Praha, 2002), *Znárodněné Československo* [Nationalized Czechoslovakia] (Praha, 2010). Together with Jan Němeček, he has published: *Hodža versus*

Beneš (Praha, 1999), *Proti Benešovi!* [Against Beneš!] (Praha, 2004), *Osvobozené Československo očima britské diplomacie* [Liberated Czechoslovakia through the Lenses of British Diplomacy] (Praha, 2005), *Od národního státu ke státu národností?* [From the Nation State to the State of Nationalities?], *Dlouhé stíny Mnichova* [Long Shadows of Munich] (also with Jaroslav Šebek, Praha, 2011) and the documentary edition *Frontiers, Minorities, Transfers, Expulsions. British Diplomacy towards Czechoslovakia and Poland during WWII* (Prague, 2015).

Jan Láníček is a senior lecturer in Jewish history at the University of New South Wales, Sydney, Australia. He specializes in modern European history and Jewish/non-Jewish relations during the Holocaust. He is the author of *Czechs, Slovaks and the Jews, 1938–1948: Beyond Idealisation and Condemnation* (Basingstoke, 2013), *Arnošt Frischer and the Jewish Politics of Early 20ᵗʰ-Century Europe* (London, 2016), and he is a co-editor (with James Jordan) of *Governments-in-Exile and the Jews during the Second World War* (London, 2013).

Zdenko Maršálek is a researcher in the Institute of Contemporary History, Czech Academy of Sciences. He is an expert in military history of Czechoslovakia and other Central European countries in the period of 1918–1945, he particularly deals with the revision of "national stories" of resistance movements during the Second World War, and with problems of nationality and ethnic identification and self-identification in Czechoslovakia. He led a team preparing a unique personal e-database of the Czechoslovak units-in-exile 1939–1945. His publications include: *Dunkerque 1944–1945. Ztráty Československé samostatné obrněné brigády během operačního nasazení ve Francii* [Dunkirk 1944–1945. Casualties of the Czechoslovak Independent Armoured Brigade during its Operational Deployment in France] (together with Petr Hofman, Praha, 2011), and *"Česká" nebo "československá" armáda? Národnostní složení československých jednotek v zahraničí v letech 1939–1945* ["Czech," or "Czechoslovak" Army? The Ethnic and Nationality Composition of the Czechoslovak Military Units-in-Exile in 1939–1945] (Praha, 2017).

Jan Němeček is the deputy director of the Institute of History, Czech Academy of Sciences in Prague. He specializes in political history of the 20ᵗʰ century, primarily the international situation and the Czechoslovak resistance movement (both at home and in exile) during the Second World War. Apart from the books written together with Jan Kuklík (see above), he is the author of: *Mašínové: zpráva o dvou generacích* [The Mašíns: A Report on Two Generations] (Praha, 1998), *Od spojenectví k roztržce* [From Alliance to Quarrel] (Praha, 2003), *Soumrak a úsvit československé diplomacie: 15. březen 1939 a československé zastupitelské úřady* [The Dawn and the Dusk of Czechoslovak

Diplomacy: 15 March 1939 and the Czechoslovak Legations] (Praha, 2008), *Prototyp zrady: životní příběh Augustina Přeučila* [Prototype of Treason: The Life Story of Augustin Přeučil] (together with Daniela Němečková, Praha, 2015). Since 1996, he is the head of the research and editorial project *Documents of Czechoslovak Foreign Policy 1918–1945*. Together with Jan Kuklík, Ivan Štovíček, Helena Nováčková and Jan Bílek, he also edited *Zápisy ze schůzí československé vlády v Londýně* [Records of the Meetings of the Czechoslovak Government in London] (Praha 2008–2016).

Doubravka Olšáková is a senior research fellow at the Institute of Contemporary History, Czech Academy of Sciences in Prague, where she leads the working group for environmental history. She is interested in the history of science and environmental history. She published the book *Věda jde k lidu! Československá společnost pro šíření politických a vědeckých znalostí a popularizace věd v Československu ve 20. století* [Science Goes to People! The Czechoslovak Society for Popularization of Sciences in Czechoslovakia in the 20th Century] (Praha, 2014) on relations between the dissemination of sciences, ideology and communist propaganda in Czechoslovakia in the 20th century. She is the principal editor of *In the Name of the Great Work: Stalin's Plan for the Transformation of Nature and Its Impact in Eastern Europe* (New York, 2016).

Richard Overy is a professor of history at the University of Exeter, UK. He is a fellow of the British Academy and a member of the European Academy for Sciences and Arts. He has published more than 30 books on the age of the World Wars and on European dictatorships, including *Why the Allies Won* (London, 1995), *Russia's War* (London, 1998), *The Dictators: Hitler's Germany and Stalin's Russia* (London, 2004), and most recently *The Bombing War: Europe 1939–1945* (London, 2013). He is currently completing a major new study of the Second World War. He was awarded the Samuel Eliot Morison Prize in 2001, the Wolfson Prize for History in 2004 and the Cundill Award for Historical Literature in 2014 for his book on bombing.

René Petráš works at the Faculty of Law, Charles University in Prague – the Institute of Legal History. He mostly focuses on the development of the legal status of national minorities in the Czech Lands in the 20th century. He is the author of a number of books – e.g. *Menšiny v meziválečném Československu* [Minorities in interwar Czechoslovakia] (Praha, 2009), *Menšiny v komunistickém Československu* [Minorities in Communist Czechoslovakia] (Praha, 2007), *Cizinci ve vlastní zemi* [Foreigners in Their Own Country] (Praha, 2012), and, together with Jan Kuklík, *Minorities and Law in Czechoslovakia 1918–1992* (Praha, 2017).

Anita Jean Prażmowska is a professor of history in the Department of International History, London School of Economics and Political Science. She is an expert on Polish foreign relations during the Second World War and the establishment of Communism in Poland. She has published the following books: *Britain, Poland and the Eastern Front, 1939* (Cambridge, 1987), *Britain and Poland 1939–1943. The Betrayed Ally* (Cambridge, 1995), *Eastern Europe and the Origins of the Second World War* (London, 2000), *A History of Poland* (Basingstoke, 2004 and 2011), *Civil War in Poland* (Basingstoke, 2004), *Ignacy Paderewski: Poland* (London, 2009, and Paris, 2014), *Poland. A Modern History* (London, 2010) and *Władysław Gomułka. A Biography* (London, 2016), which was also translated into Polish. She is a member of the Research Council of the European University Institute, Florence. She is currently working on a project entitled "The Cold War Jigsaw. Poland's role in the Angolan Civil War, 1976–1986," which is funded by a Leverhulme Major Research Fellowship, 2016–2018.

Mark Seaman is a government historian with the Cabinet Office in London. Prior to taking up this appointment in 2002, he was a senior historian with the Imperial War Museum. He has specialized in various aspects of Britain's secret activities during the Second World War, notably in the fields of intelligence, special operations, the Royal Air Force's special duties squadrons and British support to European resistance movements. He has coordinated major international conferences on the Special Operations Executive (Imperial War Museum, 1998) and "Secret Services-in-Exile" (Lancaster House, 2013). His published works include *The Bravest of the Brave. The True Story of Wing Commander "Tommy" Yeo-Thomas, SOE, Secret Agent, Codename "White Rabbit"* (London, 1997), *Secret Agent's Handbook of Special Devices: World War II* (Richmond, 2000), and *SOE – A New Instrument of War* (London – New York, 2006). In 2014 he was awarded an MBE for services to the history of espionage.

Dušan Segeš is a research fellow at the Institute of History (Department of Contemporary History) of the Slovak Academy of Sciences in Bratislava. His research interests focus on various aspects of the history of Central Europe, such as foreign policy and political culture, Czech-Slovak and Polish-Czech-Slovak relations, exile politics, national minority issues and roots of federalism in Central Europe. He wrote the award-winning book *Dvojkríž v siločiarach bieleho orla: Slovenská otázka v politike poľskej exilovej vlády za 2. svetovej vojny* [Double-Cross in the Field of Interest of the White Eagle. The Slovak Issue in the Policies of the Polish Government-in-Exile during the Second World War] (Bratislava, 2009), which was also translated into Polish (Gdańsk, 2012). He is the editor-in-chief of the documentary edition *Slovensko a slovenská otázka v poľských a maďarských diplomatických dokumentoch v rokoch 1938–1939* [Slovakia and the Slovak Question in Polish and Hungarian Diplomatic Documents in the Years 1938–1939] (Bratislava, 2012).

Vít Smetana is a senior research fellow at the Institute of Contemporary History, Czech Academy of Sciences, and teaches modern international history at the Faculty of Social Sciences, Charles University in Prague. His area of expertise includes the history of international relations during the Second World War and the first phase of the Cold War, particularly the international role of Czechoslovakia in that period. He is the author of *In the Shadow of Munich. British Policy towards Czechoslovakia from the Endorsement to the Renunciation of the Munich Agreement (1938–1942)* (Prague, 2008) and *Ani vojna, ani mír. Velmoci, Československo a střední Evropa v sedmi dramatech na prahu druhé světové a studené války* [Neither War, nor Peace. Great Powers, Czechoslovakia and Central Europe in Seven Dramatic Stories on the Eve of the Second World War and the Cold War] (Praha, 2016). Together with Mark Kramer, he edited the book entitled *Imposing, Maintaining, and Tearing Open the Iron Curtain. The Cold War and East-Central Europe, 1945–1989* (Lanham – New York – Plymouth, 2014).

Matěj Spurný is an assistant professor at the Institute for Economic and Social History of the Faculty of Arts, Charles University in Prague, and a research fellow at the Institute of Contemporary History of the Czech Academy of Sciences. He is currently (2017/18) a fellow at the Imre Kertész Kolleg in Jena, Germany. He was working as a research fellow at the Institute for Contemporary History (ZZF) in Potsdam and collaborated with the Berlin Social Science Centre (WZB). For his dissertation *Nejsou jako my* [They Are Not Like Us] (Praha, 2011) on ethnic minorities in postwar Czechoslovakia, he was awarded prestigious Czech academic and research prizes. His latest book is *Most do budoucnosti: Laboratoř socialistické modernity na severu Čech* [Making of the Most of Tomorrow: The Laboratory of Socialist Modernity in North Bohemia] (Praha, 2016). For nearly two decades he has also been acting in the field of civil society, especially dealing with the postwar forced displacement of Germans from Czechoslovakia. He has also taken part in the Czech debate about socialist dictatorship.

Blaž Torkar is a lecturer and researcher at the Military Schools Centre / Military Museum of the Slovenian Armed Forces. His research interests include the history of intelligence services, the Isonzo front, Allies in Yugoslavia during the Second World War, the Yugoslav People's Army and territorial defence or Slovenian "Independence War 1991." His publications include two books: *Prikriti odpor: ameriška obveščevalna služba na Slovenskem med drugo svetovno vojno* [A Hidden Resistance: The American Intelligence Service in

Slovenia during the Second World War] (Maribor, 2012) and, together with Bajc Gorazd, *Ivan Rudolf in padalci = Ivan Rudolf e i paracadutisti = Ivan Rudolf and parachutists)* (Maribor, 2009). He is currently preparing a book on the 12th Isonzo Offensive.

Victoria Vasilenko is an assistant professor of contemporary history in the Department of World History at Belgorod State University, Russia. Her research interests include the international history of the Second World War (focusing mostly on Polish and Czechoslovak questions), the genesis of the Cold War, and contemporary Russian-Polish relations. Most recently, she published: "The Polish-Czechoslovak Confederation Project in British Policy, 1939–1943: A Federalist Alternative to Postwar Settlement in East-Central Europe," in *Canadian Journal of History / Annales canadiennes d'histoire*, Vol. 49, No. 3 (2014), pp. 203–223.

Radosław Paweł Żurawski vel Grajewski is a professor at the History Institute of the University of Łódź, and he is also the head of the Chair of Contemporary General History. His research interests cover the history of diplomacy in the 19th century, with a particular reference to the British Empire in the first half of the century, the history of the Great Emigration after the 1830–31 November Rising (especially the Hôtel Lambert), the history of diplomacy in the period of the Second World War, especially British-Czechoslovak relations, and the issues of myths, stereotypes and national traditions. He is the author of four monographs (e.g., *Brytyjsko-czechosłowackie stosunki dyplomatyczne: październik 1938 – maj 1945* [British-Czechoslovak Diplomatic Relations: October 1938 – May 1945], Warszawa, 2008), 49 articles and 22 other academic publications. He also held fellowships from the J. and S. Brzękowski Foundation, the Foundation for Independent Polish Literature and Culture, and the Lanckoroński of Brzezie Foundation.

INDEX

French Institute in Prague, 285–286

French Ministry of Foreign Affairs, 285

French National Committee, 79, 228

French North Africa, 79

Friedman, Julius, 232

Front de l'Independance, 27

Fürth, Julius, 232

G

De Gaulle, Charles, General, 44, 62–63, 79, 95, 287

de Geer, Dirk Jan, 34–35

Gaullism, 30

General Plan Ost, 134

General Staff (Belgian), 29

Geneva, 191, 194

Gerbrandy, Pieter Sjoerds, 35–37, 42

German Führer see Hitler, Adolf

German Technical University (Brno), 288

German University (Prague), 288

Germany, 7, 16–17, 22, 32–34, 39, 41, 44, 46–55, 60, 64–65, 74, 76–78, 80–81, 86, 88, 108, 110, 122–125, 127, 134–144, 146–149, 151–152, 154–155, 157–158, 160, 167, 171–173, 176, 184, 187, 197, 204, 206–208, 210–215, 218, 221–223, 240, 244, 250

Gestapo, 140, 207, 258

Gibiansky, Leonid, 90–91

Gibson, Harold, 123

Glassheim, Eagle, 179–180, 186

Goebbels, Josef, 223, 229

Goldberger (Gross), Louis, 286

Gordon-Walker, Patrick, 211

Gotovitch, José, 96, 99–100, 103

Grand, Laurence, Major, 123

Great Britain see Britain

Greater Croatia, 18

Greece, 7, 105, 120, 132, 149, 153, 155, 193, 195–197, 216

Greek army, 12, 102

Greek-Bulgarian exchange of population, 152

Greek government, 18, 228

Greek merchant fleet, 106

Greek-Turkish exchange of population, 145, 147–148, 152, 155

Grigg, James, 272

Gubbins, Colin, Liutenant-Colonel, 123–128

Gutt, Camille, 25

H

The Hague, 33, 38

Hácha, Emil, 72, 77, 241

Haifa, 114

Haifa Oil refinery, 116

Halfaya Pass, 116

Halifax, Lord, Edward Frederick Lindley Wood, 77, 149, 187

Halifax bomber, 128

Harriman, Averell William, 69

Harris, Arthur, Air Chief Marshal, 206

Hartmann, Pavel, 86

Haslop, Vera, 68

Havel, Václav, 174–175

Hazemeyer control firing system, 107

Heydrich, Reinhard, 103, 128, 139, 146, 167–168, 187, 222, 231, 236–237, 239, 245–246

Hildprandt, Robert, 258, 269

Hilsner affair, 237

Historical Commission of E. Baker, 286

Hitler, Adolf, 17, 24, 26, 134, 136–137, 147–148, 152, 155, 212, 227, 229, 235, 237, 244–246, 250–251, 256, 261, 266, 288

Hlas svobodné republiky [Voice of the free Republic], 218, 244

HMS Prince of Wales, 108

HMS Repulse, 108

Hockey, Ron, 122, 128

Hodža, Milan, 13, 63, 74–76, 258, 270–271, 275, 278

Holland, 32, 37, 47, 103, 129, 132

Holocaust, 172, 227–229, 241, 243, 254

Holy See, 41

Home Army (Polish) see *Armia Krajowa*

Home Army (Yugoslav), 15

Hope-Simpson, John, 187

Hopkins, Harry, 43

Horstmann, Margaret, 43

Hot Springs Conference on Food and Agriculture (1943), 45

House of Commons (of the British Parliament), 68, 184, 273

Hovory s domovem [Conversations with the homeland], 218

Hull, Cordell, 46, 65–66

Hungary, 14, 17, 60, 64, 74, 80–81, 91, 105, 138, 140–141, 149, 154, 167, 193, 197, 249

Hurban, Vladimír, 72–73

Hus, Jan, 222

Huysmans, Camille, 24–25

VÍT SMETANA
KATHLEEN GEANEY
(eds)

EXILE IN LONDON
THE EXPERIENCE
OF CZECHOSLOVAKIA
AND THE OTHER OCCUPIED
NATIONS, 1939–1945

Published by Charles University
Karolinum Press
Ovocný trh 560/5, 116 36
Prague 1, Czech Republic
www.karolinum.cz
Prague 2017
English language supervision by Kathleen Geaney
Copyedited by Martin Janeček
Cover and layout by Jan Šerých
Typeset and printed by Karolinum Press
First English edition

ISBN 978-80-246-3701-3
ISBN 978-80-246-3732-7 (pdf)